Automated Machine Learning for Business

Automated Machine Learning for Business

Kai R. Larsen and Daniel S. Becker

OXFORD
UNIVERSITY PRESS

OXFORD
UNIVERSITY PRESS

Oxford University Press is a department of the University of Oxford. It furthers
the University's objective of excellence in research, scholarship, and education
by publishing worldwide. Oxford is a registered trade mark of Oxford University
Press in the UK and certain other countries.

Published in the United States of America by Oxford University Press
198 Madison Avenue, New York, NY 10016, United States of America.

Library of Congress Cataloging-in-Publication Data
Names: Larsen, Kai R., author. | Becker, Daniel S., author.
Title: Automated machine learning for business / Kai R. Larsen and Daniel S. Becker.
Description: New York, NY : Oxford University Press, [2021] |
Includes bibliographical references and index.
Identifiers: LCCN 2020049814 (print) | LCCN 2020049815 (ebook) |
ISBN 9780190941659 (hardback) | ISBN 9780190941666 (paperback) |
ISBN 9780190941680 (epub)
Subjects: LCSH: Business planning—Data processing—Textbooks. |
Business planning—Statistical methods—Textbooks. | Machine learning—
Industrial applications—Textbooks. | Decision making—Statistical methods—Textbooks.
Classification: LCC HD30.28 .L3733 2021 (print) |
LCC HD30.28 (ebook) | DDC 658.4/030285631—dc23
LC record available at https://lccn.loc.gov/2020049814
LC ebook record available at https://lccn.loc.gov/2020049815

DOI: 10.1093/oso/9780190941659.001.0001

Hardback printed by Bridgeport National Bindery, Inc., United States of America

Contents

SECTION V: INTERPRET AND COMMUNICATE

Preface

According to PricewaterhouseCoopers, there will be an enormous demand for professionals with the skills you will develop through this book, as the clear majority of future jobs will be *analytics-enabled* (Ampil et al., 2017). Machine learning is at the core of such jobs and how they are transforming business—no wonder some have termed "data scientist" the sexiest job of the twenty-first century (Davenport & Patil, 2012). While you may have no desire to become a data scientist, at a minimum, you must know conceptually what machine learning is, but to thrive you should be able to use machine learning to make better and faster decisions.

Automated Machine Learning for Business is for these readers (hereafter often referred to as "analysts"):

- Businesspeople wanting to apply the power of machine learning to learn about their business environment and extract visualizations allowing the sharing of their newfound knowledge.
- Businesspeople and developers wanting to learn how to create machine learning models for automating high-quality decisions.
- Subject matter experts assigned to a machine learning project. The book will help you understand the process ahead and allow you to better communicate with your data science colleagues.
- Students in introductory business analytics or machine learning classes, whether as part of a business analytics program or a stand-alone course wholly or in part focused on machine learning, in either the undergraduate or master-level curriculum.
- Machine learning experts with no previous exposure to automated machine learning or who want to evaluate their machine learning approach against the industry-leading processes embedded in DataRobot, the automated machine learning platform used for this book.

The tools and processes in this book were developed by some of the best data scientists in the world. Even very successful colleagues with decades of experience in business analytics and machine learning had useful experiences while testing material for the book and the DataRobot automated machine learning (AutoML) platform.

This book is not about artificial intelligence (AI). AI can be thought of as a collection of machine learning algorithms with a central unit deciding which of the ML algorithms need to kick in at that time, similar to how different parts of the human brain specialize in different tasks. Machine learning is in the driving seat as AI is becoming a reality at blinding speeds. This accelerated pace of AI development is due to recent improvements in deep learning neural networks as well as other algorithms that require less fine-tuning to work. While this book does not cover AI, it may be one of the gentlest introductions to machine learning, and as such will serve as a great starting point on your journey toward AI understanding.

Automated Machine Learning (AutoML)

In this book, we teach the machine learning process using a new development in data science; automated machine learning. AutoML, when implemented properly, makes machine learning accessible to most people because it removes the need for years of experience in the most arcane aspects of data science, such as the math, statistics, and computer science skills required to become a top contender in traditional machine learning. Anyone trained in the use of AutoML can use it to test their ideas and support the quality of those ideas during presentations to management and stakeholder groups. Because the requisite investment is one semester-long undergraduate course rather than a year in a graduate program, these tools will likely become a core component of undergraduate programs, and over time, even the high school curriculum.

It has been our experience that even after taking introductory statistics classes, only a few are capable of effectively applying a tool like regression to business problems. On the other hand, most students seem capable of understanding how to use AutoML, which will generally outperform logistic and linear regression, even in the cases where regression is the right tool for the problem. If we start with the assumption that machine learning is in the process of transforming society in the most radical way since the Industrial Revolution, we can also conclude that developing undergraduate and graduate business degrees that do not cover this material will soon be considered akin to educational malpractice. Moreover, several master's degree programs in Analytics have started introducing their students to AutoML to speed their learning and capabilities. When AutoML outperforms whole teams of experienced data scientists, does it make sense to exclude it from analytics program training, whether at the undergraduate or graduate level?

A Note to Instructors

The full content of this book may be more than is desired for a class in the core of an undergraduate curriculum but perhaps not enough content desired for an intro to data science or business analytics class, as those classes would likely spend more time on Section III, *Acquire and Explore Data*, and also cover unsupervised machine learning. While this book will stick to easy-to-use graphical interfaces, the content of the book is transformable to a class teaching AutoML through a coding approach, primarily with *R* or *Python*. Moreover, once your students understand the concepts covered in this book, they will avoid many pitfalls of machine learning as they move on to more advanced classes.

Acknowledgments

We are exceedingly grateful to Jeremy Achin and Tom De Godoy, who first built a system for automating the data science work necessary to compete in Kaggle data science competitions, a system that over time morphed into the DataRobot platform. The process taught in this book owes much to their original approach. The book also could not have become a reality without the support of many world-leading data scientists at DataRobot, Inc. We are particularly indebted to Zachary Mayer, Bill Surrette, João Gomes, Andrew Engel, John Boersma, Raju Penmatcha, Ina Ko, Matt Sanda, and Ben Solari, who provided feedback on drafts of the book. We are also grateful to past students Alexander Truesdale, Weston Ballard, and Briana Butler for support and editing, as well as Alex Truesdale, Briana Butler, Matt Mager, Weston Ballard, and Spencer Rafii for helping develop the datasets provided with this book. The following students helped improve the book during its first use in the classroom at the University of Colorado (in order of helpfulness): Mac Bolak, Gena Welk, Jackson McCullough, Alan Chen, Stephanie Billett, Robin Silk, Cierra Hubbard, Meredith Maney, Philip Bubernak, Sarah Sharpe, Meghan McCrory, Megan Thiede, Pauline Flores, Christine Pracht, Nicole Costello, Tristan Poulsen, Logan Hastings, Josh Cohn, Alice Haugland, Alex Ward, Meg O'Connell, Sam Silver, Tyler Hennessy, Daniel Hartman, Anna La, Ben Friedman, Jacob Lamon, Zihan Gao, and August Ridley.

Finally, but no less important, Kai is grateful to his children, and especially his youngest daughter, Katrine, who would have received more of his attention had he not worked on this book.

Book Outline

Section I discusses the ubiquitous use of machine learning in business as well as the critical need for you to conceptually understand machine learning's transformative effect on society. Applications and websites you already use now rely on machine learning in ways you will never be aware of, as well as the more obvious cases such as when the car next to you has no driver, or that the driver is watching a video (with or without holding his hands on the steering wheel). We then discuss automated machine learning, a new development that makes machine learning accessible to most businesspeople.

Section II begins with *Define Project Objectives*, where we specify the business problem and make sure we have the skill sets needed to succeed. We can then plan what to predict. In this section, we will carefully consider the inherent project risks and rewards, concluding with the truly difficult task of considering whether the project is worthwhile or, like most ideas, belongs in the cognitive trash pile.

Section III focuses on how to *Acquire and Explore Data*. It starts with a consideration of internal versus external data, asking the question of whether the data we have is the data we need while keeping benefit/cost considerations in mind. With all key data collected, the data can be merged into a single table and prepared for exploratory analysis. In this process, we examine each column in the dataset to determine what data type it is. The most common types of data are either numeric or categorical. For numeric data, we examine simple statistics, such as mean, median, standard deviation, minimum value, maximum value. For categorical data, we examine how many unique categories there are, how many possible values there are in each category, and within each category, which value is the most common (referred to as the *mode*). For both types, we examine their distribution—are they normally distributed, left- or right-skewed, or perhaps even bimodal? We will also discuss the potential limitations of categories that have few values.

Traditionally, detailed knowledge of your data has been very important in data science, and this will still be true when using AutoML. However, with AutoML, the data knowledge needed shifts from understanding data to understanding relationships. A critically important task in data science is to remove *target leakage*. Target leakage can occur when we collect a dataset over an extended period such that you have unrealistic data available at the time of prediction within a model. We will discuss this in further depth in Chapter 3, but for now, imagine the following: you have access to information on a potential customer who just arrived at a website for which you have contracted to place one of two available ads. You have information on the previous 100,000 customers who arrived at the website and whether they bought the product advertised in each ad. You used that information to create a model that "understands" what leads a customer to buy that product. Your model has an almost uncanny ability to predict non-purchasing especially, which means that you will never place the ad in front of the group predicted not to buy, and you will save your company quite a bit of money. Unfortunately, after you have convinced your CEO to place the model into production, you find that not all the features used to create the model are available when a new visitor arrives, and your model is expected to decide which ad to place in front of the visitor. It turns out that in your training data, you had a feature that stated whether visitors clicked on the ad or not. Not surprisingly, the visitors who did not click the ad also did not buy the product that was only accessible through clicking the ad. You are now forced to scrap the old model and create a new model before explaining to upper management why your new model is much less effective (but works). In short, the amount of humble pie eaten by data scientists who did not remove target leakage before presenting to management could power many late-night sessions of feature engineering.

While knowledge of your data is still where you must go to tease out small improvements in your ability to predict the future, automated machine learning has moved the line on the gain from such exercises. The platform we will use to demonstrate the concepts in this book, DataRobot, does most of the feature engineering automatically. We have found that for well-executed automated machine learning, additional manual feature engineering is much more likely to reduce the performance of the algorithms than to improve it. While even the DataRobot platform will not take away the need for target leakage examination, for AutoML tools embedded into another platform, such as Salesforce Einstein, target leak data is removed automatically.

Section IV, *Model Data*, focuses on creating the machine learning models. Much of the process of becoming a data scientist emphasizes the aspects of developing machine learning models, which one does by going through classes on math, statistics, and programming. Once you have completed your undergraduate degree, as well as a specialized program in data science or business analytics, you qualify as a fledgling data scientist, which is admittedly *very* cool. Then you start building models and following a process. Often, a machine learning project will take three to six months before you see your model in production. For example, say that your university wants you to create a model to predict which students will have trouble finding a job after achieving their undergraduate degree. While working on the project, approximately every month you will hear about a new algorithm that is rumored to be much better than the ones you've tried, and you might take a detour into trying out that algorithm. It has been our experience that often the biggest problems regarding the accuracy of a machine learning project involve the data scientist being unaware of a class of algorithms that could have outperformed the algorithms used.

As part of the modeling process, it is typical to try out different features and perhaps remove those that are not very predictive or that, due to random variations in the data, initially seem to offer some predictive ability. Sometimes less is more, and less is certainly easier to explain to your leadership, to deploy, and to maintain. In this book, we will focus on the concepts of machine learning rather than the math and statistics. We will focus on the results of applying an algorithm rather than an algorithm's innards. In other words, each algorithm is treated merely regarding its performance characteristics, each ranked by its performance. Section IV is by far the most important because here we are working toward an understanding of something called the *confusion matrix* (appropriately named). The confusion matrix is a comparison of whether decisions made by an algorithm were correct. The confusion matrix gives rise to most of the metrics we use to evaluate models and will also help drive our business recommendations.

Section V explains how to *Interpret and Communicate* the model. In this section, we move beyond creating and selecting a model to understand what features drive a target—in other words, which statistical relationships exist between the target and the other features. For example, the model you develop will dictate your management's trust in the course of action you propose as well as in you. Hence, "we should invest $100 million in loans to the consumers that the model indicates as least likely to default" will require strong faith in either the model or the data scientist who developed the model.

Given that faith in the person develops over time, our focus will be on developing faith in and understanding of the extent to which the AutoML platform itself not only finds problems with the model but also clarifies the reason(s) it works when it does and fails in some cases. Moreover, when specific data turns out to be predictive, we want to know if this is data to which we can entrust the future of our business. For example, the purchase of floor protectors (those cheap felt dots placed under furniture) was in one project found to be as predictive of credit-worthiness as an individual's credit score (Watson, 2014). This feature has instinctive appeal because one can easily reason that someone who buys floor protectors not only has a wood floor (more expensive than carpeting) but also cares enough about their property to protect it from damage. A feature like this could be worth gold if it picked up on variance unaccounted for by other features associated with credit-worthiness. However, a manager would be likely to push back and ask how sure we are that we have data from all the places a potential customer would buy floor protectors. This same manager could reasonably worry that the feature only helps us predict the credit-worthiness of the top 5% of income earners, a societal segment for which loans come readily, and competition is fierce. The manager may then worry that over time, word would get out about the importance of buying $5 floor protectors before applying for loans, whether one needs them or not. The short story is this: the more of these unanswered worries your model generates; the slower trust will develop in you as a data scientist.

Finally, Section VI, *Implement, Document and Maintain*, sets up a workflow for using the model to predict new cases. We here describe the stage where we move the selected model into production. For example, let's say a consumer's cell phone contract is set to expire next week. Before it does, we feed the information on this consumer into the model, and the model can provide the probability for that consumer to move their service to another cell phone provider. We must then translate this probability into business rules. For each consumer so scored, we weigh the *income* from keeping them against the *risk* of losing them, and then different retention programs are considered against that risk-weighted income. It could be that the consumer will be offered nothing because the risk of losing them is negligible, or it could be that they will be offered an extra gigabyte of broadband each month, or perhaps a $200 discount to stay on if the risk-weighted income is high. Once this risk-weighted income is established, the whole process is documented for future reproducibility and re-evaluation of rules. The likelihood of a data source changing becomes a major issue. Just a simple renaming of a column in an Excel spreadsheet or a database can prevent the whole model from working or lead to significantly worsened performance, as the model will not recognize the column and all its predictive capability is lost. We then create a process for model monitoring and maintenance. Simply put, over time, the external world modeled by the machine learning algorithm will change, and if we do not detect this change and retrain the model, the original assumptions that may have made the model profitable will no longer be true, potentially leading to major losses for the company.

We move forward with the above worries in mind, knowing that we will learn a framework named *the machine learning life cycle* to keep us relatively safe by providing guard-rails for our work.

Dataset Download

The datasets for the book (described in Appendix A) are available for download at the following link. The zip file contains one zip file for each dataset (listed as Assets A.1–A.8, each referencing the similarly labeled Appendix A datasets). The Zip file containing the datasets is 131.6MB, and the unzipped files take about 524MB of space. Download link: https://www.dropbox.com/s/c8qjxdnmclsfsk2/AutoML_DatasetsV1.0.zip?dl=0.

Copyrights

All figures and images not developed for the book, including the cover page image, are under open usage rights.

Kai Larsen is an Associate Professor of Information Systems at the Leeds School of Business with a courtesy appointment as an Associate Professor of Information Science in the College of Media, Communication, and Information at the University of Colorado, Boulder. In his research, he applies machine learning and natural language processing (NLP) to address methodological problems in the social and behavioral sciences. He earned a Ph.D. in Information Science from the Nelson A. Rockefeller College at SUNY, Albany.

Daniel Becker is a Data Scientist for Google's Kaggle division. He has broad data science expertise, with consulting experience for six companies from the Fortune 100, a second-place finish in Kaggle's $3 million Heritage Health Prize, and contributions to the Keras and Tensorflow libraries for deep learning. Dan developed the training materials for DataRobot University. Dan earned his Ph.D. in Econometrics from the University of Virginia.

SECTION I

WHY USE AUTOMATED MACHINE LEARNING?

1

What Is Machine Learning?

1.1 Why Learn This?

Machine learning is currently at the core of many if not most organizations' strategies. A recent survey of more than 2,000 organizations' use of machine learning and analytics found that these tools are integral for knowing the customer, streamlining existing operations, and managing risk and compliance. However, the same organizations were only marginally confident in their analytics-driven insights in these areas, including their processes for managing such projects and evaluating outcomes (KPMG, 2017). In the coming decade, there will be two classes of organizations: those that use machine learning to transform their capabilities and those that do not (Davenport, 2006). While barely beyond its inception, the current machine learning revolution will affect people and organizations no less than the Industrial Revolution's effect on weavers and many other skilled laborers. In the 1700s, weaving required years of experience and extensive manual labor for every product. This skill set was devalued as the work moved into factories where power looms vastly improved productivity. Analogously, machine learning will automate hundreds of millions of jobs that were considered too complex for machines ever to take over even a decade ago, including driving, flying, painting, programming, and customer service, as well as many of the jobs previously reserved for humans in the fields of finance, marketing, operations, accounting, and human resources.

The organizations that use machine learning effectively and survive will most likely focus on hiring primarily individuals who can help them in their journey of continuing to derive value from the use of machine learning. The understanding of how to use algorithms in business will become an essential core competency in the twenty-first century. Reading this book and completing any course using it is the first step in acquiring the skills needed to thrive in this new world. Much has been made of the need for data scientists, and data scientist salaries certainly support the premium that industry is placing on such individuals to create and support all the above applications. A popular meme once decreed that you should "always be yourself, unless you can be Batman, then always be Batman." Akin to this: if you can find a way to be a data scientist, always be a data scientist (especially one as good at his or her job as Batman is at his), but if you cannot be a data scientist, be the best self you can be by making sure you understand the machine learning process.

Automated Machine Learning for Business. Kai R. Larsen and Daniel S. Becker, Oxford University Press. © Oxford University Press 2021.
DOI: 10.1093/oso/9780190941659.003.0001

Despite the current doubt within many organizations about their machine learning capabilities, the odds are that many use one or several technologies with machine learning built-in. Examples abound and include fitness bands; digital assistants like Alexa, Siri, or Cortana; the new machine learning–powered beds; and the Nest thermostat, as well as search assistants like Google, where hundreds of machine learning models contribute to every one of your searches.

You are the subject of machine learning hundreds of times every day. Your social media posts are analyzed to predict whether you are a psychopath or suffer from other psychiatric challenges (Garcia & Sikström, 2014), your financial transactions are examined by the credit-card companies to detect fraud and money laundering, and each of us logs into a unique, personalized Amazon Marketplace tailored to our lives by their highly customizing machine learning algorithms. Companies have weaved machine learning into everyday life with unseen threads. For example, machine learning models perform the majority of stock trades, and even judges contemplating the level of punishment for convicted criminals make their decisions in consultation with machine learning models. In short, machine learning algorithms already drive hugely disruptive events for humanity, with major revolutions still to come.

1.2 Machine Learning Is Everywhere

Everywhere? While there is likely not an ML algorithm at the top of Mount Everest unless there are also climbers there, there are plenty of machine learning algorithms working through satellite imagery to put together complete maps not hampered by clouds (Hu, Sun, Liang & Sun, 2014). These algorithms also predict poverty through nighttime light intensity (Jean et al., 2016), detect roads (Jean et al., 2016), detect buildings (Sirmacek & Unsalan, 2011), and generate most of the 3D structures in Google Earth. If you have tried Google Earth and have floated through a photo-realistic Paris or Milan wondering what happened to the cars and those incredible Italians who still manage to look marvelous despite riding mopeds to work, an ML algorithm erased them. They simply were too transient and irrelevant for Google Earth's mapping purpose. Zoom in far enough, though, and you'll see ghost cars embedded in the asphalt. The important point is that while machine learning algorithms work wonderfully for most large-scale problems, if you know where to look, you'll find small mistakes. Finding these slips and learning from them could become one of your defining strengths as an analyst, and you will need to develop skills in figuring out which features of a dataset are unimportant, both for the creation of ML models and for determining which results to share with your boss.

We started to create a complete list of all the areas machine learning has taken over or will soon take over, but we soon realized it was a meaningless exercise. Just within the last 24 hours of this writing, news has come of Baidu machine learning that finds missing children in China through facial recognition; Microsoft is developing machine learning–powered video search that can locate your keys if you fill your home with cameras; Facebook announced that their latest language-translation algorithm is nine times faster than their competitors' algorithms; researchers announced an autonomous robot that uses machine learning to inspect bridges for structural damage; and apparently we will soon be able to translate between English and Dolphin (!?). In the meantime, albeit less newsworthy, dozens if not hundreds of teams of data scientists are engaged in making our lives better by replacing teen drivers with artificial intelligence that is ten times better drivers than adolescents right now, with the potential to be 50–100 fold safer. Cars have traditionally been 4,000-pound death machines when left in the care of people who are sometimes poorly trained, tired, distracted, or under the influence of medications or drugs. If we leave the driving to machines, car travel will one day become safer and less stressful.

Currently, machine learning is involved when you ask Alexa/Cortana/Siri/Google Assistant to search for anything. ML translates your voice to text, and the Google Assistant uses ML to rank all the pages that contain the keywords you specified. Increasingly, your very use of the Internet is used to figure you out, sometimes for good purposes, such as offering treatment when you are likely to be depressed (Burns et al., 2011) or recognizing when you are likely to drop out of college (Baker & Inventado, 2014). Questionable use of ML-driven identification exists, such as when Facebook infamously shared insights with a potential customer about when children were most likely to be emotionally vulnerable and presumably also more open to certain kinds of ads (Riley, 2017). While such stories are explosive, the reality is that they remain in the territory of poor PR practices. The sad truth is that it likely is impossible to conduct large-scale machine learning to predict what and when to market a product based on something as emotionally driven as social media posts and likes without taking advantage of human weaknesses. Machine learning algorithms will zero in on these weaknesses like a honey badger on the prowl.

In potentially dubious practices, analysts apply machine learning with a training set of past consumers that either bought or didn't buy a given product to predict new purchasers. Analysts create of a model (a set of weighted relationships) between the act of buying (vs. not buying) and a set of features (information on the consumers). These features could be "likes" of a given artist, organization, the text of their posts, or even behaviors and likes of the person's friends. If liking an industrial band (a potential sign of untreated depression) on a Monday morning predicts later purchase of leather boots, the model will target the people inclined toward depressions on the day and time that feeling is the strongest. In this case, the machine learning will not label these consumers as depressed, or ever know that they posess a clinical condition, but will still take advantage of their depression. To evaluate the existence of such unethical shortcuts in models requires tools that allow careful examination of a model's "innards." Being able to evaluate what happens when a model produces high-stakes decisions is a critical reason for learning the content of this book.

1.3 What Is Machine Learning?

Machine learning was defined by Arthur Samuel, a machine learning pioneer, as "a field of study that gives computers the ability to learn without being explicitly programmed" (McClendon & Meghanathan, 2015, 3). A slight rewrite on that suggests that machine learning enables computers to learn to solve a problem by generalizing from examples (historical data), avoiding the need explicitly to program the solution.

There are two types of machine learning: supervised and unsupervised. The main difference between the two simplifies as supervised machine learning being a case of the data scientist selecting *what* they want the machine to learn, whereas unsupervised machine learning leaves it to the machine to decide what it wants to learn, with no guarantee that what it learns will be useful to the analyst. This dichotomy is a gross simplification, however, as over decades of use, humans have figured out which unsupervised approaches lead to desirable results.[1] An example of supervised machine learning might be where a model is trained to split people into two groups: one group, "likely buyers," and another group, "likely non-buyers." The modeling of relationships in historical data to predict future outcomes is the key central concept through which machine learning is transforming the world. This is due to the relative clarity of the idea and the ever-expanding business potential available in its implementation. This book will focus exclusively on supervised machine learning because we as authors believe this is where most of the benefit of machine learning lies. From here out, we will refer to supervised machine learning as "machine learning."

As humans, we create models all the time. Think back to how you learned to be funny as a child (potentially a life-saving skill to ensure survival). You were probably sitting in your high chair being spoon-fed mashed beans by your father. Realizing that puréed beans taste horrible, you spit the food back into his face, resulting in your mom bursting out in laughter. Your brain kicked into predictive mode, thinking that there must be a relationship between spitting stuff out and getting a positive reaction (laughter). You try it again and spit the next spoonful out on the floor. This does not elicit a reaction from mom (no laughter). On the

---

[1] In unsupervised machine learning, models are created without the guidance of historical data on which group people with certain characteristics belonged to in the past. Examples of unsupervised machine learning is *clustering*, *factor analysis*, and *market basket analysis*.

third spoonful, you decide to replicate the original process, and again your mom rewards you (laughter). You have now established the relationship between spitting food in the face of a parent and a positive outcome. A few days later, being alone with your mother, you decide to show once again what a born comedian you are by spitting food into *her* face. Much to your surprise, the outcome (no laughter) indicates that your original model of humor may have been wrong. Over time, you continued spitting food in adult faces until you had developed a perfect model of the relationship between this behavior and humor. This is also how machine learning works, constantly searching for relationships between features and a target, often as naively as a toddler, but with enough data that the model will outperform most human adults.

In machine learning, there is a *target* (often an outcome) we are trying to understand and predict in future cases. For example, we may want to know the *value* of a house given that we know the number of bedrooms, bathrooms, square footage, and location. Being good at predicting the value of a home (and typically exaggerating it quite a bit) used to be the main criterion sellers used to select a realtor. Now, websites such as Zillow.com predict home prices better than any individual realtor ever could. In business, there are other important targets such as *churn* (will this customer stop being a customer?). We also may want to know if a website visitor will click on an ad for Coach handbags, or whether a job applicant will perform well in your organization. Healthcare management organizations may want to know *which* patients return to the emergency department (ED) within a month of being released, as well as *why* they are likely to return. Both the *who* and the *why* are important to improve services and preserve resources. We will return to the example of diabetes patients released by a hospital ED in this book and use it to understand the aspects of good patient care. We will also share several datasets covering most business disciplines, including finance (lending club loans), operations (part backorders), sales (luxury shoes), reviews (Boston Airbnb), and human resources (HR attrition, two datasets), as well as some datasets of more general interest, such as student grades and college starting salaries.

In this book, we will step through a process that will tease out a set of conclusions about what drives an organizational goal. The process will apply to almost any process that has a definable and measurable *target*. For now, think of machine learning as analogous to the process you've developed through a long life—the ability to decide whether a meal is going to taste good before the first bite (those mashed beans served you well in many ways). Every day, we use our already honed sense of taste to determine which restaurants to go to and which ones to avoid, as well as which of mom's meals are worth visiting for, and which ones require a hastily conjured excuse for escape. Our brains contain an untold number of models that help us predict the outside world ("I'm really hungry, but this berry looks a lot like the berry that killed my cousin"). If our forebears had not developed such abilities, we would have long since died out.

1.4 Data for Machine Learning

More Data Beats a Cleverer Algorithm

ML principle: With the best of feature engineering, results may still not be adequate. Two options remain: finding/designing a better algorithm or getting more data. Domingos (2012) advocates for more data.

AutoML relevance: With AutoML, more data represents the only realistic path to practical and significant improvements.

Let's use an example to outline how to use machine learning algorithms in business. Your CEO just received a report (most likely from you) that 75% of your eCommerce site customers make only one purchase and that most repeat customers return within a week. He would like for you to explain what drives a customer to return. It is now your job to quickly gather as much data as possible starting with what you know. You are aware that a year ago the organization made large design changes to the website that changed the traffic patterns quite a bit, so you decide to start collecting data on customer visits starting a month after that change, allowing for the stabilization of traffic patterns. Next, you begin processing account creations from eleven months ago and discard data on accounts created that never led to sales (a different question that your CEO is sure to ask about later). For each account, you add a row to a file of customers for your analysis. For each row, you examine whether the customer made another purchase during the next seven days. If they did, you code a value of *True* into a new column called "Retained," and if not, you code that customer as *False*. You stop the addition of customers who created accounts a week before today's date to avoid labeling the most recent customers as non-retained because they have not had a whole week to return for a second purchase.

Your next task is to gather as much data as possible for both "retained" and "lost" customers. As such, the specifics of the second purchase are of no interest because that information is only available about your retained customers. However, the specific details on the first purchase are important. Likely information that will require new columns (we call those *features*) includes:

1. Which site sent them to you? Was it a Google search, Bing search, or did they come directly to your site?
2. Did this customer come to us through an ad? If so, which ad campaign was it (presumably each has a unique identifier)?
3. How many different types of products did the customer buy? Was one of the products a high-end shoe? Was one of the products a kitchen knife? (Yes, depending on your company's product mix, this set of features can become

quite large, and often, we must operate at the product category level and generalize, saying for example that we sold *footwear* or *kitchen equipment*.)

4. How long did it take the customer after creating an account to make a purchase?
5. What was the customer's purchasing behavior? Did they know what they wanted to purchase, or did they browse several products before deciding? If so, what were those products?
6. Which browser did they use? What language pack do they have installed on their computer?
7. What day of the week did they make their purchase?
8. What time of day was the purchase made?
9. What geographic location did they come from (might require a lookup on their Internet Protocol (IP) address and the coding of that location with a longitude and latitude)?

The process of feature creation continues as the particular case demands. You may create dozens if not hundreds of features before considering the use of a customer's email address, credit card information, or mailing address to purchase additional information. Such information may be purchased from the likes of Equifax (credit reports and scores), Towerdata (email address–based data like demographics, interests, and purchase information), Nielsen (viewing and listening patterns recorded via television, internet, and radio behavior), or Acxiom. A variety of data on consumers is available in categories such as:

1. Demographic data including gender, educational level, profession, number of children;
2. Data on your home including the number of bedrooms, year built, square footage, mortgage size, house value;
3. Vehicle data including car make and model;
4. Household economic data including credit card type(s) and household income;
5. Household purchase data including what kind of magazines are read;
6. Average dollars spent per offline purchase as well as the average spent per online purchase; and
7. Household interest data.

Datafiniti is another data provider that provides data on consumers, scraped competitor data from websites, business location data, as well as property data. You may also buy data from aggregators like DemystData, which provides access to the above data vendors as well as many others. Returning to your role as an analyst, you generally will not make an argument to purchase additional data until you have examined the usefulness of internal data. Note also the case for retaining a healthy skepticism of the quality of paid-for data. With your table containing several features and a target (customer retained or lost), you now have everything you need to start your machine learning adventure.

Later in the book, we will go through a generalizable procedure for analyzing the gathered data and finding the answer to your CEO's question: what drives a customer to return and other related questions? You will also become familiar with the business decisions that follow from creating a model. A model is a set of relationships between the features and the target. A model is also the strength of these relationships, and it becomes a "definition," if you will, of what drives customer retention. Beyond being usable for answering your CEO's question, the most exciting part of the model you just created is that it can be applied to first-time customers while they are still on the website. In a matter of milliseconds, the model can provide a probability (from zero to one) of whether or not this customer is likely to be retained (for example, 0.11, or not very likely). In the case of low probability, a coupon for their next visit may be provided to increase their motivation to return to the site. Before getting to that point, however, we will learn how to interpret the ML results. We cover which features are most important (for your presentation to the CEO as well as for your understanding of the problem) and finally, the level of confidence in the model (can its probabilities be trusted?) and what kinds of decisions can be driven by the model (what probability cutoffs may be used?). In the end, we hope that while you will still be yourself after completing this book, your CEO will think of you as Batman due to your ability to solve these kinds of problems with relative ease.

1.5 Exercises

1. List areas in which machine learning likely already affects you, personally.
2. What is machine learning?
3. What is a *target*?
4. What is a *feature*?
5. What is *target leak*?

2
Automating Machine Learning

Follow a Clearly Defined Business Process

ML principle: "Extracting useful knowledge from data to solve business problems can be treated systematically by following a process with reasonably well-defined stages" (Provost & Fawcett, 2013, 14).

AutoML relevance: Machine learning is at its core a tool for problem-solving. AutoML drastically reduces the necessary technical skills. This can leave more time and attention available for focusing on business process.

Davenport and Patil (2012) suggested that coding was the most basic and universal skill of a data scientist but that this would be less true in five years. Impressively, they predicted that the more enduring skill would be to "communicate in the language that all stakeholders understand"—and to demonstrate the special skills involved in storytelling with data. The next step for us, then, is to develop these abilities vital for the data scientist or a subject matter expert capable of doing some of the work of a data scientist.

True to Davenport and Patil's vision, this book does not require coding skills unless your data is stored in complex databases or across multiple files. (We will provide some exercises allowing you to test your data skills if you are so inclined.) With that in mind, let's review the content of the book laid out visually now in Figure 2.1. The machine learning life-cycle has its roots in extensive research and practitioner experience (Shearer, 2000) and is designed to be helpful to everyone from novices to machine learning experts.

The life cycle model, while figured linearly here, is not an altogether linear process. For every step in the process, lessons learned may require a return to a previous step, even multiple steps back. Unfortunately, it is not uncommon to get to the *Interpret & Communicate* stage and find a problem requiring a return to *Define Project Objectives*, but careful adherence to our suggestions should minimize such problems. In this book, each of the five stages is broken down into actionable steps, each examined in the context of the hospital readmission project.

This book takes advantage of Automated Machine Learning (AutoML) to illustrate the machine learning process in its entirety. We define AutoML as any machine learning system that automates the repetitive tasks required for effective machine learning. For this reason, among others, AutoML is capturing the

Automated Machine Learning for Business. Kai R. Larsen and Daniel S. Becker, Oxford University Press. © Oxford University Press 2021.
DOI: 10.1093/oso/9780190941659.003.0002

Figure 2.1. Machine Learning Life Cycle Model.

imagination of specialists everywhere. Even Google's world-leading *Google Brain* data scientists have been outperformed by AutoML (Le & Zoph, 2017). As machine learning progress is traceable mostly to computer science, it is worth seeing AutoML initially from the code-intensive standpoint. Traditionally, programming has been about automating or simplifying tasks otherwise performed by humans. Machine learning, on the other hand, is about automating complex tasks requiring accuracy and speed beyond the cognitive capabilities of the human brain. The latest in this development, AutoML, is the process of automating machine learning itself. AutoML insulates the analyst from the combined mathematical, statistical, and computer sciences that are taking place "under the hood," so to speak. As one of us, Dan Becker, has been fond of pointing out, you do not learn to drive a car by studying engine components and how they interact. The process leading to a great driver begins with adjusting the mirrors, putting on the seat belt, placing the right foot on the brake, starting the car, putting the gear shift into "drive," and slowly releasing the brake.

As the car starts moving, attention shifts to the outside environment as the driver evaluates the complex interactions between the gas, brake, and steering wheel combining to move the car. The driver is also responding to feedback, such as vibrations and the car's position on the road, all of which require constant adjustments to accommodate, focusing more on the car's position on the road rather than the parts that make it run. In the same way, we best discover machine learning without the distraction of considering its more complex working components: whether the computer you are on can handle the processing requirements of an algorithm, whether you picked the best algorithms, whether you understand how to tune the algorithms to perform their best, as well as a myriad of other considerations. While the Batmans of the world need to understand the difference between a gasoline-powered car and an electric car and how they generate and transfer power to the drivetrain, we thoroughly believe that the first introduction to machine learning should not require advanced mathematical skills.

2.1 What Is Automated Machine Learning?

We started the chapter by defining AutoML as the process of automating machine learning, a very time- and knowledge-intensive process. A less self-referential definition may be "off-the-shelf methods that can be used easily in the field, without machine learning knowledge" (Guyon et al., 2015, 1). While this definition may be a bit too optimistic about how little knowledge of machine learning is necessary, it is a step in the right direction, especially for fully integrated AutoML, such as Salesforce Einstein.

Most companies that have adopted AutoML tend to be tight-lipped about the experience, but a notable exception comes from Airbnb, an iconic sharing economy company that recently shared its AutoML story (Husain & Handel, 2017). One of the most important data science tasks at Airbnb is to build *customer lifetime value models* (LTV) for both guests and hosts. This allows Airbnb to make decisions about individual hosts as well as aggregated markets such as any city. Because the traditional hospitality industry has extensive physical investments, whole cities are often lobbied to forbid or restrict sharing economy companies. Customer LTV models allow Airbnb to know where to fight such restrictions and where to expand operations.

To increase efficiency, Airbnb identified four areas where repetitive tasks negatively impacted the productivity of their data scientists. There were areas where AutoML had a definitive positive impact on productivity. While these will be discussed later, it is worth noting these important areas:

1. Exploratory data analysis. The process of examining the descriptive statistics for all features as well as their relationship with the target.
2. Feature engineering. The process of cleaning data, combining features, splitting features into multiple features, handling missing values, and dealing with text, to mention a few of potentially hundreds of steps.
3. Algorithm selection and hyperparameter tuning.[1] Keeping up with the "dizzying number" of available algorithms and their quadrillions of parameter combinations and figuring out which work best for the data at hand.
4. Model diagnostics. Evaluation of top models, including the confusion matrix and different probability cutoffs.

In a stunning revelation, Airbnb stated that AutoML increased their data scientists' productivity, "often by an order of magnitude" (Husain & Handel, 2017). Given data scientist salaries, this should make every CEO sit up and take notice. We have seen this multiplier in several of our projects and customer projects; Airbnb's experiences fit with our own experiences in using AutoML for research. In one case, a doctoral student applied AutoML to a project that was then in its third month. The student came back after an investment of two hours in AutoML with a performance improvement twice that of earlier attempts. In this case, the problem was that he had not investigated a specific class of machine learning that turned out to work especially well for the data. It is worth noting that rather than feel defeated by this result, the student could fine-tune the hyperparameters of the

[1] Hyperparameter is a fancy word for all the different settings that affect how a given algorithm works.

discovered algorithm to later outperform the AutoML. Without AutoML in the first place, however, we would not have gotten such magnified results. Our experience tracks with feedback from colleagues in industry. The Chief Analytics Officer who convinced Kai to consider the area of AutoML told a story of how DataRobot, the AutoML used in this book, outperformed his large team of data scientists right out of the box. This had clearly impressed him because of both the size of his team, their decades of math and statistics knowledge, and their domain expertise. Similarly, AutoML allowed Airbnb data scientists to reduce model error by over 5%, the significance of which can only be explained through analogy: consider that Usain Bolt, the sprinter whose name has become synonymous with the 100-meter dash, has only improved the world record by 1.6% throughout his career (Aschwanden, 2017).

For all the potential of AutoML to support and speed up existing teams of data scientists, the potential of AutoML is that it enables the democratization of data science. It makes it available and understandable to most, and makes subject matter expertise more important because it may now be faster to train a subject matter expert in the use of AutoML than it is to train a data scientist to understand the business subject matter at hand (for example, accounting).

2.2 What Automated Machine Learning Is Not

Love Improves Accuracy

ML principle: "An expert in some particular [algorithm]—maybe the person who developed it—can squeeze more performance out of it than someone else" (Witten et al., 2011, 378).

AutoML relevance: AutoML companies level the playing field by giving many algorithms a chance to perform for massive sets of data in different contexts. Only algorithms that perform are retained.

AutoML is not automatic ML. That is, there are still several decisions that must be made by the analyst and a requisite skill set for evaluating the results of applying machine learning to any dataset. For example, a subject matter expert must decide which problems are worth solving, determine which ideas are worthy of testing, and develop a solid understanding of common pitfalls and model evaluation skills. We base this book on a belief that most machine learning will be executed by subject matter experts who understand the machine learning life-cycle process (Figure 2.1) and have been trained to understand machine learning *conceptually* rather than mathematically. While some readers might sigh in relief, the more mathematically inclined among you may be thinking that you are about to be cheated out of essential details. We will recommend great resources for deepening your knowledge on specific machine learning algorithms but will focus on developing a deep under-standing of the machine learning process for business and the evaluation of machine learning results. For the first time, the existence of industrial-strength AutoML systems makes this possible without giving up the accuracy associated with expert-driven machine learning.

The fledgling data scientist may worry that AutoML will take away his or her job. Over time, the job market for data scientists will be greatly affected as AutoML takes over some of the most knowledge-based and time-intensive tasks currently performed by data scientists. However, given a quadrupling of interest in machine learning during the three-year period from 2014–2017,[2] it is currently hard for educational programs to keep up with demand. The tools are likely to affect data scientists disproportionately if they have neither deep subject matter knowledge in key business areas (e.g., accounting or marketing) nor cutting-edge skills in optimizing hyperparameters for the latest and best algorithms. Generally speaking, AutoML is good news for data scientists because it frees them from manually testing out all the latest algorithms, the vast majority of which will not improve the performance of their work. Less obvious, it also frees up time for the data scientist to focus on difficult problems not yet solved by AutoML applications, such as time series motifs (repeated-segments long time-series data) and trajectory mining (in which direction is something headed). With AutoML, data scientists can shift focus to the effective definition of machine learning problems, and the enrichment of datasets through location and addition of data. AutoML also saves time on process design and improves efficiency when handling some current tasks of the data scientist, monitoring dozens to hundreds of different algorithms while trying out different hyperparameters, a task at which algorithms have been found to be better than humans (Bergstra, Bardenet, Bengio, & Kégl, 2011).

2.3 Available Tools and Platforms

While there are as many different types of AutoML as there are AutoML tools and platforms, in general, there are two types: context-specific tools and general platforms. Context-specific tools are implemented within another system or for a specific purpose. For example, as mentioned above, Salesforce Einstein embeds AutoML tools within the existing Salesforce platform. The tool scores "leads," or potential customers regarding the likelihood of sales, and uses customer sentiment, competitor involvement, and overall prospect engagement to examine the likelihood of a deal to close. Another context-specific tool, *Wise.io*, now owned by

---

[2] Result from http://trends.google.com when searching for "machine learning." The plot represents the relative level of Google search for the term from May 13, 2014, to the same date in 2017. Interestingly, News search for the same term increased by a factor of 10 in the same period, indicating some hype in the news media.

General Electric, focuses on AutoML in the customer service arena, specifically through matching customers with personalized offers, identifying customers at risk of leaving, developing plans to "fortify loyalty," and prioritizing prospects to help attract customers. As such, Wise.io is a more general tool than Salesforce Einstein, but we place it in the context-specific category. A third example is *Distillery*, an AutoML company focusing on digital advertising. The focus here is on bringing awareness to how consumers experience your organization, increasing consumer awareness of your brand, prospecting for new customers, and retaining existing customers. It seems likely that context-specific AutoML applications will exist in almost every context, but for now, the focus is on customer interactions.

The second type of AutoML called general platforms, those designed for general-purpose machine learning, split into two types: open-source and commercial. In the open-source category, tools tend to be developed by and for computer and data scientists and generally require knowledge of programming languages, such as Python and R, these programming languages being the tools through which data scientists access data and algorithms. Contenders include *Spearmint, Auto-sklearn, Machine-JS, Hyper opt, TPOT, H2O.ai,* and *Auto-WEKA*. Auto-WEKA comes closest perhaps to not requiring programming skills. For the technically savvy reader, exploring these tools may be fun. Should you be interested, we recommend starting with Auto-sklearn due to its high precision in at least one competition (Guyon et al., 2016). However, these tools require an understanding of both coding and machine learning, which the tools themselves will not be very good for developing. Additionally, these tools are often not set up for visualization of results and decision-making in organizations.

The second subcategory of general platform AutoML, commercial platform, is provided by a commercial vendor, presumably for a price. Several of the available commercial general tools for machine learning also require coding skills, such as the *Google Prediction API* and *Amazon ML*. Others were, in our opinion, implemented around a less transparent process, may leave model comparisons opaque, or may have been bought by a major company for internal use, such as was the case with *Turi* (bought by Apple), *Prediction.io* (bought by Salesforce and turned into part of Einstein), and *Nexosis* and *Nutonian* (both acquired by DataRobot). As mentioned in this book, we use one of the general commercial tools that, in our experience, has transformed our ability to explain data science to novices: DataRobot. When teaching machine learning, DataRobot has even been helpful in some cases when grizzled veterans, who, despite extensive experience, may not always have used optimal processes in their work.

Before we continue to the machine learning life cycle, let's spend a bit of time discussing what we expect from a robust general machine learning tool. While organizational and human factors will influence what tools work best in a given business scenario, we focus here on the system factors, listed as the "eight criteria" in the following subsection.

2.4 Eight Criteria for AutoML Excellence

Many feature areas enable AutoML to have a significant impact on businesses. The following list is not a complete account of important AutoML features, particularly as they develop for the future, but provides a concrete start. All should apply to both context-specific and general tools, even though not all AutoML platforms are developed to be contenders in all areas. For example, some tools are developed to optimize hyperparameters and little else. These are designed specifically for use with code-based machine learning approaches, requiring knowledge of Python, R, or JavaScript. The eight criteria considered essential for AutoML to have significant impact are *accuracy, productivity, ease of use, understanding and learning, resource availability, process transparency, generalization,* and *recommended actions*. Reviewing these will allow us to define the concept of automated machine learning. After each criterion will follow a short explanation within the context of the hospital readmission project.

1. *Accuracy*.[3] By far the most important criterion. Without accuracy, there is no reason to engage in the use of AutoML (or any machine learning for that matter). Accuracy stems from the system selecting which features to use and creating new ones automatically, as well as comparing and selecting a variety of relevant models and tuning those models automatically. The system should also automatically set up validation procedures, including cross validation and holdout, and should rank the candidate models by performance, blending the best models for potential improvements. If a model predicts readmission of ten patients within a month, but only one is readmitted, then the accuracy may be too low for use.

2. *Productivity*. A large part of the productivity improvements of AutoML will come from the same processes listed under *accuracy* in large part because a data scientist's job is to constantly hunt for accuracy improvements. This hunt means perpetually living with a voice at the back of their head whispering that if only they could find a better algorithm or could tune an existing algorithm, the results would improve. Being freed from that voice is the single greatest productivity impact available. Other factors improving productivity include graceful handling of algorithm-specific needs. For example, some algorithms, such as regression, will throw out any case with even a single missing value, so we "impute" missing values (e.g., by setting all values to the mean of the feature) before such algorithms get the data. Other types of algorithms work better without such imputation, or with information on which cases have had a

---

[3] Later, we will learn about a variety of measures used to evaluate a machine learning solution. One of these measures is termed "accuracy." For right now, accuracy is used in a more general way to refer to all these measures, or more precisely the measure(s) the analyst decides are important for their context.

given feature imputed. Assuming good-quality data and existing subject matter expertise, the analyst should be able to conduct the analysis and be ready (PowerPoint and all) to present results to top management within two hours. Without subject matter expertise, the requisite time will be closer to one week. Without access to an AutoML, the timeline may be closer to three months. For the hospital readmissions project, productivity gains come from being able to run different projects per disease group at a vastly improved pace.

3. *Ease of use.* Analysts should find the system easy to use, meaning that an open-source system designed for coding data scientists should integrate easily into their process flow and be easily understandable. For non-coding analysts, the requirements are entirely different. Here the analyst must be guided through the data science process, and visualization and explanations must be intuitive. The system should minimize the machine learning knowledge necessary to be immediately effective, especially if the analyst does not know what needs to be done to the data for a given algorithm to work optimally. Once a model has been created and selected for use in production, operationalizing that model into production should be easy. For the hospital project, this means that the health management organization's analysts should all have the prerequisite skills to oversee AutoML, and that upon selection of a model, it is simple to implement it into the hospital's decision flow such that when a patient is ready for release, the system automatically uploads their record to the ML model, the model produces a prediction, and recommendations are provided to the user of the hospital system. For medium-range predictions of the likelihood of being readmitted, perhaps a cheap intervention prescribed as half an hour of watching a video on how to manage one's diabetes is likely to improve outcomes?

4. *Understanding and learning.* An AutoML platform or application should improve an analyst's understanding of the problem context. The system should visualize the interactions between features and the target and should "explain" so that the analyst can stand her ground when presenting findings to management and difficult questions rain down from above. One way this may be accomplished by the system would be through interactively allowing the analyst to experiment with different decisions. In short, the system should support thinking around business decisions. For the hospital project, the analyst may find that patients admitted for *elective* procedures are six percentage points more likely to be readmitted than *emergency* admits, potentially prompting some reflective thinking. A good AutoML system will allow the analyst to uncover such potentially useful findings, but only subject matter expertise will allow confident evaluation of this finding.

5. *Resource availability.* The AutoML system should be compatible with existing business systems and easily integrated with other tools in the business intelligence ecosystem. Such compatibility means that it should be able to connect to existing databases and file formats when ingesting data. A system developed

around a proprietary file format that requires turning existing data into that file format before use by the system will rate poorly on this criterion. The system should also allow easy use of the resulting model, either through an application programming interface (API) or through code that can be placed easily into the organizational workflow. A solid AutoML should address memory issues, storage space, and processing capabilities in a flexible manner. While this will differ depending on the intended use, for a subject matter expert user of AutoML, this means that a cloud-based system or an enterprise system on a powerful cluster of servers is probably necessary as an analyst's individual computer could not be expected to scale up to handle any problem in a reasonable amount of time. An AutoML for the coding data scientist could, on the other hand, expect the analyst to set up "containers" or virtual machines. Finally, support for the system should be available, either through online forums or customer service, allowing the analyst access to support from experienced machine learning experts. For the hospital project, the data, which is available as a stand-alone file should be easily uploadable to the AutoML platform where we should not have to worry whether the file is too large or there is enough "memory" and processing power available to handle the data and analytical processes.

6. *Process transparency.* Because AutoML insulates the analyst from the underlying complexity of the machine learning, it can be harder to develop trust in such systems. It is critical, therefore, that for analysts who seek to understand machine learning, as we will do in this book, it is possible to drill into the decisions made by the system. Process transparency interacts with the earlier criterion of *understanding and learning* in that without transparency; learning is limited. It is worth noting that process transparency focuses on improving the knowledge of the machine learning process, whereas the *understanding and learning* criterion focuses more on learning about the business context. Finally, process transparency should enable evaluation of models against each other beyond just their overall performance; which features are the most important in the neural network vs. the logistic regression; and in which cases each excels. For the hospital readmission project, details such as which algorithm produced the best model and the transformations applied to the data should also be available to the analyst.

7. *Generalizable across contexts.* An AutoML should work for all target types, data sizes, and different time perspectives. In other words, it can predict targets that are numerical (regression problems), as well as targets that contain categorical values (classification problems), both whose values have two categories and those with multiple categories. Additionally, the system should be capable of handling small, medium, and big data. When data is too big, AutoML should automatically sample down the dataset as necessary or perhaps even automate the selection of the optimal sample size. Finally, an AutoML should be able to handle both cross-sectional (data collected at one time, or treated as such) and

longitudinal data (data where time order matters). Time is a complex point that we will return to in Chapters 25 and 26. For the hospital readmission project, time is not a factor as we focus on the first interaction with any patient, specifically their discharge, and then examine the next month to find out whether they were readmitted or not. Our dataset is on the higher end of small (10,000 records), and its target has two values (readmitted=*True* or readmitted=*False*). We expect the AutoML system to work as well for the hospital setting as for other business settings.

8. *Recommend actions.* This criterion is mostly for context-specific AutoML. With specific knowledge of the analytical context, the system should be able to transfer a probability into action. For example, as the user of an AutoML, you may decide to analyze employee turnover data. The system returns robust predictions on which employees are likely to stay and who will leave over the next year. Let's say two employees come back with the same probability of leaving, .90 (90% likely to depart the organization). One is an employee you know to be the backbone of the company, and one is a slacker. The AutoML cannot understand this unless it has also been programmed to "know" the context of the problem.

Further, let's say you want recommendations about how to reduce turnover. Without background information, the system would return with a manipulation recommendation for the most potent feature. However, if the top feature is someone's age, the system must first know that age is unmanipulable and furthermore that a less effective but still valuable feature, *hours of overtime*, may be changed by management through policy or hiring. From this point, the AutoML is still not free from the need to provide facilities for profit calculation, given that the analyst supplies context information on fixed costs, variable costs, and earnings. For the hospital readmission project, this criterion is not relevant because we are not using a context-specific AutoML, so we must become the subject matter experts ourselves to take the findings from the platform and recommend actions.

With these criteria outlined, we should be better equipped to evaluate an AutoML for use within an organization.

2.5 How Do the Fundamental Principles of Machine Learning and Artificial Intelligence Transfer to AutoML? A Point-by-Point Evaluation

The manner of introduction of critical principles is a defining characteristic of any educational or instructional book. The approach taken in this book is to cover central technical and theoretical topics organically—that is, without defining them explicitly, as is often seen in university textbooks. This decision has been made due the way in which these subjects carefully fit together as equal-value components of the machine learning life cycle. Without an understanding of the whole process, a meaningful grasp of the individual parts is difficult to achieve. Nevertheless, more experienced readers may be interested in understanding which of these conceptual points we cover. Such readers may also be interested in how adding AutoML to the mix affects the approach one might take to understanding these topics.

2.6 Exercises

1. Which repetitive tasks did Airbnb identify as especially appropriate for AutoML?
2. Rank the eight criteria for AutoML excellence according to their importance for your setting and justify the order.
3. Reading through the eight criteria, make a note of every word you did not understand. Google these and discuss with a colleague.

SECTION II
DEFINING PROJECT OBJECTIVES

Focus on the Solution

ML principle: Use machine learning with a consultant focus rather than researcher approach. Focus on solving real problems rather than reporting model statistics and performance characteristics (Breiman, 2001).

AutoML relevance: A model is no better than the problem it solves. Because AutoML moves from problem statement to model implementation 10–100 times faster than traditional ML, it is easier to cycle between problem and solution.

Here we move into the details of Step 1 of the Machine Learning Life Cycle Model (Figure II.1), starting with the specification of the business problem or opportunity. We base the model on the Cross Industry Standard Process for Data Mining (CRISP-DM; Wirth & Hipp, 2000). CRISP-DM has been found to be useful to experts and beginners alike, and especially

> useful for planning, communication within and outside the project team, and documentation. The generic check-lists are helpful even for experienced people. The generic process model provides an excellent foundation for developing a specialized process model which prescribes the steps to be taken in detail and which gives practical advice for all these steps. (Wirth & Hipp, 2000, 1)

Here, updated and focused on supervised machine learning, the Machine Learning Life Cycle Model will help keep us on track by providing "guard-rails" for our projects and our skill acquisition. We outline the remainder of the book according to this process.

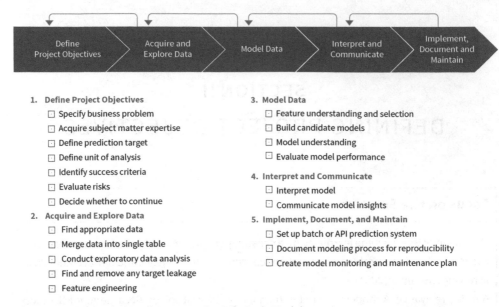

1. **Define Project Objectives**
   - ☐ Specify business problem
   - ☐ Acquire subject matter expertise
   - ☐ Define prediction target
   - ☐ Define unit of analysis
   - ☐ Identify success criteria
   - ☐ Evaluate risks
   - ☐ Decide whether to continue
2. **Acquire and Explore Data**
   - ☐ Find appropriate data
   - ☐ Merge data into single table
   - ☐ Conduct exploratory data analysis
   - ☐ Find and remove any target leakage
   - ☐ Feature engineering

3. **Model Data**
   - ☐ Feature understanding and selection
   - ☐ Build candidate models
   - ☐ Model understanding
   - ☐ Evaluate model performance
4. **Interpret and Communicate**
   - ☐ Interpret model
   - ☐ Communicate model insights
5. **Implement, Document, and Maintain**
   - ☐ Set up batch or API prediction system
   - ☐ Document modeling process for reproducibility
   - ☐ Create model monitoring and maintenance plan

Figure II.1. Expanded Machine Learning Life Cycle Model.

3
Specify *Business* Problem

3.1 Why Start with a Business Problem?

While we use the word "problem" in this chapter, the word "opportunity" is equally appropriate. As we humans love to fix problems, we'll use these words interchangeably since many data science opportunities come from problems in current business processes. For example, not knowing who among your customers will leave you for a competitor tomorrow is a problem, but figuring out your customer churn or attrition yields an opportunity to improve your competitive position in the marketplace.

We emphasized the importance of model accuracy in Chapter 2.4; however, flawless accuracy is of no value if we address the wrong problem. While no project is ever complete, the later in the process errors are detected, the costlier those mistakes are to fix (Mochal & Mochal, 2012). Since this is the first step in our machine learning process, it is essential to get it right. When we specify the correct problem from the start, most results are immediately useful. Problems (worded here as *opportunities*) encountered by companies are manifold. Companies would generally like to know:

1. Which customers are likely to buy a product? Most companies cannot afford to contact every person in existence and may need help finding the most likely buyers.
2. Why customers do not purchase the company's products.
3. Why customers purchase the company's products.
4. Why customers are dissatisfied.
5. Why customers do not renew their contracts (whether satisfied or not).
6. What leads to extensive use of a product (e.g., extra bandwidth use among customers on a cellular data plan).
7. For ad placement, which Internet users are likely to respond positively.
8. From which pages on the company website would a specific visitor benefit most.

These examples provide but a small problem set compared to what a subject matter expert might generate. In each of the above cases, it should be possible to begin the opportunity statement with "I want to predict . . . ."

By carefully specifying the problem, we can evaluate our options in a precise manner: should we proceed to address this problem, or is there a better problem in which to invest our time and resources? Finally, is ground truth for the problem

Automated Machine Learning for Business. Kai R. Larsen and Daniel S. Becker, Oxford University Press. © Oxford University Press 2021.
DOI: 10.1093/oso/9780190941659.003.0003

available? In other words, can we access data on the behavior or phenomenon we are trying to predict? Do we know which customers left our company in the past as well as some additional information on these customers? If not, there is no road forward for machine learning unless we can purchase the missing information.

Once we ensure that we have the requisite data, we create and share a project brief with stakeholders. It is essential to outline the case in the language of business rather than the language of modeling. At this point, the specific algorithms you plan to use, as well as the process of accessing data and transformations, are unnecessary unless you are presenting to a very sophisticated modeling-focused audience. Even then, focusing on technical details is likely to distract from agreeing on overall goals. The description should include specific actions that may result from the project with a focus on definitive metrics, such as the number of customers affected, the costs, and the benefits, including innovations and cost savings. In short, how will this project improve the bottom line?

Evaluate any proposed project against three criteria:

1. Is the problem statement presented in the language of business?
2. Does the problem statement specify actions that should result from the project?
3. How could solving this problem impact the bottom line?

3.2 Problem Statements

In this part of the chapter, we will outline "best practices" for constructing a problem statement. For this, we will analyze the following sample problem statements, beginning with the following statement related to providing loans (Figure 3.1):

"Our hedge fund is considering investing in loans on the website LendingClub.com. We don't have any models to use for this."

Figure 3.1. Lending Club Investment Problem Statement.

Take a minute to evaluate the statement carefully. How many of the criteria below does the statement address?

1. Is the problem statement presented in the language of business?
2. Does the problem statement specify actions that should result from the project?
3. How could solving this problem impact the bottom line?

Immediately, you may have noticed that the statement focuses on the lack of models, rather than on the business goals of the hedge fund. Moreover, it neither specifies what actions would result nor does it address how the project would improve the hedge fund's bottom line. Let us evaluate another problem statement against the three criteria.

Let us consider the problem statement in Figure 3.2. Our organization is now a hospital worried about readmission rates for all its patients, but have decided to start with diabetes patients. Take a minute (really) to evaluate the statement carefully. How many of the three criteria does the statement address?

1. Is the problem statement presented in the language of business?
2. Does the problem statement specify actions that should result from the project?
3. How could solving this problem impact the bottom line?

The problem statement in Figure 3.2 takes a significant step forward in outlining that we care about both readmissions and the cost of those readmissions. However, it still fails to address each criterion in the following ways: while it states the overall toll to the hospital for patient readmission, the statement fails to specify the total number

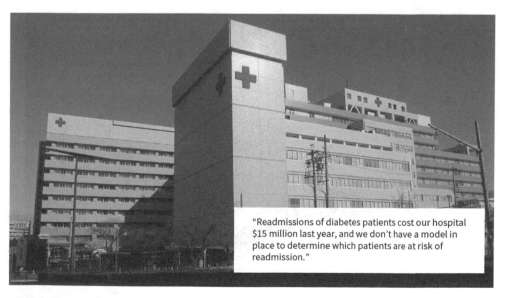

"Readmissions of diabetes patients cost our hospital $15 million last year, and we don't have a model in place to determine which patients are at risk of readmission."

Figure 3.2. Hospital Readmissions Problem Statement.

of readmissions and the avoidable portion of readmissions. Second, it does not lay out possible actions that should result from taking on the project. For example, if you knew with near-absolute certainty that a patient would be readmitted within a month, what actions would you take to provide proactive care for that patient? Would you keep him or her in the hospital? Run more tests? Send a nurse out to visit them on days 2, 4, 8, and 16 after their discharge? How would the project improve the bottom line?

Let us turn now to a third problem statement, in which warehouse logistics operators seek to improve efficiency in unloading goods from cargo trucks.

The problem statement in Figure 3.3 clarifies the action that will result from the successful analysis (tell incoming drivers when the warehouse bay will be ready), but it fails on the other two criteria. Consider the statement and think about *how* it fails. Is it presented in the language of business? We are missing key details about how often trucks show up at the warehouse, the distribution of those visits, as well as how long it takes the warehouse team to unload a vehicle.

We also do not know the cost of extended delivery waiting times or that of each truck delivery in general. Without this information, we do not see the potential for cost savings from better knowledge sharing among stakeholders. If complete transparency and prediction were possible, how would truck drivers use this information? Would they deliver their goods to other warehouses first? Are they able to do so? What if many of the trucks drive 10 or more hours to deliver the products, but our algorithms can only predict the availability of a delivery bay within three hours?

Going back to the Lending Club example (Figure 3.2), we might provide an improved problem statement by outlining how much the hedge fund is willing to invest annually, what kinds of interest rates may be received, and what problems investors

"Warehouse operators want to know how long each truck will take to unload so they can tell drivers of subsequent deliveries when the warehouse bay will be ready."

Figure 3.3. Warehouse Operators Problem Statement.

Our hedge fund is considering investing $40 Million/year in loans on LendingClub.com.
These loans are an appealing investment with interest rates averaging 17%.
However, 5% of invested money on the site is lost due to borrower defaults.
We propose building a model to screen out the riskiest borrowers. If successful,
our organization will use the model to justify

Figure 3.4. Updated Lending Club Problem Statement.

face (Figure 3.4). Even here, we can see that missing details, but most data science projects are processes of discovery, so focus on specifying the problem to the level expected by your organization. If your organization has undefined or relaxed expectations, or you are a student, go as far as you can by following our recommendations.

Reviewing the problem statement in Figure 3.4, it now seems to appropriately fulfill two of the three criteria to provide an excellent project starting point. We have *stated it in the language of business* (investment amount, interest rates, loss percentage), and it *specifies actions that should result* (screen out the riskiest borrowers, invest on the site, use model to automatically choose which loans to fund). However, it is still not without fault, doing a poor job of addressing how the project will improve the bottom line, which will require calculating the return on investment and comparing that return to other opportunities available to the organization.

Chapter 4 takes the understanding of the problem and brings in subject matter expertise to critically evaluate the assumptions made in the problem statement. The subject matter expert(s) will also help set realistic expectations for model performance and start thinking about the necessary data to collect for the project.

3.3 Exercises

To do:

1. Select either the warehouse or the hospital readmission example and write a problem statement that addresses all three criteria.
2. How would you address the potential impact on the bottom line? Consider the information in Figure 3.5 and its impact on your decision to invest $40 million through Lending Club. Additional statistics are available to review at https://www.lendingclub.com/info/demand-and-credit-profile.action.

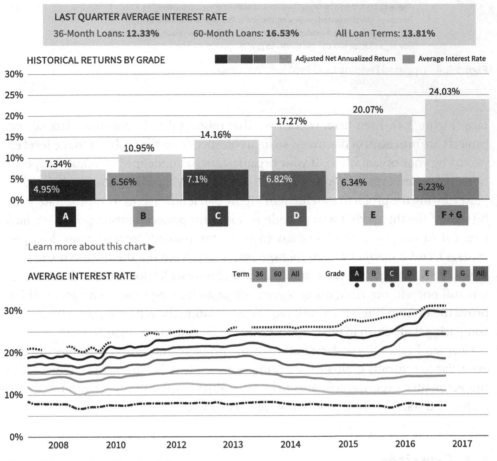

Figure 3.5. Lending Club Statistics.

4

Acquire Subject Matter Expertise

4.1 Importance of Subject Matter Expertise

Context Is King

ML principle: "Formulating [ML] solutions and evaluating the results involves thinking carefully about the context in which they will be used" (Provost & Fawcett, 2013, 15). Does the model perform well against a default alternative?

"Focus on the data and understand the business" (Williams, 2011, 9).

AutoML relevance: Context determines the appropriate type of AutoML to apply. Proper evaluation of a model requires domain knowledge. In time series analysis, using a validation measure that evaluates performance relative to naïve models is recommended.

While identification of the business problem is an important starting point, it is probable that without subject matter expertise or access to it, you will not be capable of providing complete insights. Subject matter expertise constitutes deep experience in a specific domain such as accounting, marketing, supply chain, or medicine, and supports early identification of potential obstacles and opportunities.

Throughout this book, we will use datasets that will benefit from subject matter expertise. We consider this a good exercise in developing the curiosity necessary to be a good data scientist. Sooner or later, the machine learning algorithms will provide an answer that may puzzle you. For example, you may find that patients transferred to hospice care are seldom readmitted. A careless data scientist could easily walk into a presentation and explain to the management at a hospital that we should transfer more patients into hospice care because they seem to do so well there. It would likely be the last time you were invited to do such a presentation.

Beyond knowledge of what the features mean, another important task for which we need a subject matter expert is setting realistic expectations for model performance. Most models are not going to be completely wrong, and similarly, no model is ever going to be entirely correct. A typical model will perform somewhere in the middle of the road, which is probably also where past processes performed, whether automated or not. An expert with knowledge of what constitutes success will be

Automated Machine Learning for Business. Kai R. Larsen and Daniel S. Becker, Oxford University Press. © Oxford University Press 2021.
DOI: 10.1093/oso/9780190941659.003.0004

invaluable in evaluating whether this project should proceed and in convincing management that an eventual solution is worth implementing.

We also expect the subject matter expert to suggest ideas for data collection, that is, to know where relevant data resides, including any external data. The expert should advise on ideas for modeling and even alternatives *to* modeling. Through examples and data, we will make clear the importance of experiences of subject matter experts that otherwise would take quite some time for a data science team to acquire. The preferable process is to bring an expert on board early to maximize their effectiveness in shaping the project. Of all possible machine learning practitioners, we now consider the subject matter expert the most appropriate machine learning user since AutoML has become an option for organizations. We here assume that training a subject matter expert to use AutoML will yield greater and faster returns than to prepare a machine learning expert in accounting, marketing, finance, or any subspecialty areas therein.

That said, if a subject matter expert (SME, pronounced "smee") is not available, the data scientist has the following options: discussing the domain to be modeled with data science colleagues, interviewing SMEs, reading trade journals, reading Internet sources on the subject, or even reading the definitions of available features found in data dictionaries around the web. A motivated data scientist can walk the shop floor or work in the relevant domain for a time (days or weeks) to understand the problem's context further.

4.2 Exercises

Public organizations have increasingly started evaluating hospitals based on readmission rates (Ross et al., 2009). That is, after visiting a hospital, how likely is a patient with a specific disease, or a patient visiting a given hospital, to return within some specified interval of time? The assumption is that high readmission rates are indicative of inadequate care. To learn more about this subject, use Google and Google Scholar to research why diabetes patients return to the emergency room within a commonly specified time interval after leaving the hospital (focus on articles with full text available). What are the keywords allowing you to find articles on this topic?

Alternatively, if your interests lie more in the operations domain, you may prefer to research warehouse loading and unloading processes and their average duration. What are the factors that determine the turnaround time for both loading and unloading?

5
Define Prediction Target

5.1 What Is a Prediction Target?

Learning to see the potential prediction targets of the world is a critically important skill to develop, and may enable the inspiration to use machine learning in new and ingenious ways. The prediction target is often the behavior of a "thing" (e.g., person, stock, organization, etc.) in the past that we will need to predict in the future (for example, using information about Microsoft's stock performance the last 24,000 hours to predict how it will perform during the next hour). If we return to the case of Lending Club, it is possible to get a target right out of the dataset. If our goal was to predict how much of a loan a person was likely to have paid back by the end of the loan period, that target is available to us. Figure 5.1 shows the target feature titled *loan_is_bad*. While this is a common prediction target, it is not a feature provided by Lending Club. A data scientist or subject matter expert had to decide how this feature should be defined.

As seen in data row one in Figure 5.1 *(loan_id: 1038292)*, the value for *loan_is_bad* is FALSE, which means that it was a good loan. We could have changed the target to *loan_is_good* with the first row of Figure 5.1 containing a TRUE value. It does not matter for the analysis, so let us keep the *loan_is_bad* target and examine the loan status information provided to us by Lending Club. These are the values stored for a given loan at the time we download the data:

1. Fully paid
2. Current
3. In Grace Period
4. Late (16–30 days)
5. Late (31–120 days)
6. Default
7. Charged Off

Given a value of *true*, which of these values would you classify as bad loans, and which would you classify as good? Different subject matter experts may disagree on these values, so we will proceed with the assumption that only status 1 and 2 are indicative of good loans (logged as *loan_is_bad*: FALSE) and that status 3–7 are indicative of bad loans (logged as *loan_is_bad*: TRUE).

Automated Machine Learning for Business. Kai R. Larsen and Daniel S. Becker, Oxford University Press. © Oxford University Press 2021. DOI: 10.1093/oso/9780190941659.003.0005

loan_id	loan_amnt	funded_amnt	funded_amnt_inv	term	loan_is_bad
1038292	12000	12000	12000	36 months	FALSE
1038293	15000	15000	15000	37 months	FALSE
1038294	5500	5500	5500	38 months	FALSE
1038295	22000	22000	22000	39 months	FALSE
1038296	27700	27700	27700	40 months	FALSE
1038297	12650	12650	12650	41 months	TRUE
1038298	10500	10500	10500	42 months	FALSE

Prediction target

Figure 5.1. Lending Club Target.

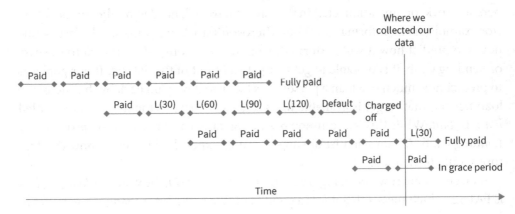

Figure 5.2. Transforming Loan Data into Classification Targets.

Consider the four loans in Figure 5.2. Over time, depending on the date you se-lect as the cutoff for collecting data, these loans will have different opportunities to succeed or fail. The first loan has been steadily paid down and was fully paid off before the date we collected data. We coded this loan as *good*. Loan number two was charged off before the collection date, so we coded this loan as *bad*. The lendee on the third loan steadily paid, but we collected data on the first day of the new period, at a time when this loan payment was not received. At the time of collecting the data, this loan was received as "In grace period (1–15 days)," and later that month switched into "Late (16–30 days)." The lendee then paid the loan in full during one of the last days of that data-collection month, and its status changed to "Fully paid," but we could not know this at the time of data collection and as such coded this row as *bad*. The fact that we are here forced to code something we later know to be a good loan as bad due to our data selection criteria is worrisome and may be an indi-cation that we did not allow the data enough time to mature before collection. More specifically, if we truly had to collect data at the vertical line in Figure 5.2, we would have been better off excluding the last two loans because they have yet to reach maturity. If maturity is not important to us, our criteria for selecting rows of data to exclude can be modified to include the fourth loan with "Paid" status at the time of data collection. We would then code the fourth loan as *good*.

5.2 How Is the Target Important for Machine Learning?

Why do we need a target? The answer to this question will become clearer as we continue to dig into machine learning models. In simple terms, without a target, there is no (easy) way for humans or machines to learn what associations drive an outcome. Take, for example, a favorite data science learning tool, the *Titanic Competition* on Kaggle.com. In this competition, you work with 891 rows of passenger information as your training data (the data you will use to create a model), including family size, ticket cost, passenger class, embarkation location, age, and sex (gender), as well as the target, *survived*.

The machine learning algorithms will soon determine that thanks to the chivalrous norms of society in the time of the *Titanic*, the most critical relationship to survival comes from the feature named *sex*. If we knew nothing more than the sex of a person and whether they survived or not, we could still make a pretty good model predicting whether people *not* in this set of 891 passengers survived or perished. As a whole, this sample shows that only 38.4% of all passengers survived (the actual figure is 31.6%), so if we had to guess with no further information, it would be wise to put our money on any given passenger *not* surviving (with a 61.6% chance of being correct based on the training data). In the training data, there are 577 males and 314 females. It turns out that the males were only 18.9% likely to survive, whereas the females were 74.2% likely to survive. This data allows us to create a model that always guesses that women survive and always guesses that men die. With these likelihoods of survival, our model should be correct 78.7% of the time, that is, if the data we haven't seen is distributed precisely like the data we used to create the model (exceedingly unlikely for such a small dataset; and later we'll learn not to use the whole training dataset to build our model). In other words, without more detailed knowledge of the relationships between a feature like *sex* and a target like *survived* (i.e., understanding the impact of features), we cannot train the machine learning algorithms to predict the future. To note as well, the *Titanic* competition on Kaggle.com is a somewhat limited exercise in that all we can do is explain the past rather than predict the future. Trans-Atlantic passenger liners collide with icebergs so infrequently these days, and even if they did crash with icebergs every day, societal norms have changed precipitously. This societal change in the value assigned to chivalry represents a significant divergence from the central relationship allowing the model to predict who will survive. As such, the competition is less about predicting further scenarios but rather to practice creating models that generalize to a smaller set of people who were also on the same ship.

We have discussed two kinds of targets here without explicitly noting their defining characteristics. The first kind is *classification*, which predicts the category to which a new case belongs. For example, we might build a model of divorce during the first ten years of marriage (our target is *divorced: TRUE or FALSE*). Alternatively, we can use machine learning to conduct *regression*, that is, to predict the target's numeric value. With this second kind of target, we might, for example, target how many years of blissful union a couple has ahead of them. Datasets with regression targets are still available in the book's appended exercises. When working through a dataset for classification, we carefully examine the possible states in which a variable can exist and consider options for simplification, as with the Lending Club question of predicting good loan prospects. Remember that for Lending Club, we had to decide whether to code a loan as good or bad and whether to throw away data.

When training a car, for example, to predict the likelihood that the light the car is moving toward is *red*, *yellow*, or *green*, the target would be one of classification. It is possible to simplify the choice to either *red* or *green* but doing so would overlook crucial information that would inform more steady and smooth braking behavior. If we choose to focus on the number of meters to the intersection rather than the light color, we are now working with a numeric value and therefore, a regression problem. If simplified into quantitative categories (sometimes called *buckets*), we can turn regression problems into classification problems. The number of meters to the intersection is as such turned into a regression problem of whether it is time to start braking or not. For the diabetes patient readmissions example, we had information on how soon (if at all) a person was readmitted based on the difference between the date they were released and the date they were next admitted (number of days). If the number were 30 or less, we would code it as a 1, indicating readmission, and if 31 or larger, we would code it as a 0 for non-readmission. Here we opted to categorize the outcome of readmission with binary TRUE/FALSE values. The alternative might have been to consider the number of days between release and readmission as a regression target to predict what leads to immediate versus more delayed readmission (if readmission at all).

With the target variable of a machine learning problem in mind, we can move forward to discussing the level of analysis of the target to create the datasets needed for prediction.

5.3 Exercises/Discussion

1. Earlier, we considered the implications of different loan status for the Lending Club data in defining the target. What do you think about status 3: In the grace period (1–15 days)? Is it bad to be in the grace period? Some people consider this period a mortgage company's gift to them, so to speak, and might be surprised to learn that they would be regarded as delinquent. Where would you place this status (good or bad) and why?

6

Decide on Unit of Analysis

6.1 What Is a Unit of Analysis?

Machine learning sometimes involves an intricate understanding of a problem's real-world context. Keeping the *target* in mind, we now deal with the fact that a given target may appear multiple times in the dataset. For example, for the hospital readmissions project, where we cared about whether a patient was readmitted or not, we must consider whether the patient or the visit is the unit of analysis. If we collect data over a whole year, the same person may be readmitted a dozen or more times. If the visit is the unit of analysis, we are fine. Each visit will be coded as a new row in the training dataset. Alternatively, if the patient is the level of analysis, we will have to decide which of a patient's visits to include.

A unit (of analysis) is the *what*, *who*, *where*, and *when* of our project. The *what* could be whether a visitor did indeed click on an ad. The *who* could be readmitted (or not) patients. An example of the *where* could be the location of a future crime, and *when* might be the time we expect a piece of machinery to break down.[1] For each unit of analysis, there can be numerous outcomes that we might want to predict. If the customer is the unit of analysis and you work for Netflix, you may want to predict whether they would be likely to accept an upgrade offer, whether they are likely to cancel their contract next week, and whether they are more likely to enjoy watching *Stranger Things* or *House of Cards*. Alternatively, Google has long engaged in a massive effort to predict the future performance of job applicants (Davenport, Harris & Shapiro, 2010). The intended outcome of this effort is that Google will glean insight on what information (at the time of application) made that person likely to become a great employee. Was it a high score on the extroverted aspect of their personality test? Their college GPA? Whatever the variables turn out to be, Google can employ a model containing these critical indicators of future performance to new applicants to predict their likelihood of becoming great employees. In the related HR challenge of managing employee turnover, machine learning can be applied to variables related to existing employees to understand better why people are leaving currently, or even which people are likely to quit over the next year. Finally, we turn to an example from the highly automated finance world. Bridgewater Associates, the world's largest hedge fund, is planning to take a further step in employing machine learning,

---

[1] Interestingly, to round out the W5's of journalistic fame, we'll later add *why* and *how*.

Automated Machine Learning for Business. Kai R. Larsen and Daniel S. Becker, Oxford University Press. © Oxford University Press 2021.
DOI: 10.1093/oso/9780190941659.003.0006

replacing most employees with models that will make the trading decisions with the remaining employees being those that "design the criteria by which the [models] make decisions, intervening when the something isn't working" (Copeland & Hope, 2016).

6.2 How to Determine Unit of Analysis

The previous section gives us a general sense of a *unit of analysis* as a concept. One way to identify the appropriate unit of analysis is to first think about what the prediction target is, which will then often supply an obvious choice. If a data scientist wants to predict whether a patient is likely to be readmitted, we have two options: patient or readmission event. In this case, one can easily see that every admission and the treatment received will be different. We would therefore, in this case, treat the readmission as the unit of analysis, and treat every readmission by the same patient in the dataset as separate rows (units). Similarly, if an insurance company is determining the price of various types of policies (house, car, life), the unit of analysis is the policy rather than the person requesting the policy; it would not make sense to use the person as the unit of analysis and then offer the same price regardless of the kind of policy the person seeks.

Another example involves Lending Club. We are big fans of Lending Club, not because we have money to invest with them but because they share a lot of data about the loan prospects they make available for investment. Figure 6.1 shows this data on a few loans. Here, the row serves as the unit of analysis, but what does that row represent? Arguably, you are interested in the loan prospect rather than the person requesting the loan. The information on the person will be the same for two loans that they ask for during a given period. However, it is the loan amount that determines whether the algorithm is likely to recommend funding the loan. For example, you're a fool if you offer to lend your friend Slackey $100,000, but $5 for coffee is generally safe if you keep reminding him to pay you back. So, the unit of analysis in this situation is the loan itself.

Sometimes it is far from obvious what the unit of analysis should be. In such cases, you lean on your subject matter expert and work with him or her to share knowledge

	loan_id	loan_amnt	funded_amnt	funded_amnt_inv	term	loan_is_bad
	1038292	12000	12000	12000	36 months	FALSE
	1038293	15000	15000	15000	37 months	FALSE
Unit of analysis →	1038294	5500	5500	5500	38 months	FALSE
	1038295	22000	22000	22000	39 months	FALSE
	1038296	27700	27700	27700	40 months	FALSE
	1038297	12650	12650	12650	41 months	TRUE
	1038298	10500	10500	10500	42 months	FALSE

Figure 6.1. Lending Club Data.

of the problem context—you will likely be able to figure it out together. Take the following example: your company has 100 open jobs, and you consider developing a model to determine whether a person is likely to be a good fit for one of those jobs. You may question whether or not you should develop a model to predict job fit at the position level or the company level (is this person a good company culture fit vs. are they a good fit for the specific position?). It is a good idea to factor in that each application is likely to be different, even when they come from the same person. As we start thinking through this problem, it becomes clear that a good model would distinguish whether an applicant is right for a job as a personal assistant or as a coder.

6.3 Exercises

Respond to the following questions:

1. For the warehouse example from Chapter 4, is the driver, the truck, or the specific delivery the unit of analysis regarding loading/unloading times? Is there another possible unit of analysis?
2. For the hospital diabetes readmission example, what is the unit of analysis? Discuss with a colleague or in class.
3. Say you want to send out mail advertisements to people in your database for upcoming events. You want to send the mailers only to people likely to respond, so you want a model to give the likelihood of response so that you can sort people by probability and mail the ones with the highest probability. You have posted many advertisements to the same people over the years, and all of this information is in your database, allowing you to create a model. What is the unit of analysis? Is it a person or is it the mailing? *A proposed answer to this problem is available in Appendix D.

7
Success, Risk, and Continuation

7.1 Identify Success Criteria

When evaluating project objectives, a better understanding of success criteria will develop over time, both within an individual project and across many projects. Having access to an AutoML can drastically cut down on the investment necessary to complete a project. As such, the availability of an AutoML presents a vital success criterion in considering project workflow and completion speed. To place a fully developed model into the workflow of a company, the best practice is to start small with clear questions and goals. Consider the following factors:

1. Who will use the model?
2. Is management on board with the project?
3. Can the model drivers be visualized?
4. How much value can the model produce?

The users of the model may already be involved in the project as subject matter experts. Early involvement of subject matter experts has been associated with project success (Bano & Zowghi, 2015). Also, support from management will make the difference between success and failure at every stage of the project (Turban, 1990). For machine learning, especially for projects without access to AutoML, management support is especially crucial at the end of a project when decisions are made about model implementation into the information workflow. As well, if the model truly drives value, that value must be specified and communicated relative costs and benefits. Model value will be discussed further in Chapter 17.4. Visualization of model drivers can be an essential tool for clarifying and communicating value. It is worth noting that there is no easy way to evaluate the extent to which a model will drive value until after the data has been collected and cleaned (real-world data can often be quite messy), and models have been run and evaluated. That said, we are not released from the responsibility of starting this process early enough to evaluate different projects against each other.

Automated Machine Learning for Business. Kai R. Larsen and Daniel S. Becker, Oxford University Press. © Oxford University Press 2021.
DOI: 10.1093/oso/9780190941659.003.0007

Break the Problem Down

ML principle: A business problem is often not directly solvable by implementing just one model (Provost & Fawcett, 2013).

AutoML relevance: The road to solving a business problem often takes a circuitous path. For example, to determine the number of employees needed at a store, it may instead be necessary to predict the number of customers. This is true for both traditional ML and AutoML.

7.2 Foresee Risks

Risks are difficult to calculate. To get at the risks, you will need to be creative and often play the devil's advocate—a model that makes unsound recommendations is far worse than no model at all. Model risks might relate to the model being insufficiently predictive or "simple" mistakes such as target leakage features in the model, which result in models that are too predictive but with no practical value. Of further concern, data may be missing or be of insufficient quality. Some topic areas that will help in thinking through potential risks are *model risks*, *ethical risks*, *cultural risks*, *business process risks*, and *environmental risks*.

Let's assume you work at a bank that has been offering consumer loans for several decades, and you have convinced your new manager that you are capable of developing a model that can outperform the current labor-intensive method for application evaluation. It is hard to see how you could lose this bet on your career, given the massive amount of available data from past loans. However, even a "shoo-in" project like this holds unexpected risks. In all likelihood, the bank does not have access to information on applicants who were rejected but would have been great customers had they been given loans. This scenario would be indicative of a *data* or *model risk*. However, there are ways of getting around this problem, most commonly by training the model based on the data you have and hoping for the best. You can sidestep the issue altogether by buying data on the rejected applicants and the loans they received. The concern with this approach is the possibility that the historical data includes subjective remnants of an earlier social paradigm where racism and sexism possibly existed as a component of the decision-making process.

Now, we must consider *ethical risks*. Was race an (unwitting) evaluation feature in the original process? Is it possible that our historical data of applicants that were given loans excluded certain ethnicities, genders, or ages? In this case, the model will not react appropriately to these groups of applicants in prediction cases. Having data with a category of people underrepresented can wreak havoc with a model, as Google discovered when deploying a model for labeling the content of photos. You do not want to be the data scientist responsible for your company's spokesperson having to apologize to the world by using words like "appalled" and "genuinely sorry" (Guynn, 2015). It is, unfortunately, the case that certain types of data are so driven by historical bias that it is nearly impossible to develop models that are bias-free. Predictive policing is a good example, which, in at least one case, was found to target black neighborhoods disproportionately (Isaac & Dixon, 2017). It is worth noting that an algorithm does not need access to age, gender, or race to become racially discriminatory, as was the case with Microsoft's Tay chatbot after using interactions with Twitter users to model human behavior (Risley, 2016).

One important type of ethical risk is that of *privacy*. Many countries have strong privacy laws, and even for those countries that are not as strict (such as the United States), news of a privacy scandal concerns many companies that have access to sensitive personal information. While this data should be held firmly by individuals, even today, few understand how much of ourselves we are giving away online. Even seemingly innocuous acts such as liking Harley-Davidson on Facebook can help algorithms decide that your IQ is low (Kosinski, Stillwell & Graepel, 2013), and mentioning *God* in a loan application has been found to be indicative of someone less likely to pay the loan back (Stephens-Davidowitz, 2017). Perhaps hitting closer to home for privacy worriers, Kosinski et al. found that liking "Britney Spears" and "Desperate Housewives" were predictive of male homosexuality, and the algorithm was quite capable of finding gay Facebook users who were not yet "out" themselves. As one of the authors of this book is a fan of both Britney and Susan of Wisteria Lane, he may be due for a chat with his wife, according to this particular algorithm. Beyond the pages liked by an individual, the act itself of "liking" something on Facebook may carry signals and significance to those analyzing user data.

Similar to these correlations in social media data that reveal sensitive information, health insurers at this time engage in massive machine learning exercises to understand the health risks and costs of American citizens based on purchased data. Perhaps the essential feature that keeps returning in stories about these exercises is that poor people require expensive healthcare (Allen, 2018). Further, someone's poor finances are reflected in so many other features that it is likely impossible to keep this information out of a model when purchasing external data. In other words, applying models predicting the healthcare costs of individuals based on purchased data will inevitably propose the highest prices for the poorest people. The central point here: do not be flippant when dealing with data likely to have a detrimental effect on another human being's life. Carefully consider the risks in such cases, not only to individuals (an ethical consideration) but the financial risks to your company as well.

Organizations often settle into ways of thinking about mission and factors leading to success that can be stifling for future growth and innovation. In these cases, processes designed around a methodology that has worked in the past will prevent an organization from becoming what Davenport and Harris (2007) term "analytics competitors." Considering your current organization (if you are a student, consider your college as that organization), ask yourself whether it fits these hallmarks of analytics competitors (Davenport, 2006):

1. Analytics is used not only for core capabilities but also in related functions like marketing and human resources.
2. The top management team recognizes and drives use of analytics and innovative measures of success.
3. Fact-based decision-making is part of the organizational culture.
4. Copious data exists, and analytics is performed, and results are shared both internally and with partners and customers.
5. A "test and learn" culture exists where opportunities to learn from data and test hypotheses is a natural part of the workplace environment.

If all of these describe your company, congratulations! AutoML is likely to be useful to you in the same way it further enabled Airbnb in speeding up data science workflows (Husain & Handel, 2017). Even if only one or a few of the criteria describe your organization, you may still be able to benefit from introducing AutoML. AutoML can be a perfect starting point in working toward becoming an analytics competitor. However, if none (or few) of the above hallmarks describe your company, you must first address the significant cultural risks to your project. In a case such as this, your first job is to put together a coalition of analytics-savvy managers to support the project throughout all of its stages. You may also need to plan educational workshops on AutoML within your organization to foster interest and explain the potential benefits to the company. Doing so will also help you understand who is excited about analytics and might support you and the project in times of need. In scenarios of high cultural risk, project success relies on the tenacity of project owners and interested stakeholders in advocating for AutoML as a means for business growth.

Business process risk derives from the possibility that many business problems cannot be directly solved. For example, to predict sales at a given location, we may need to predict sales in several categories as well as sales of individual products. To be confident in those estimates, we must ensure that these products are actually available for sale, so separate predictions of product shortages must be addressed and combined with a product reordering system. If these other systems fail, our own predictions fail. If a Starbucks coffee shop runs out of coffee at 2 p.m. and we have business system in place to replenish that store, our predictions are likely to fail. Similarly, for that same coffee shop, we may have been tasked with predicting how many employees are needed for every hour of the day. The solution here may be to instead predict the number of customers during each of those hours, but doing so imposes business process risks in that the predicted number of customers must somehow be converted into a set of employees, and those decisions will need to be carefully monitored so that lines are never or seldom long enough to discourage customers.

The last type of risk, environmental risk, comes from your organization's external environment. The primary external concern is that during or shortly after completion of a data-science project, the external environment that provided data for your analysis changes drastically. The "black swan" phenomenon represents one such risk, where one's very understanding of reality can change from one moment to the next with the introduction of new information. The concept of the black swan dates back to the moment in history when word traveled from Australia that not all swans are white, citing the existence of black swans in Australia. Previously, all swans were thought to be white, and the news of black swans required a complete rethink of the very concept of what defines a swan. Such events are highly uncommon, and it is nearly impossible to prepare for or anticipate them. One oft-cited example of such a black swan event was the "flash crash" of May 6, 2010 (Kirilenko, Kyle, Samadi & Tuzun, 2017). The US stock market lost a trillion dollars in 36 minutes, raising questions about the machine learning–based trading, often referred to as "algorithmic trading," that drives most trades today (Hendershott & Riordan, 2013). As a data scientist evaluating environmental risks, put yourself in the right frame of mind by considering the following Quora[1] examples of black swan events: the sinking of the *Titanic*, the Fukushima nuclear disaster, the unexpected Viking raids across Europe, the black death in Europe, and the 9/11 attacks. Then consider the following potential situations: a super volcano eruption, global nuclear war, or even a superhuman self-aware artificial intelligence taking control of every device connected to the Internet. While these events are all highly unlikely, they would result in a fundamental reshaping of the general understanding of global institutions and social structures. The data scientist must be prepared to remodel their target should (likely less dire) black swan events occur.

7.3 Decide Whether to Continue

After weighing the risks against the rewards, seriously evaluate whether to move forward with your project. Fortunately, AutoML changes the cost/benefit analysis currently associated with conducting machine learning. If you already have access to some of the data that would go into a machine learning project, you might consider running a pilot project if you can do so fast (under a day or two). Getting feedback from subject matter experts on that pilot should help establish whether it has the requisite potential to warrant further support. It is essential here to evaluate whether additional data could move a project above the required threshold for success. Quick pilot projects can also be an excellent way of garnering interest and buy-in for your project idea, mainly because it immediately communicates the minimum level of success management and the company can expect. We want our projects to either succeed or fail quickly to minimize risk (Shore, 2004).

---

[1] Quora is a popular question-and-answer site available at Quora.com.

7.4 Exercises

1. What are some reasons management may not be on board with your modeling project?
2. How can you best simplify machine learning outcomes to management to improve the chances of moving the project forward?
3. Outline risks when modeling hospital readmissions.

SECTION III

ACQUIRE AND INTEGRATE DATA

Love Thine (Data) Asset

ML principle: "Data should be considered an asset, and therefore we should think carefully about what investments we should make to get the best leverage from our asset" (Provost & Fawcett, 2013, 332).
AutoML relevance: Same for ML and AutoML.

For those of you who have taken a database class or know Structured Query Language (SQL; a language for communicating with almost every database in the world), most of what this section covers will be a review. If you have access to technical staff capable of providing the data you need, we recommend you jump forward to Section IV (read the rest of this paragraph first for some notable exceptions to that rule). Once you have done a few projects, you may find that you'd like to learn how to access data on your own. You can always return to this section as a starting point for developing this knowledge. Regardless, we recommended that all readers pay attention to Chapter 8.2 on purchasing data. Purchasing data has the potential to improve your ability to predict a given target feature. As of the date this book was written, there has not been a significant amount of information available on the purchasing of data, so unless your company is already purchasing data, Chapter 8.2 will be an essential introduction to this topic. We will reference Chapter 10.1.1 on one-hot-encoding in Section IV.

The concepts covered in this section apply equally to tools such as *Excel*, *SQL*, *Alteryx*, *Paxata*, *R* (we recommend the *plyr* package or *sqldf* for those comfortable with SQL), and *Python* (preferably with the *Pandas* package). We cover the following material because of its central importance to machine learning. Many of these steps are required even for AutoML because data must be found, integrated, and aggregated. Further, sometimes AutoML has blind spots that you will need to address manually. A possible such blind spot: categorical variables that look to be numeric variables. For example, the Insurance Company Benchmark dataset[1] contains customer subtypes (often referred to as affinity codes) numbered from 1–41, which

---

[1] Easily found through Googling: COIL 2000 UCI.

indicate codes such as: "1: High Income, expensive child," "29: Porchless seniors: no front yard," and "41: Mixed rurals." It is hard (though not impossible) for any kind of machine learning system to realize that each number refers to a different subset of people, the treatment of each should be different. A related problem is an inverse: when numeric variables look to be categorical. For example, if the data contains survey responses of "agree," "somewhat agree," "neutral," "somewhat disagree," and "disagree," most AutoML systems will recognize that these are categories, but not that they have a logical order––these are called *ordinal* numbers, meaning a series of numbers where the order matters but there is not an equal difference between each number.

It is also important to consider the regularity of the data. Inconsistent coding of data can reduce machine learning's ability to predict a target. One of the most common problems that data scientists encounter is missing information encoded as a numeric quantity of zero rather than as a NULL (a code indicating that a value is missing). For example, Kai is 39 years old (and always will be). If you are involved in a machine learning exercise where Kai is represented as a row of data, and you don't know his age, treating him as a newborn is likely to lead to problems in predicting his behavior.

Regarding data consistency, medical records are among the most difficult data to handle. A large number and variety of medical professionals update each record for a patient and often use different language and codes to describe the patient's condition or symptoms. There is also the case of customer service calls where a representative may code the conversation in a unique or non-standard manner. Extensive training is necessary for two employees to characterize the multiple different aspects of even the same discussion consistently.

Turning to e-commerce, sites like Amazon place significant value on the number of stars a customer assigns a given product; however, this can be an imperfect metric. A better way to evaluate the ratings for that product is to examine each customer who provided a star rating and rescale their ratings based on how many standard deviations they are from their mean. That is, when always-angry John rates products, his upper level of satisfaction may be three stars, and thus this should be taken into account when qualifying the true meaning of ratings. The same applies for always-happy Trish who never gives less than three stars.

One final concern is the practice of making a poorly designed information system that functions with the introduction of so-called *hidden flags*: codes the system was not designed to handle. An example of a hidden flag is customer service employees coding in the "age" field any customer whose behavior was exceedingly difficult as their real age + 200 (i.e., 239 for a 39-year-old). Another example is as follows: a company has just released a new product but has not yet updated its listings to include that product in the customer service application used by call-center employees. Say the company recently introduced the new Mega-phone 3000 smartphone, but in the data storage system, the *product* column does not show the new phone name as an option. Because of this, employees may have been told to start the *Notes* field with the text *Mega-phone 3000* before recording general opinions and recollections of the customer interaction. Such a notes field may state: "Mega-phone 3000: Battery exploded, but luckily in a hilarious way. Recorded by the customer and shared over 10 million times on Instagram."

8

Accessing and Storing Data

8.1 Track Down Relevant Data

When tracking down relevant data, it is vital to review the project objectives (covered in Section II). These objectives will inform what data is needed. Specifically: What is the business problem we are examining? What is the unit of analysis and prediction target? With answers to those questions, we are ready now to evaluate potential sources of data. As expected, most data sources will make little sense for a given problem. For example, data on supply chain partners will likely be of little value when the business problem involves customer lifetime value. With a clearly articulated problem (it should be at this point), scan through available data sources and inspect the ones that may be potentially useful for the project's context. For most of these data sources, do additional research on how to access the data, possibly requiring help from an IT-department staff member, as well as support from a subject matter expert.

Many analytics problems start with *internal data,* often found in a database table containing customer information, patient records, financial market information, marketing spend, or Internet of Things records. In the case of a customer analytics project, information on the customers such as addresses, payment information (credit card or bank account), and any other information provided during the registration process or in later customer interactions may be stored in different databases or tables within the same database. Beyond this information, account history such as length of the customer relationship, transactional data (payment history), and web logs providing information on products or pages a customer has visited frequently are all potential indicators of future behavior. Take, for example, a customer's unsubscription from a cloud storage company after a six-year customer relationship. Over the last few months, careful examination of his use of the company's service would have provided data indicating that the subscription was coming to an end. The customer's patterns of use changed dramatically after the movement of large quantities of data to a competing product's servers.

Figure 8.1 provides a visualization of the process we are exploring in this section, that of accessing one or more data sources and turning each source into a matrix (if it wasn't already in matrix form, as is true for databases). In non-technical terms, we will access data from different sources and create one or more tables from each source. When reviewing Figure 8.1, note the hatched column, which is there to

Automated Machine Learning for Business. Kai R. Larsen and Daniel S. Becker, Oxford University Press. © Oxford University Press 2021.
DOI: 10.1093/oso/9780190941659.003.0008

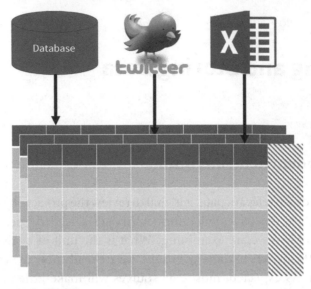

Figure 8.1. Creation of Initial Files.

illustrate the removal of superfluous data in a table. If you anticipate collecting quite a bit of data for your project, it is good practice to remove unnecessary columns. While AutoML will flag columns that are not helpful to the analysis—especially when dealing with large datasets—early detection and removal of unneeded columns reduce processing cost and time.

Each type of data generally comes with an "identity" field enabling the eventual integration of the data with other tables. An identity field is a column uniquely identifying the case (row), in databases referred to as a primary key. To combine tables, identity columns (such as email addresses) must exist in two or more tables.[2] As you review additional sources of data, keep in mind whether it is possible to find identity field combinations on which to join the sources. For example, if we start with customer data, each customer may have a *customer_id* field. This identity field will enable us to integrate all data on this customer stored in the customer database, but will not enable a connection to the customer's Twitter posts. For that, a Twitter handle must be available in the customer record. We must ask the customer to volunteer it, or we must engage an external data integrator. With information like email address, telephone number, or social security number, the data integrator can provide Twitter handles, or, even further, all Twitter posts made by a given customer during a defined period.

---

[2] This topic is a bit more complex than we make it out to be. Integration of data is also possible where no identity fields exist. For example, a person's address can be turned into a longitude and latitude, and this location used to connect to someone who according to our app spends most nights at the same longitude/latitude. When exact identity fields for connecting data do not exist, fuzzy matching may be employed (matching based on a certain level of similarity).

Twitter data represents a move away from internal data. Similarly, if the problem at hand is related to a financial or credit problem, we may purchase credit scores, information on financial transactions, and general fiscal history for the customer such as trade lines—any credit accounts held by a customer, including credit cards, mortgages, lines of credit, and so on. Telecommunications companies have access to increasingly valuable data about individuals' space-time coordinates, billing history, and call details, including whom someone calls, how long they talk, how often, and what websites they access via cellphone broadband connection. Increasingly, such information is available for purchase.

In the realm of individuals' online history, we use Web search, such as Google or Duckduckgo (for the privacy-conscious who are willing to suffer subpar search performance). While Google uses their extensive information aggregation capabilities to power an advertising empire, they are quite unlikely to sell this information to other organizations, at least for as long as their bottom line remains strong. Duckduckgo does not store or sell anything about their users (befitting of a "privacy"-oriented search engine). Other sources of online history include online blogs, social site postings, likes, and interactions. While almost the entire $430 billion market capitalization of Facebook at the time comes from the potential to use social information for marketing and related purposes, it takes careful digging to get access to such information, though it is available both in raw and summarized form. As the world gets flatter, the somewhat stricter privacy laws of the European Union are benefiting citizens of other countries.[3]

A whole ecosystem exists of companies collecting online blog and media postings and, in some cases, supplementing the postings with additional analytics, such as sentiment analysis or personality types. To see this at work (and if you have a Twitter account) head to IBM Watson's personality insights demo.[4] Although such tools do not adequately represent an individual's personality in daily life, they often quite closely describe the personality we present online. Here is a selection from the IBM Watson summary for Kai:

> You are dispassionate: you do not frequently think about or openly express your emotions. You are solemn: you are generally serious and do not joke much. And you are philosophical: you are open to and intrigued by new ideas and love to explore them.

Quite often, getting access to external data such as Tweets or financial data, or even internal data, requires the use of one or more APIs (Application Programming Interfaces). APIs are communication protocols that allow you to connect to an external provider of data and, by authenticating with a provided username and password, upload parameters for the kinds of data you want to download. The process

---

[3] To download and examine the data held on you, Google *download my private data* for quick links to the data held by Facebook, Google, and Apple. Consider reading the articles returned by the search for additional companies holding such data.

[4] https://personality-insights-livedemo.mybluemix.net/

is relatively simple: you upload identifiers and a list of the types of data you want. It is advisable to run a pilot project with a smaller part of the data you are considering purchasing before paying for thousands of columns, only a few of which are likely to be predictive for your given project.

Next, we will examine in greater depth the different kinds of data available for purchase for your modeling project.

8.2 Examine Data and Remove Columns

At this point, ideally, you have identified one or more tables in a database, one or more *Excel* spreadsheets, or a set of files containing data. If you have one of these available to you, you can turn now to the task of transforming data into one solitary table ready for machine learning analysis.

First, you will need a tool for interacting with the data. Though many machine learning experts hesitate to admit it, many of us dip into *Microsoft Excel* at times, so if your expected number of rows (cases) for analysis is below 200,000 and you feel comfortable with *Excel*, stick with it.[5] If your data are more substantial than that and you are not a programmer, we would recommend a tool like *Alteryx*.[6] Alternatively, for the programmers among you, we recommend *Python* and then *R* (in that order). Thanks to the availability of *R Studio*, R may require less effort to learn. However, there seems to be a clear and steadily increasing advantage to working with Python.[7] If your data is in a database and you are comfortable with *SQL*, you should be able to do what you need to within *SQL*.

It is now time for initial data exploration. For each of your tables or files, carefully examine their column names, data types, and number of rows. It is essential to understand the content of your data in relation to the project objective. For each file you have, now is the time to remove any column that is not relevant to either combining the files or predicting the target. For example, if you are predicting sales, the geographic region is of import, but if you already have the identifier (code) for a region, adding the name of that region is not likely to add further predictive ability (though information on longitude and latitude might). While understanding what data may help us predict a target takes time and experience, there may be data in your tables or files that are irrelevant to the project goal. If in doubt, keep the columns and let the AutoML guide you. If you are dealing with multiple tables or files, write down the identity columns; these will allow you to combine data from the different sources.

---

[5] Yes, while Excel can handle a million rows, it is our experience that it starts breaking down somewhere above 200,000 rows if you add enough formulas or columns. Explore to find Excel's breaking point for your own data.

[6] A 14-day free version is available at Alteryx.com. There are many videos and online classes available for training in its use. If you are part of a data science class, your instructor can generally get you a free version for much longer.

[7] For updated confirmations, go to https://trends.google.com and start by inserting the search term "*Machine Learning*" to see how interest in machine learning has more than quadrupled during the last five years (change time parameter to five years). To evaluate Python vs. R, compare the search terms "Python Programming" vs. "R Programming". Just comparing Python vs. R is not recommended because of the many meanings of "R". Remember to remove the "Machine Learning" search before comparing the two.

8.3 Example Dataset

Machine learning generally requires one table or matrix of data, but organizations store data in many tables. We must therefore learn how to combine data.

The Microsoft *Northwind* database will be used as a learning example in this section. It is a small-scale company database containing example data ranging from customer and employee information to products and sales. This database will reappear throughout the section as a way of gaining experience with the process of preparing the data for machine learning. Figure 8.2 displays what is generally called a database diagram. Each box represents a table of data stored in a database. We have information on *customers*, their *orders*, and *order details* for each order (think of *order details* as the different things you put in your Amazon shopping cart before checking out). There is also information on company *employees*. For each table, there is a set of attributes that we will simply call column names for the time being. For example, each new order has a unique *OrderID* assigned to it. It also has a *CustomerID* to track which customer placed this order, as well as an *EmployeeID* to track which employee oversaw completion of the order. The order also has an *OrderDate*, *ShippedDate*, and information on where it was shipped.

Table 8.1 contains a cut-out of the first few rows in the *Orders* table. Reviewing the columns gives us more information on the data. For example, many of the shipping addresses for products are international. Each table should be examined separately in this manner.

Each table in the database diagram is tied together with relationships, in this case anchored by a key on one side and an infinity sign on the other. This refers to what is called a "one-to-many relationship." The infinity sign denotes the "many" side, which, in this case, means that for each record on the "one" side, there *may* be many records related to it in the connected table. For example, for every single customer, there may be many orders. These one-to-many relationships are relevant in our case and refer back to the unit of analysis. If the order is the unit of analysis here, order detail information will have to be rolled up to the order level (each order detail row must contain any information relevant to predicting future orders—such as whether the order contained *Chai* or not). This will require a "summarize function," which we cover in Chapter 11.

A key learning point from Figure 8.2 is that regardless of the source of your data, you must be able to connect the data from the different sources. In that figure, we must have identity connections across the tables, which allows all the data to be connected. For example, if the *Order Details* table did not have a *ProductID* in common with the *Products* table, there would be no way of combining and using the data.[8] In this case, data is chained together one step at a time, but an equally likely scenario will be that you will have one table containing information on a person or

---

[8] This is generally true for a well-designed database.

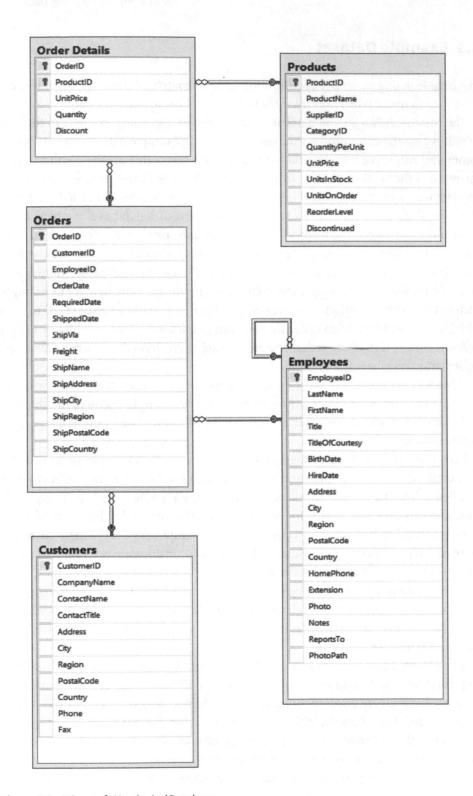

Figure 8.2. Microsoft *Northwind* Database.

Table 8.1. First 10 Rows in Orders Table.

Order ID	Customer ID	Employee ID	OrderDate	RequiredDate	ShippedDate	Ship Via	Freight	ShipName	ShipAddress	ShipCity	Ship Region	ShipPostal Code	Ship Country
10248	VINET	5	2018-07-04	2018-08-01	2018-07-16	3	32.38	Vins et alcools Chevalier	59 rue de l'Abbaye	Reims	NULL	51100	France
10249	TOMSP	6	2018-07-05	2018-08-16	2018-07-10	1	11.61	Toms Spezialitäten	Luisenstr. 48	Münster	NULL	44087	Germany
10250	HANAR	4	2018-07-08	2018-08-05	2018-07-12	2	65.83	Hanari Carnes	Rua do Paço, 67	Rio de Janeiro	RJ	05454-876	Brazil
10251	VICTE	3	2018-07-08	2018-08-05	2018-07-15	1	41.34	Victuailles en stock	2, rue du Commerce	Lyon	NULL	69004	France
10252	SUPRD	4	2018-07-09	2018-08-06	2018-07-11	2	51.30	Suprêmes délices	Boulevard Tirou, 255	Charleroi	NULL	B-6000	Belgium
10253	HANAR	3	2018-07-10	2018-07-24	2018-07-16	2	58.17	Hanari Carnes	Rua do Paço, 67	Rio de Janeiro	RJ	05454-876	Brazil
10254	CHOPS	5	2018-07-11	2018-08-08	2018-07-23	2	22.98	Chop-suey Chinese	Hauptstr. 31	Bern	NULL	3012	Switzerland
10255	RICSU	9	2018-07-12	2018-08-09	2018-07-15	3	148.33	Richter Supermarkt	Starenweg 5	Genève	NULL	1204	Switzerland
10256	WELLI	3	2018-07-15	2018-08-12	2018-07-17	2	13.97	Wellington Importadora	Rua do Mercado, 12	Resende	SP	08737-363	Brazil
	HILAA	4	2018-07-16	2018-08-13	2018-07-22	3	81.91	HILARION-Abastos	Carrera 22 con Ave. Carlos Soublette #8-35	San Cristóbal	Táchira	5022	Venezuela

thing you want to predict. This table may including some identifying characteristics, such as name, address, social security number, student ID number, customer ID, several email addresses, phone number, website cookie ID, and so on.

A short note: we will not worry about the self-referential column in the *Employees* table (the link from *Employees* to *Employees* itself). This column states which manager an employee reports to, which is likely irrelevant for our business case. We will now move forward to the topic of performing "joins" and "unions" on data.

8.4 Exercises

1. What are the types of data discussed in this chapter?
2. Download the data available on yourself from Google, Facebook, and Apple. Examine what details they hold and for what period. Discuss your experience with a colleague.

9
Data Integration

Access to additional and relevant data will lead to better predictions from algorithms until we reach the point where more observations (cases) are no longer helpful to detect the signal, the feature(s), or conditions that inform the target. In addition to obtaining more observations, we can also look for additional features of interest that we do not currently have, at which point it will invariably be necessary to integrate data from different sources. This chapter introduces this process of data integration, starting with an introduction of two methods: "joins" (to access more features) and "unions" (to access more observations).

A "join" combines two datasets (or tables) with a shared identity value, such as a customer identifier.[1] For example, you might "join" the row containing your customer record (*CustomerID*, name, address, etc.; A in Figure 9.1) with your login information on a website (*CustomerID*, visit time, products purchased, etc.; B in Figure 9.1). After a join, one or more new rows are created, each containing customer information from A on the left and website behavior from B on the right. Because a customer generally visits a website many times or has many valuable or noteworthy behaviors during each session (i.e., visiting multiple web pages), there are likely to be many rows in B containing this particular customer's *CustomerID*. If there is only one customer record in A and 50 rows containing that customer's various behaviors in B, the join will result in 50 rows represented as a new table, D.

A *union* is based on the assumption that there are multiple columns in common between A and C. A union lines up each column containing similar information on top of another (zip code existing in A and C, for example), creating a new table, E. For example, if a company has multiple customers, and we store their records in various databases, a union will create one table containing all customers for that company.

---

[1] This is a simplification. There are several different types of joins, including the "Cartesian join," which will combine every row in one table with every row in another table. For example, joining two tables with 100 and 1,000 rows will lead to 100,000 rows. This content is better learned in a database class and is not covered in this book, but can be crucial for network analysis.

Automated Machine Learning for Business. Kai R. Larsen and Daniel S. Becker, Oxford University Press. © Oxford University Press 2021.
DOI: 10.1093/oso/9780190941659.003.0009

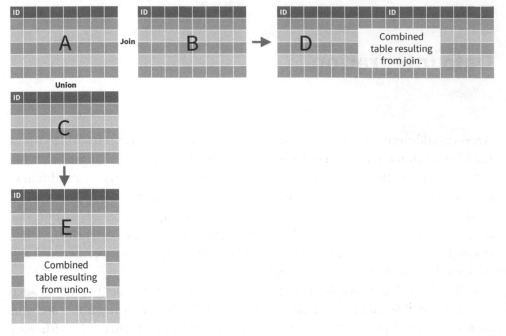

Figure 9.1. Joins and Unions.

9.1 Joins

Joins are complicated concepts for many and take quite a bit of practical experience to understand. Let's use the language of "tables" here with the assumption that a table can be any rectangular matrix containing data in column form where each column begins with a descriptive name of the data in that column (i.e., *SocialSecurityNumber*; see Figure 9.2).

There are two types of joins that are most relevant for our purposes; one has three subtypes:

- Inner join
- Outer join
  - Left outer join
  - Right outer join
  - Full outer join

Let's discuss all four types with some simple examples. A *customer* table (left table) contains *CustomerID* 1 with *Name* Kai and *CustomerID* 2 with *Name* Dan. A *purchases* table (right table) contains *CustomerID* 1 in two rows, one time purchasing the *Product* pants and one time purchasing the *Product* "bouncing castle." The table has one record for *CustomerID* 3, who bought *Product* sunglasses. The joins will all produce four columns, as shown in the *Example* column of Table 9.1.

When dealing with carefully curated databases, we will use the inner join most commonly for our data integration process. Such databases will generally be designed not

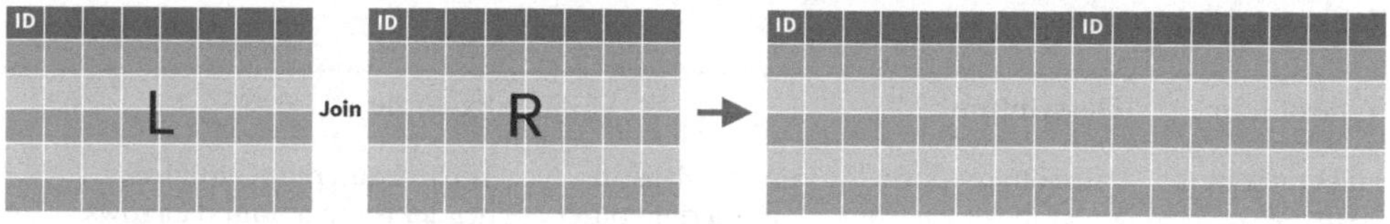

Figure 9.2. The Join.

Table 9.1. Types of Joins.

Type of Join	Description	Example
Inner Join	Each row in the left table is combined horizontally (see Figure 9.2) with any row in the right table that has the same identity value. For example, if we join based on the identity *CustomerID*, which both the *Customers* and the *Orders* tables contain, the customer information and order information for each customer is combined into a third table, containing repeated information on the customer for each order they have made.	The inner join produces a header row and two data rows (here shown in CSV format, spaces after commas for readability): CustId, Name, CustId, Product 1, Kai, 1, pants 1, Kai, 1, bouncing castle
Left Outer Join	This join produces the same result as an inner join but also adds any rows from the left table that do not have corresponding rows in the right table. Below the rows outlined in the above cell, we will also get rows containing customers who never placed an order. For such customers, the order-related columns will contain NULLs (a sign that there is nothing there). We may use left outer joins if our goal is to find out why some customers place orders and some do not. An inner join would exclude all the customers that did not place an order.	The left outer join produces a header row and three data rows: CustId, Name, CustId, Product 1, Kai, 1, pants 1, Kai, 1, bouncing castle 2, Dan, NULL, NULL The NULLs here indicate that Dan bought nothing yet.
Right Outer Join	This join produces the same result as an inner join, but also adds any rows from the right table that do not have corresponding rows in the left table. In the customer and order case, this type of join might be used to combine orders or near-orders, such as the common problem of abandoned shopping carts. Such shopping carts will be filled by an anonymous user and registered in our system as an incomplete order when the potential customer leaves the site without registering as a customer and paying for the products. This kind of data would be critical if we suspected that the specific products themselves led to the abandonment of shopping carts.	The right outer join produces a header row and three data rows: CustId, Name, CustId, Product 1, Kai, 1, pants 1, Kai, 1, bouncing castle NULL, NULL, 3, sunglasses The NULLs here indicate that we do not know who the person who bought the sunglasses is.

Continued

Table 9.1. Continued

Type of Join	Description	Example
Full Outer Join	This join produces the same result as an inner join + a left outer join + a right outer join. This means that any customer without orders is added to the resulting table, and any order not connected to a customer is also added to the resulting table.	The full outer join produces a header row and four data rows: CustId, Name, CustId, Product 1, Kai, 1, pants 1, Kai, 1, bouncing castle 2, Dan, NULL, NULL NULL, NULL, 3, sunglasses Now we get all information from both tables combined.

Table 9.2. Customers Table.

customerid	CompanyName
ALFKI	Alfreds Futterkiste
ANATR	Ana Trujillo Emparedados y helados

Table 9.3. Orders Table.

orderid	customerid	employeeid	orderdate
10643	ALFKI	6	2019-08-25
10692	ALFKI	4	2019-10-03
10702	ALFKI	4	2019-10-13
10835	ALFKI	1	2020-01-15
10952	ALFKI	1	2020-03-16
11011	ALFKI	3	2020-04-09
10308	ANATR	7	2018-09-18
10625	ANATR	3	2019-08-08
10759	ANATR	3	2019-11-28
10926	ANATR	4	2020-03-04

to accept an order unless a customer account exists for that order (something called "referential integrity" forces the database and any system using it to adhere to rules of conduct like this). If we are engaged in a project with the goal being to collect as much customer data as possible, then the *left outer join* is most useful. Beginning with the table containing the information most related to the project unit of analysis (see Chapter 5), the inner join and the left outer join together will take care of 99% of our needs.

Joins are based on relational algebra, so, as when learning math, the best way to get a sense of how joins work is to practice performing them. Let's go through an example of using inner joins to integrate all five tables in the database diagram in Figure 8.2. Table 9.2 contains a small sample of the columns in the *Customers* table.

Let's look now at a small set of rows from the *Orders* table in Table 9.3. These are the orders belonging to the two customers in the *Customers* table (Table 9.2), and while we see the *customerid*, only the *Customers* table contains the *CompanyName* column.

Table 9.4. The Result of Inner Join of Customers and Orders.

customerid	companyname	orderid	customerid	employeeid	orderdate
ALFKI	Alfreds Futterkiste	10643	ALFKI	6	2019-08-25
ALFKI	Alfreds Futterkiste	10692	ALFKI	4	2019-10-03
ALFKI	Alfreds Futterkiste	10702	ALFKI	4	2019-10-13
ALFKI	Alfreds Futterkiste	10835	ALFKI	1	2020-01-15
ALFKI	Alfreds Futterkiste	10952	ALFKI	1	2020-03-16
ALFKI	Alfreds Futterkiste	11011	ALFKI	3	2020-04-09
ANATR	Ana Trujillo Emparedados y helados	10308	ANATR	7	2018-09-18
ANATR	Ana Trujillo Emparedados y helados	10625	ANATR	3	2019-08-08

Table 9.5. Employees Table.

EmployeeID	LastName	City
1	Davolio	Seattle
2	Fuller	Tacoma
3	Leverling	Kirkland
4	Peacock	Redmond
5	Buchanan	London
6	Suyama	London
7	King	London

Now, let's integrate the two tables with an inner join. As Table 9.4 illustrates, each column in the *Customers* table is placed in front of the corresponding rows in the *Orders* table, contingent on the shared information in their *CustomerID* columns. We now know the *CompanyName* and order information for each customer. Notice that the *CustomerID* from both tables is included in the result. To save space, we can remove any identical columns from the resulting table.

The next step is to find out a bit about which employee made the sale for a given order. Let us look at a reduced version of the employee table in Table 9.5.

Now, joining the result of the first join (Table 9.4) with the employee information in Table 9.5, we can include the *LastName* and the *City* of each employee (and drop the second *CustomerId* column). Before looking at the table below, try to guess how this new table will look. Which employee sold the most recent order in Table 9.6? We will join the tables using the shared *EmployeeID* columns (and also drop the second *EmployeeId* column).

As may be seen from Table 9.6, the most recent order was fulfilled by employee *Peacock* (probably in the conference room with a telephone).

From here, the next step is to find out what information is available in the *Order Details* table. We see here that, judging by values in the *OrderID* column, there are ten unique orders, many of which comprised several rows. Each order row has a *ProductID* linking that row to information on the purchased product; *UnitPrice*, the

Table 9.6. Combined Table.

customerid	companyname	orderid	customerid	employeeid	orderdate	lastname
ALFKI	Alfreds Futterkiste	10643	ALFKI	6	2019-08-25	Suyama
ALFKI	Alfreds Futterkiste	10692	ALFKI	4	2019-10-03	Peacock
ALFKI	Alfreds Futterkiste	10702	ALFKI	4	2019-10-13	Peacock
ALFKI	Alfreds Futterkiste	10835	ALFKI	1	2020-01-15	Davolio
ALFKI	Alfreds Futterkiste	10952	ALFKI	1	2020-03-16	Davolio
ALFKI	Alfreds Futterkiste	11011	ALFKI	3	2020-04-09	Leverling
ANATR	Ana Trujillo Emparedados y helados	10308	ANATR	7	2018-09-18	King
ANATR	Ana Trujillo Emparedados y helados	10625	ANATR	3	2019-08-08	Leverling
ANATR	Ana Trujillo Emparedados y helados	10759	ANATR	3	2019-11-28	Leverling
ANATR	Ana Trujillo Emparedados y helados	10926	ANATR	4	2020-03-04	Peacock

Table 9.7. Sales Table.

OrderID	ProductID	UnitPrice	Quantity	Discount
10308	69	28.80	1	0
10308	70	12.00	5	0
10625	14	23.25	3	0
10625	42	14.00	5	0
10625	60	34.00	10	0
10643	28	45.60	15	0.25
10643	39	18.00	21	0.25
10643	46	12.00	2	0.25
10692	63	43.90	20	0
10702	3	10.00	6	0
10702	76	18.00	15	0
10759	32	32.00	10	0
10835	59	55.00	15	0
10835	77	13.00	2	0.2
10926	11	21.00	2	0
10926	13	6.00	10	0
10926	19	9.20	7	0
10926	72	34.80	10	0
10952	6	25.00	16	0.05
10952	28	45.60	2	0
11011	58	13.25	40	0.05
11011	71	21.50	20	0

cost of each unit of the product; *Quantity*, how many units the customer bought; and any *Discount* applied to the sale (Table 9.7).

Now, let us join the current record of our customers to the order information using the *OrderID* for the result shown in Table 9.8.

Table 9.8. The Result from Joining Customer Record (Table 9.6) with Sales (Table 9.7).

Customer id	companyname	Order id	Employee id	Orderdate	lastname	City	Product ID	Unit Price	Quantity	Discount
ALFKI	Alfreds Futterkiste	10643	6	2019-08-25	Suyama	London	28	45.60	15	0.25
ALFKI	Alfreds Futterkiste	10643	6	2019-08-25	Suyama	London	39	18.00	21	0.25
ALFKI	Alfreds Futterkiste	10643	6	2019-08-25	Suyama	London	46	12.00	2	0.25
ALFKI	Alfreds Futterkiste	10692	4	2019-10-03	Peacock	Redmond	63	43.90	20	0
ALFKI	Alfreds Futterkiste	10702	4	2019-10-13	Peacock	Redmond	3	10.00	6	0
ALFKI	Alfreds Futterkiste	10702	4	2019-10-13	Peacock	Redmond	76	18.00	15	0
ALFKI	Alfreds Futterkiste	10835	1	2020-01-15	Davolio	Seattle	59	55.00	15	0
ALFKI	Alfreds Futterkiste	10835	1	2020-01-15	Davolio	Seattle	77	13.00	2	0.2
ALFKI	Alfreds Futterkiste	10952	1	2020-03-16	Davolio	Seattle	6	25.00	16	0.05
ALFKI	Alfreds Futterkiste	10952	1	2020-03-16	Davolio	Seattle	28	45.60	2	0
ALFKI	Alfreds Futterkiste	11011	3	2020-04-09	Leverling	Kirkland	58	13.25	40	0.05
ALFKI	Alfreds Futterkiste	11011	3	2020-04-09	Leverling	Kirkland	71	21.50	20	0
ANATR	Ana Trujillo Emparedados y helados	10308	7	2018-09-18	King	London	69	28.80	1	0
ANATR	Ana Trujillo Emparedados y helados	10308	7	2018-09-18	King	London	70	12.00	5	0
ANATR	Ana Trujillo Emparedados y helados	10625	3	2019-08-08	Leverling	Kirkland	14	23.25	3	0
ANATR	Ana Trujillo Emparedados y helados	10625	3	2019-08-08	Leverling	Kirkland	42	14.00	5	0
ANATR	Ana Trujillo Emparedados y helados	10625	3	2019-08-08	Leverling	Kirkland	60	34.00	10	0

Continued

Table 9.8. Continued

Customer id	companyname	Order id	Employee id	Orderdate	lastname	City	Product ID	Unit Price	Quantity	Discount
ANATR	Ana Trujillo Emparedados y helados	10759	3	2019-11-28	Leverling	Kirkland	32	32.00	10	0
ANATR	Ana Trujillo Emparedados y helados	10926	4	2020-03-04	Peacock	Redmond	11	21.00	2	0
ANATR	Ana Trujillo Emparedados y helados	10926	4	2020-03-04	Peacock	Redmond	13	6.00	10	0
ANATR	Ana Trujillo Emparedados y helados	10926	4	2020-03-04	Peacock	Redmond	19	9.20	7	0
ANATR	Ana Trujillo Emparedados y helados	10926	4	2020-03-04	Peacock	Redmond	72	34.80	10	0

Table 9.9. Products Table (Top 10 Rows Only).

ProductID	ProductName	CategoryID
3	Aniseed Syrup	2
6	Grandma's Boysenberry Spread	2
11	Queso Cabrales	4
13	Konbu	8
14	Tofu	7
19	Teatime Chocolate Biscuits	3
28	Rössle Sauerkraut	7
28	Rössle Sauerkraut	7
32	Mascarpone Fabioli	4
39	Chartreuse verte	1

Finally, add the names of products sold from the *Products* table shown in Table 9.9 before joining the product names with the rest of the data for the result shown in Table 9.10. Note that while we don't have the name of the categories that products are rolled up in, the *CategoryID* number will work as well for our predictive purposes.

After that final join, we have an (in this case, reduced) version of the table containing all the data we will need. To fit the data on the page, we have removed *CompanyName* as it is not useful in machine learning since every company name is unique and the *CustomerID* provides the same information.

Unions allow us to combine two datasets, shown as the top (T) and bottom (B) in Figure 9.3. Generally, we perform unions when we have datasets that contain unique sets of cases sharing the same or very similar columns. For example, upon first implementing a Salesforce system, it is not uncommon for an organization to find that different parts of the organization have been keeping separate lists of internal and external data. For example, a college may be tracking students in one system and faculty in another whereas we follow guest lecturers, members of the school's board, and other industry contacts in yet another system. To create a consistent system of tracking the entirety of a college's interactions, all of these different data sources need to be integrated. Having the aggregate of a given person's information available within a single system is critical to performing high-quality analytics and machine learning.

As discussed in Chapter 8, the full outer join is excellent for connecting different lists *if* there are shared identifiers to allow for integration and to indicate that rows refer to the same units (e.g., people). However, if the tables refer to different units, a union is a more appropriate tool for combining lists that consist of different people. However, the distinction between a join and a union can at times be difficult. Take, for example, the union of lists of parishioners at 20 different churches, synagogues, and mosques in a small city. Use of the union in this situation will not make clear which individuals on the combined list are, in fact, the same people. If extensive

Table 9.10. Final Join Result.

Customer id	orderid	Employee id	orderdate	lastname	City	Product ID	UnitPrice	Quantity	Discount	ProductName	Category ID
ALFKI	10643	6	2019-08-25	Suyama	London	28	45.60	15	0.25	Rössle Sauerkraut	7
ALFKI	10643	6	2019-08-25	Suyama	London	39	18.00	21	0.25	Chartreuse verte	1
ALFKI	10643	6	2019-08-25	Suyama	London	46	12.00	2	0.25	Spegesild	8
ALFKI	10692	4	2019-10-03	Peacock	Redmond	63	43.90	20	0	Vegie-spread	2
ALFKI	10702	4	2019-10-13	Peacock	Redmond	3	10.00	6	0	Aniseed Syrup	2
ALFKI	10702	4	2019-10-13	Peacock	Redmond	76	18.00	15	0	Lakkalikööri	1
ALFKI	10835	1	2020-01-15	Davolio	Seattle	59	55.00	15	0	Raclette Courdavault	4
ALFKI	10835	1	2020-01-15	Davolio	Seattle	77	13.00	2	0.2	Original Frankfurter grüne Soße	2
ALFKI	10952	1	2020-03-16	Davolio	Seattle	6	25.00	16	0.05	Grandma's Boysenberry Spread	2
ALFKI	10952	1	2020-03-16	Davolio	Seattle	28	45.60	2	0	Rössle Sauerkraut	7
ALFKI	11011	3	2020-04-09	Leverling	Kirkland	58	13.25	40	0.05	Escargots de Bourgogne	8
ALFKI	11011	3	2020-04-09	Leverling	Kirkland	71	21.50	20	0	Flotemysost	4
ANATR	10308	7	2018-09-18	King	London	69	28.80	1	0	Gudbrandsdalsost	4
ANATR	10308	7	2018-09-18	King	London	70	12.00	5	0	Outback Lager	1
ANATR	10625	3	2019-08-08	Leverling	Kirkland	14	23.25	3	0	Tofu	7
ANATR	10625	3	2019-08-08	Leverling	Kirkland	42	14.00	5	0	Singaporean Hokkien Fried Mee	5
ANATR	10625	3	2019-08-08	Leverling	Kirkland	60	34.00	10	0	Camembert Pierrot	4
ANATR	10759	3	2019-11-28	Leverling	Kirkland	32	32.00	10	0	Mascarpone Fabioli	4
ANATR	10926	4	2020-03-04	Peacock	Redmond	11	21.00	2	0	Queso Cabrales	4
ANATR	10926	4	2020-03-04	Peacock	Redmond	13	6.00	10	0	Konbu	8
ANATR	10926	4	2020-03-04	Peacock	Redmond	19	9.20	7	0	Teatime Chocolate Biscuits	3
ANATR	10926	4	2020-03-04	Peacock	Redmond	72	34.80	10	0	Mozzarella di Giovanni	4

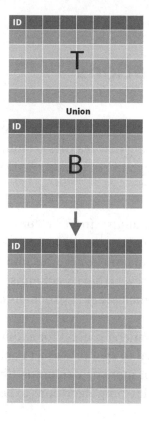

Figure 9.3. Union.

overlaps are expected, a first step may be to join units in the list based on names and addresses. Testing for these duplicate records (whether two records in a database refer to a single person) is a very challenging problem faced by most companies.[2]

9.2 Exercises

1. What is the difference between an inner join and a left outer join?
2. What is the relationship between joins and unions? Are they logically related in some way?

---

[2] In fact, "a friend of ours" relentlessly took advantage of as a child to join the same book club about 20 different times for the sign-up offer of three free books before canceling the memberships within the trial period. Between the many book clubs available, a sizable collection of free children's literature was amassed.

10

Data Transformations

This chapter focuses on creating new features (columns) based on the data we acquired in Chapter 8 and integrated in Chapter 9. Depending on the type of data available we'll do the following:

- Text: Extract new columns from columns containing text. Several transformations are generally necessary to find predictive ability within the text.
- Categorical: Combine numerous categories into fewer categories, turn multi-categorical columns into several binary columns.
- Numerical: Add, subtract, multiply, etc. two or more columns to create new columns.

Figure 10.1 illustrates the general process for adding new columns. We will start by discussing approaches used to split or extract content from an existing column and place this data into one or more new columns. These transformations have the potential of helping machine learning algorithms to better predict the target.

10.1 Splitting and Extracting New Columns

10.1.1 IF-THEN Statements and One-hot Encoding

IF-THEN statements are among a data scientist's best friends during data transformations. They allow for the examination of a value in a column and the ability to make changes to this value or other values elsewhere in the dataset. For example, we could create an IF-THEN statement that evaluates every value in a column *TitleandName*. Every time it finds the German title of "Herr" before a name, it writes "Mr" into the same row for the column *EnglishLanguageTitles*, a potentially helpful addition of data for target prediction, especially if we can standardize the titles across the whole dataset.

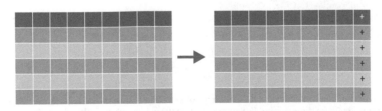

Figure 10.1. Data Transformation (Creating New Columns).

Automated Machine Learning for Business. Kai R. Larsen and Daniel S. Becker, Oxford University Press. © Oxford University Press 2021.
DOI: 10.1093/oso/9780190941659.003.0010

IF-THEN statements allow you to create content in a new column depending on what exists in one or more other columns. For example, if say we want to promote information about whether an employee was involved in the sale of a given order. We have an *EmployeeID* column containing the unique identity for each employee.

IF *EmployeeID* = 1
THEN Emp_1 = 1
ELSE Emp_1 = 0
ENDIF

The above example of an IF-THEN statement examines the content in a cell of the *EmployeeID* column and places a one or a zero in a cell of the same row but in the column named *Emp_1*. After running such a statement on a table of data, one would expect results similar to those in Table 10.1, where only rows for *EmployeeID* 1 are tagged as belonging to the new column *Emp_1*.

Table 10.1 shows the first step of splitting a column, part of perhaps the most well-known approach for dividing column data: *one-hot encoding*.[1] One-hot encoding is the conversion of a categorical column containing two or more possible values into discrete columns representing each value. For each unique category in this column, we create a new column with binary values of *1* or *0* (TRUE or FALSE). In statistics, this is known as "dummy" encoding. We use this approach because some machine learning tools are not able to accurately analyze the content of multi-categorical features.

Recall that our goal is to discern from the dataset developed in Chapter 9 what the drivers of large sales are. Table 10.2 shows the result of using IF-THEN statements to create new TRUE/FALSE columns for each of the possible *EmployeeId* values. Each employee is tagged with the numeral "1" if they made a given sale, and a "0" if they

Table 10.1. Applying Simple IF-THEN to Data.

CompanyName	Order ID	Employee ID	Emp _1
Alfreds Futterkiste	10643	6	0
Alfreds Futterkiste	10692	4	0
Alfreds Futterkiste	10702	4	0
Alfreds Futterkiste	10835	1	1
Alfreds Futterkiste	10952	1	1
Alfreds Futterkiste	11011	3	0
Ana Trujillo Emparedados y helados	10308	7	0
Ana Trujillo Emparedados y helados	10625	3	0
Ana Trujillo Emparedados y helados	10759	3	0
Ana Trujillo Emparedados y helados	10926	4	0

[1] If you really are interested in the etymology, go to Wikipedia.Org and search for *One-hot*.

Table 10.2. The Result from One-Hot Encoding.

CompanyName	Order ID	Employee ID	Emp _1	Emp _2	Emp _3	Emp _4	Emp _5	Emp _6	Emp _7	Emp _8	Emp _9
Alfreds Futterkiste	10643	6	0	0	0	0	0	1	0	0	0
Alfreds Futterkiste	10692	4	0	0	0	1	0	0	0	0	0
Alfreds Futterkiste	10702	4	0	0	0	1	0	0	0	0	0
Alfreds Futterkiste	10835	1	1	0	0	0	0	0	0	0	0
Alfreds Futterkiste	10952	1	1	0	0	0	0	0	0	0	0
Alfreds Futterkiste	11011	3	0	0	1	0	0	0	0	0	0
Ana Trujillo Emparedados y helados	10308	7	0	0	0	0	0	0	1	0	0
Ana Trujillo Emparedados y helados	10625	3	0	0	1	0	0	0	0	0	0
Ana Trujillo Emparedados y helados	10759	3	0	0	1	0	0	0	0	0	0
Ana Trujillo Emparedados y helados	10926	4	0	0	0	1	0	0	0	0	0

didn't. For example, notice that *Emp_3* sold to both customers, *Alfreds Futterkiste* and *Ana Trujiilo*, so this employee shows up multiple times throughout the dataset.

By one-hot encoding employee identity values, your predictive ability will likely improve, and, if you are trying to understand which employees were your highest performers in the past, it makes sense to include employee identities. However, if you are creating a system that is designed to understand better and predict future performance, you are better off including the characteristics of your employees, such as age, personality factors, and geographic background, to mention a few. Such additional information will better indicate to which employee a new customer should be assigned to create the highest likelihood of a successful sale. For example, an algorithm may find that, while Emp_7 is your best salesperson overall, Emp_4 is the better fit for a new customer in Atlanta where she grew up. Why? The algorithm had discovered that when an employee grew up near the location of the customer, the probability of a sale increases dramatically. Knowing this information would, of course, require setting up your data transformation workflow to always calculate the distance between a customer's location and a salesperson's past and current living location(s).

10.1.2 Regular Expressions (RegEx)

Understanding Regular Expressions (RegEx) is likely the best investment you can make in your data transformation skills. While a full introduction to RegEx is beyond the scope of this text (many books exist on the subject), this section will cover some highlights and essentials to understand the capabilities of Regular Expressions. We strongly recommended that you read the section while having access to a RegEx tool.[2]

Regular expressions are a powerful and flexible language for finding, replacing, or extracting content from text. You may recognize a simple version of regular expressions when searching for content in Microsoft (MS) Word. When you search for a specific word like *one* in a document such as this chapter, MS Word will mark all instances of *one* throughout the text, often in highlight. In this case, Word will find all our mentions of one, including the first word in "One-hot" but also as a part of the word "mentioned." This example is the simplest version of a RegEx statement. The specified pattern, in this case, "one," prompts the RegEx system to examine the available text and detect all text that fits the pattern.

The RegEx language can be further used to specify the context in which a pattern exists (beginning of a line, end of a line, only as a stand-alone word, etc.). Some concrete examples of RegEx use include detection and extraction of phone numbers (which are often stored in non-uniform formats; including with or without dashes and parentheses). Any text that has a predictable form can be extracted. For example, emails are predictable due to the @-symbol in the middle of a text with no spaces in it, followed by some characters, a period, and a few more characters. Does your email address follow these rules? That's because someone once set up a system of logic to make sure that every email address is unique and easily routable through the Internet. Tables 10.3–10.7 contain examples of RegEx commands.

Now comes the first difficulty in understanding RegEx. RegEx allows general commands. For example, rather than "abc" you may be looking for any three-character string starting with *a* and ending with *c*, such as *adc* or *atc*. For this string to work, we need an *escape* character. This escape character will indicate that the next character in the RegEx pattern should be interpreted as a special command. In RegEx, that escape character is the backslash (\). For example, \d does not mean

Table 10.3. Examples of RegEx Patterns and Results.

Command	Example text	Result	Comment
555	(555) 932-9382	*found*	Any set of numbers may be specified. If the command was 720, RegEx would find any set of three numbers fitting the exact number for one of Colorado's telephone area codes.
	(720) 828-8382	*not found*	
abc	abc Plumbing	*found*	Any combination of letters can be specified. This is similar to the MS Word search for a specific word or pattern. RegEx is case-sensitive, so a search for "Abc" would not find abc.
	ab1 Plumbing	*not found*	

Table 10.4. More Examples of RegEx Patterns and Results.

Pattern	String	Result	Description
a\dc	a1c	*found*	The \d shows the capability of RegEx as we now have a way to find any three-letter text starting with "a" and ending with "c" having a number between 0 and 9 between them.
	a5c	*found*	
	abc	*not found*	
a\Dc	aGc	*found*	The \D augments our search to find patterns where a part of the string is anything *but* a digit.
	a-c	*found*	
	a1c	*not found*	
a\wc	aGc	*found*	The \w command finds any single alphanumeric character. If you need more, specify how many. If you need any three-character alphanumeric string, specify \w\w\w.
	a-c	*not found*	
	a1c	*found*	
a\Wc	aGc	*not found*	The \W character finds any non-alphanumeric character. Some examples include: !%&'()*;=+./{}^~. \W also finds space and return characters.
	a-c	*found*	
	a@c	*found*	
a.c	aGc	*found*	The period (.) command finds any character.
	a-c	*found*	
	a@c	*found*	
abc?	abc	*found*	The question mark (?) makes the character before it optional. In this example, RegEx finds a match whether the "c" is there or not. This may seem wasteful because we could have matched by just using the "*ab*" pattern, but we will soon learn about capturing patterns, in which case capturing the "c" (if it is there) will be important.
	abd	*found*	
	adb	*not found*	
a\sc	a c	*found*	The \s matches any whitespace.
	aa c	*found*	
	abc	*not found*	
a\Sc	a c	*not found*	Any three-character pattern starting with "a" and ending with "c," as long as the second character is not a whitespace.
	aa c	*not found*	
	abc	*found*	

Table 10.5. Even More Examples of RegEx Patterns and Results.

Pattern	String	Result	Description
a[Ga]c	aGc	*found*	Hard brackets specify that one character in the specific position can be any character listed inside the brackets.
	aac	*found*	
	a@c	*not found*	
a[^Ga]c	aGc	*not found*	Same as hard brackets, but caret (^) at start inside bracket specifies that the characters listed cannot exist.
	aac	*not found*	
	aTc	*found*	
ab|cd	abc	*found*	The pipe command means that the pattern on the left of the pipe *or* the pattern on the right is acceptable. In this case, either the "ab" or the "cd" will qualify as a match, but only sets of two characters will be found.
	bcd	*found*	
	adc	*not found*	
^ab	aab	*not found*	Caret (^) specifies the beginning of the examined string.
	abc	*found*	
	bcab	*not found*	
ab$	aab	*found*	The dollar sign ($) specifies the end of the examined string. The pattern must be at the end of the string. In this case, the pattern we are looking for is *ab*, so only those characters are found in each string.[3] Note that RegEx would find none of the strings if had you specified ^ab$.
	abc	*not found*	
	bcab	*found*	

[3] If you are using https://RegEx101.com, test one string at a time.

Table 10.6. Yet, Even More, Examples of RegEx Patterns and Results.

Ab*	a	found	The pattern begins with "a" and may or may not contain any number of "b's."
	aab	found	
	abbb	found	
ab+	a	not found	The pattern begins with "a" and must be followed by at least one "b." "aab" will be found, but just the last two letters of it.
	aab	found	
	abbb	found	
a{3}	a	not found	The pattern is three "a."
	aa	not found	
	aaa	found	
a{2,4}	a	not found	The pattern is between two and four "a's."
	aa	found	
	aaa	found	

Table 10.7. A Final Example of RegEx Patterns and Results.

(Mrs?)	Mr	"Mr" captured	Use the parentheses around a pattern to capture whatever substring is matched by the pattern.
	Mrs	"Mrs" captured	
	Miss	not found	

that we are looking for the letter *d* but that any digit (0–9) will do. If you want to find all combinations of three digits, the pattern is \d\d\d. Table 10.4 contains additional pattern examples. While \d returns any digit character, \D does the opposite. This command will find any character except for digits, including any characters between a lowercase and an uppercase Z, as well as characters such as dashes. To find the 7-character Scrabble word AARRGHH in a list of words use \D\D\D\D\D\D\D (note that this will return any other 7-character word as well). Composite words such as "one-half" will also be found using this \D character, as it returns punctuation marks among other non-digit characters.

Now, consider the command \w, which accepts any alphanumeric character (digits from 0–9 and letters from a–Z). If you specify seven characters by using \w\w\w\w\w\w\w, this command will find "aband1r" (abandoner––where "one" has been replaced with the digit 1). If you need to find words, like &*%$, then you will use the \W character (specifically, \W\W\W\W for four-character words), which returns any non-alphanumeric character. So far, these special characters have parameters, returning only specific groupings of characters possibly found in a given text. Conversely, the period (.) is the royalty of RegEx, in that it has the widest scope. Using the period will return any character.

Finally, let us discuss a bit of magic: how to make a character optional and how to find invisible characters such as spaces. The question mark character (?) means that the character directly preceding it is not necessary for a match. Consider the differences in British-English relative to American-English. Often, the Brits follow an "o" with a "u," such as in the word "color," or rather "colour." A pattern can be created that works for both by specifying the pattern *colou?r*. Sometimes, we need to look for what is called whitespace (\s). What qualifies as whitespace can differ a bit between different RegEx engines (which vary slightly from one programming language to another), but often space, tab, new line, and carriage return qualify.[4] Alternatively, we can specify anything *but* whitespace (\S). Look now to Table 10.4 for examples of these special characters in use.

Now, what if the desired pattern is a bit more restricted? For example, in the county of Boulder, Colorado, there are two telephone area codes: 303 and 720. A Regular Expression that matches specifically these two three-digit numbers requires additional specificity; enter square bracket characters []. Square brackets allow for the specification of a list of allowable characters for a specific character position. In this case, a pattern that will enable either a "3" or a "7" as the first number followed by any two digits is needed: [37]\d\d or [73]\d\d. Alternatively, in the case of the Hawaiian words Kai and Lai, the expression could specify [KL]\D\D.

Furthermore, to be sure that only lowercase characters from "a" to "z" are returned for the second and third positions, the pattern [KL][a-z][a-z] would be suitable. Notice that the dash allows us to specify a range of allowable values. It is also possible to specify anything *but* the alphanumeric values listed by putting a caret (^) in the first position *inside* the square brackets (note: the caret must be inside the brackets, as it has a separate function outside). Returning to the example of finding the two specific Boulder county area codes, another acceptable method would be to use the *or* command, which in RegEx syntax is the pipe symbol: "|." By putting a pipe between two different patterns, either pattern will be selected. For example, 303|720 will capture both relevant area codes.

Let us add two more crucial special RegEx characters to those already mentioned. We now want to match a pattern only if it occurs at the beginning or end of a string. By using both, the pattern must be the only thing inside the string being searched. The caret (^), when not in square brackets, indicates the beginning of the string and the dollar sign ($) indicates the end of a string (Table 10.5).

This series of command instructions may feel a bit overwhelming at this point, but don't give up. We will cover two additional sets of commands before a fun online exercise that will help to solidify this knowledge. The final two types of patterns are *repetitions* and *captures*. Captures refer to the explicit notation (capturing) of any substring matching a RegEx pattern that can then be used to create a new column for use in machine learning.

Repetition refers to occurrences in which it makes sense to specify that a pattern repeats a certain number of times within a string. We accomplish this specification in several ways. The first method is to use the asterisk (*) character, which declares

---

[4] Carriage return originally referred to the manual action of moving the typing head to the beginning of a new line on something called a typewriter.

that the RegEx pattern preceding it can be matched zero to an infinite number of times. The asterisk allows for a RegEx pattern to be skipped if it does not exist in a string (zero matches), or to be matched many times; for instance, \w* will match a string of letter characters a–z of any length (infinite matches). To change this lower bound from zero to one, the plus character (+) can be used instead. The plus char-acter is similar to the asterisk except that it specifies that the pattern must occur at least once. There remains no upper limit on the number of matches allowed. Finally, curly brackets "{}" specify precisely how many times a pattern can appear with the possibility of including lower and upper bounds (Table 10.6).

The capturing of patterns is one major application area for RegEx. We may sur-round all these examples of patterns with parentheses to capture any substring that fits the profile specified (Table 10.7). The primary goal of using RegEx for data sci-ence is to extract instances of a specified pattern in a string, thus allowing for the creation of a new column containing either a TRUE or a FALSE value (is the pattern matched or not). Through capturing, new columns can also be created containing the actual values of the captured substring. In the *Titanic* project mentioned in Chapter 6, RegEx can be used to extract the titles of all those who traveled on the *Titanic*. The resulting feature is quite predictive following some minor cleaning.

Table 10.8 contains a quick overview of the patterns and special characters discussed. Use this as a reference for the assignment at the end of this chapter.

Table 10.8. Overview of Some Key RegEx Patterns.

Pattern	Explanation
0–9	RegEx looks for the exact digit or set of digits you specify.
a–z A–Z	RegEx looks for the exact set of characters you specify, including uppercase and combinations of uppercase and lowercase.
\d	Any one digit
\D	Any one character except for digits
\w	Any alphanumeric character
\W	Any non-alphanumeric character
.	Any character
?	The character following question mark is optional
\s	Any whitespace
\S	Anything but a whitespace
[]	Any alphanumeric character listed within the brackets
[^]	Any alphanumeric character not listed after the caret
|	The pattern on either side of the pipe, if found, constitutes a match
^	Any pattern must begin from the start of the string being examined
$	Any pattern must be adjacent to the end of the string being examined
*	Zero or more repetitions
+	One or more repetitions
{m}	The pattern preceding the curly brackets should repeat "m" times
{m,n}	The pattern preceding the curly brackets should repeat "m" to "n" times
()	Capture the strings that fit the pattern

10.2 Transformations

Sometimes it can feel as though there is an infinite number of feature transformations possible. Getting a firm grasp on which features should be transformed for optimal performance by various models can take years of experience; however, many machine learning books do not fully cover this material. The following is an introduction to the various transformations available to create new features. Often, the comparison of two columns can create a new column that provides an additional predictive ability for machine learning algorithms. Table 10.9 covers these pairwise transformations.

Table 10.9. Operators Applied to Two Columns.

Transformation	Symbol	Comment
Addition	+	By adding different columns, predictive signals can be increased. For example, by adding a person's number of spouses (usually one) with their number of children and adding one for the focal person, the resulting number is family size, which might help to understand a person's behavior in certain situations. For example, air travel might become unaffordable for large families.
Subtraction	–	By subtracting one column from another, the similarity or difference between them becomes more apparent; the closer the number is to zero, the more similar. For example, to predict whether a person is likely to engage in outside activities, subtracting their preferred inside temperature (gathered from their thermostat) from the current outside temperature can be an indicator. A positive number would indicate that it is colder outside than they prefer and a negative number would indicate that it is warmer than they prefer. The closer to zero the number is, the closer to their preference, and the more likely they will be to engage in outside recreational activities.
Absolute	Abs()	Similar to subtraction but used in cases where the actual distance between two numbers rather than whether it is negative or positive is of importance. Carnies offering to guess your weight take advantage of this one.
Multiplication	*	Sometimes two related columns interact with a target in a way that is only detectable through their product. This interaction effect is often called a moderated relationship between a column and the target. The moderation comes from the size of another feature. For example, having a bad interaction with a customer service representative does not necessarily mean that someone will cancel their customer relationship (churn). However, if the person also has a bad temper, it is much more likely that the bad customer service interaction will result in churn.
Division	/	By dividing one column by another, sometimes information that is otherwise hidden from some types of algorithms can be made available. For example, income divided by number of kids might reveal aspects of available funds of a family.
Less than	<	If the number of seats available in a family's largest car is smaller than their family size after the birth of a new child, this feature may be predictive of the purchase of a new car.
Less than or equal	<=	If the number of bedrooms in a family's home is smaller than or equal to the family size one year after the birth of a new child, this feature may be predictive of the purchase of new bunk beds.

Table 10.9. Continued

Transformation	Symbol	Comment
Greater than	>	If the family unit is larger than the number of seats in the largest car owned by the family, fun, summer camping vacations to national parks become less likely.
Greater than or equal	>=	If the number of available seats in a car is greater than or equal to the family size, the likelihood of purchasing a new van may be lower.
Not equal	!=	When two data points are not the same, this can affect a prediction. For example, the vibration of a machine if different during operation from its vibration the day before.
Equal	==	If two data points *are* the same, they may cancel each other out in some cases, or they may indicate a higher likelihood of a target phenomenon occurring.
Exponentiation	**	When dealing with financial data, the current interest of a continuously compounded loan or bond may be of interest. To represent $P = C\,e^{(rt)}$ in data transformations, $C*e**(r*t)$ can be used to capture the exponential relationship between e and (r*t).

Table 10.10. Operators Applied to One Column.

Transformation	Symbol	Comment
Natural logarithm	Log()	Log transformations are generally used to linearize exponential data. The higher a family's total income, the less likely they may be to visit national parks because they can afford other experiences. But at some point, love for national parks would trump doubling of income. For example, doubling a family's income from $500,000 to $1,000,000 is not likely to negatively impact their desire to visit national parks.
Square root	Sqrt()	Similar to a log transformation. Works for a different distribution of data. Compare ability to linearize data vs. log.
Square	Square()	Makes large values even larger. For example, if a column you are working with contains the standard deviation of an engine's vibrations, you might square it to find the variance.

Finally, Table 10.10 lists a small set of transformations applicable to one column at a time.

The next chapter will cover two different approaches to summarization of data. This content is critical because the data needed is seldom at the right level of analysis.

10.3 Exercises

1. What is one-hot-encoding? Where did the name come from?
2. Go to https://regexone.com and complete the 15 lessons and the 8 practice problems to reinforce your understanding of RegEx.

11
Summarization

Earlier in the book the term "unit of analysis" was discussed, for example, the customer. Quite often, data does not exist at that level, meaning that, while we may have information directly about the customer, such as age, gender, and personality factors, most information will be about interactions with that customer, or perhaps even about their friends on a social network. We aggregate or summarize data that is not available at the right unit of analysis. If the customer called a support line five times, this information will not exist in the customer table, but instead in a customer support table. After joining these together, the data is summarized to get a new column about each customer stating how many times they called the customer support line.

In the Northwind dataset, the order details level was the depth required to work with the data even though it may be preferable to stay at the *order* unit level. Getting the data back to the order level of analysis can be managed through summarization. Figure 11.1 illustrates how summarization reduces both the number of columns and the number of rows.

11.1 Summarize

Summarize is a feature available in most programming tools and is also known under the names *group* and *group by*. When summarizing, one or more columns by which to group data is selected, essentially creating a virtual "bucket" for each unique group. For example, if you are interested in employees, you would summarize

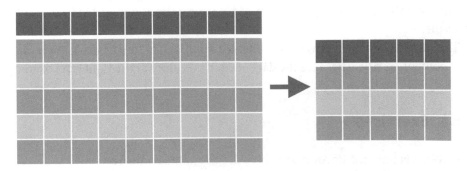

Figure 11.1. Summarization.

Automated Machine Learning for Business. Kai R. Larsen and Daniel S. Becker, Oxford University Press. © Oxford University Press 2021.
DOI: 10.1093/oso/9780190941659.003.0011

by *EmployeeID*, and in the given case, the nine unique employees in the dataset would each be assigned a bucket. Every row belonging to that employee would then be placed inside the bucket. Once all the relevant rows for that employee are in the bucket, the data within are available to be summarized. For example, if the number of rows belonging to a given employee is needed, the *Count* function with the *Summarize* function returns a table that contains each *EmployeeID* from 1–9 as the first column and the count of how many rows belong to each employee as the second column.

It is possible also to summarize by more than one column. For example, if we need the number of rows referring to a given employee on each day, the data would be summarized by the two columns *EmployeeID* and *OrderDate*. This way, more digital buckets would be created, each referring to an individual employee on each given day. The following is a list of typical functions that can be applied to data inside each bucket:

- Count
- Sum
- Min
- Max
- First
- Last
- Average
- Median
- Mode
- Standard Deviation

In this case, for every *Order Detail* row, each order's detail's costs should be summarized into an overall order cost. In this case, Table 11.1 contains the result of (*UnitPrice*Quantity*)*(1-Discount)* stored in the column *OrderDetailPrice*, and no longer contains *UnitPrice, Quantity,* and *Discount.*

Let us visualize a simplified representation of what this would look like in a summarize tool. In Table 11.2, only *OrderID* and *OrderDetailPrice* remain.

In this case, it is logical to group by *OrderID*, meaning that each row with the same *OrderID* ends up in the same "bucket" (Figure 11.2).

With each set of order details placed in the appropriate bucket, the preferred function is now applied across the buckets, for example, a sum, count, average, max, min, and so on. In this example, the second column (*SalePrice*) is summed, resulting in a new table, which operates at the correct level of analysis for the order, as illustrated in Table 11.3.

An important point: the summarize function could have been run with any information above the level of analysis of *OrderID*. As shown in Table 11.4, any column that does not change within each *OrderID* could be placed as the grouping

Table 11.1. Order Detail Level.

customerid	orderid	employeeid	orderdate	lastname	City	ProductID	ProductName	CategoryID	SalePrice
ALFKI	10643	6	2019-08-25	Suyama	London	28	Rössle Sauerkraut	7	513
ALFKI	10643	6	2019-08-25	Suyama	London	39	Chartreuse verte	1	283.5
ALFKI	10643	6	2019-08-25	Suyama	London	46	Spegesild	8	18
ALFKI	10692	4	2019-10-03	Peacock	Redmond	63	Vegie-spread	2	878
ALFKI	10702	4	2019-10-13	Peacock	Redmond	3	Aniseed Syrup	2	60
ALFKI	10702	4	2019-10-13	Peacock	Redmond	76	Lakkalikööri	1	270
ALFKI	10835	1	2020-01-15	Davolio	Seattle	59	Raclette Courdavault	4	825
ALFKI	10835	1	2020-01-15	Davolio	Seattle	77	Original Frankfurter grüne Soße	2	20.8
ALFKI	10952	1	2020-03-16	Davolio	Seattle	6	Grandma's Boysenberry Spread	2	380
ALFKI	10952	1	2020-03-16	Davolio	Seattle	28	Rössle Sauerkraut	7	91.2
ALFKI	11011	3	2020-04-09	Leverling	Kirkland	58	Escargots de Bourgogne	8	503.5
ALFKI	11011	3	2020-04-09	Leverling	Kirkland	71	Flotemysost	4	430
ANATR	10308	7	2018-09-18	King	London	69	Gudbrandsdalsost	4	28.8
ANATR	10308	7	2018-09-18	King	London	70	Outback Lager	1	60
ANATR	10625	3	2019-08-08	Leverling	Kirkland	14	Tofu	7	69.75
ANATR	10625	3	2019-08-08	Leverling	Kirkland	42	Singaporean Hokkien Fried Mee	5	70
ANATR	10625	3	2019-08-08	Leverling	Kirkland	60	Camembert Pierrot	4	340
ANATR	10759	3	2019-11-28	Leverling	Kirkland	32	Mascarpone Fabioli	4	320
ANATR	10926	4	2020-03-04	Peacock	Redmond	11	Queso Cabrales	4	42
ANATR	10926	4	2020-03-04	Peacock	Redmond	13	Konbu	8	60
ANATR	10926	4	2020-03-04	Peacock	Redmond	19	Teatime Chocolate Biscuits	3	64.4
ANATR	10926	4	2020-03-04	Peacock	Redmond	72	Mozzarella di Giovanni	4	348

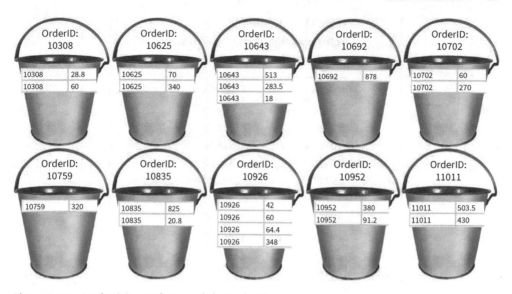

Figure 11.2. Bucketizing Order Details by OrderId.

Table 11.2. Reduced Dataset at Order Detail Level.

orderid	SalePrice
10643	513
10643	283.5
10643	18
10692	878
10702	60
10702	270
10835	825
10835	20.8
10952	380
10952	91.2
11011	503.5
11011	430
10308	28.8
10308	60
10625	69.75
10625	70
10625	340
10759	320
10926	42
10926	60
10926	64.4
10926	348

Table 11.3. The Result from Applying Summarize with Sum Function.

orderid	OrderCost
10308	88.80
10625	479.75
10643	814.50
10692	878.00
10702	330.00
10759	320.00
10835	845.80
10926	514.40
10952	471.20
11011	933.50

Table 11.4. Summarize with Additional Columns Included.

CustomerID	CompanyName	EmployeeID	orderid	OrderCost
ANATR	Ana Trujillo Emparedados y helados	7	10308	88.8
ANATR	Ana Trujillo Emparedados y helados	3	10625	479.75
ALFKI	Alfreds Futterkiste	6	10643	814.5
ALFKI	Alfreds Futterkiste	4	10692	878
ALFKI	Alfreds Futterkiste	4	10702	330
ANATR	Ana Trujillo Emparedados y helados	3	10759	320
ALFKI	Alfreds Futterkiste	1	10835	845.8
ANATR	Ana Trujillo Emparedados y helados	4	10926	514.4
ALFKI	Alfreds Futterkiste	1	10952	471.2
ALFKI	Alfreds Futterkiste	3	11011	933.5

(bucketizing) condition (and thereby become part of the output table), including *CustomerID, CompanyName,* and *EmployeeID.* To understand whether a column is above the desired level of analysis, examine whether any row ever changes for the same *OrderID.* You may notice that a specific order (for example, *OrderID* 10835) is always made for the same customer and is always sold by the same employee, which is why these additional columns can be included without affecting the summarized result.

The next section focuses on a similar tool: summarize's cousin, the crosstab.

11.2 Crosstab

Where summarize provides summary and aggregate information on existing columns, crosstab uses the content inside columns to create new columns.

Crosstab is a way to deal with data that is currently in "skinny" form and transform what is currently listed in rows to column form. This kind of "skinny" data is seldom at the right level for analysis, and crosstab makes data available in an intuitive and readable fashion, sometimes also creating new features for machine learning to better predict a target. For example, let's say Kjetil (the Norwegian), Richard (the Brit), and John (the American) work for a startup that provides free drinks to employees. They have the choice between tea (low caffeine), coffee (medium caffeine), or an energy drink (high caffeine) from a machine that responds to the RFID chip in their company badge. Every time one of them selects a drink, their name, date/time, and drink type is recorded as a row in a database table. After a year of free drinks, their boss would like to learn more about what their drink choices suggest about them as employees. She accesses the table (shown here in Table 11.5) and notices that it contains 4,869 rows (not all shown here).

Now she applies a crosstab to the table by selecting the *Name* column to become the new row, and she specifies the *DrinkType* column to expand into three separate columns (coffee, tea, energy drink). After deciding that she wants "count" as her function, she receives results akin to Table 11.6. Now she has an immediate understanding of why John has received the nickname "Jumpy John" by his coworkers.

The skinny table is a typical shape for data to take. It happens with data from sales when one or more customers make many purchases over time. It also occurs with Internet of Things devices[1] that report their status back to their owner every sub-second. At the time a database is designed, we often do not know how data will

Table 11.5. Skinny Table with 4,869 Rows (first six shown).

Name	Date	DrinkType
Kjetil	01/02/2019 08:51	Coffee
Kjetil	01/02/2019 08:59	Coffee
Richard	01/02/2019 09:00	Coffee
John	01/02/2019 09:01	Energy Drink
Richard	01/02/2019 09:51	Tea
Richard	01/01/2019 10:15	Tea
...	...	...
...	...	...
...	...	...
Kjetil	12/30/2019 17:05	Coffee

[1] Internet of Things (IoT) is a fancy term for all devices connected to the Internet. In the future, your thermometer and just about any other tool you use will be connected to the Internet and report its status to a central server, allowing the manufacturer to know the temperatures recorded and suggest actions based on readings from other thermometers in the same geographic area.

Table 11.6. Crosstab on Drink Types.

Name	Tea	Coffee	Energy Drink
Kjetil	0	2,159	10
Richard	785	50	0
John	38	25	1,802

Table 11.7. Order Detail Product Information.

orderid	ProductID	ProductName	CategoryID	CategoryName
10248	11	Queso Cabrales	4	Dairy Products
10248	42	Singaporean Hokkien Fried Mee	5	Grains/Cereals
10248	72	Mozzarella di Giovanni	4	Dairy Products
10249	14	Tofu	7	Produce
10249	51	Manjimup Dried Apples	7	Produce
10250	41	Jack's New England Clam Chowder	8	Seafood
10250	51	Manjimup Dried Apples	7	Produce
10250	65	Louisiana Fiery Hot Pepper Sauce	2	Condiments
10251	22	Gustaf's Knäckebröd	5	Grains/Cereals
10251	57	Ravioli Angelo	5	Grains/Cereals
10251	65	Louisiana Fiery Hot Pepper Sauce	2	Condiments
10252	20	Sir Rodney's Marmalade	3	Confections
10252	33	Geitost	4	Dairy Products
10252	60	Camembert Pierrot	4	Dairy Products
10253	31	Gorgonzola Telino	4	Dairy Products
10253	39	Chartreuse verte	1	Beverages
10253	49	Maxilaku	3	Confections
10254	24	Guaraná Fantástica	1	Beverages
10254	55	Pâté chinois	6	Meat/Poultry
10254	74	Longlife Tofu	7	Produce

be combined, so each "event" (a sale, a sensor reading, or a visit to a web page) is stored as a row in a database table or file. This means that every customer, device, or user of the Web is involved in different *types* of events. For example, a grocery store customer over time will purchase products from multiple different categories, such as *Dairy Products*, *Produce*, *Seafood*, and so on, but this information does not exist at the individual customer level; it exists at the order detail level (inside the shopping cart). Joining data about what products someone placed in their shopping cart could provide access to valuable information about a customer and his or her shopping habits. Now, in all honesty, a lot of information about the customer will be lost by generalizing a specific dairy product such as Geitost (genuinely disgusting Norwegian brown cheese) to the *Dairy Products* category, but for this exercise, it will do. Table 11.7 contains the starting point; for each order detail line, what was the product ordered? To which category does that product belong?

Table 11.8. Order Detail Product Information.

orderid	Beverages	Condiments	Confections	Dairy_ Products	Grains_ Cereals	Meat_ Poultry	Produce	Seafood
10248	0	0	0	2	1	0	0	0
10249	0	0	0	0	0	0	2	0
10250	0	1	0	0	0	0	1	1
10251	0	1	0	0	2	0	0	0
10252	0	0	1	2	0	0	0	0
10253	1	0	1	1	0	0	0	0
10254	1	0	0	0	0	1	1	0

In this case, in applying the cross-tab tool, *OrderID* will become the rows of interest and *CategoryName* will provide the content for the columns. Apply the count function again to determine how many of each type of product category were part of each order. A cutout of the result in Table 11.8 gives a strong sense of which orders contained various categories—data that can be used for the prediction exercise.

Now the two tables from the chapter may be joined to create a larger table for machine learning. The next chapter will cover data sampling and splitting, processes that are critical to machine learning.

11.3 Exercises

1. For Figure 11.2, what would Table 11.3 look like if we ran summarize with the *average* function?
2. In Table 11.8, can you confirm that *OrderID* 10248 contains the right number of dairy products?

12
Data Reduction and Splitting

We will now focus on removing rows from the dataset or splitting the dataset into different parts. In Chapter 10, the process of splitting columns into multiple columns was explained. The topic now is similar: splitting rows. In Chapter 9, it was suggested to use a union to combine training and test data (if the test data has been provided by an outside entity). This chapter will examine different reasons and approaches for splitting the data once more.

12.1 Unique Rows

It is not uncommon for data to contain duplicate rows, which need to be removed. There are two ways to remove duplicates:

1. Partial match removal: Removal of full rows based on the identical content of a few columns.
2. Complete match removal: Removal of full rows based on identical content in all columns.

Since complete match removal is just a special case of partial match removal, the following examples will utilize the partial match. First, we sort the data in the order listing the rows *to keep* first. Second, we specify which columns should be identical for duplicates to be removed.

For example, assume that a business seeks to determine someone's home address based on location data from their cellphone. The organization's app reports device ID—a unique cellphone identifier—date, time, longitude, and latitude of the cell phone every time the app is used. To find a user's home address, it is necessary to know their home longitude and latitude, but because each user moves around regularly, app data suggests hundreds of locations for each user. For this exercise, assume that an app user's first interaction with the app each day occurs in their home. One possible method to find the individual's home following this assumption is to sort the data by device ID and then by date and time.

Having the data in sorted order, we now have a list of every person's app usage reports, starting with the first date they used the app and the first time they used it that day, followed by additional uses in chronological order. The next step is to select only the device ID and date columns and applying a *unique* function (a function that keeps just unique rows, discarding any row containing data already encountered),

Automated Machine Learning for Business. Kai R. Larsen and Daniel S. Becker, Oxford University Press. © Oxford University Press 2021. DOI: 10.1093/oso/9780190941659.003.0012

retaining only the first row from each day. Presumably, this leaves us with one record from each day at a time when the app user was quite likely to be at home.

While the data now displays a single record for every day the user interacted with the app, it is still unknown with full certainty which location represents their home location. Using the *summarize* function, we can now group each unique device ID with its unique configuration of longitude and latitude into discrete buckets. From here, we can count the number of occurrences of each location. With enough days of data and a few assumptions, we can determine that the most frequent location of usage is likely to be where a person lives. Another round of partial match removal may be required after sorting by device ID and count (descending) of call location to retain only the most frequent site for each device. Following this procedure, we can label the resulting table containing one row per device ID with associated longitude and latitude as *Home Location*.

Since partial match removal is a complex process, let us try one more example, this time with the Northwind data. Table 12.1 shows a set of sales information.

Table 12.1. Original Sales Data in the "Dairy Products" Category.

orderid	productid	ProductName	CategoryId	CategoryName
10248	11	Queso Cabrales	4	Dairy Products
10248	72	Mozzarella di Giovanni	4	Dairy Products
10248	42	Singaporean Hokkien Fried Mee	5	Grains/Cereals
10249	14	Tofu	7	Produce
10249	51	Manjimup Dried Apples	7	Produce
10250	65	Louisiana Fiery Hot Pepper Sauce	2	Condiments
10250	51	Manjimup Dried Apples	7	Produce
10250	41	Jack's New England Clam Chowder	8	Seafood
10251	65	Louisiana Fiery Hot Pepper Sauce	2	Condiments
10251	22	Gustaf's Knäckebröd	5	Grains/Cereals
10251	57	Ravioli Angelo	5	Grains/Cereals
10252	20	Sir Rodney's Marmalade	3	Confections
10252	33	Geitost	4	Dairy Products
10252	60	Camembert Pierrot	4	Dairy Products
10253	39	Chartreuse verte	1	Beverages
10253	49	Maxilaku	3	Confections
10253	31	Gorgonzola Telino	4	Dairy Products
10254	24	Guaraná Fantástica	1	Beverages
10254	55	Pâté chinois	6	Meat/Poultry
10254	74	Longlife Tofu	7	Produce
10255	2	Chang	1	Beverages
10255	16	Pavlova	3	Confections
10255	59	Raclette Courdavault	4	Dairy Products
10255	36	Inlagd Sill	8	Seafood
10256	77	Original Frankfurter grüne Soße	2	Condiments

Table 12.2. Reduced Dataset.

orderid	productid	ProductName	CategoryId	CategoryName
10248	11	Queso Cabrales	4	Dairy Products
10248	42	Singaporean Hokkien Fried Mee	5	Grains/Cereals
10249	14	Tofu	7	Produce
10250	65	Louisiana Fiery Hot Pepper Sauce	2	Condiments
10250	51	Manjimup Dried Apples	7	Produce
10250	41	Jack's New England Clam Chowder	8	Seafood
10251	65	Louisiana Fiery Hot Pepper Sauce	2	Condiments
10251	22	Gustaf's Knäckebröd	5	Grains/Cereals
10252	20	Sir Rodney's Marmalade	3	Confections
10252	33	Geitost	4	Dairy Products
10253	39	Chartreuse verte	1	Beverages
10253	49	Maxilaku	3	Confections
10253	31	Gorgonzola Telino	4	Dairy Products
10254	24	Guaraná Fantástica	1	Beverages
10254	55	Pâté chinois	6	Meat/Poultry
10254	74	Longlife Tofu	7	Produce
10255	2	Chang	1	Beverages
10255	16	Pavlova	3	Confections
10255	59	Raclette Courdavault	4	Dairy Products
10255	36	Inlagd Sill	8	Seafood
10256	77	Original Frankfurter grüne Soße	2	Condiments
10248	42	Singaporean Hokkien Fried Mee	5	Grains/Cereals
10249	14	Tofu	7	Produce

Here, our goal is to retain only information on only one order row that contains a dairy product. We believe the lowest *productid* is the best product to display (hard to construct a business case for this rule, but let's just go with it for now). There are many ways to do this, but one is to apply a *unique* function based on the *orderid* row and the *CategoryId* row. Assuming the data is ordered by *orderid*, *CategoryId*, and *productid*, as is shown in Table 12.2, this leaves only one dairy product per order, enabling a straightforward count of the number of dairy orders. In Table 12.2, after removing the second dairy product for each unique order, we lost a few rows. For example, row 2 in Figure 12.1 is now gone.

We mentioned that *complete match removal* is a special case of partial match removal. To remove a row, all values in all columns must match the same values in a prior row. Notice that by this logic, no two rows in Table 12.1 is removed due to the unique combination of *OrderID* and *CategoryId* values. In the case of complete match removal, sorting the data is often not required because the only rows removed will be identical to a retained row.

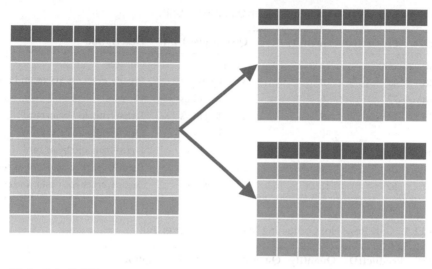

Figure 12.1. Data Splitting.

12.2 Filtering

Filtering is an often necessary and convenient tool for splitting up a set of data into two separate tables based on characteristics of that data. Looking again at the Northwind dataset, starting with the example dataset in Table 12.3, it could be reasonable to split the data to examine the quantity type in further detail, the goal being to understand better the types of content and packaging sold by the company.

After applying a filter tool, Table 12.3 is filtered into Table 12.4 and Table 12.5 based on the criterion of whether the *QuantityPerUnit* column contains the string

Table 12.3. Order Details Example Table after Joining in Product Information.

OrderID	ProductID	Quantity	QuantityPerUnit	Description
10248	11	12	1 kg pkg.	Cheeses
10248	42	10	32–1 kg pkgs.	Breads, crackers, pasta, and cereal
10248	72	5	24–200 g pkgs.	Cheeses
10249	14	9	40–100 g pkgs.	Dried fruit and bean curd
10249	51	40	50–300 g pkgs.	Dried fruit and bean curd
10250	41	10	12–12 oz cans	Seaweed and fish
10250	51	35	50–300 g pkgs.	Dried fruit and bean curd
10250	65	15	32–8 oz bottles	Sweet and savory sauces, relishes, spreads, and seasonings
10251	22	6	24–500 g pkgs.	Breads, crackers, pasta, and cereal
10251	57	15	24–250 g pkgs.	Breads, crackers, pasta, and cereal
10251	65	20	32–8 oz bottles	Sweet and savory sauces, relishes, spreads, and seasonings

Table 12.4. Only Rows Containing "kg" in QuantityPerUnit.

OrderID	ProductID	Quantity	QuantityPerUnit	Description
10248	11	12	1 kg pkg.	Cheeses
10248	42	10	32–1 kg pkgs.	Breads, crackers, pasta, and cereal
10248	72	5	24–200 g pkgs.	Cheeses
10249	14	9	40–100 g pkgs.	Dried fruit and bean curd
10249	51	40	50–300 g pkgs.	Dried fruit and bean curd
10250	51	35	50–300 g pkgs.	Dried fruit and bean curd
10251	22	6	24–500 g pkgs.	Breads, crackers, pasta, and cereal
10251	57	15	24–250 g pkgs.	Breads, crackers, pasta, and cereal

Table 12.5. Only Rows Not Containing "kg" in QuantityPerUnit.

OrderID	ProductID	Quantity	QuantityPerUnit	Description
10250	41	10	12–12 oz cans	Seaweed and fish
10250	65	15	32–8 oz bottles	Sweet and savory sauces, relishes, spreads, and seasonings
10251	65	20	32–8 oz bottles	Sweet and savory sauces, relishes, spreads, and seasonings

"kg" (kilogram). It is immediately clear that this initial criterion is flawed as it picks up on the "kg" in "pkgs." It is not completely useless, however, because the remaining table contains only cans and bottles measured in oz (ounces). We are also getting an indication that if we filter by "kg" with spaces on the side, we'll get all the products sold in kilogram measures. The next step here would be to split Table 12.4 based on whether it contains the "g" (grams) measurement (Table 12.4) or not (Table 12.5).

12.3 Combining the Data

We have now examined a lot of different data transformation options. While not all are directly useful to our goal of conducting machine learning on this dataset—and we will move on to another dataset for the next section—all of the transformations described are part of a data scientist's daily task list. At the end of this process, we might end up with a dataset much like that in Table 12.5.

For Table 12.5 we assume the predictive task to be a prediction of sales at the order-level of analysis. We have here collected and one-hot encoded some features. To save space, the table shows only the column headers and one example row.

It is worth noting that we can go quite far in developing features. For example, we created three features called *Measure_* suggesting whether the proportion of order detail lines referring to products represented in kilos, grams, ounces, milliliters, or centiliter. The *Cat_* features suggest whether a given category was part of this order.

Table 12.6. Dataset for Machine Learning (Only Partial One-hot Encoding Shown).

CustomerID	CompanyName	EmployeeID	orderid	Emp_1	Emp_2	Emp_3	Emp_4	Emp_5	Emp_6	Emp_7	Customer_ANATR
ANATR	Ana Trujillo Emparedados y helados	7	10308	0	0	0	0	0	0	1	1

Customer_ALFKI	Measure_kg	Measure_g	Measure_oz	Measure_ml	Measure_cl	Cat_1	Cat_2	Cat_3	Cat_4	Cat_5	Cat_6
0	1	0	0	1	0	1	0	0	1	0	0

Ship_Mexico	Ship_US	Ship_Canada	Empl_years_empl	Discount	OrderCost
1	0	0	24	0	88.8

In this case, categories 1 (Beverages) and 4 (Dairy Products) were present in the given order. We also developed features such as which country the product was shipped to and the number of years of employment for the salesperson. Hundreds or thousands of features may be developed in this fashion, but luckily the AutoML we will use does most of the feature engineering itself, such as creating all the features through one-hot encoding.

We also created a feature named *Discount*, which we are currently a bit worried about as it could constitute target leak, as a discount directly affects the target (*OrderCost*) negatively (price is lower if a discount is given). However, a discount may also have a positive effect on sales volume, and we need to understand what effect a discount has.

12.4 Exercises

1. What is the difference between partial match removal and complete match removal?
2. Develop the RegEx pattern that would filter out only quantity information measured in kilograms from Table 12.3.
3. What additional features may we add to the dataset in Table 12.6?

SECTION IV

MODEL DATA

After preparing your dataset, the business problem should be quite familiar, along with the subject matter and the content of the dataset. This section is about modeling data, using data to train algorithms to create models that can be used to predict future events or understand past events. Figure IV.1 shows where data modeling fits in the overall machine learning pipeline. Traditionally, we store real-world data in one or more databases or files. This data is extracted, and features and a target (T) are created and submitted to the "Model Data" stage (the topic of this section). Following the completion of this stage, the model produced is examined (Section V) and placed into production (Section VI). With the model in the production system, present data generated from the real-world environment is inputted into the system. In the example case of a diabetes patient, we enter a new patient's information electronic health record into the system, and a database lookup retrieves additional data for feature creation.

The system now creates features for the new patient (but without a target, as this data is unknown until later). This row of data (the new patient) is then submitted to the model, which predicts an outcome value of the target variable and a subsequent recommendation depending on the level of confidence in the model's prediction.

In this textbook, we provide several practice datasets. In all likelihood these datasets will be new and unfamiliar, so do not be afraid to open the files and examine their structure and content. Most files are small and may be opened in Excel. We structured the in-book lessons around the premier AutoML tool: DataRobot. If you are an avid open source enthusiast,[1] the processes and evaluative techniques should translate well into the open source world.

For those less enthusiastic about the years of coding, statistics, and math experience needed to conduct high-quality data science, DataRobot takes care of most of these requirements. It currently fulfills almost every one of the criteria for AutoML excellence outlined in Chapter 2.4. Among other tools tested, DataRobot performed the best on the AutoML criteria and was therefore selected as the tool of

---

[1] Open source software is software that can freely be downloaded and used, often for any purpose. It is notable for making sharing of knowledge and progress much easier. One of the most popular sites for sharing and working on open source software is Github.com.

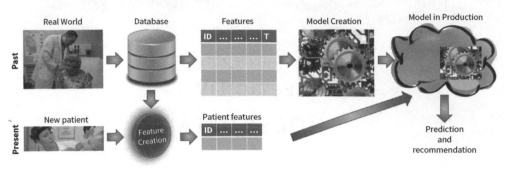

Figure IV.1 The Machine Learning Pipeline.

choice. Please note that DataRobot is a "living" tool that is continuously updated and improved. There is every chance that by the time you get your hands on this book, there will be small changes to the system that might change the exact results of the following analysis. In those cases, take our outlined process as a guide or as a map that while not 100% accurate will get you to the goal line.

In Section III, we referred to columns in a given dataset as *columns*. As we now transition to the use of machine learning tools on our data, these columns will be denoted as *features*, following the language of machine learning. The column containing the target variable will be known as the *target*. It is now time to move from business logic and data preparation to the actual machine learning.

13

Startup Processes

If this is your first time logging into DataRobot, note the starting point for analysis in Figure 13.1. To see all visualizations correctly and to avoid startup frustrations, make sure you use the latest version of the *Chrome* browser. If you are a student, you should have access to a fully functioning DataRobot account through your professor/class or bookstore. If you are an independent learner, Oxford University Press and DataRobot have collaborated to provide you a 14-day version of DataRobot that works with datasets developed for this book.[2] Alternatively, contact your organization's information technology group to see if they have access to an account.

13.1 Uploading Data

If this is not your first time logging into DataRobot, the opening page of DataRobot is often the most recent project. In this case, click the DataRobot logo in the upper left corner to get to the screen in Figure 13.1. The top black menu bar will be discussed in further detail later in this chapter. For now, begin by taking note of the kinds of data that can be uploaded into DataRobot.

The easiest way to bring a dataset into DataRobot is to read in a *local file*. The local file can be a file carefully prepared through the approaches outlined in Section III or one that has been provided and described in Appendix A. Generally, the datasets provided for this book consist of several files or tables. For example, for the Lending Club dataset, the raw data (a large dataset of more than 300,000 rows) is made available, downloaded from Lending Club in July 2017. We also share a second dataset that has been prepared for machine learning with a specified unit of analysis, target, and unsuitable rows removed. This set remains as large as the raw dataset. Finally, we share a dataset that we downsampled to around 10,000 rows. It is *strongly* recommended to stick to the smaller downsampled datasets while learning. There is little more to be learned from analyzing a larger dataset and abusing DataRobot's servers is not good for our educational agreement with them. The next chapters will focus on the Hospital Diabetes Readmission dataset, another dataset supplied with the book. This set began as 100,000 rows but has since been reduced to 10,000 rows.

---

[2] At the time of writing, such an account may be requested at this URL: https://www.datarobot.com/lp/request-a-demo/.

Automated Machine Learning for Business. Kai R. Larsen and Daniel S. Becker, Oxford University Press. © Oxford University Press 2021.
DOI: 10.1093/oso/9780190941659.003.0013

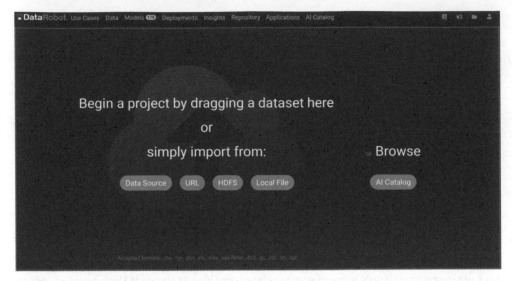

Figure 13.1. New Project Screen.

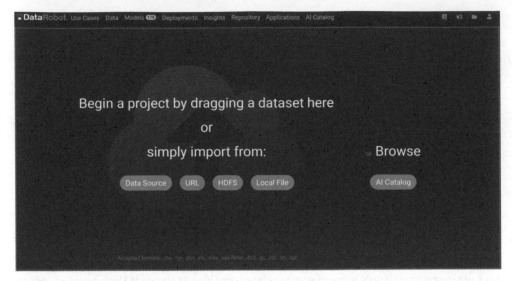

Figure 13.2. Small CSV File Opened in Text Editor (*left*) and Excel (*right*).

DataRobot will accept comma-separated values files (CSV; files with a .csv extension). These are text files where the first row contains the column names with a comma between each, and the following rows contain data, again with a comma between each. Scanning down the left side of a CSV file, anything listed before the comma on its line belongs to column 1, etc. We illustrate such files in Figure 13.2 where a .csv file is opened first in a text editor and then in Excel.

The column name and data between the first and the second comma corresponds to the second column. With text data that needs to be analyzed, be careful with this approach, as a comma inside a text field can cause the reading of a .csv file to fail. In such cases, it may be better to store the data as a tab-separated file (.tsv) where instead of commas, tabs are used to separate columns. With tab-separated files, text data is less likely to be problematic. Excel files (.xls and .xlsx) may be the safest bet, mainly if the data is small enough to be read into Excel (about one million rows or less).

If the desired data is available in any of the formats just described, is on the web, and has a direct URL (web link) linking to it, the URL button is an option as well. If the data is stored in a database such as PostgreSQL, Oracle, or MySQL, select ODBC

A managed healthcare organization believes they suffer from over $30 million in preventable losses annually due to the readmission of patients who are discharged from the hospital too soon. However, keeping all patients in the hospital longer is costly and inconvenient to patients. The organization has hired you to develop a model of readmission risk that doctors can consider when determining when to discharge a patient (if you find anything else in the data that helps reduce readmissions, they will appreciate that too).

They want you to start by focusing on readmissions among their diabetic patient population, and they have provided a dataset (10kDiabetes.csv) from a large set of hospitals, including their own, which describes admissions of this patient population. Predicted readmission risks from the model are only useful if the doctors believe in you and your model. To help the doctors gain trust, you have been invited to create a presentation for the doctors. Sketch out the content of this report or whitepaper. Focus on the conclusions and exhibits you will show them to support those conclusions.

Figure 13.3. Hospital Diabetes Problem Statement.

(Open Database Connectivity—a standard for connecting to just about any database). If the data is in a Hadoop system and you have an Enterprise DataRobot account, select HDFS. For these last two options, discuss access with your database administrator if you are not already a database expert. It is worth noting that if you are on a slow Internet connection, compressing the data as one of the following can help speed up the data upload: .gzip, bzip2, or zip archive (note that .zip, .tar, .gz, .tgz, and tar.bz2 files are the preferred compression approach because they give DataRobot access to the actual file size for some early process choices while reading the file).

Now, with basic knowledge of how to upload data to the AutoML, let us start a project. This project will be the primary example for the rest of the book (See Figure 13.3).

Begin first by loading the data into DataRobot. For this first exercise, use the *Hospital Diabetes Readmission* dataset described in Appendix A.1. This dataset is a 10-year, reduced sample of a public dataset for 130 US hospitals for the period 1999–2008. In the dataset, the unit of analysis is *patients that visited an emergency room for diabetes-related treatment.* The target is whether the patients returned to the hospital in less than 30 days of being released and were readmitted (*target: readmitted with values true or false).* A journal article describing the data and findings is available along with the dataset (Strack et al., 2014).

It is generally assumed that feature names are unique, whether you created the dataset yourself or downloaded it from an outside source. Be aware that joining different tables will invariably generate columns with identical names, so either rename or remove features with identical names. If the content of the columns is identical, remove the column; otherwise, rename it.

The current data limit for DataRobot is that the uploaded dataset must be 100 data rows or more, less than or equal to 20,000 columns, and less than or equal to

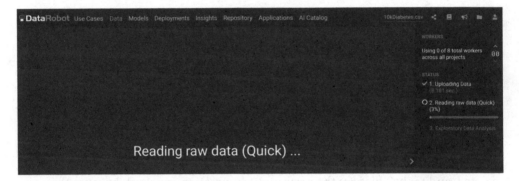

Figure 13.4. Accessing a Local File.

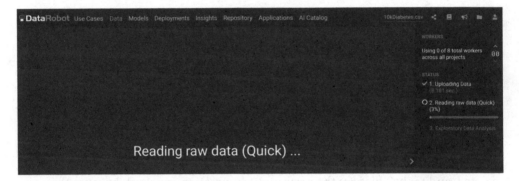

Figure 13.5. Startup Processes.

1.5 gigabytes of an uncompressed text file (though this is likely to change to be more accommodating).[3]

Select *Local File* as shown in Figure 13.4. To select the appropriate file, navigate to the directory where data for this book is stored and open the *A.1 Hospital Readmissions directory.* (The screen capture shown in the figure is from a Windows computer. Mac file structure should not vary greatly.) Select the file named 10kDiabetes.csv and click *Open*.

Now, as shown in Figure 13.5, the system is going to rapidly upload the data to the DataRobot cloud platform (step 1), read the data out of the file (step 2), and prepare exploratory data analysis results (step 3).

While the data is being processed, click on *Untitled Project* in the upper right part of the screen and name the project. This project can be titled *Hospital Diabetes Project*. After creating multiple projects, consider creating *tags* to keep track of them. To do this, click the file folder inside the circle symbol in the upper right area of the screen. Clicking the folder brings up a menu where new projects can be created (+

---

[3] If you deal with large datasets, we recommend that you read up on DataRobot's handling of such data. Go to the documentation and search for "working with large datasets."

Figure 13.6. Tagging a Project.

Figure 13.7. A Tagged Project.

Figure 13.8. Menu Bar.

Create New Project) and managed (Manage Projects). Following this step is an alternative to clicking the DataRobot icon for starting a new project.

Click on *Manage Projects*. Doing so will list all prior and currently running projects. Click on *Tags* and type in a more general name for the type of project that can be applied to similar ones. In this case, an appropriate tag might be *Patient Decisions*, per Figure 13.6. Assign the tag the blue color and click the plus symbol to create it.

Next, select the project by clicking the checkmark left of it (☑ Hospital Diabetes Project), and then click tags again (🏷 Tags). Apply the tag to the project by clicking *Apply*. Once several projects have been created, tags become increasingly important tools for managing them. Note that each project may have multiple tags. Try to create a new tag, *Diabetes*. Perhaps later projects will involve the topic of diabetes in a less patient-centric manner. Assign it a color different from blue. Your project should now show up as in Figure 13.7.

Exit the project menu now by clicking the *Data* (Data) link in the upper left corner to then return to the data screen in preparation for the next chapter. Notice that the link turns blue (Data) to illustrate that this is the screen currently being displayed. Figure 13.8 shows this in the context of the rest of the menu bar. The other menu links will be addressed in time as needed. For now, be aware that any project can be shared with collaborators by clicking the share icon (◁), DataRobot documentation is accessible through the documentation icon (▤), customer support and the DataRobot community are available through the megaphone (◁),[4] and account

---

[4] If you are a student in a course taught using DataRobot, contact your instructor instead of DataRobot support.

and settings can be managed with the user icon (◼). We recommend you start by exploring the community, where you will find training resources.

Chapter 14 introduces the initial exploration of the data. Now the fun starts!

13.2 Exercise

1. Review Appendix A datasets. Consider which is most relevant to your life for future reference. Plan to analyze this dataset once you have completed the book with the Diabetes Readmissions dataset.

14

Feature Understanding and Selection

Now that the project and data have been set up in DataRobot, the next step is to interpret the data contained in each feature (*feature understanding*). This chapter covers several parts of feature understanding, including *descriptive statistics*, *data types*, *feature content*, and *missing data*. Your screen should now look like Figure 14.1. DataRobot is now waiting to be instructed on what the target to be predicted is, but there are essential steps to take before doing so. Target selection will be covered in Chapter 15. If you are an experienced data scientist, it may be tempting to jump ahead, but consider scanning this chapter for potential divergences from your personal experience.

14.1 Descriptive Statistics

First, scroll down to see the list of features. Alternatively, click the link at the bottom of the screen to go to the features (**Explore 10kDiabetes.csv**). In Figure 14.1, notice that DataRobot lists all features in rows with their names under the *Feature Name* header and the order they were read into DataRobot under the *Index* header. The index number will be used to specify which feature is being discussed.

Unique is listed after *Var Type* (covered in the next subsection) and notes how many unique values exist for each specific feature. For example, the *rowID* column has unique numbers from 1 to 10,000, so there are 10,000 unique values. The next feature, *race*, has only five unique values. Hover over the *race* feature name with the mouse.

DataRobot offers to expand feature details if the feature name is clicked, as shown in Figure 14.2. Now click on *race*. The feature list will expand to show details about the *race* feature, as shown in Figure 14.3. Note that any feature name can be clicked to display more details about the feature. When a new feature is selected, DataRobot will close the previous feature detail screen.

Notice that the feature has five unique values according to the *unique* column. In the bar chart expanded by looking into the feature details, there are six bars, initially sorted by size (number of rows). The third bar shows the number of missing values. Hovering the mouse pointer over the blue bar, the number of missing values is displayed. This number (221) is the same as the number listed in the *Missing* column. In this case, DataRobot detected 221 question-marks (?) in the 10,000 cells for the *race* feature and converted the question marks to their code indicating *Missing* data.

Automated Machine Learning for Business. Kai R. Larsen and Daniel S. Becker, Oxford University Press. © Oxford University Press 2021.
DOI: 10.1093/oso/9780190941659.003.0014

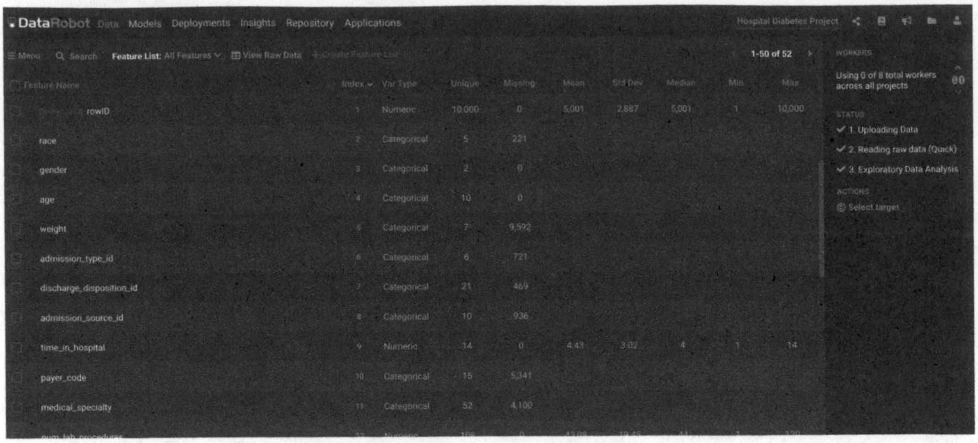

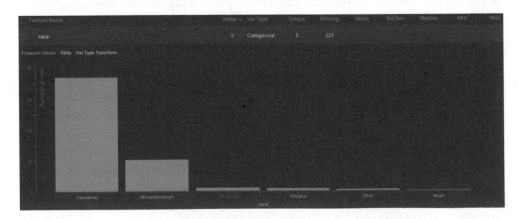

Figure 14.1. Starting Point for Data Types and Exploratory Analysis.

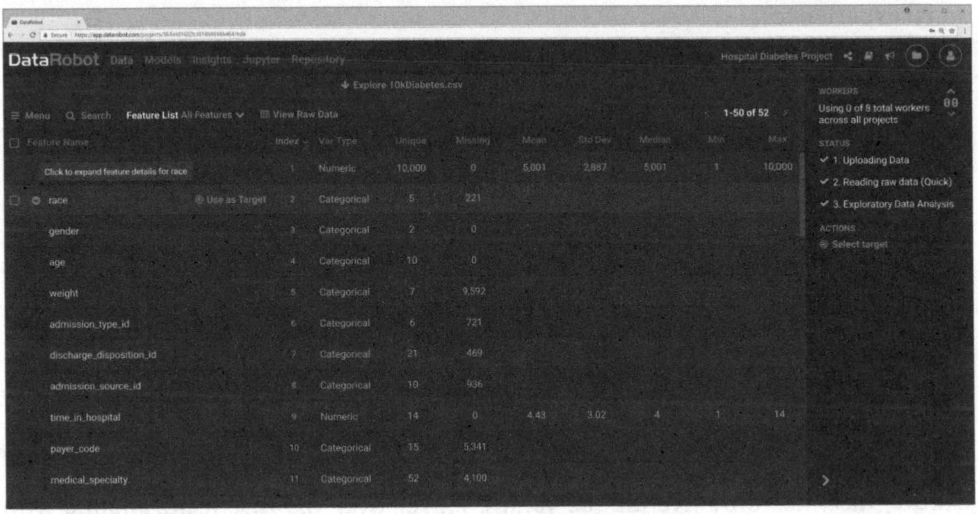

Figure 14.2. Option to Expand Feature Details.

Figure 14.3. Race Feature Details.

They did this to ensure handling of the variety of different codes that may indicate a missing value (this topic will be covered further in following paragraphs). Take note as well of the *Other* bar in this view. "Other" is a specific value present in the original data received. Hover over the bar to find that 121 patients were coded as race: *other*.[1] Click on *race* again to close the visualization.

To the right of the *Unique* column lies information on standard descriptive statistics such as *Mean*, *Std Dev* (standard deviation), *Median*, *Min*, and *Max*. Notice that these stats are only available for numeric columns, as one would expect (for categorical values, mean would be replaced with mode—the most common value—which can be displayed visually by clicking the feature name to enter the details screen). Take a look now at the numeric feature at index 9 in Figure 14.1, *time_in_hospital*.

The detailed view in Figure 14.4 shows how long the patients stayed in the hospital before being released. When using histograms like this one in future presentations, be ready for the question about where the cutoffs exist between bars. To do this, select the orange down-arrow next to **Showing 7 bins**, and change it to 14 bins. This results in the view shown in Figure 14.5.

Since there are fourteen separate values and fourteen bars, this is now a better position from which to understand the cutoffs between each value. These cutoffs can be confusing since the "2" shows up after the first bar, but the "14" shows up before the last bar. Hover over the first bar of this histogram, which should look like the chart Figure 14.5. The screen should now show the information in the rightmost part of Figure 14.6.

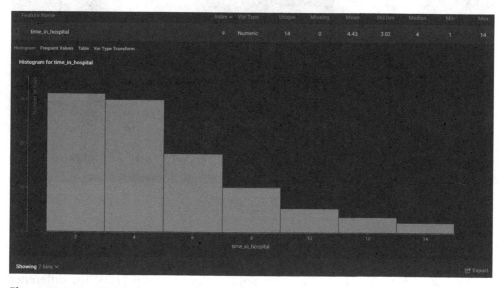

Figure 14.4. Detail View for *time_in_hospital* Feature.

---

[1] Some have different concepts of race and gender, and not all data suits all ideologies. Being aware of the potential for bias in machine learning is paramount, and there are often cases where certain features should not be included in a machine learning exercise (a topic for later discussion).

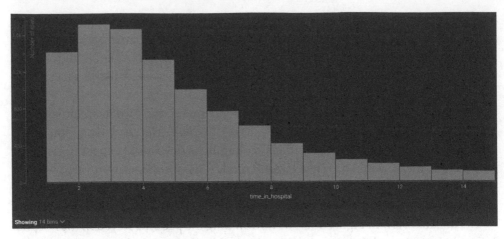

Figure 14.5. Detail View of *time_in_hospital* with 14 Bins.

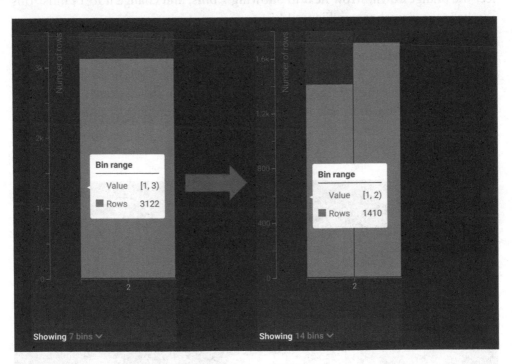

Figure 14.6. The Content of First Bar for 7 Bins and 14 Bins.

The visualization in Figure 14.6 shows that, for the first bar, the original seven bins "bin range" is between [1,3), while the range of the 14 bins is [1,2). The difference between brackets [] and parentheses () is important. A bracket denotes an inclusive range whereas a parenthesis denotes an exclusive range. In other words, the range includes the number next to a bracket, but not the number next to a parenthesis. Here are all possible values for the first bin in the 7-bin range:

- (1, 3) = 2
- (1, 3] = 2, 3
- [1, 3) = 1, 2
- [1, 3] = 1, 2, 3

DataRobot will only present the data in the third position above, bracket followed by parenthesis, meaning that the first number is counted in this bar on the histogram, whereas the last number is not. In Figure 14.6, the left figure shows that for the 7-bin case, the first bar contains all ones and twos. In the right part of Figure 14.6, in the 14-bin case, the [1, 2) indicates that it contains a count of only the ones, as one would expect. So, there are 1,410 values of "one" in this feature.

Moving on to the rest of the descriptive statistics, the *mean* is listed as 4.43, suggesting that the average hospital stay is a bit more than four days with a *standard deviation* of 3.02, which indicates that, if this had been a normal distribution[2] (it is not), the 68–95–99.7 rule would apply. This means that 68% of the data is within the −1 to 1 standard deviation, 95% of the data is within −2 to 2 standard deviations, and so on. In this case, the median value is 4. The median represents the number that is at the exact middle point of the sorted range of values.[3] The descriptive statistics end with *min* and *max* statements showing that the patients in question stayed a minimum of one day in the hospital and a maximum of 14 days.

To summarize, for these patients in this dataset, the most frequent value for the length of hospital stay was two days. The mean duration was 4.43 days, and the median was 4, suggesting that this data is an example of a right-skewed distribution (the "tail" on the right side of the distribution is longer or fatter). In such cases, one can generally expect the mode to be smaller than the median, which will, in turn, be lower than the mean.

14.2 Data Types

A data type indicates the nature of the data inside of a feature. Notice that the feature at index 3 in Figure 14.1 is *gender*, and it is listed as a categorical feature. Gender is listed as having two categories, male and female, per Figure 14.7 and noted in the adjacent *unique* column. While this variable has only two categories (binary categorical), it is also common to have many categories (multi-class categorical).

The other most common data type is numeric, which can be any number, including integers and decimals. Figure 14.5 covered *time_in_hospital*, a numeric feature. In some cases, we can code categorical features as numeric (1 = Caucasian;

[2] Google "bell curve" at images.google.com if you want to see a "normal" distribution.
[3] At the risk of having all third-grade math flood back into your consciousness, this statement is true only if you have an odd number of rows. If the number of rows is even, as in this case, take the two values on either side of the result of the dividing number of rows by two, which is 5,000.5 in this case: rows 5,000 and 5,001 and average the two numbers. Both numbers were clearly a four in this case.

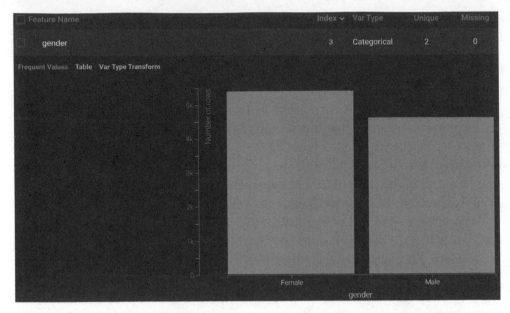

Figure 14.7. Example Categorical Data Type.

2 = African American; 3 = Asian, etc.). It is in these cases essential to scrutinize the automatic coding done by a machine learning system (automated or not) so that it correctly codes these as categorical rather than numeric. If the machine learning algorithm treats a categorical feature as numeric, it may look for evidence suggesting that African American patients are twice as likely to be admitted relative to Caucasian patients, or perhaps that Asian patients are somehow three times as likely. Such strong patterns are unlikely to exist and otherwise useful information about categorical differences is possibly lost.

Moving now further down the list of features, nearly at the end, lies the *readmitted* feature. Notice that it is listed as a *Boolean*, a type of categorical feature that always holds one of two values: true or false. Finally, the last data type present in this dataset is the *Text* type. The first example of this data type is at index 50 (not shown in Figure 14.1, so scroll down further in your view screen) for feature *diag_1_desc*, as shown in Figure 14.8. This is simply a case where we joined in the name of each diagnosis as its own feature (a separate table with diagnosis code and diagnosis name).

It may be apparent that the bar chart in Figure 14.8 is decidedly less useful than the numeric and categorical cases we examined, but there remain some valuable findings here. The most common value is *All Others*, which means that counting the 48 most common diagnostic descriptions and adding one bar for *Missing* (invisible because there are only two rows missing this value), DataRobot represents the remaining 409 (457 −48) types of values as *All Others*. However, it is immediately visible that, since the 10,000 cells contain only 457 unique values, or an average of about 22 cases per category, the *diag_1_desc* feature must be a standardized choice for the

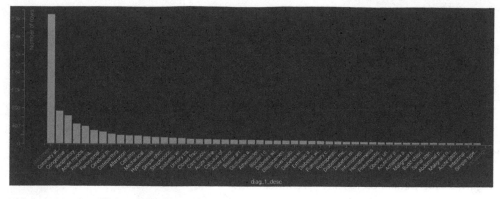

Figure 14.8. Detail View for *diag_1_desc*.

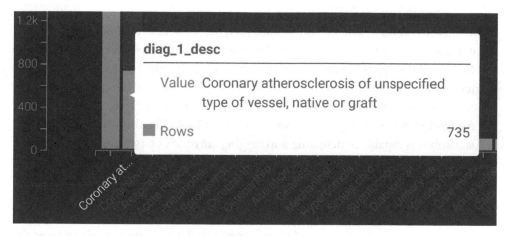

Figure 14.9. Example Diagnostic Description.

medical record system. While DataRobot does not care about whether the values inside a categorical feature were part of a standardized pre-set choice or not, having access to data that is carefully organized like this will often improve the AutoML's ability to find patterns. To see the most frequent diagnostic description, hover over the second bar from the left to get the view in Figure 14.9.

This code, *coronary atherosclerosis of . . .*, means that a case of plaque buildup in an artery supplying the heart with blood. As can be seen, this most common code exists in 735 columns, so it is possible that the machine learning algorithms could benefit from knowing which rows belong to the same category. In this case, it turns out that the feature *diag_1* (which can be found as index 18) already contains this information. The coronary code shows up in *diag_1* as number 414. Because this feature should clearly be categorical, go to it and check that the AutoML coded it correctly, as this will matter during analysis.

As seen in Figure 14.10, the bar chart for *diag_1* is identical to the bar chart for *diag_1_desc* in Figure 14.8. Furthermore, DataRobot already tagged this code as a

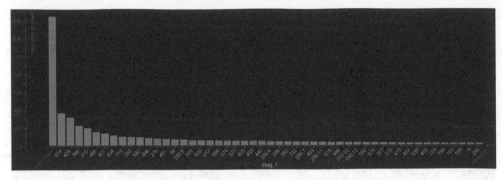

Figure 14.10. Detail View for *diag_1* Feature.

categorical data type (not something we should take for granted for a feature exclusively containing numbers).

Before moving on to discuss additional data types, be sure to take note of one somewhat hidden feature in DataRobot. The feature *diag_1*, at index 50, appears to be the last feature of the uploaded data; however, there are two more features in this dataset at index 51 and 52. DataRobot shows the first 50 features by default, and it is good to be aware of how to view features beyond index 50. Find the last two features by using the navigation at the top right of the window, which looks like this: **< 1-50 of 52 >**.

DataRobot is capable of detecting and tagging currencies based on the existence of currency symbols such as $ (dollar), € (euro), EUR (also euro), £ (pound), and ¥ (yen). It will also detect measurement length based on information such as <feet>'<inches>," which is important because it can then be converted to a consistent measurement. For example, 6'2" will be converted to 74 inches. Such conversions are, of course, unnecessary for metric distance measurements due to the brilliant introduction of the meter in 1799. Finally, DataRobot also does some nice work with dates. For each date, DataRobot will extract the day of the week and code each as 0–6, where 0 = Monday, 1 = Tuesday, and so on. It will then obtain the day of the month as a new feature, coded from 1–31, and month of the year as 1–12, as well as the year coded as the actual year.[4,5]

DataRobot does examine whether any auto-generated features already exist in the dataset and, in such cases, does not generate a new feature, for example, if a *Year* feature already exists and an auto-generated feature is found to contain the same year values.

14.3 Evaluations of Feature Content

Take note that the feature *rowID* at index 1 in Figure 14.1 has been detected as a unique identifier and marked with [Reference ID]. This means that the system will

---

[4] Note that these coding transformations are done only if, in each case, there are at least three weeks (for week transformation), three months (for month transformation), and three years (for both month and year transformations).

[5] If there are 10 or more date features, DataRobot does nothing to them, presumably to avoid overfitting. If the dataset exceeds this limit of 10 date features, make sure you remove unnecessary dates before uploading to get to nine or fewer dates.

not use it to predict your target because there should be no predictive value in a unique identifier. Scan through the whole list of features for other such feature codes; another one lies at index 29. DataRobot has tagged here *acetohexamide* (whether patients are on the medication Dymelor, a medication used to treat type 2 diabetes) with the code [Few values]. It is immediately visible that there is only one *unique* value in this feature (no one seems to be on this medication). DataRobot will ignore this feature during modeling.

At index 32 and 36, two more features are tagged with [Few values] in spite of these features having two and four unique values, respectively. As is clear from Figure 14.11, while there are four unique values for this feature, *No* is the only value with a significant number of responses. To see the other three, the display type needs to be changed to the table form (click "Table" Frequent Values   Table), per Figure 14.12. It can now be seen that

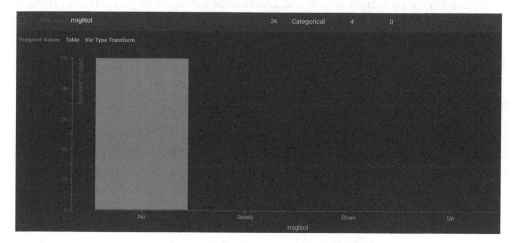

Figure 14.11. Index 36, *miglitol* Feature.

Values	Count
No	9995
Steady	3
Down	1
Up	1

Figure 14.12. Exploring *miglitol* Using the Table Display.

Steady (3), *Down* (1), and *Up* (1) do not occur frequently enough to warrant use of this feature in modeling. In other words, since only five of 10,000 patients (0.05%) are on the diabetes drug Miglitol, no conclusions can be drawn about its effectiveness in preventing patients from returning.

At index 40 (not shown in the figures, but can be found by scrolling down in the window), the feature *citoglipton* (probably a misspelling of Sitagliptin, an antidiabetic drug) is tagged both as [Few values] and [Duplicate]. It is labeled as a duplicate because several other features contain the same values, including the feature *examide* (medication for congestive heart disease and other conditions). One might worry that two features are identical (same data throughout) when they are different features, as in this case. An AutoML would not know which one to remove correctly, and it is possible that a researcher might draw incorrect conclusions about which drug had the positive or negative effect.

When the target feature is selected, DataRobot will tag it as [Target], and that's it for this dataset. In future datasets, however, the code [Too many values] may also be encountered, which applies to non-numeric columns, for example, *customer names*.

14.4 Missing Values

In many previous figures, the *Missing* column outlined how many of the values (out of 10,000 cases in this dataset) are missing from a specific feature. Remember also that the question mark (?) was coded as a missing value by DataRobot. Why care about missing values? The reality is that there are many ways for missing values to be handled even within the same dataset. By converting them all to one consistent type for missing values, an analyst can avoid them being categorized as multiple unique values during an analysis. This also prevents the machine learning tool treating a missing value, such as a question mark, as text and thereby treating a whole numerical column as categorical or textual (sadly, quite a common problem in machine learning). Even when a missing value is handled correctly, some algorithms will ignore a whole row if there is a single missing value in any cell of that row, leading to deleterious effects for the model. Algorithms struggling with missing values include *regression*, *neural networks*, and *support vector machines*.

Other codes converted to missing values by DataRobot are *nulls*. Nulls are values that were never entered or retrieved. How is this different from a zero? Considering a person's involvement in Yoga, a subject's value would be zero if they have done Yoga zero times. However, if others who are also part of this dataset have unknown Yoga habits, they would have to be coded as a *null*.

When different datasets or tables are joined through tools, such as Structured Query Language (SQL), many types of joins (left outer, right outer, full outer) generate null values whenever there is no connection between a row that exists in one table and the joining table. For example, a hammer was sold, but that sale had no specific employee number attached to it. In this case, when the order table is joined with the employee table, that particular sale is listed with a null for the *EmployeeId* and any other columns retrieved from the employee table. If you do not know SQL, no worries. It is not necessary for machine learning (that said, knowing SQL is a valuable skill in the world of technology). Null values will show up in some different ways, including null, Null, NULL, and sometimes as the text "null."

When a cell in a table or matrix is *not applicable*, not available, or there was no response, it may have been coded as character values that mean *missing* or *null*, but quite often they will be stored as a text code that means they are missing, such as "N/A," "na," "n/a," "#N/A." In the system that provided the data, some mathematical operations (such as any non-zero number divided by zero) result in a number that is *infinite* or at least beyond the computer's ability to represent, often coded as "inf," "Inf," or "INF." Empty fields, such as a single space, a blank, or a "None" will also be coded as missing values.[6] As painful as this chapter may have been, it contains content that is important for spotting and debugging troublesome errors in traditional machine learning systems. To be seen later, DataRobot will automatically impute missing values (calculate replacements, for example, by replacing a missing value with the average for the feature) before running the data through algorithms that cannot handle missing values. If you have special domain knowledge and believe yourself better capable of imputing missing values, you may try to do so before uploading data to DataRobot. We recommend that you carefully evaluate your imputation against the DataRobot imputation regarding their relative performance.

Next comes the truly good stuff: picking a target and starting to run the algorithms. Time for you to feel at the top of the world as you do work that is typically reserved for people with years of coding experience and advanced degrees.

14.5 Exercises

1. Use the search function to find the *diabetesMed feature*. Make sure you can find any specific feature for which you know the name.
2. Examine the *age* feature. It is stored currently as a categorical data type. Is this correct? Check the raw data to confirm. Consider going back to the original data to fix it if it should be an ordinal feature. What could your analysis gain from this?

---

[6] The full set of values DataRobot converts to missing: "null," "na," "n/a," "#N/A," "N/A," "?," ".", "," "Inf," "INF," "inf," "-inf," "-Inf," "-INF," "," "None," "NaN," "-nan," "NULL," "NA," "-1.#IND," "1.#IND," "-1.#QNAN," "1.#QNAN," "#NA," "#N/A N/A," "-NaN," and "nan."

15
Build Candidate Models

The Multiplicity of Good Models

ML principle: For any problem, a number of different models are likely to have similarly high accuracy (Breiman, 2001).

Build multiple models: most give very similar performance (Williams, 2011).

AutoML relevance: Because the top models in the AutoML leaderboard often arrived at their answers in different ways, blending them frequently improves accuracy further.

Corollary: There are always many more poor models than good models, but you don't know which are which until you try them.

At last! The data is ready to be used in creating a first deep-learning, neural network model (and many others). We will build many "candidate" models in this chapter. In other words, most of these models will serve primarily to improve understanding of what combinations of data, preprocessing, parameters, and algorithms work well when constructing models. Because there is no way to know which algorithms will work best for the data at hand, this step is essential.

Errors, Big and Small

ML principle: "Errors are not simply present or absent; they come in different sizes" (Witten et al., 2011, 180).

AutoML relevance: Same for ML and AutoML, though AutoML guard-rails helps avoid many typical errors.

It is important to distinguish between process errors, such as target leakage, and model errors, such as classification mistakes.

15.1 Starting the Process

At this stage, it is time to select the target feature. As with earlier chapters, this process will be a walkthrough of the DataRobot interface alongside an explanation, hopefully providing a deeper understanding of these steps. The point is not to

Automated Machine Learning for Business. Kai R. Larsen and Daniel S. Becker, Oxford University Press. © Oxford University Press 2021.
DOI: 10.1093/oso/9780190941659.003.0015

become a DataRobot expert, but rather to understand the machine learning process. The desired target feature can be found directly in the feature list; hover over it, and then click on the "Use as Target" text (). Alternatively, the name of the feature can be typed into the target area, as shown in Figure 15.1. This field will auto-populate possible features based on text input. Type until the intended target shows up and then select it.

Once we select the target, the top of the window changes, as depicted in Figure 15.2. The distribution of the target feature is displayed. See that the two options (True and False) are (relatively) well distributed. Had this not been the case, DataRobot automatically deals with it by downsampling (randomly removing cases) the majority class (that which is most common). See also that there are three sets of choices to

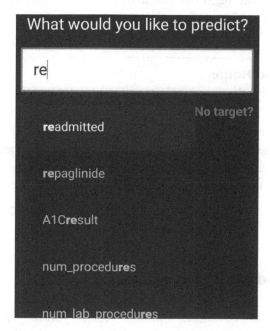

Figure 15.1. Selecting the Target.

Figure 15.2. Start Screen.

make here. It would be okay to click the big *Start* button without worrying much about it, but let us instead use this opportunity to learn a few more useful lessons before doing so.

First, note that DataRobot offers the option of which metric for which to optimize the produced models. In general, DataRobot can be trusted to select a good measure, but sometimes a customer or client has a preference for another measure on which they will evaluate the performance of the resulting models, in which case, consider using their measure. In the next section, we'll examine the alternatives. Second, note that by default, DataRobot will run with the *Informative Features*. If you scroll down to the feature list, you will see that DataRobot shows all features (`Feature List: All Features ▾`). Select the orange down-arrow and change the view to Informative Features (`Feature List: Informative Features ▾`). Note that DataRobot now displays only those features it had not marked for removal. These are the features that DataRobot will use for our first analysis.

Generalize or Go Home

ML principle: Use "an independent test set rather than the training set for performance evaluation, the holdout method, cross-validation" (Witten et al., 2011, 180).

Use training/validation/ testing datasets to build/tune/evaluate models (Williams, 2011). AutoML relevance: Both ML and AutoML models are evaluated on data they have not encountered before, but for which the target value is known.

15.2 Advanced Options

Next, examine the advanced options. Click "Show Advanced Options" (`⚙ Show Advanced Options`), and the options in Figure 15.3 will appear. Click on "Additional."

By selecting the orange down-arrow, the options for additional metrics are displayed, per Figure 15.4. Note that these are just the top options for this dataset and for this specific target, which is a binary classification problem (True/False). For regression problems (predicting a numeric value), other measures will be proposed.

LogLoss (Accuracy) merely means that rather than evaluating the model directly on whether it assigns cases (rows) to the correct "label" (False and True), the model is instead assessed based on probabilities generated by the model and their distance from the actual answer. For example, DataRobot treats an actual value of False as zero here, and an actual value of True as a one. For a case where the model assigns a probability of 0.9 (90%) to a case that is actually True, the model is considered to have done better than if it had calculated a probability of 0.8 (80%) to the same case. Had the model assigned a probability of .1, *LogLoss* would punish the model greatly

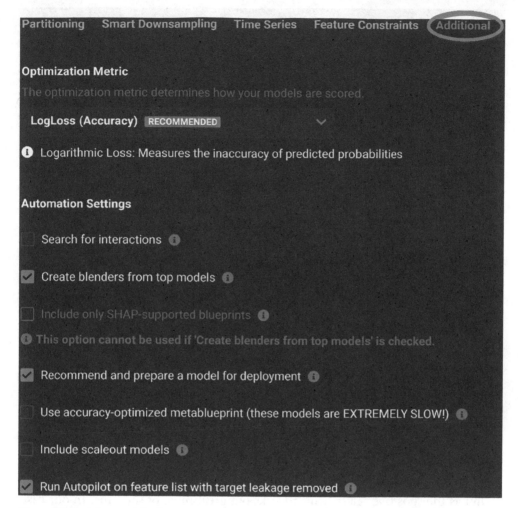

Figure 15.3. Advanced Options.

for being confident (close to zero) *and* wrong. Appendix B contains a full listing of the available measures from the DataRobot documentation. For the time, keep the recommended optimization measure: *LogLoss (Accuracy)*. If you become a regular user of DataRobot, consider reading up on these measures to better understand how models are selected.

Note that the "Additional" advanced options provide alternatives such as using accuracy-optimized metablueprints, which will potentially lead to better results, but at the cost of processing power and time. We recommend you ignore this and most of the advanced options under this section, including random seed[1] unless you are

---

[1] It is worth noting that computers cannot generate random numbers, and given the same starting point, DataRobot has been set to start with the random seed of 0, which means that given identical datasets, your results should be the same as those outlined in this book, unless relevant changes are made to the software in the meantime. Expect things to change if you add or remove rows from your data.

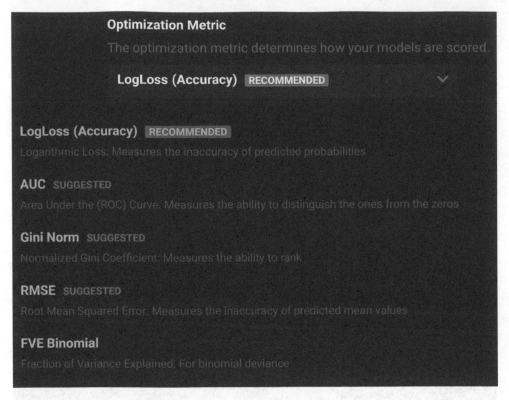

Figure 15.4. Optimization Metric.

already a data scientist. A notable exception to this is the positive class assignment. DataRobot will generally assign the highest target value (alphabetically or numerically) as the "positive" class, which works out great most of the time. In our case, we are trying to detect patients likely to be readmitted, so those patients are our positives, which works in a medical sense where a "positive" is often a negative for you as a patient, and the "positives" are the ones we will want to treat. However, when working with a dataset of lenders who are likely to default on their loans, it makes more sense to change the positive class to those who have a False value for loan default, as those are the ones you want to lend money.

Select "Partitioning" under advanced options, as this gives us another screen related to one of the most fundamental parts of machine learning, partitioning of data into training and validation groups (folds). Figure 15.5 shows the options available through selecting a partitioning method.

Click back and forth between the four available types of partitioning methods a few times. Notice that *Random* and *Stratified* give identical options. The only difference between *Random* and *Stratified* is that the *Stratified* option works a bit harder to maintain the same distribution of target values inside the holdout as the other samples (approximately the same percentage of *True* values inside each sample).

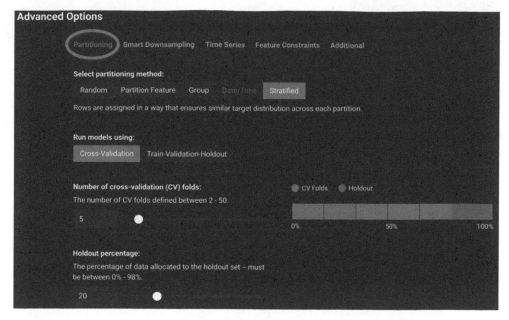

Figure 15.5. Partitioning.

In the DataRobot default, and as is commonly done in data science, 20% of the data is assigned to the holdout sample (the red, rightmost, part of Figure 15.5). Since there are 10,000 rows (cases) in this dataset, a random set of 2,000 cases will be pulled out of our dataset and stored in a "lock-box." These 2,000 cases will be unlocked right before making the final decision about whether to place this system into "production" (start predicting cases from the real world). The holdout cases protect us against risks that will be discussed later in the book.

You may change the holdout percentage to another number. Try it out with 50% by pulling the holdout percentage slider bar to the right or typing 50 into the input field. There are occasions where it makes sense to increase the holdout sample to more than 20%, such as when you have a lot of data, and you want to ensure that the holdout evaluation is as accurate as possible. For this dataset, it is best to stick to 20.

Once the lock-box has been filled with holdout cases and appropriately locked, the remaining cases are split into n folds. The (n)umber of folds can also be set manually. For small datasets, it may make sense to select more folds to leave the maximum number of cases in the training set. That said, be aware that picking more folds comes with drawbacks. The validation sample (the first fold) will be less reliable if it contains a small set of cases. In short, DataRobot makes very consequential decisions based on the first validation fold, such as picking which algorithms are given a chance to succeed. If the intent is to run cross validation on the data, each extra fold leads to one more run-through of creating models. This concept will be covered in detail later. Five and ten are the most commonly chosen numbers of folds, and since the DataRobot folks swear by five, keep the number of folds at five for this

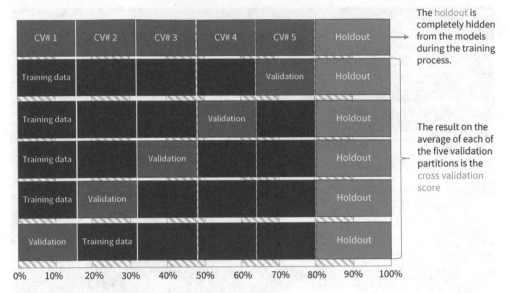

Figure 15.6. Cross Validation and Holdout Overview.

exercise. With 10,000 cases in total and 2,000 cases set aside for the holdout, there are 8,000 cases left that, when divided by five, leave 1,600 cases in each of the five folds.

Read Figure 15.6 in conjunction with Appendix C. It illustrates two things: first, it is a reminder of the distribution between the various samples split into five folds and a holdout. Second, it specifies that the cross validation scores to come from the system are combined validation scores for the number of models used (including the original validation model). This means that for the first set of models created for CV#1, 4 * 1,600 = 6,400 cases are combined for training a model, and 1,600 cases are used to validate that model.

Moving now to the *Partition Feature*, this is a method for determining which cases to use in different folds. *Partition Feature* is different from the other approaches in that the user must do their own random or semi-random assignment of cases. You must here manually specify which cases belong in *train*, *validation*, and *holdout*. Three different values in your selected feature are required. If more than three unique values exist in the selected feature, you may only select *train* and *validation* folds, with all other values assigned to *holdout*. This option is helpful when analyzing graph (network) data where it may be necessary to make sure that there was no overlap between friendship networks (groups of people directly connected to each other) in the *train* and *validation* sets.

The *Group* approach accomplishes much of the same as with the partition feature, but with some fundamental differences: first, it allows for the specification of a group membership feature. Second, DataRobot makes decisions about where a case is to be partitioned but always keeps each group (those with the same value in the selected feature) together in only one partition. Finally, the *Date/Time* option deals with a critical evaluation issue: making sure that all validation cases occur in a period *after* the time of the cases used to create models. In our case, this option is not available because we have not selected time-aware modeling. Time-aware modeling and time series modeling are covered in Chapters 25 and 26, respectively.

Think of time-aware modeling this way: a data scientist claims to have created a model that flawlessly predicts the weather according to his cross validation score. After some immediate disbelief from his audience, he clarifies that all he needs is an hour-by-hour accounting of the weather in his training set. His prediction model becomes far less impressive, as knowing the weather an hour from now is less of a feat (as well as less useful) than knowing it 24 hours into the future. Upon digging into his validation procedure, it becomes apparent that there is another problem. Cross validation randomly samples from different parts of the training set, and he was working with a dataset that was a time series (weather proceeds along a time-line). Simply put, the misguided data scientist used information about future weather to train and evaluate his model. In some instances he gave his training algorithm this type of data: on day 15, it rained during hour 5, and it rained during hour 7. He then validated his model by checking whether it could predict that it also rained during hour 6 on that same day. Any prognosticator that will offer to tell you what the weather will be like tomorrow if you will first show them the actual state of the weather the day after tomorrow is not going to have a future in the business. One of the authors once participated in a grant review process where not being aware of this basic fact cost a team a $1 million grant. This situation is a special case of something called *target leakage*, which will be covered further in Chapter 20.6. The *Date/ Time* option ensures that the models' *training* and *validation* data are appropriately split by time to avoid this.

Search for the Right One

ML principle: "Search for a model that gives a good solution, either algorithmic or data" (Breiman, 2001, 202).
AutoML relevance: AutoML carries out that search for the user.

15.3 Starting the Analytical Process

It is now time to start the analytical process, which will prepare the data through the prescribed options: *Autopilot*, *Quick*, and *Manual*, per Figure 15.6. Before doing so, make sure to reset the options to where they were initially before this little exploration: *Stratified* partitioning method with *5-fold cross validation* and 20% *holdout* sample. Note that if you have the student version of DataRobot, Autopilot is not available.

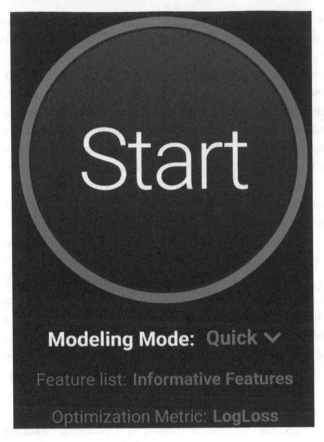

Figure 15.7. Start Button.

Imagine briefly working with data to create a model predicting when a customer is likely to abandon a shopping cart with products in it rather than complete the purchase. There are two hours before the presentation starts, and the client expects an explanation of which features drive the behavior. In this situation, select the *Quick* run option (see Figure 15.6) to leave more time to create a presentation. *Quick Run* is an abbreviated version of *Autopilot* that produces almost as good models (on average) by shortcutting the DataRobot best practice machine learning process.

This chapter describes the *Quick* option because all readers will have it, but if you have the professional version, the Autopilot option is also available to you. *Autopilot* and *Quick* are similar, except that for *Autopilot* DataRobot starts the analysis at 16% of the sample and uses that information to determine which models to run with 32% of the sample. *Quick* begins right at 32% with models that have historically performed well. One other difference is that in *Quick*, only four models are automatically cross validated, and only one blender algorithm applied. For the dataset we are using, the top models in *Autopilot* vs. *Quick* turn out to have near identical performance characteristics on the *LogLoss* measure. We, therefore, recommend that you stick to *Quick* while you are learning, even if you have the Autopilot option.

For now, set aside the *Manual* option to try out later with one of the many datasets prepared in later chapters. As mentioned, know that *Informative Features* represents all the data features except for the ones automatically excluded and tagged, for example, as [Duplicate] or [Too Few Values]. We will now explore the modeling process in depth. *Please be aware that because DataRobot is developing this product and adding algorithms and features at blinding speed, some details in this book may be wrong. In such cases, be sympathetic with these poor authors working in a format thousands of years old (the book). Try to generalize from our points to what shows on your screen.*

Keep the *Quick* option selected and click the Start button. Doing so will start a lot of processes. First, the right sidebar will begin to show a rapid succession of steps 1–7, as seen in Figure 15.8. Step 1, "Setting target feature," transfers the user's target feature decision into the analysis system. Step 2, "Creating CV and Holdout partitions," uses the decisions we made in the advanced settings (or the default if we did nothing) to randomly or semi-randomly assign cases to the holdout and various cross validation folds. Step 3, "Characterizing target variable," is where DataRobot will save the distribution of the target to the analysis system for later use in decisions about which models to run.

Step 4, "Loading dataset and preparing data," is relevant if (a) the dataset is large (that is, over 500MB); (b) all the initial evaluations before this step will have been conducted with a 500MB sample of the dataset (or the whole dataset is smaller than 500MB); and (c) now the rest of the dataset is loaded. Step 5, "Saving target and partitioning information," is where the actual partitions are stored in cross validation folds, and holdout sets are stored in a separate file on a disk. In Step 6, importance scores are calculated (we discuss these in the next paragraph). The features have now been sorted by their importance in individually predicting the target. Step 7, "Calculating list of models," is where information from steps 3–6 is used to determine which blueprints to run in the autopilot process.[2]

As soon as DataRobot completes these seven steps, a new column is added to the feature list: *Importance* (Importance ⌄), providing the first evidence of the predictive value of specific features (see Figure 15.9).

The green bar in the *Importance* column indicates the relative importance of a particular feature when examined against the target independently of all other features. Each feature is compared to the target by a logistic or linear regression using the Alternating Conditional Expectation (ACE) algorithm (Breiman & Friedman, 1985; Wang & Murphy, 2004) on the training and validation sets. Doing so produces numbers that when scaled between zero and one and are equivalent to R^2-scores (0 = feature has no relationship to target; 1 = the feature entirely predicts the target, with .5 indicating that the feature predicts 50% of changes in the target). DataRobot refers to this as the *normalized value*. The approach works well even for non-linear relationships. The

---

[2] Blueprints are combinations of pre-processing of data, a specific algorithm, and specific parameters. We will examine blueprints in Chapter 16.5.

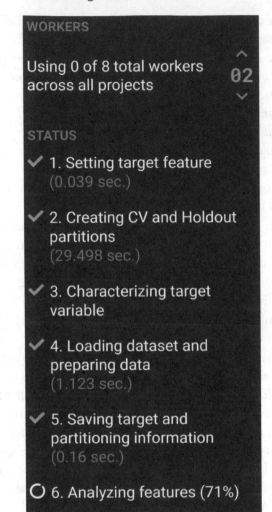

Figure 15.8. Startup Process Initialization.

most important feature is given a fully green bar. The other bars are filled in based on their relative importance compared to the most important feature.

If you hover over the bar, two numbers appears, per Figure 15.10. This number is not the ACE number. Instead, it is the ACE number converted into a chosen optimization measure, in this case, *LogLoss* (Accuracy), but still derived from only the relationship between that feature and the target. It might be worthwhile comparing the LogLoss of 0.658 from the top feature to the best model created later. This LogLoss is not tremendous, but one generally does not expect one feature alone to carry a model.

A final point worth making is that now that you have committed to a target and DataRobot has finished locking away the holdout sample, it provides additional

Feature Name	Data Quality	Index	Importance ⌄	Var Type	Unique	Missing	Mean	Std Dev	Median
readmitted	TARGET	49	Target	Boolean	2	0	0.40	0.49	0
discharge_disposition_id		7	▬▬	Categorical	21	374			
number_diagnoses		21	▬▬	Numeric	9	0	7.03	2.02	7
number_inpatient		17	▬▬	Numeric	11	0	0.39	0.86	0
diag_2_desc		51	▬▬	Text	398	48			
diag_3_desc		52	▬▬	Text	426	164			
medical_specialty		11	▬▬	Categorical	52	3,286			
admission_source_id		8	▬▬	Categorical	9	761			
diag_3		20	▬▬	Categorical	426	164			
admission_type_id		6	▬▬	Categorical	6	574			
num_lab_procedures		12	▬▬	Numeric	108	0	43.11	19.52	44

Figure 15.9. Importance Column Added to Feature List.

Feature Name	Data Quality	Index	
			Value: 0.658632
			Normalized Value: 0.018254
readmitted	TARGET	49	Open documentation
⌄ discharge_disposition_id		7	▬▬▬ Cate

Figure 15.10. Optimization Measure Score.

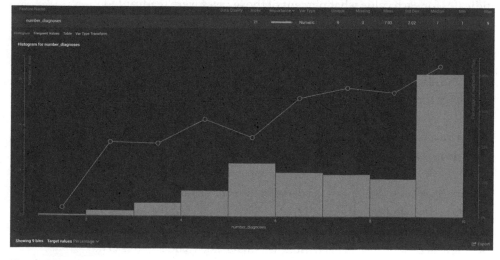

Figure 15.11. Histogram with Target Proportions.

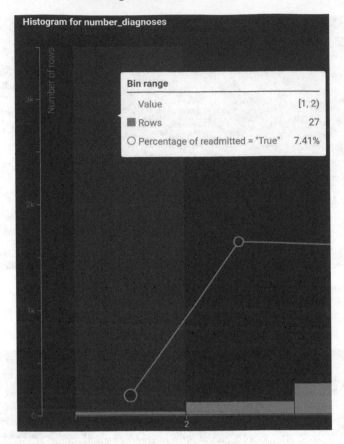

Figure 15.12. Information from Bar 1.

information in the feature detail screens. Click on *number_diagnoses* for the histogram in Figure 15.11. This histogram now shows a new Y-axis to the right that indicates for each value what percent of those cases were readmitted.

On your screen, hover over the first bar to get information suggesting that, per Figure 15.12, patients with only one diagnosis had the lowest rate of readmission, with only 7.41%. Unfortunately, only 27 patients out of 8,000 (0.3%) had such a small number of diagnoses, so the particular value may be less useful in predicting outcomes than one would hope.

Assume That Assumptions Are Everywhere

ML principle: Every algorithm is built around assumptions and knowledge that determine its ability to generalize (Domingos, 2012).

AutoML relevance: In AutoML this can be taken advantage of by trying several algorithms and letting their performance characteristics determine which model(s) to select.

15.4 Model Selection Process

The second change to the screen (as seen in Figure 15.13) is the introduction of a sidebar showing several algorithms running on the Amazon Cloud environment. This will include the running of almost every useful type of algorithm invented for machine learning. Earlier in the process, the original data uploaded to DataRobot is then uploaded to Amazon servers where all the DataRobot algorithms also reside. Now at the present moment, even though each different type of algorithm has very different run times and processing needs, each is assigned here to a "worker." We can think of a worker as a dedicated computer. Notice that in Figure 15.13, the worker running the

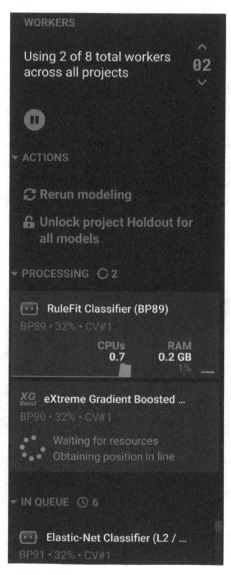

Figure 15.13. 32% Samples for Validation Starting Run.

TensorFlow Neural Network Classifier is using only 0.3 CPUs at the time of the screen capture. These allocations will change over time, but generally, algorithms requiring more processing power will be assigned many more CPUs. Some will run with 10 or more CPUs as needed to even out processing time across algorithms.

Another worthwhile piece of information in Figure 15.13 is that the algorithms are run with a *32% sample, CV #1*. Recall from earlier in this chapter that combining the four folds not used for validation produces a 64% sample of the whole dataset. The 32% sample being used right now is half of that data randomly selected from each of the four folds, or 3,200 cases used to *train* each model, with the full set of the final fold's cases being used to *evaluate* the models (1,600 cases). Think of the DataRobot *Quick* process as a four-round tournament to determine the best approach and algorithm (which we will later refer to as blueprints).

15.4.1 Tournament Round 1: 32% Sample

In this case, a total of 14 algorithms are running or scheduled to run. This may be a good time to check how many workers you have access to by clicking the up-arrow next to the worker number. Even if you have access to more workers, set it back to two for now since there is a fair amount of explaining to do as things move forward here. If DataRobot gets ahead of your reading, feel free to pause the algorithms by hitting the pause button next to the *Worker* number.

At this point, a few algorithms should be finished. Click on *Models* in the upper middle of the screen to view these finished models. This click opens the model leaderboard, Figure 15.14. It is a busy screen with many details, so here is

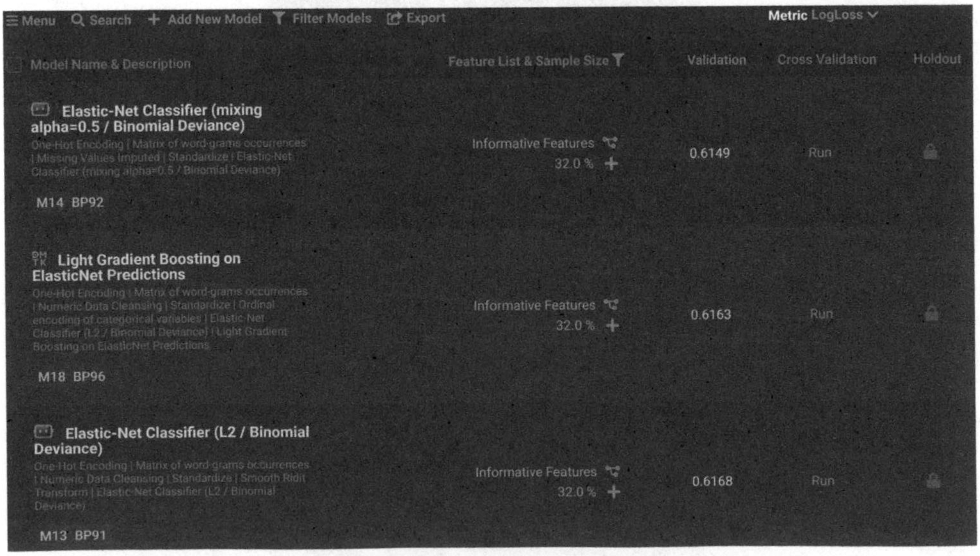

Figure 15.14. Models Leaderboard Screen.

a breakdown of what is going on. While the algorithms are running on Amazon and completing one by one, they are reported and ranked on the leaderboard. Here they are ordered by their validation score. Since LogLoss measures something "bad" (loss), small numbers are a good thing, so DataRobot places the algorithms with the lowest scores on top. In Figure 15.14, with 14 algorithms finished running at 32% of the training set, something called the *Light Gradient Boosting on ElasticNet Predictions* leads with *Gradient Boosted Trees Classifier* rounding out the bottom of the leaderboard (if we ignore the three text models at the bottom). It is noteworthy that both algorithms represent approaches for combining hundreds or thousands of decision trees. A decision tree classifier will be examined in Chapter 17 because decision trees are easy to understand and often work well.

The distinction between algorithms that perform well in the leaderboard and those that do not is important because DataRobot will use the information on which algorithms work well with 32% of the data to make decisions about which algorithms will be selected for further "participation." There is one notable exception to this rule. Any text feature will be assigned its own algorithm. In this case we have three text features, the diagnosis descriptions (*diag_1_desc*, *diag_2_desc*, and *diag_3_desc*). At the bottom of the leaderboard you will find three *Auto-Tuned Word N-Gram Text Modeler using token occurences* models. These will always be selected for participation because they provide features for other models.

Figure 15.14 shows the whole DataRobot process that has just unfolded. Each combination of preprocessing steps before application of the algorithm and its parameters is called a "blueprint." Consider the list of individual algorithms, such as the *Light Gradient Boosting on ElasticNet Predictions* listing.

Figure 15.15 outlines a few different things: First, the light-blue DMTK symbol (![DMTK]) means that this algorithm came from the Microsoft Distributed Machine Learning Toolkit. The other types of models used by DataRobot are Python-based models from the scikit-learn package, R-based models, DataRobot-created models, Nutonian Eurequa models, Apache Spark MLlib models, Vowpal Wabbit models,[3] TensorFlow models, XGBoost models, H_2O models, Keras models, and blender models. Review the symbols for your models. If you want to find some of the listed models that were not part of this DataRobot run, go to the **Repository** tab.

Figure 15.15. Top Model Information.

---

[3] Yes, computer scientists read Lewis Carroll and watch Elmer Fudd cartoons.

Second, comes the name of the classifier (in this case, "*Light Gradient Boosting on ElasticNet Predictions*"). Third are any significant options made in the implementation. DataRobot keeps a few secrets, but in this instance, they are forthcoming about all the details inside this model. We will discuss these when covering the model blueprint. Fourth, the listing states that this model implementation is Blueprint number 96 (BP96).[4] BP96 notes the specific process flow implemented for this algorithm. More blueprint examples are examined later. For now, know that the same blueprint number is used at various sample sizes so that it is clear which models "survived" the selection process. Fifth, the model number (M18) says that this particular model is model number 18. This model number will only show up once in the whole leaderboard as a unique identifier for a model. To interact with DataRobot through its *R* and *Python* application programming interfaces, knowing a specific model's number can be helpful.

Note that DataRobot offers additional "scale-out" approaches, algorithms for exceedingly large datasets with the ability to add hundreds and thousands of workers as needed, such as for running large H_2O jobs. These must be requested from DataRobot to become part of your system.[5] MONO models, which means that this model may be set up for forced directional relationships between a feature and the target. Such "monotonic constraint" approaches are useful to increase the efficiency of algorithm processing and to avoid overfitting. Rating tables means that you may export all the relationships and weights in the model and change them manually. After replacing the weights, you may upload the rating table to DataRobot as a new model. When we earlier mentioned the difficulty of avoiding bias related to gender and race, rating tables are interesting because they hint at an approach to avoiding such bias: including information on race and gender as part of the modeling, but then changing their weights to zero in the rating table. While not likely to root all effects of bias in the data, it might represent a reasonable first step.

The Beta-sign means that this model provides additional information about which features have a positive effect on the target and which features have a negative effect—often called *coefficients*. The watchful eye means that the model provides *insights* under the **Insights** menu on the top of the page.[6] The final symbol, the reference-model icon (REF),[7] means that a model is included not because it is expected to outperform other models, but because these are very simple models with little or no pre-processing to enable comparison against more advanced processing options and models. The reference models serve much the same function as a canary in a coal mine. If such models perform as well as or better than other models, then this is a sign that something is wrong.

---

[4] Note that the blueprint number may be different in your project.

[5] If you have a student account for DataRobot, please do not request access from DataRobot support. You will not need it for your class and it would eat through your processing allowance in no time.

[6] Let's run the marshmallow test: if you resist going to the *insights* menu right now, I'll give you two marshmallows later when we cover that screen.

[7] The ref symbol has recently been retired by DataRobot. However, the concept is important enough that we kept it in this section. Examples of reference models is the *Majority Class Classifier*.

15.4.2 Tournament Round 2: 64% Sample

Next, DataRobot selects the four best algorithms in the 32% round for use with the remaining set of data, 64%, and the three *Auto-tuned Word n-Grams* are rerun to provide input into the other four algorithms. The algorithms are now learning from 6,400 cases and are once more being validated against all 1,600 cases in cross validation fold #1, also known in the leaderboard as, simply, *Validation*.

15.4.3 Tournament Round 3: Cross Validation

The next step, if the validation dataset is small (<= 10,000 cases), is to run the full cross validation (CV) process on the four top models. After this is done, ensure that you always sort the leaderboard by the cross validation column. We strongly encourage you to read Appendix C to better understand cross validation before proceeding. Before finishing this round, *Feature Impacts* of the top model are calculated. We will return to feature impacts in Chapter 19.1. As a final step, DataRobot will select the top model in the leaderboard and train it with 80% of the available data (all data from the five folds), and provide estimated validation and cross validation scores, marked with asterisks. In this case, the holdout sample score is also shown. A bit of pause is provided by the lower validation and cross validation, but we will not know whether this is an issue until we unlock the holdout scores later in the process. The 80% model, which DataRobot proceeds to train with all rows of data, is recommended for deployment should you be in a hurry to get your model into production. We are not ready to go to that step yet and will ignore this model in our future deliberations. Note that DataRobot reports the performance metrics with asterisks because no true validation and cross validation is possible when training a model with all the data.

Shaken *and* Stirred

ML principle: The evolution of thinking about algorithms has moved from (1) focusing on many variations of the same algorithms, to (2) exploration of many different types of algorithms, to (3) the blending of multiple algorithms.

"This works because it greatly reduces variance while only slightly increasing bias" (Domingos, 2012, 85).

AutoML relevance: AutoML approaches often automatically select the top models and blend them together.

15.4.4 Tournament Round 4: Blending

Once the cross validation has finished running, the models are then internally sorted by cross validation score before the best models are blended. To see the order in which the models will be selected, click the *Cross Validation* column, but ignore the 80% model. There are many different ways to do this in DataRobot. Two average blenders (*AVG Blender* and *Advanced AVG Blender*) average the probability score of each model's prediction for each case. In our *Quick* process, the AVG Blender is applied to the top two models.

Another approach employed is *ENET Blenders*, one blending the three top models and the other blending the top eight models. In the DataRobot Autopilot, the three or eight probabilities are considered features, which are used along with the target value for the whole dataset to run another predictive exercise in case some models are stronger at certain probability levels. Let us create our own blender model. Sort the leaderboard by cross validation and select the top three non-blender models run on 64% of the data. Then go to the menu (≡ Menu) where several blending approaches are available and select the *ENET blender*. A new model run is now created in the right window. Figure 15.16 shows the result of creating that blender at the time of this writing. Adding blenders might not always work, but is generally worth a bit of extra effort. In this case, the DataRobot-added AVG Blender does better.

The *AVG Blender* takes predictions from the top two models (M21 and M55) and averages the probabilities as its prediction. For the *Advanced AVG Blender*, the same process is followed, but often by blending more models.

For example, if one of the *Light Gradient Boosting on ElasticNet Predictions* models is very good at predicting patient readmissions based on three of the features, and

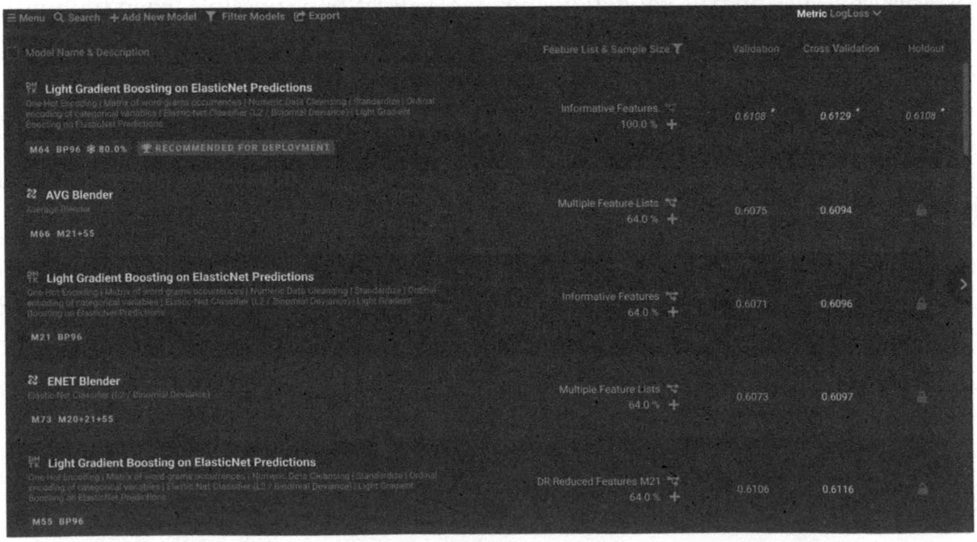

Figure 15.16. Addition of ENET Blender.

the *other model* is good at predicting readmissions based on three other features, then this new predictive exercise can pay more attention to each model when they are strong. Blending models does not always result in better models, but often, the blended models perform best or land near the top of the leaderboard.

This blending comes at a cost in terms of human understanding of what happens inside of algorithms because it is functionally impossible to explain the branches and functioning of a *Light Gradient Boosting on ElasticNet Predictions*, to begin with, not to mention the result of blending several equally complex algorithms. Any hope of explaining a model during a management presentation has long since passed. If you are an expert on one of the algorithms that produced models in the top of the leaderboard, you may decide to select that model over a more complex model because you know it and can explain it, even if it performs somewhat worse than other top models. However, one of the main advantages of DataRobot is that regardless of which model is selected, the same kind of evidence is available for explanation. This will be discussed later in Section V, where the focus shifts to model transparency tools such as *X-Ray*, *Feature Importance*, and *Insights*.

15.5 Exercises

1. Review the alternatives to the *LogLoss* optimization metric. Google RMSE and try to understand it. What would an RMSE score of .45 mean?
2. Why does DataRobot place cases in a holdout "lock-box"?
3. Explain how data is used when validating.
4. Explain how data is used during cross validation.

16

Understanding the Process

In this chapter, the focus will transition to the evaluation of whether additional cases (data) are needed to increase the accuracy of models produced in the previous chapter. We will also examine the pre-processing that went into each model to learn about machine learning at a more granular level.

16.1 Learning Curves and Speed

Before settling in with the selected models, it is critical to understand whether more data would improve the models' predictive ability. There are two forms of additional data: additional features (e.g., more information on the people you already have) and additional cases (e.g., more people). It is wise to generally work under the rule of diminishing marginal improvement: the more relevant data at the outset of a project, the less likely additional data will improve predictability.[1] We discussed access to other features in Chapter 1.4. Now the value of adding more cases will be examined.

So far, this walkthrough has focused on the *Leaderboard* tab. Now go to the menu option next to "Leaderboard" and select ***Learning Curves***. Doing so opens the screen shown in Figure 16.1, the *Learning Curves* screen. This screen shows the validation scores on the Y-axis and the percent of the available data used as the X-axis. Remember that, in this case, on the Y-axis, lower scores are preferable because *LogLoss* is a "loss" measure (every mistake in prediction increases the "loss score"). With loss measures, DataRobot will sort the best models to the bottom, so that the curves stretch from the upper left to the bottom right, generally, with an "elbow" toward the bottom left. Figure 16.1 shows the Quick analysis learning curves, which misses the 16% step available in Autopilot.

The dots in Figure 16.1 represent how a model performed with different amounts of data available to it. The lines connect the same models at each of these different amounts. Starting in the upper left corner, hover over a dot. Doing so will activate the model name represented by the dot. If you select a dot connected by a line, it will show how that model performed with double the data.

To get a true sense of the relationship between number of rows in the training set and performance, click on the two bottom-most lines and write down their

---

[1] It is possible that even if 10,000 features have been examined, feature number 10,001 could be the most predictive of all. However, it is not likely that it would bring much predictive ability beyond that already provided by the most predictive of the previous 10,000 features.

Automated Machine Learning for Business. Kai R. Larsen and Daniel S. Becker, Oxford University Press. © Oxford University Press 2021.
DOI: 10.1093/oso/9780190941659.003.0016

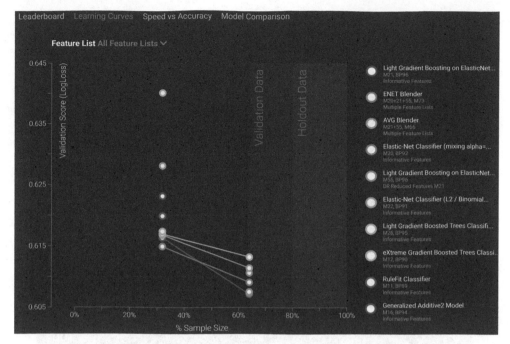

Figure 16.1. Learning Curves.

blueprint numbers. In Figure 16.1, this is M20 and M21, but this may not be the case for you. Return to the leaderboard and find those two models. They are the top two non-blender models. For both, click the orange plus (██████). Doing so will open the window in Figure 16.2. Select the *64* and instead type in *16*.

Click *Run with new sample size.* This will start up two new algorithm runs with only 16% of the original data. Allow these runs to finish before going back to the learning curves screen. Returning to the learning curves in Figure 16.3, you may select the two models.

Generally, it seems as though these models will benefit from more data. However, while doubling the dataset from 1,600 to 3,200 cases led to a definite improvement in quality, the second doubling from 3,200 to 6,400 cases turned our learning curves from a downward plunge into hockey sticks. If we imagine once more doubling our dataset to 12,800 (which may be hard or even impossible), the learning curve will likely flatten out, indicating little benefit from more data.

It is essential that we apply these numbers to reality and understand their implications.[6] Soon these models will be examined further to understand performance metrics, but for now, the performance of the LGBENP (M21) model can be addressed directly at the three data levels (16%, 32%, 64%).[2] In all cases, it is possible to get DataRobot to cross validate the three models against 8,000 patients

[2] We will soon teach you how to get these numbers yourself. Until then, enjoy the free ride and assume we shared correct numbers.

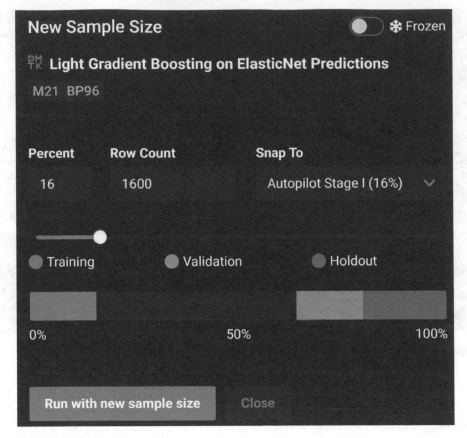

Figure 16.2. Running a Model with a Different Sample Size.

unknown to the model. At 16% of the data, the model made correct decisions for 4,658 patients out of 8,000, an accuracy of 58.23% (accuracy is the number of correct choices made by a model divided by all choices made). At 32% of the data, the model made correct decisions for 4,696 patients out of 8,000, an accuracy of 58.70%, and an improvement of 38 more patients correctly classified. At 64% of the data, DataRobot made the correct decisions for 4,563 patients out of 8,000, an accuracy of 57.04%, with a reduction of 133 patients correctly classified over the 32% model. At the first doubling of data from 16% to 32%, of the 38 additional correct classifications, the hospital saved money due to the avoidance of labeling sick patients as healthy (likely readmits) and vice versa. Considering the additional costs of caring for a readmitted patient, this is, perhaps, a worthwhile improvement. For the next doubling of available data (32% to 64%), classification improvement is −133 patients, which means that doubling our data again is not likely to lead to good results if accuracy is the measure we care about. We can now use accounting measures of the cost of incorrect classification to evaluate the likely benefit of collecting more data. We will later return to the concept that not all correct decisions have the same value to us.

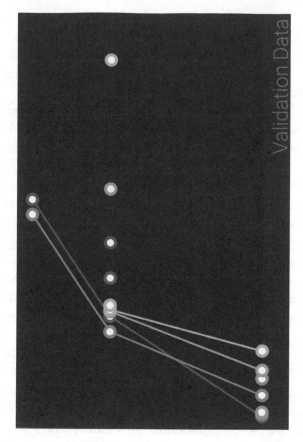

Figure 16.3. Focusing on Two Models.

It may be confusing that using more data would lead to worse results. The reality is that because accuracy is the most straightforward measure to evaluate, it is seldom the measure we care about in the end. We will later learn about more meaningful measures, including some for which this 64% model does much better than the 32% model. Regardless of measure used, when considering the addition of more data, it is important to calculate the cost, if, that is, such data is available. If the data available is data from an earlier date than what is currently used, it is not clear that the data will lead to improvements, as data gets "stale" over time. When in the position to consider adding data to a project, use the cross validation results as done here, even if that means running a few more models manually.

It is worth noting that the classification of human behavior as it relates to disease as complex as diabetes is very difficult. Data that may indicate whether or not patients are readmitted to a hospital within 30 days are plagued with errors related to any myriad of circumstances from patients dying in their home to patients being readmitted to other hospitals. Only by further immersion in studying success measures and assigning a dollar value to each type of success will it become clear whether gathering more data is worthwhile. These evaluations are covered in Chapter 17.

16.2 Accuracy Tradeoffs

Select now the Speed vs. Accuracy tab in the sub-menu under Models
(Leaderboard   Learning Curves   Speed vs Accuracy   Model Comparison).

This screen addresses an important question related to how rapidly the model will evaluate new cases after being put into production. An "Efficient Frontier" line has been added to illustrate which models are best. The Efficient Frontier line is the line drawn between the dots closest to the X- and Y-axes and usually occurs when two criteria (speed and accuracy in this case) are negatively related to each other (the best solution for one is usually not the best solution for the other). This line won't show on your screen because it has been manually added for this book to illustrate which models to pay attention to when learning and when using DataRobot in a real-world application. A model must be capable of producing predictions as rapidly as new cases are arriving. To evaluate the best models, the speed vs. accuracy screen shows the top 10 models by validation score. The Y-axis, as in the case of the learning curves explanation, displays the validation *LogLoss* score (the optimization measure selected), and the X-axis shows the time to score 1,000 records in milliseconds, one-thousandth of a second (ms). In this case, the slowest model (furthest to the right on the bottom), the *ENET blender*, requires the scoring by three other models first before computing the result, so it should come as no surprise that it is a bit slower than the individual models. Hovering over the dot, the time to score 1,000 records will be displayed, in this case, 4,490 milliseconds. This model scores 1,000 records in just over 4 seconds, or 222 cases per second (see Figure 16.4).[3]

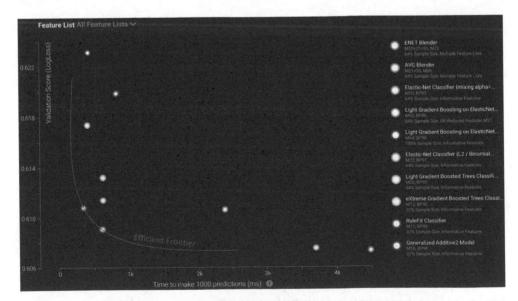

Figure 16.4. Speed vs Accuracy with Efficient Frontier Added.

---

[3] Note that if no model reaches your business needs in terms of speed (but is accurate enough), it is generally possible to set up multiple prediction servers to speed up predictions.

As before, start by calculating the speed of the slowest model by converting the numbers into cases per second. Compare this result with the reality of the predictive needs required by the given project at hand. If the slowest model produces results more rapidly than needed, ignore speed as a criterion in model creation. Speed must be evaluated against peak-time prediction needs. If fast responses are not required, it may be all right if the model is not able to keep up with peaks in case arrival. Some use cases do not allow the model to ever fall behind the outside world. For example, if a self-driving car is traveling at 65 miles per hour, a model must be able to predict whether an intersection light is red, yellow, or green at the appropriate speed. For example, if the model can detect the state of the light 222 times per second, detecting that the light changed from green to yellow would occur in the time taken for the car to travel 5.1 inches (about 13 centimeters).

Always look for the efficient frontier line (imaginary). If time is a factor, the efficient frontier will need to be followed to the left until the most efficient model is found that is still reasonably accurate. Do note, however, that not all speed issues are unchangeable. One can add more prediction servers as a method to increase prediction speed. Take as an example the prediction of whether a visitor to a website is one who might react positively to an ad. If the action requires a bid within 0.01 seconds from the visitor arriving, our most accurate model (as evaluated by cross validation) requires only 0.0045 seconds (1 second divided by 222 predictions per second), which is fast enough. However, if the website receives thousands of visitors per second, more prediction servers will be needed to keep up, or a faster model is required.

Goldilocks Wins

ML principle: "Controlling complexity is necessary to find a good trade-off between generalization and overfitting" (Provost & Fawcett, 2013, 332).

AutoML relevance: In ML, the data scientist is often responsible for finding the trade-off. In AutoML, the system controls the trade-off, and algorithms that do not perform well are not in contention for selection.

16.3 Blueprints

After seeing the model creation and scoring process, the model blueprints addressed at the start of this chapter can now be more readily understood. Each of the models seen prior employs a different set of pre-processing steps unique to that type of model. For an executive or manager using DataRobot in daily decision-making, this section is generally not necessary, as it is quite granular in its focus.

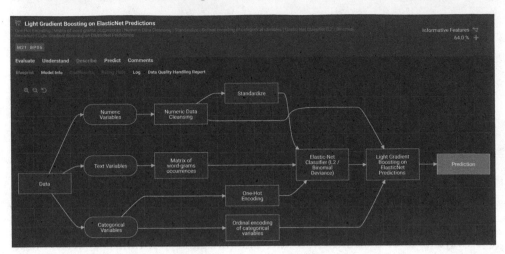

Figure 16.5. Blueprint for LGBEP Model.

To consider the blueprints, start by clicking on the name of the 64% *LGBEP* model. This will lead to the screen shown in Figure 16.5. Right at the bottom of the blue line stating the name of the algorithm used to create this particular model is a sub-menu showing the option "Describe." This again has a Blueprint option. If this is not already selected, click on "Blueprint."

Figure 16.5 shows that our top non-blender model at 64% is one for which DataRobot tells us a lot about their process. We here learn that DataRobot applies different operations to categorical variables, text variables, and numeric variables. We learn that common pre-processing approaches such as one-hot encoding, numeric data cleansing, and standardization are employed along with a few other approaches. Note that a blueprint is a generalized approach to creating high-quality predictive models. If you examine other blueprints, these tend to employ many of the same basic elements, but these may be combined in different ways. We will next examine some of the most common pre-processing approaches.

16.3.1 Numeric Data Cleansing (Imputation)

Take a look at the *LGBEP* blueprint and click on the box stating "Numeric Data Cleansing." As you do this, a new box should appear as in Figure 16.6.

The dialog box states the parameters used in this specific case and provides a link to the "DataRobot Model Docs." Click on the link to examine the documentation shown in Figure 16.7. Here, information related to DataRobot's code base is displayed (such as which class this function is in). By reading the first paragraph starting with "Impute missing values . . .," we learn that the median value of the feature is used and that, for each feature imputed, another feature is created called an "indicator." Addition of these indicator features is a step often missed even by seasoned machine learning experts.

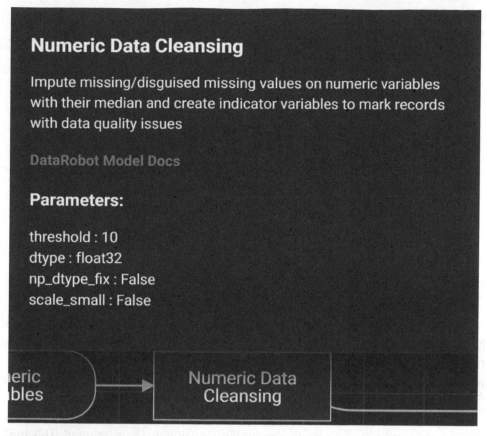

Figure 16.6. Information on How Missing Values Are Imputed.

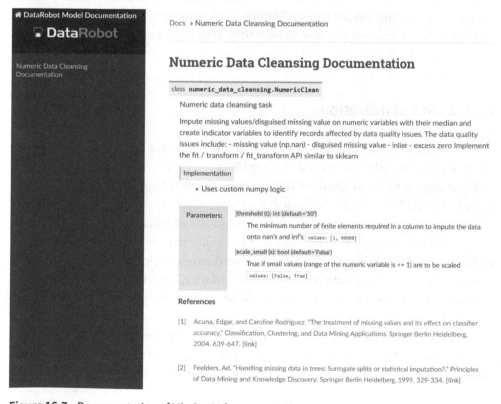

Figure 16.7. Documentation of Missing Values Imputation.

num_lab_ procedures		num_lab_ procedures_ imputed	Indicator
27		27	False
10		10	False
18		18	False
missing	⟶	27	True
28		28	False
35		35	False
missing	⟶	27	True
11		11	False
45		45	False

Figure 16.8. *num_lab_procedures* Imputation.

For further reading, there are also references to articles explaining the approach and its justification as well as information on what open source software (numpy) originated the code. By combining the information on the parameters, such as *threshold*, we learn that this parameter may stop the imputation from happening unless there are 50 or more finite numbers in the feature. Figure 16.8 shows an example of median imputation.

As in Figure 16.8, the indicator feature will simply contain a *False* if that row was not imputed and a *True* if a given row contains a value that was imputed. This indicator variable allows the algorithm to look for predictive value about which patients are missing information for a given feature. For example, it is possible that the fact that *age* was not entered was due to how they arrived at the hospital, which might help us predict whether they will be readmitted.

16.3.2 Standardization

Now, click on the *Standardize* box to see that after imputing missing values, the numeric features are all standardized (Figure 16.9).

What does it mean to standardize a numeric feature? By reading the language in Figures 16.9 and 16.10, it becomes clear that some algorithms, such as *Support Vector Machines* and some linear models that are regularized (including one used in this blueprint), will struggle with features that have different standard deviations. Each feature is, therefore "scaled," which means that the mean value of the feature is set to zero and the standard deviation is set to "unit variance," which is a fancy way to say 1.

Figure 16.11 shows an example of how standardization of the *num_lab_procedures_imputed* feature leads to the creation of a new feature named *num_lab_procedures_imputed_std* with values having a mean of zero and a standard deviation of one. After imputing age and standardization of the feature, only the imputed and standardized feature is used by the *Elastic-Net Classifier*.

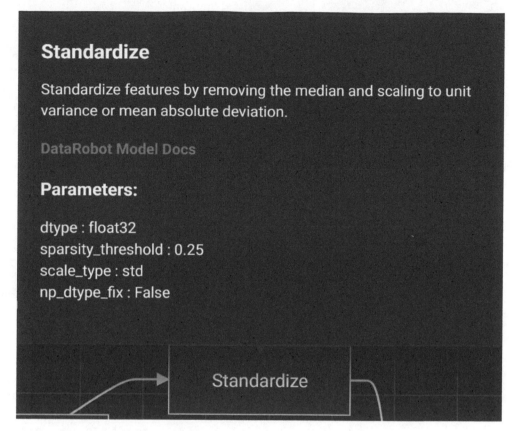

Figure 16.9. Standardize Numeric Features.

16.3.3 One-hot Encoding

Click on the *One-Hot Encoding* box shown in Figure 16.12 to view the information on this particular step in the DataRobot feature engineering. Then open the DataRobot Model Docs.

One-hot encoding was discussed briefly in Chapter 10.1.1. Consider re-reading this section before continuing if you do not fully remember what one-hot encoding is. In short, for any categorical feature that fulfills specific requirements, a new feature is created for every category that exists within the original feature. Figure 16.13 shows that if the original feature has only two values (for example, "yes" and "no"), it is turned into one new feature with *True* and *False* values. Such conversion is necessary for many algorithms (termed "estimators") to function as designed. In Section V, how DataRobot provides insights into the model based on these one-hot encoded values will be covered in greater detail. For now, one-hot encoding can be further demystified by examining the specific parameters therein.

First, we see that the parameter *min_support* specifies "the minimum number of records for a category to be represented in one hot encoding." In this case, the

Standardize Documentation

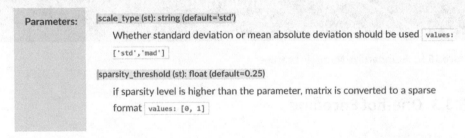

class `standardize.Robust_Standardize`

Standardize task

Standardize features by removing the median and scaling to unit standard deviation or the mean absolute deviation

Centering and scaling happen independently on each feature by computing the relevant statistics on the samples in the training set.

Standardization of a dataset is a common requirement for many machine learning estimators: they might behave badly if the individual feature do not more or less look like standard normally distributed data.

For instance many elements used in the objective function of a learning algorithm (such as the RBF kernel of Support Vector Machines or the L1 and L2 regularizers of linear models) assume that all features are centered around 0 and have variance in the same order. If a feature has a variance that is orders of magnitude larger that others, it might dominate the objective function and make the estimator unable to learn from other features correctly as expected.

Parameters:	scale_type (st): string (default='std') Whether standard deviation or mean absolute deviation should be used `values:` `['std','mad']` sparsity_threshold (st): float (default=0.25) if sparsity level is higher than the parameter, matrix is converted to a sparse format `values: [0, 1]`

References

Marquardt, Donald W. "Comment: You should standardize the predictor variables in your regression models." Journal of the American Statistical Association 75.369 (1980): 87-91.

Figure 16.10. Documentation for Standardization.

value 5 was used, meaning that when one-hot encoding the *admission_type_id* (see Figure 16.13), DataRobot one-hot encoded the *Not Mapped* category (32 rows) into a new feature but did not initially one-hot encode *Newborn*, which has only 1 row. When multiple categories, each containing fewer than ten rows, are combined, a new feature is created named *=All Other=*, even if the new category contains fewer than ten rows. After this operation, *Newborn* is then one-hot encoded as it is the only category with less than ten values (see Figure 16.14). Typically, this grouping would be renamed *=All Other=*; however, because *Newborn* is the only category included in this grouping, its name is retained.

num_lab_ procedures_ imputed		num_lab_ procedures_ imputed_std
27	⟶	0.15
10	⟶	−1.38
18	⟶	−0.66
27	⟶	0.15
28	⟶	0.24
35	⟶	0.87
27	⟶	0.15
11	⟶	−1.29
45	⟶	1.77
25.33	*Mean*	*0*
11.12	*StDev*	*1*

Figure 16.11. Example of Standardization.

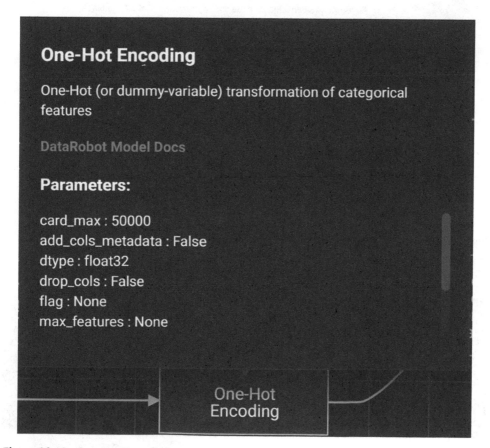

Figure 16.12. One-Hot Encoding.

One-Hot Encoding Documentation

---

class **cat_converters.DesignMatrix3**

One Hot encoding task

This transformer will do a binary one-hot (aka one-of-K) coding. One boolean-valued feature is constructed for each of the possible string values that the feature can take. For inputs with only 2 unique values, only one boolean-valued feature will be constructed

This encoding is needed for feeding categorical data to many estimators, notably linear models and SVMs.

Parameters:	min_support (sc): int (default='5')
	The minimum number of records for a category to be represented in one hot encoding. If a category has fewer counts it will be grouped with other small cardinality values `values: [1, 99999]`
	card_min (cmin): int (default='1')
	An integer that specifies the minimum number of unique values `values: [1, 99999]`
	card_max (cm): int (default='100')
	An integer that specifies the maximum number of unique values `values: [1, 99999]`
	drop_cols (dc): bool (default='False')
	drop_cols, If True, drop last level of each feature `values: [False, True]`
	max_features (mf): int (default='None')
	If the total number of categories created across all features exceeds this value, the top `max_features` most frequent categories will persist. All others will be either thrown out or grouped. A value of None disables the limit. `values: [1, 999999]`
	flag (flag): select (default='None')
	flag, If all, add highcat-cols to metadata `values: ['None', 'all']`

Figure 16.13. Partial Documentation on One-Hot Encoding.

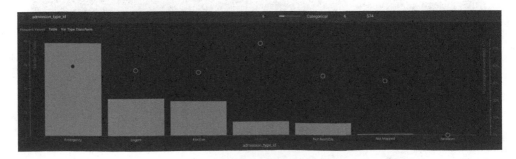

Figure 16.14. *Admission_type_id* One-hot Encoding Example.

The two parameters *card_min* and *card_max* specify how many unique values must be present in a feature for it to be eligible for one-hot encoding. In this case, no parameter for *card_min* is given in this blueprint, so a default of 1 is used. For *card_max*, a parameter of 50,000 is specified. With only 10,000 rows, this means that all categorical features will be one-hot encoded, except for the features containing only one value, earlier coded as [Few values]. These features were not allowed into the machine-learning process, so functionally, the *card_min* parameter functions as a 2 in this case, since no feature with only one value will make it to this stage.

The next parameter is *drop_cols*, which in this blueprint is set to *False*. This parameter is described as "If True, drop last level of each feature." This simply means that if true, DataRobot removes the smallest category. The smallest category is removed because, when encoding, for example, three values into three new features, as demonstrated in Figure 16.15, all information available in the final feature, *Age_[20-30)*, is available by examining the previous two features. Why is this so? Assuming that imputation has happened so that each person has an age, any row where both *Age_[0-10)* and *Age_[10-20)* are *False* must be *True* in the final feature. Conversely, if one of the first two features is *True*, then the value in *Age_[20-30)* must be *False*. DataRobot keeps this final feature because it allows visualization of this feature's impact.

16.3.4 Ordinal Encoding

It is worth noting that DataRobot here engages in another type of encoding of the categorical data. Whereas the one-hot-encoded features flow directly to the first algorithm used in this blueprint, the *Elastic-Net Classifier*, DataRobot is now trying to preprocess categorical data in another way to feed this information into another algorithm, the *Light Gradient Boosting*.

Age		Age_[0–10)	Age_[10–20)	Age_[20–30)
[0–10)	⟶	True	False	False
[0–10)	⟶	True	False	False
[0–10)	⟶	True	False	False
[0–10)	⟶	True	False	False
[10–20)	⟶	False	False	False
[10–20)	⟶	False	False	False
[10–20)	⟶	False	False	False
[20–30)	⟶	False	False	True
[20–30)	⟶	False	False	True

Figure 16.15. One-hot Encoding Example.

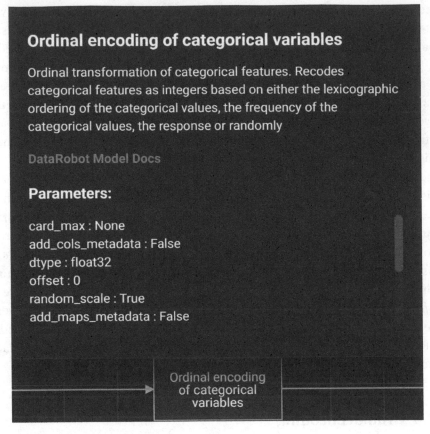

Ordinal encoding of categorical variables

Ordinal transformation of categorical features. Recodes categorical features as integers based on either the lexicographic ordering of the categorical values, the frequency of the categorical values, the response or randomly

DataRobot Model Docs

Parameters:

card_max : None
add_cols_metadata : False
dtype : float32
offset : 0
random_scale : True
add_maps_metadata : False

Ordinal encoding
of categorical
variables

Figure 16.16. Ordinal Encoding.

The ordinal encoding may turn categories into numbers. For example, our *Age* feature could be ordinally encoded to 0 (0-10) to 9 (90-100) based on alphabetical sorting. Alternatively, it could be encoded based on the number of cases in each category, or each category could randomly be assigned a value.

Click on the *DataRobot Model Docs* to once more evaluate the approach to data preparation. Here we learn that *random_scale* is True, which means that the categories here are randomly ordered into numbers. For example, *Age* [70-80) may turn into a 0 and [10-20) into a 1 with [50-60) perhaps becoming a 3, etc. Missing values are encoded as −2 and categories with low cardinality (few cases), already assigned to the =All Other= category (see *medical_specialty*, for example) are encoded as −1.

It may seem counter-intuitive to randomly assign a number to a certain category, such as patients in the [50-60) age range, and it would make no sense as input into a linear algorithm such as the Elastic-Net Classifier because it would not find a relationship between a randomly assigned number and the target, but a tree-based algorithm such as Light Gradient Boosting will split most or all numbers up and treat them separately, so this process becomes similar to a one-hot encoding.

Curse of Dimensionality

ML principle: Using a large number of features (high dimensionality) has traditionally been seen as dangerous and likely to lead to overfitted models (Breiman, 2001).
AutoML relevance: Same for ML and AutoML.

 With better approaches to avoiding overfitting and feature selection, high dimensionality is seen as a blessing rather than a curse.

 It is possible that reducing dimensionality through approaches such as factor analysis and singular value decomposition decreases accuracy.

16.3.5 Matrix of Word-gram Occurrences

The final preparatory step focuses on the text features. In this case, we had three features containing the text of the patient diagnoses. While text analytics is beyond the scope of this book, we next show a short example of what such analysis might look like for one of the diagnosis features.

When opening the details view on the "Matrix of word-gram occurrences" box, we see that this is the pre-processing step with the most parameters. This is because language is quite complex. From the parameters in Figure 16.17 as well as the model documentation, we learn that each word is lowercased and that each word (and also pairs of words that frequently co-occur) are turned into new features and each populated with a 1 if the word exists in the diagnosis and a 0 if it does not.

Figure 16.18 shows an example of creating such a word-gram occurrence matrix. It shows that the patient in RowID 12 has the words *unspecified, type,* and *diabetes* in his *diag_1_desc* field. Going to the original data, we find that this patient's diagnosis was "Diabetes with other specified manifestations, type II or unspecified type, not stated as uncontrolled," so we would expect him to also have ones in other feature columns such as *manifestations.*

It is worth noting that if you are operating outside of a carefully managed AutoML such as DataRobot, be careful with text features such as these. The three diagnosis features alone likely contributed thousands of new features for this analysis. While cross validation and the procedures designed to avoid overfitting of the model to the available evidence will allow confidence in the findings, we worry that a model that relies extensively on word-gram occurrences (or n-grams as they are often called in the literature) may not stand up well to changing language use within the analytical context.

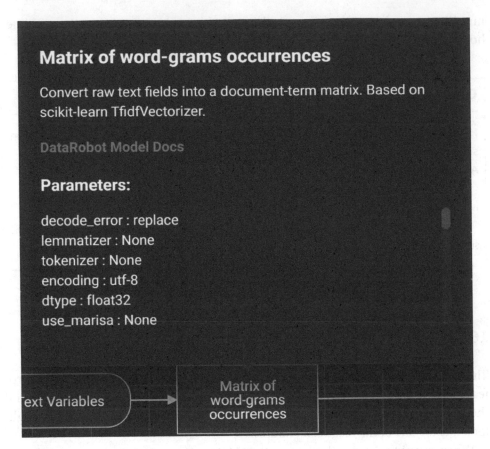

Matrix of word-grams occurrences

Convert raw text fields into a document-term matrix. Based on scikit-learn TfidfVectorizer.

DataRobot Model Docs

Parameters:

decode_error : replace
lemmatizer : None
tokenizer : None
encoding : utf-8
dtype : float32
use_marisa : None

Text Variables → Matrix of word-grams occurrences

Figure 16.17. Matrix of Word-gram Occurrences.

rowID	unspecified	type	without	acute	graft	mention	diabetes	...
1	0	0	0	0	0	0	0	...
2	1	0	0	0	0	0	0	...
3	0	0	0	0	0	0	0	...
4	0	0	0	0	0	0	0	...
5	1	0	0	0	0	0	0	...
6	1	0	0	0	0	0	0	...
7	0	0	1	0	0	1	0	...
8	1	0	0	0	0	0	0	...
9	1	0	0	0	0	0	0	...
10	0	0	0	0	0	0	0	...
11	1	0	0	0	0	0	0	...
12	1	1	0	0	0	0	1	...
...	...	...	...	...	...	...	...	...

Figure 16.18. Example Word-gram Occurrences Matrix.

Fit—Don't Overfit

ML principle: If the algorithm and data available are not sufficient to completely determine the correct classifier, a model may not be grounded in reality. Instead the model may purport to be accurate, but when tested against external data, performs poorly (Domingos, 2012). AutoML relevance: In AutoML, these models are often based on complex algorithms, yet found at the bottom of the leaderboard.

   AutoML includes validation approaches and regularization terms designed to penalize complexity.

   Evidence of overfit is also found in cases of targets are time-dependent, but where models are incorrectly evaluated using cross-validation.

16.3.6 Classification

This particular blueprint contains two predictive algorithms. The first one, an *Elastic-Net Classifier*, is a type of logistic regression that works well with data that contains a lot of zeros, which the blueprint ensured both when creating the many word-gram features as well as through the one-hot encoding. It is worth noting that the inputs to this algorithm included the one-hot encoded features, the standardized numeric variables with missing values imputed, and the matrix of word-gram occurrences. This algorithm will then generate a probability for each case.

   The probability from the *Elastic-Net Classifier* is then fed into a *Light Gradient Boosting* (LGB) algorithm along with the categorical features that have been ordinally encoded and the imputed numeric values. The details of both algorithms are beyond the scope of this book. That said, even by reading the linked DataRobot Model Docs, you will get a good sense of what these algorithms do.

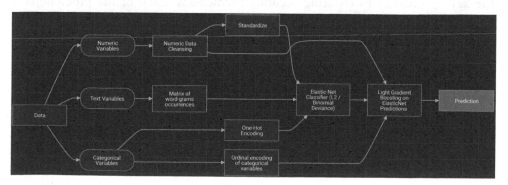

Figure 16.19. Combination of All Features into Two Algorithms.

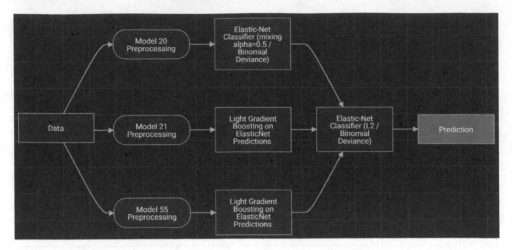

Figure 16.20. Blueprint for ENET Blender.

Because we believe it is important to develop a generalized sense of how such algorithms work, the next chapter will explain tree-based algorithm, which is a basic version of the *LGB* algorithm. This will allow us to understand the principles behind these algorithms. For now, it is worth knowing the gradient-boosting algorithms are among the most efficient and successful algorithms in data science, and function by fitting a tree to the data, and then successively fitting more trees to the residuals (the leftover values not explained by the previous trees).

Chapter 16 will close by examining the blueprint for the best model for the hospital case, the *ENET Blender*, Figure 16.20. Here it is visible that the three top models sorted by cross validation have been selected. Each of the eight models is shown in the blueprint with its preprocessing step. They all generate a probability indicating that a target was positive (readmission), which now becomes one of three features used along with the target as an input into an *Elastic-Net* classifier, which then generates predictions.

As we have now seen the *Elastic-Net Classifier* twice, we should discuss one of the key approaches to ensuring accurate predictions. Each of the predictions is conducted on data the model has never before seen. As mentioned in our list of ML principles, a good model generalizes from what it has learned to new cases it has not yet experienced.

To make this point about generalization clearer, we will examine a much simpler model. Figure 16.21 shows an attempt to model where a point will fall on the Y-axis, given that we know the x-value (the order of the points).

In Figure 16.21's upper left chart, we see a simple linear model created from the training data. This model believes itself 83% accurate in understanding the data. The algorithm that created the model would love to understand more, but it cannot do so because it is only capable of drawing straight lines. This model (line) is then applied to the validation data, which is also 83% accurate. Here, we see a model that

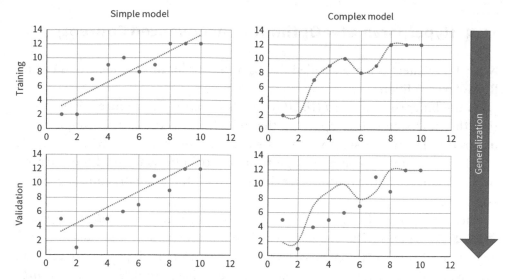

Figure 16.21. Overfitting.

is reasonably accurate but likely underfits: it is not complex enough to adequately model the data.

The same training data was given to a complex algorithm that was flexible enough to perfectly model the data. This model, when applied to the training data, is 100% accurate. Luckily, we always test machine learning models with a validation or holdout sample, so when we applied the model to the validation data, we learned that the model is only 62% accurate, indicating that the model is overfitting. Unfortunately, according to the *Goldilocks Wins* principle, there is probably a better generalizing model lurking somewhere between the simple model and the complex model.

While a simple model will generally underperform a complex model because the world is labyrinthine in its complexity, an algorithm must know when to stop adding complexity to a model. We mentioned earlier that a standard way to do this in machine learning is through regularization. Regularization techniques penalize complexity in the model; they can be thought of as a type of regression that shrinks coefficient estimates toward zero. So, for our complex model, all the variations in the model would be evaluated to examine whether they are worthwhile relative to the extra complexity added. One approach, for example, might look at whether the swoop up to capture the third through fifth data points is worthwhile, given that without them, the model becomes quite a bit simpler.

It is worth noting that if we allow the regularization penalty to become too high, we underfit models, whereas if it is too low, we create models that overfit the data. Given that a good AutoML will appropriately apply regularization for us, and that playing around with hyperparameters is seldom a productive use of time in AutoML, we will stick to this surface-level understanding of regularization—even as we proceed to share a bit about hyperparameter optimization for those who want to try it out.

16.4 Hyperparameter Optimization (Advanced Content)

Note: This content is more detailed than is necessary for most readers of the book. Read at own volition.

As the blueprint for the *LGBEP* model is examined in Figure 16.19, notice that the final step before applying the model to the validation sample is the use of the algorithm itself to create the model. This is the step where AutoML provides one of its single most significant contributions to machine learning; hyperparameter optimization (see Figure 16.22 for a small sampling of the parameters).

Click on the model's Evaluate (Evaluate) option and then select *Advanced Tuning* (Advanced Tuning) for the *LGBEP* model to see all the different parameters available for this algorithm (Figure 16.22 contains a few of the parameters). It is possible to calculate how many different parameter combinations are available for fine-tuning an *LGBEP* model. An estimate, in this case, is about one vigintillion (a 1 with 64 zeros). Given that such parameter tuning can mean the difference between a successful project

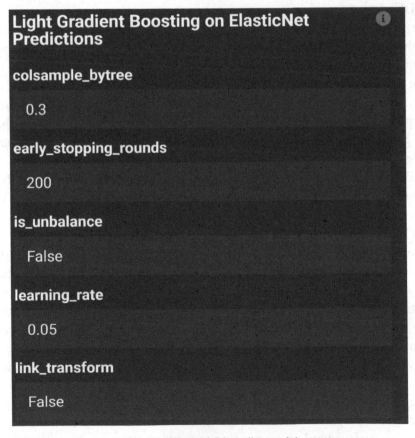

Light Gradient Boosting on ElasticNet Predictions

colsample_bytree

0.3

early_stopping_rounds

200

is_unbalance

False

learning_rate

0.05

link_transform

False

Figure 16.22. Hyperparameters for LGBEP Model (Small Sample).

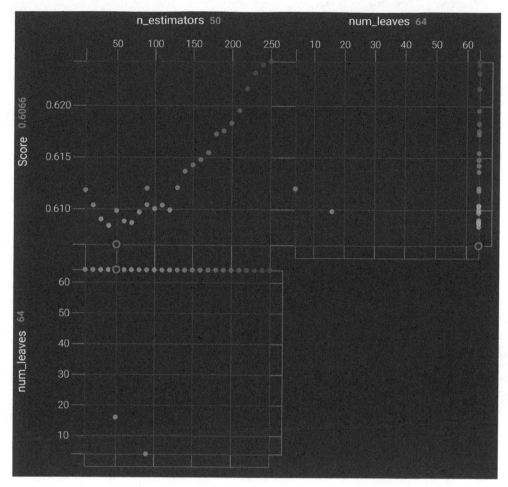

Figure 16.23. Hyperparameter Tuning Performance for Main Parameters.

and a mediocre project, this provides a sense of why companies like Google place such a premium on hiring the best-of-the-best data scientists (in one case paying more than half of a billion dollars for a startup with deep learning, neural network expertise—turning it then into the Google Brain team). As discussed earlier, even Google has found that AutoML outperforms their world-class data scientists when it comes to hyperparameter tuning.

In Figure 16.23, note that the score is best for this algorithm at *n_estimators* (models) of 50 and *num_leaves* (number of leaf nodes in a tree) of 64. This may be a bit confusing because the selected parameter listed by DataRobot for *n_estimators* is 2,500. All this means is that the algorithm generates 2,500 trees, but in the end, it makes predictions with only 20 of those trees.

This chapter covered the automated process for building candidate models and how they are assessed against one another. Next, Chapter 17 will dig deep into the models to understand their performance characteristics.

16.5 Exercises

1. Examine the blueprint for five additional models (focus on those providing details) and read about their pre-processing steps. What patterns do you detect?
2. Pick three different algorithms and read up on them in the DataRobot documentation.

17
Evaluate Model Performance

17.1 Introduction

So far, the processes of model creation and model evaluation have been covered. Unfortunately, at this juncture, there is still minimal understanding of the best models developed beyond the introductory information provided in the previous chapters. One of the AutoML criteria is *understanding and learning*, meaning that the AutoML should improve a user's understanding of the problem by providing visualization of the interactions between the features and the target. With such knowledge, a user of AutoML will be in a strong position to present the results of an analysis. With that criterion in mind, we begin the next phase of the machine learning process with an introduction to DataRobot's model creation process and, following that, a conceptual example of how the decision tree algorithm works.

In DataRobot, there is no way to know *a priori* which algorithm will be elevated to the top of the leaderboard. Therefore, as an AutoML user, one must commit to either knowing all algorithms at a technical level or knowing the function of these algorithms conceptually (meaning, in general, what happens inside an algorithm when it creates models). Think of this as an equivalent to knowing how to ride a bike. One must know how to balance their body on the bike, be capable of transferring energy from their feet to the wheels, and understand the rules of the road. Electric bikes now make biking easier in that they store up energy in a battery and then provide a bit of that energy to the wheels to assist in acceleration when pedaling. It is not crucial to understand the electric engine and battery components to effectively use an electric bike.

It stands to reason that with limited training, upgrading to a moped or even a motorcycle is within the realm of reason. In AutoML, the remaining critical skill to acquire is the one that translates across all vehicles--the ability to balance the bike (understand a model's performance) and to understand the environment (a model's business context). How energy is created and transmitted is unimportant unless the plan is to become a bike mechanic.

We spent Chapter 16 discussing the *Light Gradient Boosting on ElasticNet Predictions* (LGBEP) and explained that the gradient boosting part of this algorithm is a *tree*-algorithm. While far from the computational complexity of some algorithms, it continues to be difficult to explain, at least in a way understandable to managers and organizational leaders. If, on the other hand, a manager understands

Automated Machine Learning for Business. Kai R. Larsen and Daniel S. Becker, Oxford University Press. © Oxford University Press 2021. DOI: 10.1093/oso/9780190941659.003.0017

the *Decision Tree* algorithm, the task is easier. That said, presentations to management should never be about explaining how algorithms work, but instead, about their performance characteristics, much as riding a bike, even an electric one, should never be about the mechanics of the bike, but about maintaining balance and momentum while riding.

So far, the focus has been on the overall optimization measure (*LogLoss*). While *LogLoss* does a great job of optimizing overall success, for most users, it does not constitute a reasonable measure of how far from the target predictions are at the level of the average case (or patient, in this scenario). For example, if a model were constructed that has no better ability to predict a patient outcome (readmission) than random assignment (heads or tails on a coin), that model would have a cross validation *LogLoss* score of 0.672. There are measures, however, that make such evaluations in a more understandable manner, such as *Fraction of Variance Explained (FVE) Binomial* (Figure 17.1).

FVE Binomial provides a sense of how much of the variance in the dataset has been explained and is equivalent to an R^2-value. In simpler terms, this metric states how far off, percent-wise, the model is from fully explaining who will be readmitted (to turn an R^2-value into a percentage, multiply it by 100). To see this, change the leaderboard metric (go to the area marked with the orange oval and change to "FVE Binomial," as in Figure 17.1, and order by cross validation score). Note that changing this does not work as an optimization measure, in that the models themselves do not change, as that would require a rerun of the entire modeling process. It does, however, allow a user to reorder the leaderboard by this and several other measures to more holistically evaluate the models produced. In this case, the best 64%

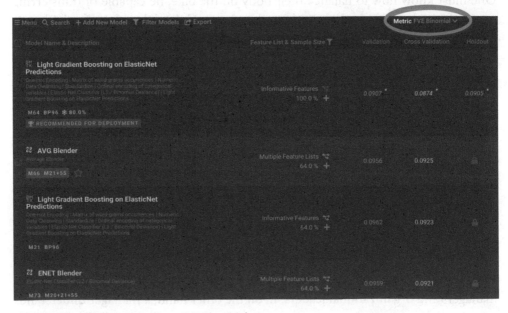

Figure 17.1. Changing Metric to FVE Binomial.

model explains only 9% of the target (0.0923 out of 1.00), providing yet another confirmation that the data available for this project is far from perfect or that the problem is quite challenging. Change the metric back to *LogLoss* and ensure that the leaderboard is still sorted by cross validation score before moving forward.

17.2 A Sample Algorithm and Model

It has been argued in this text that there is little need for the everyday business user of AutoML to understand the inner workings of the best models in the leaderboard for any given project. That said, there remains value in having a strong *general* understanding of how such algorithms work to be more effective in model creation and validation. With this nuance in mind, take as an example one of the most conceptually accessible algorithms, the *Decision Tree Classifier*. Many tree-based algorithms build on the logic of the decision-tree classifier, which is to repeatedly find the most predictive feature at that instance and split it into two groups that are as internally homogeneous as possible. The many types of tree-based algorithms are often combinations of hundreds or thousands of decision trees. Arguably, if a budding data scientist were to learn only one algorithm, the decision tree would be the one due to both its conceptual simplicity and its effectiveness.

To begin understanding the decision tree classifier, go to the **repository** at the top of the page. This is where DataRobot stores all the models it for several reasons opted not to run on your dataset. Scroll down in the list until you come to the "Decision Tree Classifier (Gini)." As shown in Figure 17.2, select the classifier (click the check box next to it), change the *CV runs* to **all**, and click *Run Task*.

DataRobot will start running five algorithms, one each for the five cross validation folds. Once these are done, return to the model tab and search for "Decision Tree." It will likely be the worst model given access to most features and 64% of the data. To confirm this, click on "Feature List & Sample Size" (Feature List & Sample Size) in the leaderboard and uncheck all but the 64% models.

As the FVE Binomial score indicates, the Decision Tree underperformed with a score of 0.0594 (Figure 17.3), but consider that it did not use the text features and is an exceedingly simple and fast algorithm.

Figure 17.2. Finding and Running a Decision Tree Algorithm.

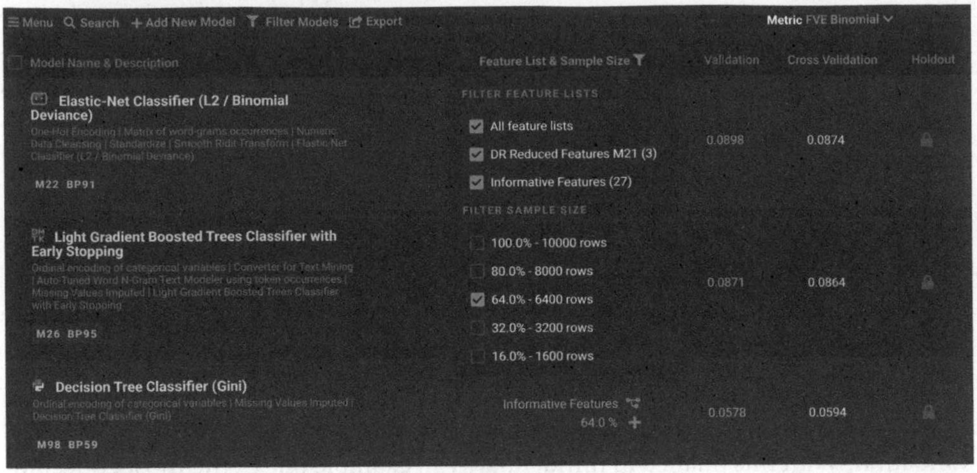

Figure 17.3. Decision Tree Classifier in the Leaderboard.

To see this, click on the *Decision Tree Classifier (Gini)* name to access the Decision Tree Classifier model's blueprint. Notice the yellow and blue symbol next to its name, which suggests that this algorithm came from a *Python* implementation. Now click on the *Decision Tree Classifier (Gini)* box in the blueprint to access the information on the model, per Figure 17.4. Here it is stated that the algorithm came from a Python package called scikit-learn (as mentioned earlier; go to http://scikit-learn.org/ for more information).

To demonstrate how a decision tree classifier works with a minimum of complexity, a reduced version of the diabetes dataset was extracted containing only three of the most important features in most of our other models: *discharge_disposition_id*, *number_diagnoses*, and *number_inpatient* (in Chapter 19, the process for selecting those three will become self-evident). To get close to the DataRobot process, *discharge_disposition_id* has been one-hot encoded for the most common values to create the following features (Dis = Discharged): *Dis_home, Dis_long_term_hospital, Disc_inpatient_care, Dis_rehab, Dis_short_term_hospital, Dis_home_service, Disc_ICF, Disc_SNF, Expired, Hospice, Left_AMA,* and *Not_Mapped*. For expediency, any row containing a missing value was also removed, leaving 9,494 rows.

After running the scikit-learn decision tree algorithm, the model in Figure 17.5 is returned. The decision tree is represented as an upside-down tree, with the 9,494 patients in the root note. The decision tree classifier works through the following steps to create this tree:

1. **Find the most predictive feature (the one that best explains the target) and place it at the root of the tree.** For example, here the decision-tree classifier selected the feature representing the *number of inpatient visits* by the patient during the year preceding their hospital visit (*number_inpatient*). This feature contains numbers from 0 to 10. The blue color of the root box indicates that the majority of patients in this box are *not* getting readmitted (the colors are somewhat arbitrary, but the depth of the color indicates how homogenous the "leaf"

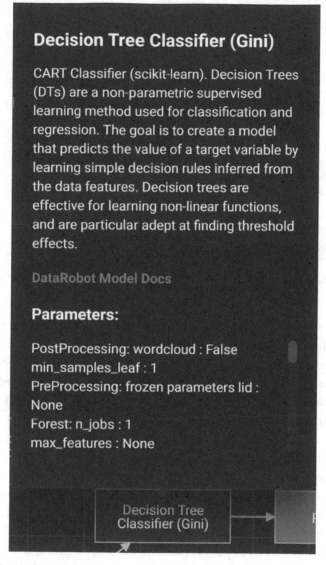

Figure 17.4. Information on Decision Tree Classifier.

is). This is shown in the brackets where 3,820 patients are readmitted (40.2%) and 5,674 patients are not readmitted (59.8%).

2. **Split the feature into two groups at the point of the feature where the two groups are as homogenous as possible.**[1] Homogeneity is, in this case, measured using the Gini impurity measure, a measure of the homogeneity of the two groups created through a split. This split should happen at the number of visits where each group contains the most unequal number of *readmits*. In this dataset, there are ten cuts available, corresponding to a split at <= 0.5 visits, a split at <= 1.5 visits, all the way up to a split at <= 9.5 visits. When using the Gini measure to evaluate the impurity

---

[1] Some decision tree algorithms allow splits into more groups at each stage.

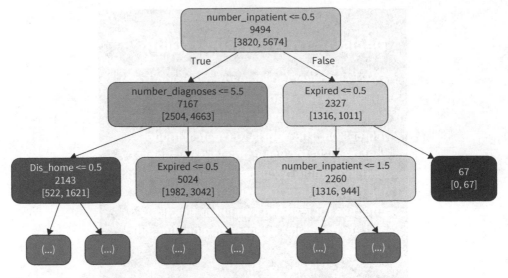

Figure 17.5. Decision Tree with Two Levels.

of the two groups (meaning the extent to which each group is not purely homogenous), the Gini measures at each cutoff point are compared, and the cutoff with the best score is selected. In Figure 17.5, the best cutoff is at *number_inpatient <= 0.5*. Follow now the arrows down to the two groups that are created based on this cutoff. The left, blue[2] box shows that there are now 7,167 patients in this branch that had no inpatient visits during the last year (75.5%), and the right, red box shows those who had 1 or more inpatient visits during the same period (24.5%). It is clear to see that just the simple act of splitting the patients based on this most predictive feature allows prediction of which patients will be readmitted.

3. **Repeat step 2 for each new branch (box)**. Travel down the rightmost arrow to the 2,327 patients that did indeed require 1–10 inpatient visits during the last year. By splitting this group once more by the feature *expired <= 0.5*, 2,260 patients are sent down the left (*True*) path because they did not expire and 67 down the right (*False*) path because they did expire. This second path leads to what is called a *leaf node*. It will not be split further because it is as pure as specified by the algorithm parameters. In this case, no expired patient was readmitted. Traveling down the left path to examine the patients who did not expire, the next most predictive feature is again *number_impatient*, applied now to a set containing only patients with 1–9 inpatient visits in the last year. This group is now split into those who had only one inpatient visit (left path) and those with 2–9 visits.

The whole model is printed in Figure 17.6. For training that includes coding of IF-THEN statements, imagine translating this entire model to a series of IF-THEN

[2] Given that the book is printed in black and white, note that only two boxes in Figure 17.5 are red: "Expired <= 0.5" and "number_inpatient <= 1.5."

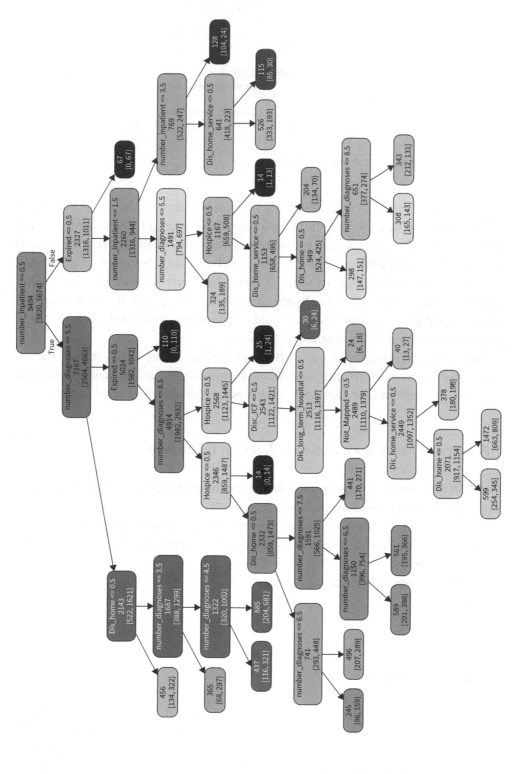

Figure 17.6. Whole Decision Tree.

```
IF number_inpatient <= 0.5 THEN
        IF number_diagnoses <= 5.5 THEN
                        Set readmitted to False
        ELSE
                        Set readmitted to False
        ENDIF
ELSE
        IF expired <= 0.5 THEN
                        Set readmitted to TRUE
        ELSE
                        Set readmitted to False
        ENDIF
ENDIF
```

Figure 17.7. Model Coded Up for Predictions.

statements. Figure 17.7 contains the first two levels of that model and is now available to make predictions. Imagine using this model to query a patient who is about to be discharged (interviewing the patient personally rather than querying the records in this case). Staff member: "Sir, before this visit, how many times were you admitted to our hospital during the last year?" Patient: "Five times." Staff member: "Since I can see that you did not expire in our care, you are in a group of patients likely be readmitted during the next 30 days. Would you please sit down while we ask a physician to come and evaluate alternatives to discharging you?"

Next, the performance of one of the best models, a tree-based model, will be examined in its performance as applied to previously unseen cross validation samples, noting model predictions vs true readmission data for each data point.

Predictive Accuracy and Generalization Is the Key

ML principle: Models must generalize beyond the training cases because identical cases are unlikely to be encountered in the future (Domingos, 2012).

Predictive and concurrent accuracy on test sets is *the* criterion for how good the model is. This is a departure from traditional statistical model testing, which focuses on internal fit statistics (Breiman, 2001).

AutoML relevance: Same for ML and AutoML.

17.3 ROC Curve

So far, the focus has been on single measures of model quality. It is now time to understand different aspects of quality so that it is possible to realistically make business decisions using the model. Return to the third-ranked model, the *LGBEP* model's blueprint. Click on **Evaluate** in the *LGBEP* menu and then the **ROC Curve**

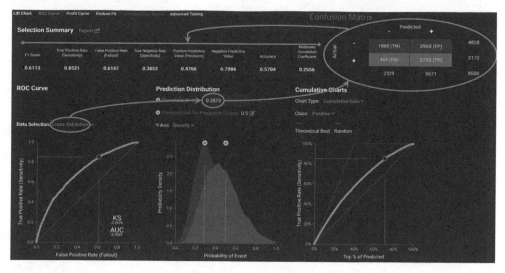

Figure 17.8. ROC Curve Screen.

link to open the dashboard seen in Figure 17.8. This is perhaps the single most important screen in DataRobot with much content to be explained.

The Receiver Operating Characteristics (ROC) Curve screen, so named because of the ROC curve in the bottom left corner, is where several central measures of model success exist beyond the original optimization metric, *LogLoss*. In Chapter 16, a few measures of success were discussed as alternatives to *LogLoss* when determining whether or not to gather further data for model construction. The numbers informing those additional measures were drawn from the contents of this screen. To break the dashboard down into individual components, orange guides have been added to assist in this walkthrough. Start with the orange oval on the left. At the moment, the screen contains measures drawn from the cross validation results. Change the pulldown value to "Validation" and note the changes in the charts and other measures. This change does not have a large impact, and this is a good thing. Generally, validation and cross validation scores should not differ wildly, given that DataRobot makes important decisions based on validation early in the AutoML process. Before continuing, change the dropdown value back to "Cross Validation."

Still in the ROC Curve screen, look now to the "Prediction Distribution." The *LGBEP* algorithm has created a model and applied that model to 8,000 patients. This visual shows the readmits (readmission = True) in green and the non-readmits (readmission = False) in purple. For each of the 8,000 cases, the target feature is either true or false, determining, therefore, which distribution "mountain" that case falls into. Also, the *LGBEP* model has assigned a probability to each case determining where on the X-axis the case is placed. This process can be visualized as follows: each case is assigned a color (green or purple depending on its true value). After its color is assigned, the specific case falls atop the existing cases at their respective assigned probabilities (location on the X-axis), building the distribution for that color.

The explanation makes less sense while looking at the density distribution (the default view). By changing the outlined option from "Density" to "Frequency," the display changes to a presentation of how many cases ended up at each probability. The density option is available to present each group as the same volume in case of an unbalanced target (more cases in one category than the other). Switching between the two views, the majority class (readmission = False) retain the same shape. In contrast, the minority class changes to the same size as the majority class, but maintains its distribution (this is sometimes more difficult to see in other cases). The goal of the algorithms is to assign high probabilities to positive cases (readmission) and low probability to negative cases (non-readmission). In this case, mountains overlap quite a bit more than is ideal, again affirming the earlier conclusion that the data is not of the best quality for predicting patient statuses. It remains early to give up, though, as amazing things can be done even with results of such seemingly poor quality as these.

In Figure 17.9, there is also another element in this chart to note: the threshold. The threshold is the probability value at which DataRobot changes a prediction from negative (no readmit) to positive (readmit). The threshold is shown with a score and a vertical line identifying the best cutoff to separate the two mountains.

DataRobot picked this threshold at the optimal F_1-score, a measure that denotes model success in predicting the positive values (readmission). We will return to the F_1-score shortly after clarifying a few further points. With the threshold at its default position, cases with probabilities at or above .2873 are classified as readmits, and those below .2873 are classified as non-readmits. Keeping these numbers in mind, follow the orange arrow in Figure 17.8 over to the two-by-two matrix, which is referred to, in common parlance, as a *confusion matrix*. This matrix did not come to its name by coincidence, and as such, the next paragraph will introduce the confusion matrix using the hypothetical example of car autopilot capabilities.

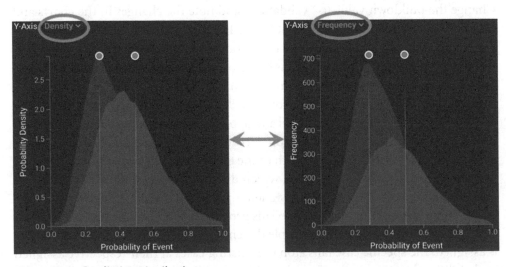

Figure 17.9. Prediction Distribution.

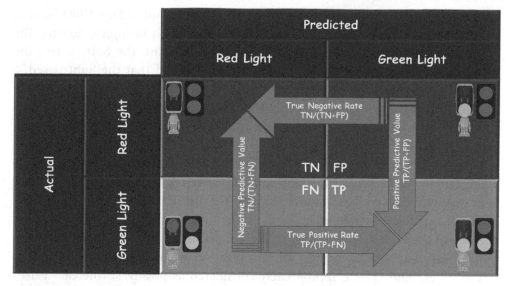

Figure 17.10. Confusion Matrix Breakdown.

Figure 17.10 shows the confusion matrix for a self-driving car's detection of traffic lights, simplified to remove that pesky yellow light scenario as confusion matrices are easier to understand for binary problems. On the left of the matrix lies what the car *should* have seen: whether the light was red or green (conveniently organized under purple and green bands in DataRobot's construction of a confusion matrix). The top of the matrix shows the actual detection made by the in-car algorithm, predicting that the light it is facing is either red or green. Take a moment to confirm that the traffic light in each quadrant reflects the actual color of the light and that the car's algorithm "sees" either a red or green light in accordance with its prediction. The red light is on top and the green light on the bottom.

Examine now each quadrant and compare the car's algorithmic perception of the color vs. the actual color. In the bottom right quadrant of Figure 17.10, the light is green, and the algorithm has determined that it is green. This is called a *true positive* (TP). In the top left, the light is red, and the algorithm has determined that it is red. This is called a *true negative* (TN). When combined, any case in these two quadrants constitutes a correct classification and provides the measure: *accuracy*, which is any correctly classified case divided by all cases categorized, or: $\dfrac{TP + TN}{all\ cases}$ In other words, what proportion of decisions made by the model are correct?

The remaining two quadrants represent the cases where the algorithm has incorrectly predicted the color of the traffic light. The top right quadrant represents the case where the traffic light was red, but the algorithm classified it as green, a *False Positive* (FP). This failure has significant consequences as the car speeds through the red light and is T-boned by a semi-trailer full of Diet Coke bottles, destroying the vehicle, causing injury, and adding insult to injury, dousing the passengers in fake-sugar soda. In the opposite quadrant, the bottom left, the traffic light was green, while the algorithm determined that the light is red, a *False Negative* (FN). The car screeches to a stop in front of the light, immediately getting tail-ended by the car behind it, leaving the passenger of the vehicle with a nasty case of whiplash and causing the can of Diet Coke in the cup holder to explode, covering the interior.

Now that we have elaborated the confusion matrix and its four quadrants, it is important to note that every case is evaluated (validated) and placed in one of these four quadrants. Secondly, recognize also that the distinction between true positive and true negative is simply whatever the system decided constituted a positive. In the case of DataRobot, it sorts target features alphanumerically and treats the lowest value as negative and the highest value as positive. Following this logic, values of "True," "Yes," and "1" are appropriately considered as positives, whereas "False," "No," and "0" are considered negative values. We recommend that you are deliberate about which values are designated to be true positives in the first few projects completed in DataRobot for the sake of results matching with logical true/false values. Remember that the advanced options covered in Chapter 15.2 allow you to change what constitutes a positive.

The third and final detail to be sure to recognize is the case-by-case importance of the kind of mistake a model makes. It matters whether the car runs a red light or stops in front of a green light, as one is more dangerous than the other. Other examples include whether an algorithm predicts that a patient has acquired a highly contagious tropical disease. In this case, a false positive (when it comes to medical tests, "positive" is seldom good) means that the patient lives in fear for a few days while the model prediction is proven wrong by way of a blood test. A false negative, however, means that the patient will think themselves safe when they shouldn't, potentially even transmitting the disease to others.

At this point, all four quadrants have been defined and discussed along with an important model assessment metric derived from the confusion matrix, *accuracy*. Next, we cover another key measure, *positive predictive value* (PPV). This measure is derived from the two rightmost quadrants and is more often called *precision*. It is calculated as $\dfrac{TP}{TP + FP}$, or the number of cases in the bottom right divided by the number of cases in the right two quadrants. Conceptually, this measure states how often the model is correct when it indicates that something is positive. Take the patient data in Figure 17.11. By dividing 2,703 by 5,671, the PPV value is 0.4766. When this model states that a patient *will* be readmitted within a month, it is correct 48% of the time. Admittedly this is not a great predictive value, given that random guesses between two options should be correct 50% of the time. Though this sounds quite foreboding, there is still a way to make good business decisions with the model.

Figure 17.11. Confusion Matrix for Hospital Diabetes Project.

The second most important measure is called *True Positive Rate* (TPR), or more commonly in Medicine, *Sensitivity*.[3] TPR measures what proportion of positive cases (readmissions) have been correctly identified and is calculated by $\frac{TP}{TP+FN}$, or the number of cases in the bottom right quadrant divided by the number of cases in the two bottom quadrants in Figure 17.11. In this case, TPR is measured by dividing 2,703 by 3,172, with a result of 0.8521. The model finds 84–85% of the readmissions, which is quite good, especially considering that this is more than double the rate of 40% of readmitted cases. Returning now to the F_1-score and understanding the components of the confusion matrix, it is possible to calculate the F_1-score by taking the harmonic mean of *Positive Predictive Value* and *True Positive Rate*. The harmonic mean is calculated through $\frac{2TP}{2TP+FP+FN}$, but it can be hard to conceptualize. Somewhat simplified, the F_1-score can be expected to be very close to the lower points of the PPV and TPR lines as shown in Figure 17.12.

Figure 17.12 shows the interaction between PPV and TPR––listing PPV from 0 to 1 and TPR as the opposite––to demonstrate how the F_1-score is consistently close to the lower of the two scores at any given point. By picking the location where the two are equal, the F_1-score is maximized. While F_1-scores play a significant role in the generation of all the other scores in DataRobot, it is not necessarily the case that a maximal F_1-score is optimal for a given business case.

This leaves two measures outlined in both Figures 17.10 and 17.11: *Negative Predictive Value* and *True Negative Rate*. *Negative Predictive Value* (NPV) is the mirror image of *Positive Predictive Value*. If the content of the target values were reversed by flipping *true* and *false values*, the two measures would simply have their scores flipped. The formula for NPV is $\frac{TN}{TN+FN}$, indicating the proportion of times the model is correct when predicting cases will be false (non-readmits—in this case, good news). The NPV in this example is 1,860/2,329 or 0.7986. When the model suggests that a patient will not return, it is right about 80% of the time. This is a decent outcome, but considering that 60% of patients will not return, this is not quite a boast-worthy result. Finally, we look at *True Negative Rate* (TNR), sometimes called *specificity*. The formula is $\frac{TN}{TN+FP}$ and measures the extent to which the model can

---

[3] Computer scientists like to refer to this measure as *Recall*.

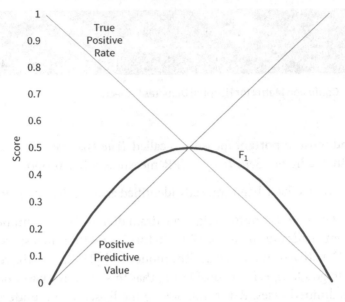

Figure 17.12. F$_1$-Score.

find all the patients who will not return within a month. Here we have 1,860/4,828 or a TNR of 0.3853. The model is finding only 39% of the patients that will not return. These are the patients of lesser interest as they will not be readmitted.

DataRobot reports two more measures out of the confusion matrix. First, there is the *False Positive Rate* (FPR), or *Fallout*, which was not added to Figure 17.10 to avoid overloading. FPR's formula is $\dfrac{FP}{FP+TN}$, or in this case 2,968/4,828 or an FPR value of 0.6147. This suggests that the model reports about 61.5% of the negative cases as positives. This measure becomes more crucial if there is a high cost to false positives, such as a mandatory follow-up test or where there is a need to evaluate the cost of mailing an expensive catalog. The importance of this measure will become clearer in a paragraph or two. The final measure, *Matthews Correlation Coefficient* (MCC) found to the left of the confusion matrix, is a correlation measure that is a strong indicator even when the target of a business case is highly unbalanced. For example, measures like PPV, TPR, and F$_1$ are of little value if 99% of the cases are positive and the model classifies all cases as positive. These measures would then all end up around 0.99. MCC is considered a reasonable evaluation of the whole confusion matrix. In this case, with a correlation at 0.2556, the MCC score offers yet another indicator that the overall model is not great. Because this correlation is derived in a different way than Pearson correlation, it cannot simply be squared, as is standard practice in statistics, to see the percent of the potential variance that has been found (and as such requires some experience with correlations to interpret).

Examining all the measures discussed so far, most take only two quadrants of the confusion matrix into account. This is true for *True Positive Rate, False Positive*

Rate, *True Negative Rate*, *Positive Predictive Value*, and *Negative Predictive Value*. As such, they provide only a partial picture of model performance. F_1-score is more holistic in this sense by carefully balancing three quadrants, but with an overriding focus on true positives. *Accuracy* provides another improvement by considering all quadrants but assumes that positives (readmits) and negatives (non-readmits) are of equal importance, which is seldom true. Finally, MCC considers all quadrants and is probably the most useful measure of overall model performance, but is hard to understand to those without experience working with correlations (see Table 17.1).

All these measures are calculated based on the confusion matrix numbers as they exist *at a single threshold*, and as such must be considered *static*, or at least incomplete because they do not provide any information about the model performance at multiple thresholds. Keep in mind that by granting the opportunity to modify the threshold, DataRobot provides the user with the opportunity to make these static measures dynamic by changing the threshold manually and recording the performance of favored measures at each threshold.

Also based on the four quadrants of the confusion matrix, the main *dynamic* measure commonly used by data scientists and displayed in the ROC Chart screen is the *Area Under the Curve* (AUC) of the ROC Curve. ROC curves are considered dynamic because they evaluate the model performance at several prediction

Table 17.1. Measures.

Measure name	Formula	What does it measure?
Positive Predictive Value (PPV; Precision)	$\dfrac{TP}{TP+FP}$	What proportion of the cases the model considers positives are actually positives?
True Positive Rate (TPR; Sensitivity; Recall)	$\dfrac{TP}{TP+FN}$ 20	What proportion of the positive cases is the model capable of finding?
F_1	$\dfrac{2TP}{2TP+FP+FN}$	The harmonic mean of PPV and TPR, punishing uneven performance (disharmony) between the two.
Accuracy	$\dfrac{TP+TN}{\text{all cases}}$	What proportion of model predictions are correct?
Negative Predictive Value (NPV)	$\dfrac{TN}{TN+FN}$	What proportion of the cases the model considers negatives are actually negatives? A flip of PPV.
True Negative Rate (TNR; Specificity)	$\dfrac{TN}{TN+FP}$	What proportion of the negative cases is the model capable of finding? A flip of TPR.
False Positive Rate (FPR; Fallout)	$\dfrac{FP}{FP+TN}$	What is the likelihood of a false alarm?
Matthews Correlation Coefficient (MCC)	$\dfrac{TP*TN-FP*FN}{\sqrt{(TP+FP)(TP+FN)(TN+FP)(TN+FN)}}$	The correlation coefficient between predicted and actual values. A measure that works well even for unbalanced targets.

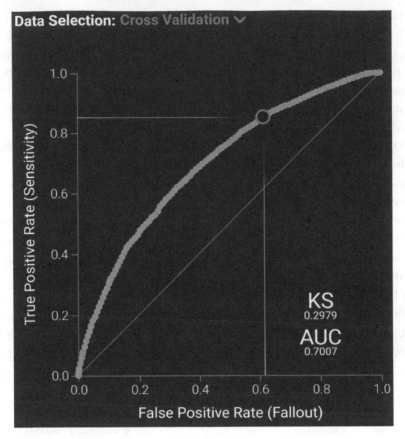

Figure 17.13. ROC Curve.

distribution thresholds (thereby changing the numbers in the confusion matrix during calculation). Often, even when reporting on the ROC Curve, most data scientists and researchers do not fully understand it. The ROC Curve, Figure 17.13, sets the *True Positive Rate* (what proportion of positive cases were found) against the *False Positive Rate* (proportion of negatives we label as positives) between the values of 0 and 1. The diagonal line shows the performance of a random assignment model. A good model will tend to curve up toward the upper left corner quite a bit more than this one. Such a model would be able to find a high proportion of the positives without admitting negatives into the set of predicted positives. However, if a model goes straight up to the top left corner and then to the right in a right angle, it is often a sign of target leakage or that the problem being addressed is not very sophisticated. A simple way to think about a good AUC score is having a low FPR and a high TPR at any given threshold.

Remember the logic of *True Positive Rate*. The TPR is the proportion of true positives found: how many patients are going to show up at the hospital again within a month relative to how many patients the model predicted. The *False Positive Rate* is how many of the negative cases are classified as positives; that is, the proportion

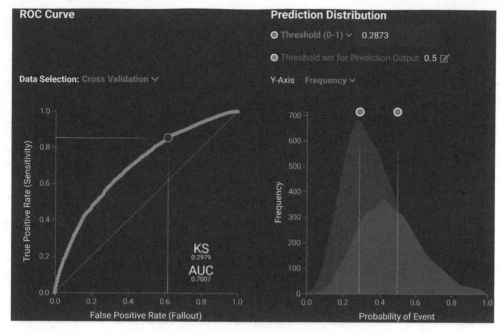

Figure 17.14. Step 1 of Visualizing the Creation of the ROC Curve.

of patients who are *not* going to return within a month but that we think will return. DataRobot has provided a useful tool for making sense of the drawing of the ROC curve. It is possible to move the threshold for the prediction distribution and then check the TPR vs. FPR. Begin by setting the threshold to 1.000. If you can't move to exactly that point by clicking on the prediction distribution, type 1.0 directly into the *Threshold (0–1)* field and hit enter, which yields a view like that in Figure 17.14. Make sure you change the Y-axis to "Frequency" so that we see a real representation of the number of patients at each probability level (X-axis).

Setting this value to 1 states that only patients predicted with a probability of 1.0 of returning to the hospital will be classified as returning patients (readmitted = *True*). Everyone else (all data points) will be classified as non-returning patients (readmitted = *False*). Examining the confusion matrix, the model predicts that no patients will return, which leaves both TPR and FPR at zero (both measures are available to the left of the confusion matrix). Now change the threshold to 0.8; a small number of positives are predicted, and the TPR (0.0227) and FPR values (0.0019) remain indistinguishable from zero in the ROC curve (red dot). Next, change the threshold to 0.6 to continue mapping out the ROC Curve shape, which yields the visual in Figure 17.15.

After placing the threshold at a probability of 0.6, those cases with a predicted probability of readmission of 0.6 or higher are placed in the confusion matrix as predicted positives, whereas all the cases to the left in the prediction distribution are placed as predicted negatives. Looking at the prediction distribution, the green squares can be imagined as making up the right side of the distribution, each representing about seven people, summing up to the TP count of 668 and the FP

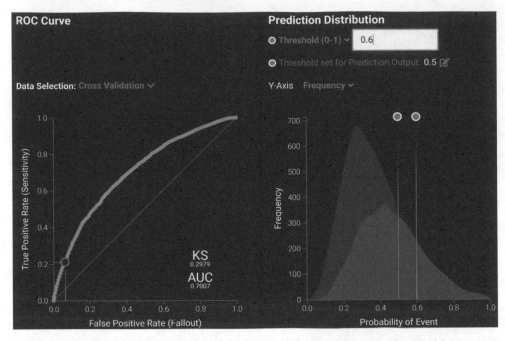

Figure 17.15. Third Step of Plotting the ROC Curve.

count of 301, per figure 17.16. The same counting happens on the left of the threshold to make up the confusion matrix.[4]

Now, continue to place the threshold to the left at intervals of 0.2, to cover 0.4, 0.2, and 0.0. Note that the red dot in the ROC curve will "trace" the shape of the curve. Being able to spot a good ROC curve is helpful and will become natural with practice. However, it is also essential to know the metric that is used to succinctly summarize the quality of an ROC curve. The measure used to communicate a single number that represents model quality according to the ROC curve is the *Area Under the Curve* (AUC) value.

As we have seen in Figure 17.17, calculating AUC is merely a matter of splitting the whole area into 100 boxes and keeping only those that are mostly or fully under the curve. Here, the result is 69 boxes out of 100, or an area of 0.69. Examining the DataRobot on-screen AUC curve, the AUC value is listed as 0.7007, so this quick assessment was slightly off. If a more accurate number is needed, the process remains the same but you might instead split the area into 100×100 (or remembering your calculus training). Of course, DataRobot provides the number, so no boxes or calculus is needed.

DataRobot has recently added the Kolmogorov-Smirnov (KS) test to the ROC curve. This test examines the separation between true positives and false positive

---

[4] You are now hopefully ready to rename the matrix the "clarity matrix," but if not, keep interacting with it as you analyze different datasets.

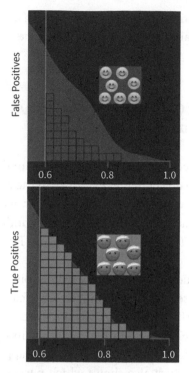

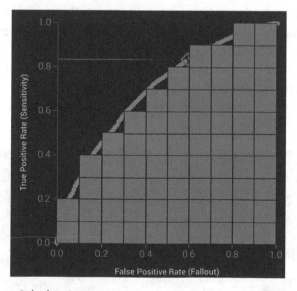

Figure 17.16 False Positives (Non-readmits) vs. True Positives (Readmits), all Predicted as Readmits.

Figure 17.17. How to Calculate AUC.

distributions. The KS test number may be used to compare different models. In this case, the LGBEP model received a score of 0.2979 out of 1.0, whereas if you examine the same score for the *Decision Tree Classifier* model we added, its score was 0.2376. It is a score that, like the AUC score, will require experience to use, so we will leave it aside for now. In DataRobot, the ROC Curve screen also contains some advanced charts: the Cumulative Gain and Cumulative Lift charts. We will leave these aside in this book.

17.4 Using the Lift Chart and Profit Curve for Business Decisions

Nearly all the elements required are now present to make business decisions. The only thing still missing is subject matter expertise in the health and hospital domain. We have several times criticized the model; however, we have also noted that this model likely still have value. To further examine the model, let us do a walkthrough. Begin by going to the *LGBEP* model menu, clicking **Evaluate**, then access the **Lift Chart**, per Figure 17.18.

The lift chart is constructed by sorting all validation cases by their probability of readmission (or in this case, cross validation, which means every case that is not part of the holdout sample). After sorting, DataRobot splits the cases into 10% bins, that is, ten bins laid out on the horizontal axis, each containing 800 cases. The ideal scenario is when blue and orange lines are entirely overlapping, indicating an accurate model (on average). This chart also shows which parts of the model are struggling the most. Is there a bigger gap between predicted and actual for certain parts of the model? In Figure 17.18, we see that the model over-predicts readmissions by a couple of percentage points in the highest-probability group (bin ten), but it underpredicts the target in bins eight and nine and then wobbles for a while. The model tends to be right on target for the cases predicted less likely to return (1–3). The true gold as found through this screen is how well the model performs at the top and bottom. First, it at the top (right) part of the model, cases in the 10th bin are 70% likely to be readmissions.

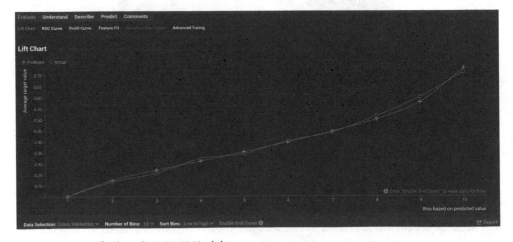

Figure 17.18. Lift Chart for LGBEP Model.

Cases in the bottom (left) bin are only 15% likely to be readmitted. Sorting cases this way allows us to target a smaller group of patients with high confidence.

A hospital may want to examine the dollar value of a campaign to reduce readmissions to weigh better the importance of implementing a machine learning model to make predictions on patients. This campaign may have been set up to text discharged diabetes patients on each of their first 30 days back home. The texts provide reminders to take medications, as well as motivational messages found to be effective in academic research, such as "Fruit, celery or carrot sticks, pretzels, plain popcorn make healthy snax" to encourage healthy eating and "Boost ur daily activity—play ur favorite music and dnz!" to encourage exercise (Franklin, Waller, Pagliari & Greene, 2006).

Next, click on **Profit Curve** to get to the core of business machine learning. This screen tells you where to draw the cutoff in a prediction distribution. This decision is based on the cost and benefits of your selected intervention. In this case, we will assume that the medication/motivation intervention is relatively cheap and has a minor effect. Figure 17.19 shows the profit curve screen after the creation of a new Payoff Matrix (click on **Add New Matrix**). The important decisions here revolve around determining reasonable costs and benefits for the four quadrants of the confusion matrix:

- True Negative: Patients in this quadrant have been correctly predicted not to get readmitted. There is no cost or benefit to this quadrant, so we set the value to 0.
- False Positive: Patients in this quadrant were never going to be readmitted, but our model predicted them as readmits. We here get no benefit from the intervention, but will be paying the cost. While it is hard to explain exactly how to get to the exact cost per false positive prediction, but think of it as the fixed costs of developing the intervention divided by the total expected positive predictions over

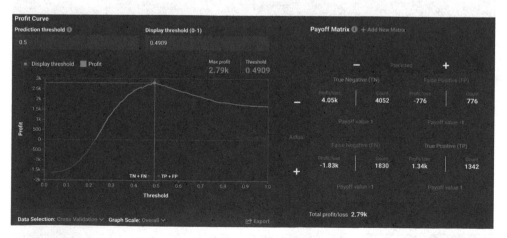

Figure 17.19. Profit Curve Screen.

the lifetime of the intervention plus the variable cost per delivery of of the intervention. We'll here assume a cost of $100 per false positive prediction, inserted as −100.

- True Positive: Patients in this quadrant were correctly predicted to need intervention, so that they will not be readmitted. We will assume that digging into the data suggested an average benefit of $400 per patient in this quadrant. Deducting the cost of the intervention ($100), we here get a benefit of $300 for this quadrant, inserted as 300.
- False Negative: This quadrant contains the patients predicted not to need intervention, but that actually will end up readmitted. The cost here may be assumed related to reevaluation and admission. While probably a lowball estimate, we will assume an average cost of only $100 per case, inserted as −100. This low estimate is due to the fact that these patients would under the old model (no machine learning) still be readmitted.

Once the new costs and benefits are added and saved, we see that the optimal probability cutoff for this intervention is at a probability threshold of .216. That is, if we target any patient with a probability of .216 or higher of being readmitted, we will optimize our profit. In this case, we would realize an improved profit of $125,500 for the 2,000 patients in the holdout sample.

Change the **Threshold** from *Probability* to *% of rows*, as shown in Figure 17.20. Note first that the X-axis direction has changed. Because we would always enagage the patients with the highest probabilities of readmission, the first 1% of patients asked to participate in the intervention will always be the patients with the highest

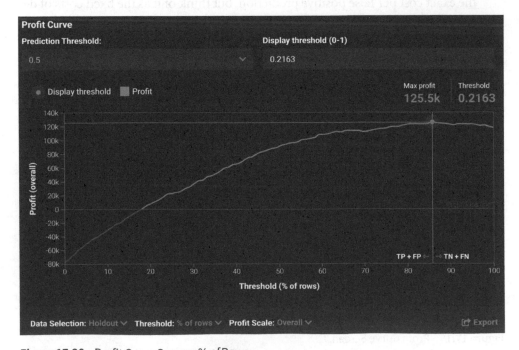

Figure 17.20. Profit Curve Screen: % of Rows.

probabilities. Notice here that our optimal profit would be reached through involving roughly 85% of our patients in the intervention. Note the ability to set the *Prediction Threshold* at the optimal level, so that when we use the model to predict readmissions probability for new patients, a patient with a probability above the threshold would be coded as a positive, suggesting that they should be offered enrollment in the intervention.

17.5 Exercises

1. What advantage does the FVE Binomial measure have?
2. Using the Decision Tree in Figure 17.7, explain how to get to two leaf-nodes. What are the characteristics of the patients in these nodes?
3. For your top model, change the prediction distribution threshold to 0.9. Explain the confusion matrix regarding what the model expected to happen to each group of patients relative to what happened.
4. What does *precision* mean? Explain it in the context of a Google search. Do the same with *recall*.

18
Comparing Model Pairs

Perfect *Is* the Enemy

ML principle: Question the "perfect" model as too good to be true (Williams, 2011, 9).
AutoML relevance: When a model has perfect or near-perfect performance characteristics, it is often due to either an inconsequential problem or target leakage.

18.1 Model Comparison

So far, this section's focus has been on an individual model selected from the top of the leaderboard. To save processing time, the model selected was the best non-blender model because blender models are generally beyond simple explanation and take longer for *Feature Effects and Feature Impacts* to calculate. To understand the difference between the overall best model (the *ENET Blender*) and the best non-blender model (*LGBEP*), DataRobot provides a way to examine the two against each other. In the upper left of the screen, select *Model Comparison* (Model Comparison). This panel allows the selection of two models from the leaderboard in addition to auto-selecting the top model, placed in the left position.

Click *Select second model+* (Select second model +) on the right-most model and search for *the model number of your LGBEP model*. Select this model and click on the chart if necessary. The left model (the *ENET Blender*) is shown in a blue color, whereas the right model (the *LGBEP* model) is shown in yellow. Select *Lift* (Lift), and make sure that *Lift Data Source* is set to *Cross Validation* (Cross Validation), and *Number of Bins* (Number of Bins : 15 ▾) is set to 15. This will produce the figure shown in Figure 18.1. The chart orders each algorithm's predictions by probability from high to low and splits each into 15 bins, calculating the average number of readmits (values of 1) in each bin and ordering those bins from right to left on the X-axis. The Y-axis displays the accuracy of each bin.

Given that about 40% of cases are readmits, a perfect model would leave the first six bins (starting from the right) at 1 (100% readmits) and the rest at 0 (0% readmits), with one middle bin somewhere in the middle, as demonstrated in Figure 18.2 with circled crosses. In contrast, a random model (one that has access to no predictive data) would produce a nearly straight line with every bin having about 40% readmits, as shown with plusses.

Automated Machine Learning for Business. Kai R. Larsen and Daniel S. Becker, Oxford University Press. © Oxford University Press 2021.
DOI: 10.1093/oso/9780190941659.003.0018

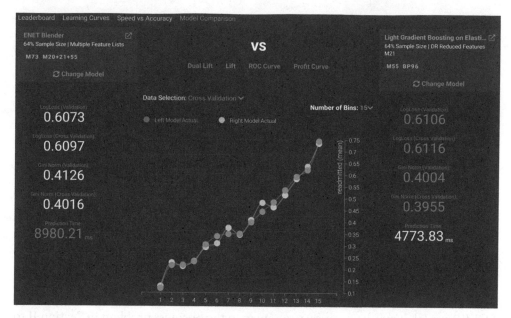

Figure 18.1. Model Comparison Lift Chart.

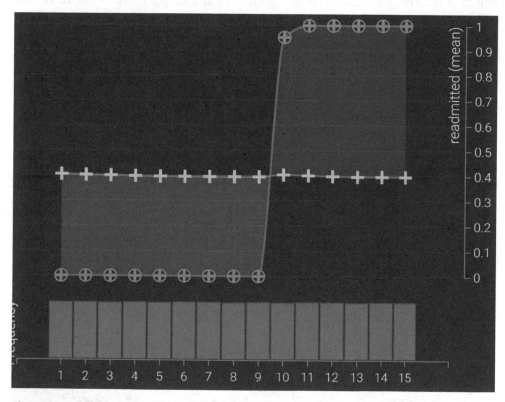

Figure 18.2. Perfect Model (Circles) and Random Model (Pluses).

The two models in Figure 18.1 are far from perfect, but it is worth recognizing that they are also significantly better than random selection. Both models portray a linear relationship between case bins sorted by probabilities and actual readmits. Starting the interpretation in of the two models in the upper right corner of the figure, note that for these bins, each representing 6.67% of all cases, the *LGBEP* model is the better performer by approximately one percentage point. This information could be significant if the goal is to find only a small set of predictions. For example, in the case of loans, an investor may want to invest only in the 1% of loans predicted to be the safest. Examining loan statistics from Lendingclub.com, the site is reported to have facilitated nearly $2 billion of lending in the first quarter of 2017 alone. This means that if the investor intended to compete for only the very safest 1% of loans in a three-month period, this group of loans might sum to as much as $20 million. This use-case suggests that to compare two models, we would want to examine their performance characteristics for much smaller bins.

Now change the number of bins for the lift chart to 60 (1.67% of total cases), and notice that the *ENET Blender* model now detects 8% points more readmits than the *LGEBP* model. It may be necessary to return to the business problem in Section II to generate ideas about what can be done for various patients depending on their probability of returning. Set the bin count again to 15 and keep it there for the rest of the exercise. Consider the top and bottom of the chart and the importance of detecting each as it depends on the business problem. The answers will help in selecting the appropriate model for implementation.

Moving on to the ROC Curve, there is little to no detectable difference between the models in Figure 18.3.

Figure 18.4 displays what a perfect model would look like in a lift chart—right up along the left Y-axis and then to the right along the upper bound of the figure. This

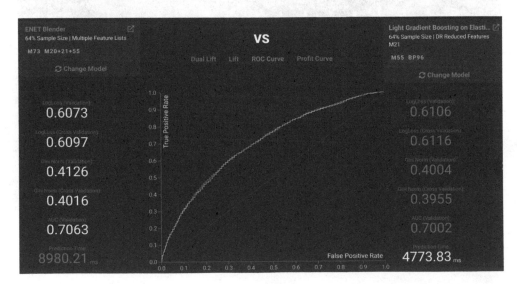

Figure 18.3. Dual ROC Curves.

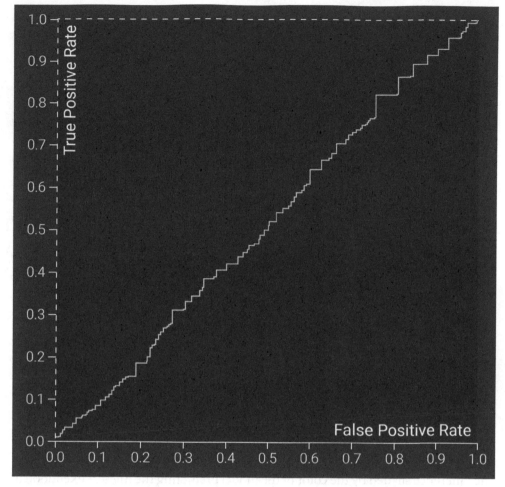

Figure 18.4. Perfect Model (dashed) and Random Model (solid) ROC Charts.

"curve" is drawn beginning with a high probability distribution threshold in which almost no cases are predicted as positives, and therefore, both the *true positive rate* and the *false positive rate* are zero. With the perfect model, at any cutoff point, one finds only true positive cases, so the "curve" travels immediately along the left bound of the chart. The "curve" remains there until the model begins predicting negative cases, which in an ROC chart will start to be predicted as positives as the probability distribution threshold moves to the left. The random model displayed here confirms that the ROC chart random line does indeed extend from the bottom left to the upper right corner.

Finally, examine now the dual lift chart by clicking on *Dual Lift* ( ), a screen displaying which model is right when two models disagree. This is the most complex of the dual model comparison screens. Click the middle bottom box with the text *Compute data for this model* (Compute data for this model). Notice that the number of bins can still be changed to get more detailed information. The dual list chart is

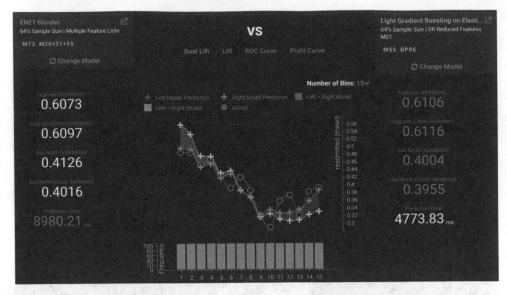

Figure 18.5. Dual Lift Curve.

calculated by subtracting the predictions made by the two models. Taking the left model's probability prediction for a case and subtracting the right model's prediction for the same case, the difference between them is produced. This difference is then ordered from lowest to highest and grouped into 15 bins with the smallest (negative) numbers to the left. This is the group where the left model, the *ENET Blender*, assigns a lower probability to readmission than the *LGEBP* model. For this bin, the average probability of each model is mapped against the Y-axis and the difference shaded by the color of the model predicting the highest likelihood of readmission (see Figure 18.5).

The orange line shows which model is closest to the average of the readmissions for the bin. In this case, when the two models disagree at the greatest magnitude on either side of the spectrum, the *ENET Blender* is closer to the correct answer. This is hardly surprising, given that the *ENET Blender* incorporates the predictions of the *LGEBP* model in addition to seven others. However, when evaluating all bins, no clear patterns emerge.

When comparing the perfect model (yellow) against the random model (blue), Figure 18.6 shows again the differences between the two as well as how the perfect model mirrors the average target score (generally either 1 or 0), whereas the random model averages probabilities of .4 based on the average readmissions.

At this point, the two top models have been examined, and their performance evaluated. It is now time to make a final decision on which model to proceed with. Because it is still quite possible that there is more to learn about that model, which might require modifying the original data, the holdout sample will remain locked for the time being.

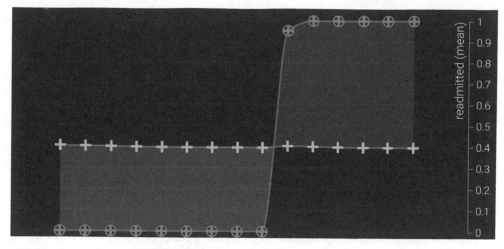

Figure 18.6. Perfect Model (circled crosses) and Random Model (crosses) Dual Lift.

Clear, Simple, and Wrong

ML principle: Simple and interpretable models generally are not as accurate as complex prediction models (Breiman, 2001; Domingos, 2012).

AutoML relevance: For every complex problem there is an answer that is clear, simple, and wrong. (H. L. Mencken).

Most models with equivalently high accuracy are now so complex that Occam's Razor no longer applies (there are many counter-examples suggesting that Occam's Razor is wrong with regard to ML) (Domingos, 2012).

18.2 Prioritizing Modeling Criteria and Selecting a Model

When deciding which model to select, there are five criteria to consider. They are:

1. Predictive accuracy.
2. Prediction speed.
3. Speed to build the model.
4. Familiarity with the model.
5. Insights.

It is now time to make an initial choice of model based on the first four criteria. All DataRobot models cast off similar insights, so, while it is important to analyze these insights for most AutoML applications, in DataRobot, insights will not significantly affect the model selection process.

So far, many of the many different measures of accuracy have been covered,[1] and at this point, it should be decided which measure DataRobot should use for its hyperparameter optimization, leaderboard ranking, and model selection. Within each model, there should also be a clear sense of the different measures generated through different prediction distribution thresholds and their impact on the confusion matrix. After deciding which measure or set of measures are best for the modeling case at hand, select a model that provides the best predictive accuracy at the most affordable price and suitable run-time requirements. While it is hard to imagine ever wanting a model that is less predictive, high accuracy often comes at a cost. These costs generally come from the other four criteria (2–5). The job of a data scientist is to find out which of the criteria affect the use of the model and pick a model based on the optimal combination of criteria.

The second criterion is the *prediction speed*. When a patient is ready to be discharged, and their data is uploaded to the model, a probability of readmission is calculated, and that probability is translated into a business decision. How long can the hospital staff afford to wait for that process to conclude? In the hospital context, patients are quite used to waiting, so the sub-second speeds by which predictions happen are not likely to matter, in which case this criterion may be ignored (to a degree). For example, the *ENET Blender* model creates a prediction on a new data record in 3.3 milliseconds (0.0033 seconds), whereas the *LGEBP* model requires only 1.25 milliseconds to make such a prediction. Expect this to be quite a bit slower when predictions are done through an Application Programming Interface (API) to a prediction server, but still, the patient will not notice the difference. Alternatively, if an organization engages in high-speed algorithmic trading between stock exchanges, for instance, in Chicago and New York, *prediction speed* will be an important criterion. In 2010, the company *Spread Networks* finished two years of laying fiber-optic cable in the ground between these two cities to shave off three milliseconds over the previously fastest route of digital communication (Steiner, 2010). Spread Networks' first 200 customers alone paid $2.8 billion for these milliseconds (Durden, 2012). Per 2017, algorithmic traders co-locate their computers with the trading computers for microsecond advantages (1 millisecond = 1,000 microseconds) over placing their computers one building further away (Frino, Mollica & Webb, 2014). For those charged with bidding for the best loans on Lending Club, a fast algorithm is a necessity. Similarly, to bid for placement of ads in front of visitors to a website, the model determining whether or not to bid for a given customer must make predictions in a fraction of the time it takes the page to load.

The third criterion, *speed to build*, reflects how long it takes to train a model. This will depend on how much data the model is trained with and the complexity of an algorithm. It is possible to build a research model that processes over a nine-month period before finishing its task; however, for business purposes, such turnarounds are not realistic. Some models must be continually retrained based on streaming data to be sufficiently accurate. For example, returning to the ad-bidding process, if a company

---

[1] The term "accuracy" is used here in a generic sense to indicate your preferred measure.

has an ad to place in front of visitors to half a million different blogs, the ad-placement model will first receive all available information on a visitor and the blog they are in the process of loading. It will then compute a probability that this visitor will click on our ad. If that probability is sufficiently high, the company will participate in an auction to bid for the right to place the ad on the visitor's browser as the page loads. If that auction is won, the ad is placed in front of the visitor. In the case that many of these users do not click the ad, frequent retraining of the model with updated data may be reasonable, which means that the speed to train the model takes on added importance.

The fourth criterion, *familiarity with model*, assumes that the data scientist (you) is an expert on one of the algorithms and can understand the exact meaning of its results. Because most models and the algorithms that created them are too complex to make much sense of, this criterion is more relevant when someone is an expert on regression (logistic or linear). However, even in this case, DataRobot provides regression-type information in the Variable Effects screen regardless of what model you create. You may need to run this model manually if you conducted a *Quick run*—go to **Repository**, scroll down to *Logistic Regression* and select **Run** followed by **Add Model**. Then find *Logistic Regression* in your leaderboard, click on it, and select **Coefficients** for that familiar regression information.

Finally, the fifth criterion, *insights*, is based on the assumption that different algorithms make different statistics available. For example, regression is commonly used to show which features drive improved prediction of the positive result of a target against the features that drive the negative result of the target. It is possible that those patients who are in the 80–90-year-old age group provide a general explanation for who will be readmitted, whereas not having a weight measurement for a patient will predict who will *not* be readmitted.

At this point, one of the models produced should stand out as a winner. Usually, there is a high demand for rationale if selecting a model that is not at the top of the leaderboard. Moving into Chapter 19, we select the *ENET Blender* model, as it has the best predictive accuracy of any of the models produced, and especially so at the high range of predictions. Prediction speed is not an issue in this specific instance of the hospital setting, the model will not need to be rebuilt often, and the current speed is acceptable, even for the *ENET Blender*. Therefore these measures can be considered secondary in model selection for this case. This decision is further justified by the fact that simpler models that are more familiar, such as the logistic regression and decision tree models, did not do well enough to be realistically considered.

18.3 Exercises

1. Explain why the perfect model vs. the random in Figure 18.2 look the way they do in the Model Comparison Lift Chart.
2. Explain the Dual Lift Curve to a friend.

SECTION V

INTERPRET AND COMMUNICATE

Having evaluated all the measures and selected the best model for this case (the *ENET Blender model*), keep in mind that while much of the machine learning process has been clarified, our understanding of the problem context is still relatively immature. That is, while we have carefully specified the problem, we still do not fully understand what *drives* that target. Convincing management to support the implementation of the model typically includes explaining the answers to "why," "what," "where," and "when" questions embedded in the model. While the model may be the best overall possible model according to selected measures, for the particular problem related to hospital readmissions, it is still not clear *why* the model predicts the readmission of some patients will be readmitted and that others will not. It also remains unknown *what* features drive these outcomes, *where* the patients who were readmitted come from, or whether or not this is relevant. In this case, access to time information is also unavailable--*when*, so it is not relevant, but it is easy to imagine that patients admitted in the middle of the night might have worse outcomes due to tired staff or lack of access to the best physicians. If we can convince management that the current analysis is useful, we can likely also make a case for the collection of additional data. The new data might include more information on past interactions with this patient, as well as date and time information to test the hypothesis about the effect of time-of-admission and whether the specific staff caring for a patient matters.

19
Interpret Model

Models Are Lenses to Understanding

ML principle: "Building models is thus fundamental to understanding our world" (Williams, 2011, 172).

AutoML relevance: AutoML generally provides the insights into models required to increase user understanding of them. While this should not differ from traditional ML, such insights have tended to require extra work and user expertise.

19.1 Feature Impacts on Target

Four kinds of relationships are commonly used for exploring why a model predicts outcomes. In DataRobot, the four types of relationships a feature can have with a target are as follows:

1. The **overall impact** of a feature without consideration of the impact of other features.
2. The **overall impact** of a feature adjusted for the impact of other features.
3. The **directional impact** of a feature.
4. The **partial impact** of a feature

Live with the Data

ML principle: It is essential to understand the data *before* starting to model it (Breiman, 2001).

AutoML relevance: AutoML makes it arguably easier to train a domain expert in ML than an ML expert in a domain. Such understanding is also crucial for selecting which data to acquire.

Because AutoML enables rapid prototyping, the suggested method to understand the data at hand is through modeling.

Because most features are not predictive of the target, detecting and discarding them is important and worthwhile.

Automated Machine Learning for Business. Kai R. Larsen and Daniel S. Becker, Oxford University Press. © Oxford University Press 2021.
DOI: 10.1093/oso/9780190941659.003.0019

19.2 The Overall Impact of Features on the Target without Consideration of Other Features

The *overall impact* of a feature without consideration for the impact of *other* features treats each feature as a standalone effect on the target. An example of this was encountered right after starting the DataRobot process, per Figure 19.1. As a reminder, each feature was individually examined in a logistic regression model against the target. The feature with the best ability to predict the target is listed first with a full green bar. All other bars represent how predictive those features are as a percent of the first bar. Hovering the cursor over the green bar, the optimization measure score for the individual feature model becomes visible (in this case, *LogLoss*), along with a normalized value between zero and one indicating the predictive value of the feature (with higher values being better).

The importance score is exceedingly useful because it allows a data scientist to focus attention on the features most likely to yield additional predictive value if misinterpreted by the AutoML, such as through misinterpretation of the variable type. This misinterpretation would include the treatment of a categorical feature as though it were a numeric feature. Unfortunately, these scores are not entirely reliable indicators of a feature's value. For example, it is quite common for a pair of features (or more) to contain the same information. In the diabetes readmission example, it turns out that the highly predictive feature, *number_diagnoses*, has quite a bit of overlapping information with *diag_3*, in that a missing *diag_3* means that the number of diagnoses is restricted to the range of 0–2. There is also overlapping information in the feature *num_medications,* as people with a lot of diagnoses also are more likely to be on one or more medications for each diagnosis. It would be a reasonable assumption to expect *age* to contain overlapping information. In short, while they provide a useful way to sort features, importance scores should not be relied on for feature selection and model interpretation.

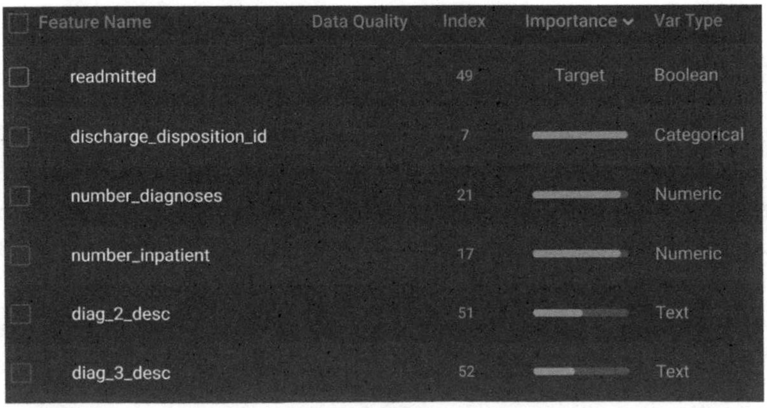

Feature Name	Data Quality	Index	Importance ⌄	Var Type
readmitted		49	Target	Boolean
discharge_disposition_id		7	▬▬▬	Categorical
number_diagnoses		21	▬▬	Numeric
number_inpatient		17	▬▬	Numeric
diag_2_desc		51	▬	Text
diag_3_desc		52	▬	Text

Figure 19.1. Importance Score.

19.3 The Overall Impact of a Feature Adjusted for the Impact of Other Features

---

Separating Signal from Noise Is the Role of ML

ML principle: Recognizing the fundamental patterns in relationships between features and the target is a fundamental ML goal (Berry & Linoff, 2004).
AutoML relevance: Same for ML and AutoML.

Click on the top model as sorted by cross validation, *ENET Blender*, and then select the **Understand** menu followed by **Feature Impact**, followed by **Enable Feature Impact**. Doing this will initiate a calculation of the value of each feature in the context of this model. DataRobot does this by randomly shuffling the values of one feature within the validation data segment (thereby removing its ability to have a meaningful impact on the target). DataRobot then examines the model's performance relative to the model that retained all the features. The extent to which the model with the randomly shuffled feature does worse than the original model is assigned as the feature's value. This procedure is done with every feature (all the features not being examined retain their original data). Once each feature has been scored this way, the most important feature is scaled to a score of 100%, and the other features are scaled relative to it.

This procedure might be difficult to follow and is best assisted by an example. To properly illustrate the process, let us return to Usain Bolt in this book's most morbid example. In 2009, he set the world record for the 100-meter dash at 9.58 seconds. Consider Bolt to have four features that contributed to his speed on that day: (1) Left arm, (2) Right arm, (3) Left leg, and (4) Right leg. The process starts by randomly scrambling the connective tissue and muscles in his left arm, rendering it a useless mass. Then he runs the race again. Assume that the left arm was not all that important, and Mr. Bolt finished the dash in 10.58 seconds. A value of 1 second is now assigned to the left arm. The next step is to reset his left arm to its original specifications and randomly scramble his right arm. In the next race, Mr. Bolt comes in at 11.08 seconds, suggesting that the right arm contributed 1.1 seconds to his speed. Reset the right arm and scramble the left leg before another race. This time the race takes him 99.58 seconds, suggesting that the importance of the left leg is 90 seconds. The procedure is repeated a final time for the right leg, after which it takes Bolt 109.58 seconds to cross the finishing line, assigning a value of 100 seconds to the right leg. It is now clear not only that the right leg was Mr. Bolt's most important feature that day, but also that its relative value as compared to the left arm is 100 times greater.[1]

---

[1] No athletes were harmed in the making of this book.

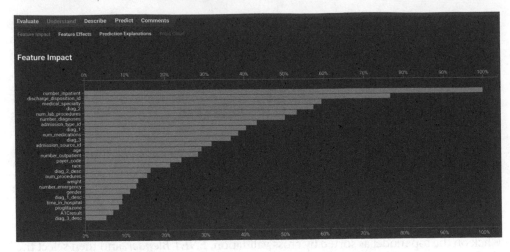

Figure 19.2. Feature Impact.

After this process is carried out, DataRobot produces the view seen in Figure 19.2. This figure shows that the number of inpatient visits during the last year (*number_inpatient*) is the most predictive feature overall. *Discharge* (*disposition_id*) is the second most predictive feature and *num_medications* the fifth most predictive feature.[2]

There is also a valuable lesson immediately present here, which is that for the models that accessed the text embedded in the diagnosis descriptions (*diag_1_desc*, *diag_2_desc*, and *diag_3_desc*), this embedded information was among the most important information available for the *ENET Blender*. This result suggests a pressing need to return to the texts and reassess their impacts more closely, as will be done in Chapter 19.5.

DataRobot has conveniently placed an option to select a set of top features as a new feature list. All that is necessary is to give the new list a name and select how many of the top features will populate it. A new model run can then be done using this feature list. Creating models with fewer features is generally a good idea to avoid overfitting,[3] and can also reduce problems due to changes in the databases and sources of data.

19.4 The Directional Impact of Features on Target

The third type of relationship is what has been termed in this book the directional impact of the feature, or whether the presence of a value helps the model by assisting it

---

[2] It was mentioned earlier that the *num_medications* feature contains a lot of information also existing in other features. In fact, if a new model building process was done without it, the best model may have a better *LogLoss* score than the model with it. This distinction is important, because the *Feature Impact* calculations do not tap into these other sources of the same information because this information is no longer used in the particular model created (*ENET Blender*). In this case, getting at the information inside *num_medications* and none of the information not available in other features works out as a benefit.

[3] While DataRobot in our experience does a good job of avoiding overfitting, including features in a model that have little effect can come back to haunt us in the future if the environment changes.

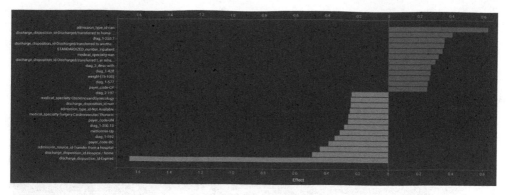

Figure 19.3. Coefficients.

in predicting readmissions or non-readmissions. Search for "Elastic-Net Classifier" using CTRL-F (PC) or Command-F (Mac). As we have experienced, the elastic-net classifiers are highly effective linear models. Select your top ElasticNet model and click the **Describe** menu option. Then select **Coefficients**, which will open the view displayed in Figure 19.3

While the DataRobot coefficients screen does not provide all the information to recreate a model, it provides the most important feature characteristics that drive a prediction decision. The red bars (those with coefficients above 0) indicate feature values that make positive cases (readmits) more likely, while the blue bars indicate feature values that make negative cases (non-readmits) more likely. One way to read this data would be to start at the top as follows: If the patient for whom the hospital is trying to predict readmission does not have an *admission_type_id* (it is missing or *nan*—a Python code for "not a number"), add 0.62 to their score (this is the score the longest red bar indicates. If the decision from the doctor was to send the patient home with home health service, then add 0.41 (hover over the name of the third red bar to see that this one is "Discharged/transferred to home with home health service"). One could continue this process all the way through to *discharge_disposition*, where they would then subtract 1.62 from the patient's total score if the value for this feature is *Expired*. The weight of this last feature value would likely wipe out almost any existing sum, but not necessarily all of it.

19.5 The Partial Impact of Features on Target

Everyone Lies (Even Data)

ML principle: "Let the data talk to you but not mislead you" (Williams, 2011,9).
AutoML relevance: In the context of AutoML, the leaderboard (validity and holdout scores) serves as lie-detectors for data.

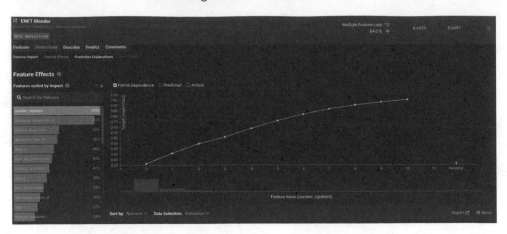

Figure 19.4. Feature Effects, *number_inpatient*.

Now navigate to the **Feature Effects** screen for the *ENET Blender* model. Click on **Understand, Feature Effects**. Then click on **Compute Feature Effects** (leave the sample size as is. If in the future we need this exhibit to be highly accurate, we can change it to 100%). This computation will take some time to process as it must consider three different models while calculating the values of the features therein. DataRobot does begin providing information on the top features as it is processing the rest. Figure 19.4 shows one of the most information-packed panel in DataRobot. The Feature Effects screen constructs a list of features ranked by feature impacts on the target as denoted by the size of the green line under each feature name in the left pane and the listed percentage. This information comes from the *Feature Impacts screen* (Chapter 19.3). Click on the feature names to examine each one. While we cover *Partial Dependence* later, it is worth noting that, somewhat simplified, the yellow line shows the importance of specific values of the feature *number_inpatient*, showing that a patient with zero past inpatient visits would be 35% likely to be readmitted whereas a patient with ten such visits is 95% likely to be readmitted. Note that the bars below the chart show how many patients possess each value. While having ten readmissions makes you easy to predict, we won't often encounter such patients, so this knowledge is less useful for predictions.

Let us start with the second most important feature, *discharge_disposition_id*.

To simplify the display a bit, some of the information can be hidden. Start by clicking on *Predicted* (☑ Predicted) and *Actual* (☑ Actual), and then uncheck *Partial Dependence* (☑ Partial Dependence) to hide that information from the Feature Effects chart.

The display should now look as is shown in Figure 19.5. The bottom bar contains the *frequency* of cases in the validation set. The X-axis contains the values of the feature *discharge_disposition_id*. Because this feature is categorical, every category is listed, starting with "Expired" discharge_disposition_ids. For this category, which in this case contains 29 patients, DataRobot averages the number *True* (1) and *False* (0) cases and places an orange circle, which represents the "Actual" score. That proportion of readmits is shown on the Y-axis. (In this case, that proportion is 0.)

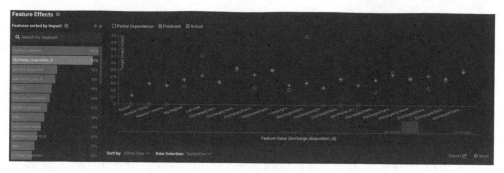

Figure 19.5. Feature Effects, *discharge_disposition_id*, No Partial Dependence.

Next, DataRobot averages its prediction probabilities of these 29 patients and places these probabilities as a blue cross, labeled "Predicted." The average probability is again found in the leftmost Y-axis (in this case, .126). Although we must examine each of these features before presenting conclusions to a management team, for now, we will focus on the last two features showing substantial differences between predicted and actual. Here, there is clear evidence that having deceased patients in the model degrades its performance as it is not able to accurately identify these patients. DataRobot algorithms are set to carefully avoid overfitting (the creation of models that fit the training data well, but fail when tested against the validation and holdout sets). Given the number of features created through one-hot encoding, it is not uncommon for all or most cases in a feature to get assigned to one of the two target values (*readmitted*, in this case). DataRobot will purposefully work to avoid the possibility of a model growing too confident based on small sets of values. Therefore, given that it is known for sure that none of these patients will ever return to the hospital, a processing step to remove such patients before training the model is necessary. Refer back to Chapter 12.2 on filtering for how to remove these rows from the dataset.[4]

Examining the third from the last feature, representing *Discharged/transferred to another rehab facility including rehab units of a hospital*, may offer an enticing indicator that rehabilitation works and that patients who are sent into rehab improve enough that their stats "fool" the model. Another hypothesis may be that those selected for rehab are patients with fewer maladies. This hypothesis was tested by creating a new feature named *sent_to_rehab* and using this new feature as a *target* to better understand these patients (removing the *readmitted* feature in the process). After running the whole DataRobot process on this dataset, we found that the major reasons patients were sent to rehab included having a fracture, seeing an orthopedic specialist, and length of time in the hospital. Being in rehab may simply mean having

---

[4] Do note that removing rows from the underlying data set *will* mean that the sampling procedures (cross validation and holdout sample selection) will assign different rows to each fold, thereby giving the algorithms access to many cases previously reserved for the holdout sample. This is not likely to be an issue, but keep an eye on the performance metrics in case they improve more than should be expected by removing a few expired patients.

Figure 19.6. Feature Effects with Partial Dependencies.

access to experts who help that patient avoid readmission. We may think of these patients as having less than 30 days in which to be readmitted, and they are therefore harder to predict for the model.

At this point, set the previously hidden *Partial Dependence* scores to be shown once again. Ensure the list is sorted by *Effect Size*. In Figure 19.6 the categories are sorted based on effect size (partial dependence) from those driving low readmission rates (*Expired*--at about .13 readmissions per patient) to those driving the highest readmission rates (*Discharged/transferred to home with home health service*--at about .45 readmissions per patient). What does the information tell us? DataRobot's partial dependence plot shows the marginal effect of a value when all other features are constant. In other words, it pretends that the value of this feature is the only known information for each patient and calculates its effect on the target as such. When interpreting a partial dependence plot, a strong result is when the locations of the yellow dot values on the rightmost Y-axis change significantly. For this to be true, the yellow dots should represent a wide range of values. Here, that range is between .15 and .45 and can be considered significant.

19.6 The Power of Language

In Chapter 19.2 we explained that the top non-blender model takes major advantage of the three text features. With this information in mind, head to the **Insights** screen (top menu) and select *Text Mining*. Once on this screen, use the orange down arrow to select the model *Auto-Tuned Word N-Gram Text Modeler using token occurrences—**diag_3_desc***, for one of the 64% sample models, as shown in Figure 19.7. It is now visible that the most important terms leading to readmissions were *valves* and *renal*, meaning, patients with heart and kidney problems. The two most important terms related to patients avoiding readmission were *diag_3_desc = nan* and *sarcoidosis*, an inflammatory disease. *Diag_3_desc* was also coded as *nan*, suggesting that not having a third diagnosis is the best thing for avoiding a readmission. The "effects," in this case, are just a relabeling of the word *coefficients*.

At this point, access to a subject matter expert (SME) will be important during evaluation of the text model(s). For example, an SME may need to examine the diagnosis codes that contain the word "valve." In this case, there are four diagnosis codes containing this term:

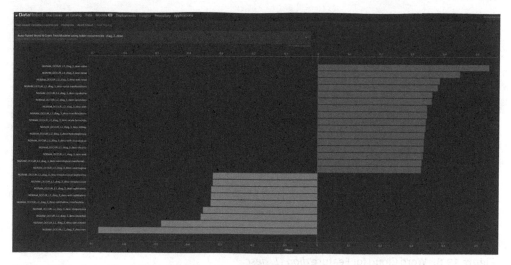

Figure 19.7. Auto-Tuned Word N-Gram Text Modeler.

- Diseases of the tricuspid valve
- Mitral valve disorders
- Congenital pulmonary valve anomaly, unspecified
- Mitral valve stenosis and aortic valve stenosis

This diagnosis information may seem overwhelming for anyone not trained as a physician. If so, this stands as evidence to support one of the initial statements of this text: AutoML makes analytics easy enough that, for the first time, it is easier to train subject matter experts in machine learning than it is to train a machine learning expert in the subject matter. This case is simple enough, however, that a Google search of the four diagnosis codes reveals that they are all associated with heart disease, as suggested earlier. A subject matter expert would examine these four diagnoses and state that they represent different *types* of heart disease related to the four separate valves of the heart.

Next, by once more going to **Insights** and selecting **Word Cloud**, and for some new information select the **diag_1_desc model**, the same information is displayed once more, but this time in a word cloud, per Figure 19.8. A word cloud represents the words that have the highest coefficients (remember adding these up to get an idea of the likelihood of a case being readmitted?). The intensity of the red or blue colors indicates the size of their coefficient. By hovering over a term (one or more words in order from the text feature), the coefficient of that specific term is shown. Hovering over "heart failure," the coefficient of 0.861 for that term appears. This means that if the term "heart failure" appears in that patient's first diagnosis description, add 0.861 to the likelihood that the person will be readmitted.[5] Below "Coefficient: ... "

---

[5] Discussion of coefficients is a bit beyond the purpose of this book and it is recommended to return to an introductory statistics book for such information. In short, it is the "slope" of a regression line and the model will have a number of positive and negative coefficients that are added up depending on which words appear in their diagnoses.

Figure 19.8. Word Cloud for Feature *diag_1_desc*.

is another piece of information: "Appears in . . ." This term appears in 452 rows out of the 6,400 rows used to create the model. Notice the barely discernable term in the bottom right corner. When hovering over this phrase, the term "obesity unspecified" is illuminated, which can be traced back to the code applied in the diagnosis containing a comma between the two words. Unspecified obesity simply means that there are patients in the sample who are obese, but their specific situation is not being specified with a defined code, such as "obesity complicating pregnancy" and so on. This term has a coefficient of −0.956, suggesting that patients with this diagnosis are *not* likely to come back. However, the information window also notes that this term appears in only 38 rows—the reason this phrase appears in such a minuscule font size. The key then, to interpreting the word cloud, is to simply analyze large terms with vivid colors.

A final note on word clouds: for any text-heavy analysis, the option **Filter Stop Words**, set to *yes* by default, but here unchecked in Figure 19.9, is an important detail to note. A stop word is a common word generally assumed to have little value. Such assumptions can be dangerous, so for every text field examined, uncheck this stop-word option to be aware of what is being filtered and ensure that they are truly stop words.

Interestingly, there was a surprise hiding inside this feature. The stop word, "of," turns out not only to be exceedingly predictive of someone not returning (coefficient of −1.000), but it is also quite frequent, appearing in 2,441 rows. As with any surprise indicator that can't be immediately explained, this requires further examination. Opening the dataset in any favored data tool of choice, select only the unique values inside this feature, leaving 440 rows. It is now possible to mark every row containing "of." After doing so, it becomes apparent that the use of the word "of" in a diagnosis is quite common—183 different diagnoses contain the word. One hypothesis to explain the predictive power of "of" is that diagnoses containing

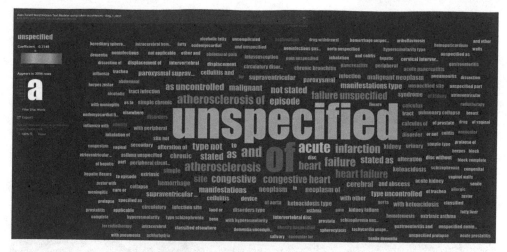

Figure 19.9. Word Cloud, Including Stop Words.

it refer to very specific problems, such as "Abscess *of* lung," which, if true, would mean that these diagnoses are longer (contain more words). Counting the number of words in each diagnosis and averaging them by whether the word "of" is present produces a value of 7.5, whereas a diagnosis lacking the word averages at only 4.3 words long. A further hypothesis might be that the more words required to specify a diagnosis, the less likely it is to be lethal or critical as common and dangerous ailments tend to have their names shortened over time. It can also be hypothesized that the more specific the diagnosis is, the more likely proper treatment can be devised. These hypotheses are difficult to confirm without access to new and different data than what is presently at hand (the 5-year survival rates for each diagnosis, for example).[6]

19.7 Hotspots

The final portion of Chapter 19 will outline the *Hotspots* view in DataRobot. To get there, navigate first to **Insights** and then **Hotspots**. This visualization uses the *RuleFit Classifier*, which is an immediate red flag, considering that this is one of the algorithms that was stalled at 32% of the data during model creation. As done before, record the model number, go back to the leaderboard, and run the same model again with access to more data. After finding the model, click on the orange "+" followed by setting snap to *Autopilot Stage III (64.00%)*. Click **Run with New Sample Size**. Once this is finished running, go back to *Insights, Hotspots*, per Figure 19.10.

---

[6] The relevance of this analysis to the final presentation given to management is unclear; however, these opportunities to dig into the data can be quite fun and offer valuable learning experiences. (We geeked out. Sorry.)

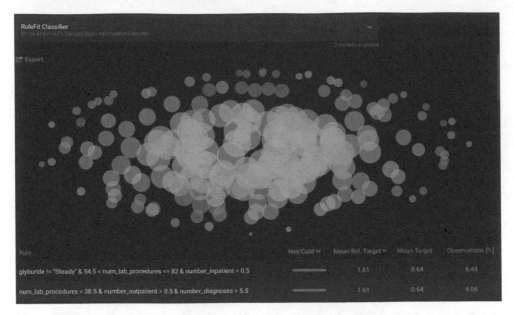

Figure 19.10. Hotspot at 64% of Sample.

The *Hotspot* screen shows the most relevant (up to four) combinations of features and their effect on the target.[7] Think of this diagram as a set of Venn diagrams where the largest and most overlapping hotspots are organized in the middle. Just as for the word cloud, the deeper the tone of the blue and the red, the more of an impact that particular combination of features that specifies a sub-group of patients has on the target. For example, by hovering over the dark red dot in the upper middle of the chart, a new window (see Figure 19.11) shows that this group of patients is 6.44% of the total (a relatively small group). It also shows that, for the feature value of *steady* (likely a one-hot encoded feature), all the members of this group are coded as [0.5 for the target, which, in this case, means zero (or *False*).

For the features in Figure 19.11, the false value for the feature *steady* indicates that these patients are not in a steady-state for the medication *Glyburide*. Further, the number of lab procedures completed in this group is greater than 54.5 and less than or equal to 82, and the number of inpatient procedures during the last year is 1 or more. It is also stated that this group of patients has a 64% (mean target value = .64) chance of being readmitted. The mean relative target is the result of dividing the target value of this hotspot group by the average number of readmits and accounts for how predictive this hotspot is.

While the *Hotspot* panel is quite visually impressive, we do not recommend its use during presentations due to its exceedingly high level of detail and complexity. Chapter 20 will cover the process of communicating model insights as an extension of Chapter 19.

---

[7] The four combinations are determined by the depth parameter of the *RuleFit* classifier (how many branches and sub-branches may the algorithm create), but, in this case at least, its depth suggests that four is the maximum number of conditions.

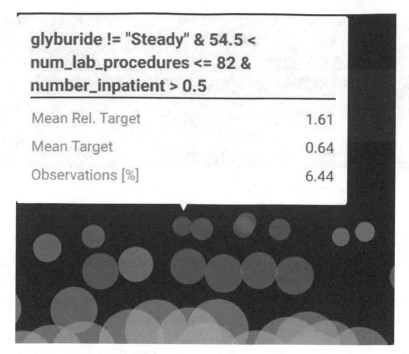

glyburide != "Steady" & 54.5 <
num_lab_procedures <= 82 &
number_inpatient > 0.5

Mean Rel. Target	1.61
Mean Target	0.64
Observations [%]	6.44

Figure 19.11. Dark Red Circle New Screen.

Find the Puppet's Strings

ML principle: "From a large mass of data, information technology can be used to find informative descriptive attributes of entities of interest." Sometimes this process is referred to
roughly as finding variables that "correlate" with [the target] (Provost & Fawcett, 2013, 15).
AutoML relevance: In ML, the set of potential relationships is reduced to the set of feature-
target relationships of a certain effect size.

Examine cases to understand *why* a given case was given a specific probability. In other
words, which features led to a patient being rated as likely to be readmitted? Was it their age,
their past admissions, or perhaps a specific blood test result?

19.8 Prediction Explanations

The focus of this chapter thus far has been on the features and feature values that
drive positive or negative changes in the target; however, understanding of the data
at the more granular individual patient level remains limited. To address the individual data points, each patient's feature values need to be examined, along with an
analysis of how these values determined that patient's probability of readmission.
These determinations are what the **Prediction Explanations** screen in Figure 19.12
shows. You may upload a new dataset, but this figure refers to the validation data.

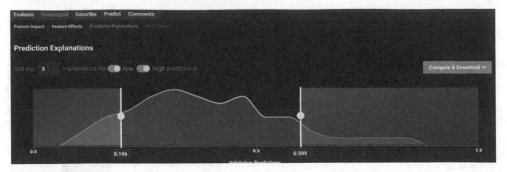

Figure 19.12. Prediction Explanations.

The left and right thresholds allow for the specification of the probability cutoffs. For example, the left (blue) threshold states that we want prediction explanations for all patients with probabilities of readmission ranging between 0.0 and 0.204. The rightmost (red) threshold specifies that we also want prediction explanations for any patient with a probability between 0.601 and 1.0. The default for the screen consists of the top three reasons for each probability (as specified in the box following "Get top"). This cutoff can be any number between 1 and 10. The default for the thresholds is to show the top and bottom 10% of cases.

The bottom preview section of the screen shows the top three cases (those with the highest probabilities of readmission) and bottom three cases (those with the lowest probability of readmission). If there are fewer than three cases within either of the selected thresholds, then fewer cases are shown in the preview area. This preview section also shows the internal ID number used by DataRobot (a number identifying the cases in the order read in from the original data file, starting at zero), the probability of readmission, and up to three pluses or minuses representing the importance of the feature and its value. The importance of each reason is valued at *strong* (+++/ −−−), *medium* (++/−−), or *weak* (+/−).[8]

For the first patient, it can be seen that the reason this person was estimated as 98.4% likely to be readmitted is that they had 13 emergencies, four inpatient visits during the last year, and was discharged to home with home health service.

The prediction explanations are a effective feature that can supplement business decisions. Take the example of predicting employee turnover. An HR manager may be told not only which of his or her most valuable employees are likely to leave, but also that the model suggests that if Janine leaves (a likely event), it would be associated with her low salary, whereas if John leaves (another likely event), it would be associated with required overtime hours. In the latter case, a simple conversation with John may confirm that his overtime hours are preventing him from spending

---

[8] It would have been preferable if DataRobot used the identified ID column from the dataset (*rowID*) instead of its own assigned id value (in this case, *row_id*). Since the DataRobot identifier starts counting records at zero, and the *rowID* from the original data starts at 1, a simple solution is to find these cases in the original dataset and add one to the ID.

time with his family. With this information, different interventions may be used to keep both John and Janine on staff. Unfortunately, discussing their salary with an employee is tricky territory. Imagine being the manager tasked with asking Janine whether she is happy with her current salary.

As a final caution, be aware that computing prediction explanations is slower than computing predictions, as prediction explanations engage in additional evaluations of *why* a prediction was set as the given probability for that case. This is, however, not likely to be a problem since prediction explanations are primarily of use in settings where human beings are involved in the decision process (unlike our earlier example of automated stocks trading).

19.9 Exercises

1. Run another analysis with *number_diagnoses* as the target. To do so, the dia-betes dataset will need to be uploaded again. Use the *manual* modeling mode rather than *autopilot* to save processing time. Select the first *eXtreme Gradient Boosted Trees Regressor with Early Stopping* model. Then examine the feature impact screen to see how many other features share predictive values with this feature.

2. In the *Feature Impact* screen, create a new feature list consisting of the top five features. Run autopilot on this feature list and compare the full-data *ENET Blender* with the best blender model from the top five models. What are the main performance differences between these models? Why are they different?

3. Access the original diabetes data and cross-tabulate *discharge_disposition_id* with the average of *readmitted* (it may be necessary to turn all *True* values into 1 and *False* values into 0). Look for another group that has a suspiciously low re-admission rate. If you do not know how to do a cross-tabulation, sort the sheet by *discharge_disposition_id* and examine the *readmitted* column.

20
Communicate Model Insights

Correlation Does Not Imply Causation. So What?

ML principle: "Whether or not causality really exists is a deep philosophical question with no definitive answer in sight" (Domingos, 2012, 87).

AutoML relevance: Whether a relationship between a feature and a target is causal or correlational is left for post-modeling presentation posturing and argumentation.

   Same for ML and AutoML.

Previous chapters have outlined all the information needed to prepare a presentation about the knowledge gained through machine-learning analysis (conducted in Sections IV and V). It is vital to distinguish between information useful for understanding the model and information useful to an audience for making business decisions. Understanding the model is important for the data scientist creating and modifying the model, but fewer model details are relevant to the final stakeholder audience.

Presentations should be adjusted based on personal experiences with the audience, as well as an understanding of the business context. For example, if you have made similar presentations to the same audience in the past, less time will be required to explain machine learning.

There are six types of information that should be communicated during a presentation:

1. Business problem
2. Model quality metrics (confusion matrix)
3. Areas where a model struggles (potential for improvement through more data, features and cases)
4. Most predictive features for model building
5. Feature types especially interesting to management (e.g., insights into the business problem and unknowns uncovered during the modeling process)
6. Recommended business actions (i.e., to implement model or not, any business decisions to execute at various probability thresholds, and assertions on how implementation will change practice?)

It takes quite a lot of experience to get to the point of accurately presenting models. Even with decades of experience, seasoned data scientists continue to encounter

Automated Machine Learning for Business. Kai R. Larsen and Daniel S. Becker, Oxford University Press. © Oxford University Press 2021.
DOI: 10.1093/oso/9780190941659.003.0020

difficult lines of questioning and skepticism from their audiences. Surprisingly, the simplest questions can be the hardest to answer. One example is the question asked after a five-minute introduction to NLP: "what is natural language processing, really?" Another might be something akin to: "how does regression *work*?" Keep in mind that these types of questions generally do not betray the person asking them as less knowledgeable, but rather that this person has a higher threshold for embarrassment, asking what many in audience are quietly wondering. These questions represent a real problem because not answering them may suggest that one doesn't know the answer while explaining them will take the entire time allotted for the presentation. What to do?

We recommend that you respond by stating that delving into foundational questions will not leave enough time remaining for the presentation and might not really help the audience follow the information displayed. State also that these questions can be discussed one-on-one with the person after the presentation. Then explain that all the algorithms being worked with function conceptually in the same way. They determine the generalizable relationship between the *features* (or *independent variables*, if your audience is used to statistics) and the *target* (*or dependent variable*) and place those relationships into a model that can be used to both understand those relationships and predict the outcome of cases not yet encountered. Over time, learning to anticipate the kinds of questions these presentations are likely to evoke will become easier. It may even be helpful to prepare separate slide sets in advance that answer these FAQs. This approach provides reliable information to compress the answers of even the most complicated questions into just a few minutes (this advice goes for any professional focused on presenting and communicating vital information).

There are many books available about presentation style and process. The goal in this book is not to replicate that material but rather to focus on what information you should share during a machine learning presentation to provide precise information that is understandable by your audience and will indicate next steps for the business problem. For this case, assume that the person or persons that this information will be presented to are in management, and, in all likelihood, are above or at your level in the organizational chart. As you prepare these presentations, keep the information simple, and help the audience learn 3–7 things they didn't already know.

20.1 Unlocking Holdout

Before heading off to convince management that the model is worth investing in, it is first vital to check that there haven't been any mistakes made in the model creation process. We do this by releasing the holdout data. Earlier, the holdout sample was discussed as a final opportunity to evaluate the constructed model against a set of data that has been untouched and unsullied by the model selection process. For example, when 16% of the data was used to select the top algorithms to evaluate against 32% of the sample, we mentioned that a small set of data could sometimes lead us in the wrong direction. The holdout sample provides an opportunity to check whether such problems may have occurred. To release the holdout data, return to the leaderboard and click **Unlock project Holdout for all models** under *Actions*, per Figure 20.1.

With the holdout sample unlocked, click on the holdout column to re-sort the leaderboard by those scores. Observe the ranking differences between the *Cross Validation* and *Holdout* scores (it may be necessary to click between the two options a few times to see the patterns emerge). The best outcome would be one in which the order of models did not change between the two sorts. The second-best outcome would be when at least the top models stay at the top of the list. If neither of these outcomes is true and the top models' holdout sample scores are substantially lower than the cross validation sample, then we have a reason to be concerned about the modeling process. At this point, expert advice may be useful in reevaluating assumptions made about how to train the models (see Advanced Options in Chapter 15.2). Small samples are more likely to lead to such issues, and when this is the case, there is cause to reevaluate the whole process because DataRobot is so dependent on *validation* and *cross validation* scores to make its decisions.

As can be seen in Figure 20.2, the second-best option just noted rings true in this case in that the top two models remain atop the leaderboard after sorting the models by the holdout column. In this case, one model outperformed the LGBEP model,

Figure 20.1. Unlock Holdout Option.

Figure 20.2. Sorted by Holdout.

but both our blender models remained on top among the 64% models. Because there were no significant changes in the ordering of the results—which would require a reexamination of the modeling process—continue forward with the best model, the *ENET Blender*. However, we must now reexamine the confusion matrix for the *ENET Blender* and examine whether the model is still profitable in case the implemented model performs as the holdout sample rather than the validation and cross validation samples.

20.2 Business Problem First

Section II (Define Project Objectives) began with the outlining of a business problem. This problem continually guides the work, and we continually refine the problem statement as the AutoML process proceeds, given that the analytics (discussed in Section IV) made clear more detailed information about the model and features of the data. For example, some specifics became clear about decisions made by the physicians in the study, including discharge decisions. Other data manipulations were considered as well, such as recreating decisions including "Discharge to home" vs. "Discharge to home with home health service." Of all patients in the training set discharged to home, 16.7% (one in six) were discharged with home health services. It was determined, therefore, that the problem statement had to be changed to incorporate this additional information.

The original belief was that all patients discharged to home could be evaluated, and the patients with the highest probability of readmission could be given home health services regardless of the physician discharge decision. However, after consulting a subject matter expert, we learned that only patients assigned home healthcare could receive these services. These are patients who, for example, require complex wound care or home intravenous antibiotics. Therefore, it was decided to focus on patients discharged to home without home health service--60% of patients. Figure 20.3 contains the updated problem statement, which we may place on the second slide of the final presentation after the title slide.

Our organization suffers over $15 million in preventable losses annually due to the readmission of diabetes patients who are discharged from our hospitals too soon or who are inadequately prepared to manage their disease on their own. However, keeping all patients in the hospital longer is costly, risky, and inconvenient to patients.

We will create a machine-learning model capable of detecting which patients are likely to be readmitted within 30 days of discharge and develop educational and support programs targeting these patients. 60% of our patients are discharged to home without home health services; this group mirrors the overall patient population in terms of average readmission. We are especially interested in detecting cases where these patients are highly likely to be readmitted.

Figure 20.3. Updated Problem Statement.

20.3 Pre-processing and Model Quality Metrics

In Chapter 16.3, model metrics from the confusion matrix were combined to better understand model performance characteristics. Because it is now time to put your career on the line with your top model, the holdout sample just released will be used. Though this model performs worse on the holdout data, in all likelihood, this result is closer to realistic model performance. Having settled on both the model to present and using the holdout sample to present evaluation metrics, it is now time to plan the model quality metrics part of the presentation.

Slide three might contain a quick overview explaining the process for procuring data, cleaning that data, and carefully addressing issues, such as removing expired patients and patients discharged to hospice. Explain that many different high-quality algorithms were run on the data, and feel free to point out examples of these, such as logistic regression and deep-learning neural networks. It may be tempting to share code or go into great details here, but it is best to restrict this data processing information to one slide without code.

For slide four, to address model quality metrics, begin with the confusion matrix for the chosen model and annotate it for the audience, per Figure 20.4. In a presentation, it is preferable to first introduce the confusion matrix without the orange add-ons. Explain that this is how the model performs on 2,000 patients it has never seen before but that this *was* data collected during the same period as data used to train the model. Add that it is possible that performance will deteriorate if we give the

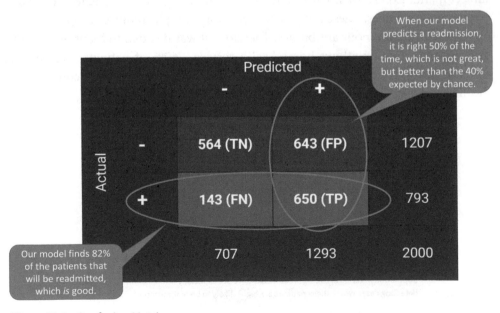

Figure 20.4. Confusion Matrix.

model new data but that this can be monitored, and, in the case of reduced effectiveness, the model can be retrained when needed.

Next, animate onto the slide the rightmost orange oval and the text within that explains the model's performance. This is the *Positive Predictive Value*, but for most audiences, focus on what the measure means rather than its name. What it means is the level of precision of a model regarding its ability to predict readmissions. Next, animate in the oval around the true positive rate along with its included text. Explain that there is limited interest in predicting non-readmits here, so the focus will remain on predicting and measuring readmitted patients. Here, the prediction distribution threshold is set at 64% of patients being predicted as readmits. This is because 64% was the percentage suggested by the original profit chart as the optimal point for investing in the educational and support programs previously planned. Since we are now dealing with the *holdout* confusion matrix, 64% means setting the model to predict approximately 1,280 patients as predicted readmits by moving the prediction threshold. Since many patients have the same predicted probability, you may not be able to get exactly that number. In this case, we ended up at 1,293 predicted positives (readmits), which is close enough.

Slide five: Now would be a good time to describe the education program intervention on a slide. These programs should be developed with the help of the subject matter expert working on the project and based on scientific findings.

For slide six, the confusion matrix with a different probability distribution threshold would typically be displayed to identify a probability above which a small set of patients would be highly likely to be readmitted. However, because it has been decided to focus on patients discharged to home without home health service (a subset of all patients), this part needs to be done manually. There were two options available in this case: (1) Go back to the knowledge developed in Chapter 10.2 and filter away all patients not in this subgroup before doing all the analysis again, or (2) simply remove all patients not in that subgroup in the holdout sample. To learn something new, and because losing that many cases could negatively impact model performance, proceed with option 2.

First, it is necessary to extract the predicted probabilities for all patients in the holdout sample. To do so, navigate to the **Predict** screen for the selected model, add the optional features *discharge_disposition_id* and *readmitted* through the **Optional Features** dropdown. Select "Holdout" from the second dropdown menu, and then select **Compute Predictions** in the field next to it. Once downloaded, it is possible to open the data in any data tool and remove any row containing *discharge_disposition_ids* that are not "Discharge to Home." In this case, 1,219 of the patients were discharged to home, and another 126 had "NA" or "Not Mapped," which we decided to include, for a total of 1,345 or 67.25% of the overall dataset. Note that the group had a 38.5% readmit rate, which mirrors the overall readmit rate.

Figure 20.5 shows a simple graph that could be created for the presentation. A spreadsheet showing how to calculate this graph is available with the data for the book, titled "Holdout for Discharged to Home 10kDiabetes.xlsx" (see data *A.1*

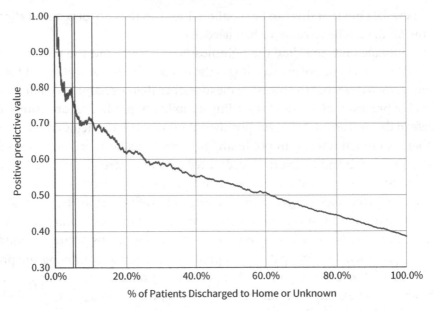

Figure 20.5. Model's Ability to Find Readmits among Patients Discharged to Home.[1]

Assets. Hospital Diabetes directory). The chart shows the positive predictive value (accuracy) at every point among the patients (ordered from left to right by probability, with each point in the graph showing what percent of patients have correctly been categorized as readmitted). Because the effect of providing home health services is not yet known and therefore cannot be used to create a profit chart, one possible proposal might be a one-month pilot program where the 60 patients (4.5% of patients we plan to discharge to home) most likely to be readmitted are given home health services (leftmost orange box). This group is about 78% likely to be readmitted before receiving these services. We can also propose to provide the same service to another set of 60 patients (rightmost orange box). This experiment will examine whether the patients with the highest probability of returning are so sick they cannot be helped. This second group of patients are about a 63% likely to return if not provided these services.[2] You have now provided management with an option for a relatively cheap experiment that will teach us much about patients highly likely to be readmitted.

This slide focuses on convincing management that the model would ultimately save money for the organization if recommendations are implemented properly.

---

[1] The graph in Figure 20.3 was created by simply sorting, in descending order, the patients who were discharged to home in the holdout sample by their probability of returning. After changing the readmit columns to 1 and 0 instead of *True* and *False*, a *Positive Predictive Value* column was created that calculated the sum of readmits from the top to the current row, divided by the count of patients from the top to the current row.

[2] Note that the PPV shown in Figure 20.5 might indicate that the chance of returning for the second window would be higher than 63%, but PPV considers all patients at a cutoff point, so we have to calculate PPV for only the group inside the second window

20.4 Areas Where the Model Struggles

For the seventh slide, arguments are stated in favor of launching a pilot project. Throughout the discussion of this dataset, we have repeatedly noted that the dataset is not a very predictive one. Trusting DataRobot's ability to find predictive value, none of the tests carried out in this book, including the use of cross validation and holdout samples, suggest any problems with the algorithms themselves. It can only be concluded, therefore, that the problem lies with the data. If we are convinced that there is value in this analysis for the patients that the model assigns high probabilities of readmission, and the proposed pilot and educational and support interventions are successes with the current data, arguing for more data is reasonable.

Earlier, two main types of data were discussed:

1. **Internal data:** for this case, we can argue that more data on past visits should be collected for patients who are repeat visitors (per Figure 20.6).[3] Are they repeat visitors for the same problem? It was also seen that predictive ability was extracted from the very limited text in the diagnosis descriptions. Patient records contain a high volume of text that could be further mined for additional features.
2. **External data:** While it is not clear that mining public external data will be a worthwhile exercise for this project, it is likely that this project could benefit from purchased data such as grocery store purchase data, financial data, distance to hospital, and so on. It might be appropriate to argue for a budget to pilot such data.

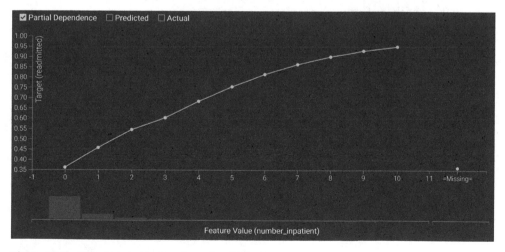

Figure 20.6. Data Related to Past Inpatient Visits Argument.

---

[3] Notice that probabilities and partial dependencies were turned off for this visual. If spending time explaining these can be avoided, all the better. Keep a visual with all the information in the back of the slide-deck, however, in case audience questions require more details.

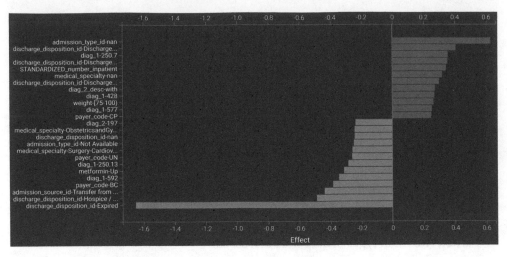

Figure 20.7. Directional Impacts.

20.5 Most Predictive Features

Turn now to slide eight. When explaining a model, directional results tend to make intuitive sense, as shown in Figure 20.7. The fact remains, as stated in earlier comments, that understanding every feature and feature value shown during a presentation is not necessary. It is likely that expired patients and the patients discharged to hospice have been removed at this point. In this case, given that the case focus is on predicting patient readmissions, discussion for this slide will focus on the red bars. Be prepared to develop a story around these findings based on the extensive examination of these features completed earlier.

Remember that while Figure 20.7 provides a wealth of information, not all of it will be of interest to the audience. Next, the discussion turns to different types of features that are useful in model evaluation and presentation.

Communicate Tersely

ML principle: Communicate discoveries effectively and visually (Williams, 2011, 9).

AutoML relevance: ML is complicated. Keep discoveries limited in any one presentation. Focus on the major ones.

20.6 Not All Features Are Created Equal

Often information that assists a model in making high-quality decisions is not helpful in changing practice. In other words, many relationships predicting diabetes patient readmission may be of limited use to the hospital Chief Executive Officer (CEO) because they are immutable (non-actionable insights). The CEO cannot change how many times a patient was admitted to in-patient care in the past, nor can they affect the diagnoses a physician will ascribe to a patient. Therefore, they may prefer presentations to focus on mutable features once model quality has been evaluated.

There are four kinds of features to consider before going into a management presentation:

1. **Features that need to be changed and therefore require a re-run of the models:** In this example, we must remove cases with a *discharge_disposition_id = Expired* or *Hospice*. Following this, it would then be best to re-run the model. As a general rule, when features need to be changed, it is often necessary to then re-run the model after making these changes. Any row with this "expired" value should be removed before generating new models.[4] These features are a special case of target leak in that, while target leak defines a model that is trained with features not available at the time of prediction, for *expired* patients, the hospital staff will never have the opportunity to run the model that will predict the deceased patient's probability of readmission. If there is no time to remove this data before presentations to management, simply be aware of this feature and the fact that, in a minor way, it has negatively affected model creation.

2. **Features requiring further examination:** Preferably examined further with the help of a subject matter expert (SME). These are features about which a manager is likely to ask follow-up questions. An example in the diabetes readmission project is the *admission_type_id = nan*. It is not enough to explain that *nan* means any patient who was not given an admission type ID. The manager is likely to ask *why* these patients were not given an admission type ID.

   If access to an SME is not possible to answer this question, go to the data and create a new column where every row contains a value of *False*, except for the rows missing data in *admission_type_id*. These are coded as *True*. After removing the original *admission_type_id* column, run a fast machine learning process with the new column as the target. Doing so, and then examining the *Variable Effects* (under Insights) will explain why some patients do not have admission type IDs. In this case, the reason is that patients with no admission type ID also are discharged with an ID of "Not Mapped." The *admission_source_id* and *payer_code* are also missing. A quick Google search with some of the values inside the *payer_code* feature suggests that this patient is not with a healthcare insurer; nor are they with a government program such as Medicaid. In other

---

[4] They are removed from the training set not because they are dead per se, but because the model is designed to figure out who is going to be readmitted at the time of release from the hospital. Deceased patients are not released in the same manner as treated patients.

words, these are patients without insurance that the hospital is required to by law provide (often minimal) support. It should come as no surprise that they often return for more help due to the underlying issues of their condition often being left unaddressed in their initial visit.

Other features to be prepared to answer questions about are any features where the feature name does not fully appear in the visuals due to its character length. See the DataRobot screen pictured in Figure 19.6 to identify any feature name ending with three dots (. . .). Hover over them to see what the full text is, and write it down. In future projects, consider shortening such feature names and values for added simplicity. Some examples of features that may need additional care are: *diag_1 = 250.7* (Diabetes with peripheral circulatory disorders), diag_2 = 250.6 (Diabetes with neurological manifestations), Metformin = Up (The person is on the Metformin drug, and their dose was increased). When presenting the model and data, the meaning of any feature/value combination placed in front of a management team *must* be known in full detail; however, do not crowd a PowerPoint presentation with this information. This information can be placed on a separate sheet to be used as notes during the presentation.

3. **Immutable features:** These are features that are good for modeling but are of no value to management if they want to implement corrective actions. An immutable feature is one that a management team cannot change, such as the number of years that have passed since someone entered a given industry after receiving their bachelor's degree (in the case of modeling employee turnover). In the diabetes readmission project, most of the features fall into this class. For example, the fact that a patient was admitted to the Emergency Room is something that cannot be changed. Even if a sign were set up pointing all diabetes patients to another door, it would not change the underlying reality that a patient or an ambulance crew felt they needed urgent attention. Management also cannot change the diagnosis for a given patient, nor can they change whether or not a patient died in the care of the hospital (this is a different modeling project altogether).

4. **Mutable features:** These are the features that management *could* potentially change. Because these are the measures that may be manipulated, it is possible that by doing so, management can improve the status (health, mood, etc.) of the subjects in a given dataset. For example, if employee turnover is predicted by the number of overtime hours worked, management may decide to hire more workers to reduce the need for overtime. In the diabetes readmission example, there are not many mutable features. The given dataset is missing some features about the state of the hospital during admission (which and how many specialists were working, as well as the wait-time in the ER, as primary examples), but there are encouraging hints of feature pliability. For example, when there is no medical specialty coded, this could be evidence of specialists not being available, meaning that the patient was treated by a generalist, a variable that could be addressed in future management decisions. There is also a

reference to the drug Metformin being "upped" for some patients (raising a patient's prescribed dosage). In this case, could it be that this drug is being undersubscribed? Given that the same drug does not show up as a missing in data for patients that are readmitted, this hypothesis may not be reliable; however, it remains worthwhile to examine. A separate listing and discussion of mutable features could be effective content for slide number nine.

Kaiser Permanente, the integrated HMO with massive access to prescription, hospital, and physician data, has saved their patients from detrimental outcomes on multiple occasions, including early detection of the "opioid epidemic," now ravaging the United States, as early as 2009 (Ostrov, 2017). For patients deemed to be at high risk for abuse, Kaiser physicians about to prescribe OxyContin will receive an alert noting this risk. The system also warns the physician when they are about to prescribe a benzodiazepine to patients already taking an opiate painkiller, a combination with potentially lethal results (Ostrov, 2017).

There is a caveat here. Management interference with mutable features often comes with complications. Any time management changes the environment in which a model operates to improve the organization, that model then loses efficacy. However, in the interest of consistent improvements, data scientists must accept this reality and carefully monitor model performance after implementation. Some interventions are less harmful to model performance than others. For example, an intervention that reduces the number of overtime hours worked is not likely to have a negative effect on the model because the underlying truth that overtime hours lead to turnover remains. The only difference in the environment is that the employees work fewer overtime hours than before, and, as such, the model will appropriately predict them as less likely to leave. If, on the other hand, the intervention focuses on making employees enjoy the overtime hours more, perhaps through catered dinners or free massages, then the model may struggle and require retraining.

20.7 Recommended Business Actions

Slide number ten addresses the final part of the presentation, which should contain explicit recommendations for next steps. In this case, three concrete recommendations are available:

1. Implement the model to find the 64% of patients most likely to be readmitted. In the case that educational and support programs have been developed and deemed effective, these at-risk patients should then be targeted as program candidates to reduce their likelihood of readmission.
2. Institute a two-month pilot program targeting 9 percent of patients discharged to home (split by probability as argued in Chapter 20.3). Add home health services to this discharge condition and evaluate the extent to which this patient

group can be further cared for. Keep the pilot program running for one month and leave the window for readmission open for one month after closing the pilot program.

3. Institute a data-extraction-and-purchase pilot program to explore how the patient readmission model can be improved and to what degree.

In the next section, it will be assumed that permission has been given to move forward on at least recommendation #1. Implementing this model will require changes to hospital routine, as well as placing the model into production.

20.8 Exercises

1. What was the reason for waiting so long to unlock the holdout?
2. How can unlocking the holdout help an analyst provide value to management?
3. If the CEO asks for the difference between machine learning and statistics, what would be a viable answer?
4. What are the two types of data that the model may struggle with?
5. Why is the leadership team not presented with the machine learning code?

SECTION VI

IMPLEMENT, DOCUMENT, AND MAINTAIN

Now comes the final section of the machine learning life cycle. Consider these the most important steps of the entire process. This is the point at which we have the greatest potential to help our organization reap the benefits of machine learning. In traditional information systems development, 60–80% of the cost of a system comes during the maintenance phase, so treat these steps accordingly.

21

Set Up Prediction System

Ploy to Deploy

ML principle: "Don't overlook how the model is to be deployed" (Williams, 2011, 9).
AutoML relevance: Same for ML and AutoML.

After a successful presentation that garners the support needed to implement the new system, it is time to set the system up. Help from the corporate IT function will likely be necessary to make system predictions available during the business decision process, as well as to help train users. Setting up a prediction system means that, at the decision point where data is available (this case is with regard to a patient about to be released from the hospital), the model is given the data on that patient to in turn provide a probability that this patient will be readmitted within a month. This probability is then formulated as a suggested decision for the user of the system. A probability above a specified threshold might qualify a patient for the educational intervention outlined in Chapter 20. A probability above a higher threshold among patients *discharged to home* may further qualify this subset of patients for the more expensive home health service.

21.1 Retraining Model

Recall the possibility that the best model developed in DataRobot may not perform entirely as well as expected when put into practice, as suggested by the holdout sample LogLoss score being lower than that of the cross validation sample. One reason a model's success rate can be lower than expected, perhaps even deteriorating over time, is that the environment being modeled changes subtly as time passes. Also, the model, in this case, was trained with data randomly selected from an unknown period (the period during which the patients selected for inclusion visited the hospital). Similarly, the performance of the model was validated with data collected during the same period. In this case, there was no alternative course of action, as this dataset provided no access to the date of the patient visit (perhaps to maintain patient privacy). That being said, there are steps that can be taken to improve predictive ability, perhaps even to the point of negative such concerns. Begin by finding the top model, and clicking the orange "plus" sign, per Figure 21.1.

Automated Machine Learning for Business. Kai R. Larsen and Daniel S. Becker, Oxford University Press. © Oxford University Press 2021.
DOI: 10.1093/oso/9780190941659.003.0021

Figure 21.1. Selected *ENET Blender*.

Figure 21.2. Top Blender Model after Rerun.

Since validation scores are no longer needed to order models, nor is holdout data necessary to evaluate for overfitting, 100% of the data can now be utilized to create a model. Click the orange plus and change the "Snap to" option from *Autopilot Stage II (64%)* to *Full Dataset (100%)*. Click **Run With New Sample Size**. DataRobot will now rerun any model used as input into the blender model at 100% of the sample size. This includes all three top non-blender models sorted by cross validation. It also includes any model required by one of those eight models.

Figure 21.2 shows the result of running the *ENET Blender* with 100% of the data. Notice that DataRobot again provides Validation, Cross Validation, and Holdout performances, this time marked with an asterisk. These are estimated numbers and therefore should be treated with a degree of caution. Note that the results for 100% of the data are better than those for the 64% sample for the holdout sample, as expected. Under the assumption that this new model is now the best model available, it can be used for the remaining work.

The next step is now to make this model available in the business process flow.

21.2 Choose Deployment Strategy

DataRobot provides several different model deployment strategies. It is the user's job to determine which one best suits the organization's needs. The deployment strategies range from very easy to implement and use to requiring extensive experience and assistance from the organization's IT department. These strategies will be discussed in approximate order of difficulty, beginning with the easiest approaches first. (Depending on user skills, these may be ordered differently.) Only the first approach, drag-and-drop scoring, requires no programming skills.

1. Drag-and-drop
2. Application Programming Interface (API)
3. DataRobot Prime
4. Batch
5. In-place with Spark

Drag-and-drop Scoring is accessed through the *Predict* screen of the selected model, per Figure 21.3. Since this screen has been addressed previously, specific details will be passed over apart from the need to upload all relevant data in a file containing the features used to create the model. The file does not need to include a target since this is what DataRobot is now preparing to predict. Go to the **Predict** menu, followed by the **Make Predictions** menu.

After uploading a file to DataRobot, click **Compute Predictions**. DataRobot will apply the model to all the uploaded data, after which the results can be downloaded by clicking **Download**. As demonstrated in Figure 21.3, if you upload a prediction dataset containing a target column, DataRobot will assume that you may want to run an *external test*, checking the model against yet another dataset unknown to the model.

Be aware that it is possible to add up to five features from the dataset to the downloadable file. It is recommended that at least the reference *id* column is included to avoid having to manually match the results based on the row *id* provided by DataRobot. Note that *drag-and-drop* is a slow approach to scoring and will not allow files larger than 1GB. This limitation should not be a problem, as it is possible to split a large file into files below 1GB and upload them separately. If a project does require such quantities of data, however, and additional data continues streaming in at a fast pace, *drag-and-drop* is not the ideal approach to scoring. Be aware that once a file is uploaded for scoring through the *drag-and-drop* interface, this file also becomes

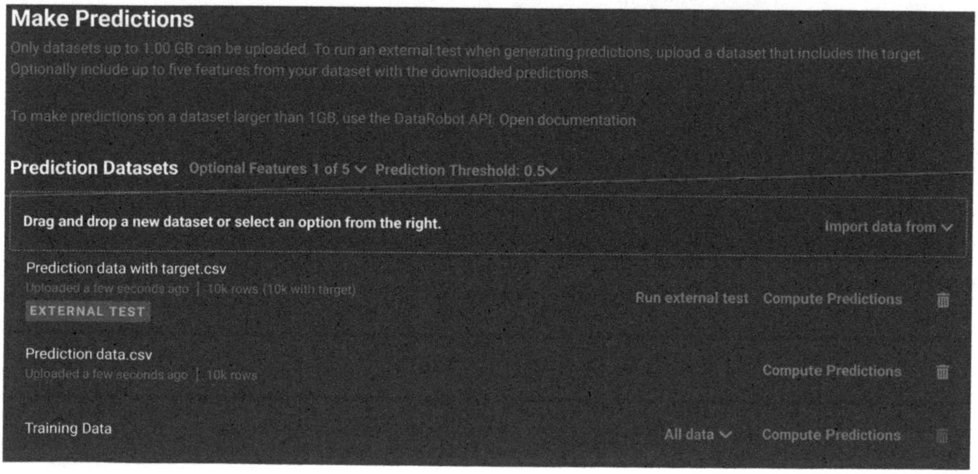

Make Predictions

Only datasets up to 1.00 GB can be uploaded. To run an external test when generating predictions, upload a dataset that includes the target.
Optionally include up to five features from your dataset with the downloaded predictions.

To make predictions on a dataset larger than 1GB, use the DataRobot API. Open documentation

Prediction Datasets Optional Features 1 of 5 ∨ Prediction Threshold: 0.5∨

Drag and drop a new dataset or select an option from the right.   Import data from ∨

Prediction data with target.csv
Uploaded a few seconds ago | 10k rows (10k with target)   Run external test   Compute Predictions   🗑
EXTERNAL TEST

Prediction data.csv
Uploaded a few seconds ago | 10k rows   Compute Predictions   🗑

Training Data   All data ∨   Compute Predictions   🗑

Figure 21.3. Predict Screen.

available in the *Prediction Explanations* window (see Chapter 19.8 for a review of prediction explanations). Note the *prediction threshold* option, which specifies the probability above which DataRobot will predict that a case is a positive case (in our setting, a patient that will be readmitted). Your selected probability may come from your profit curve evaluation or from evaluating your confusion matrix for multiple cutoff points of the Prediction Distribution figure (ROC Curve screen).

API Scoring is relatively straightforward for those able to program in *R* or *Python*. An Application Programming Interface (API) is created on the DataRobot server, allowing a developer to write a program that uploads new patient data to the API, which then returns a probability that the patient will be readmitted. Figure 21.4 shows how to deploy the model to a DataRobot server. While most student and demo accounts will not have access to deployment, clicking on **Show Example** will show example *Python* code with API connection information, which may be run with your modeling workers rather than dedicated prediction servers. Figure 21.4 shows that example code for this particular project. Although it is beyond the scope of this book to detail *Python* and *R*, many functions covered here may be programmed through *Python* and *R* by accessing the DataRobot packages. The *Python* package is available at http://pythonhosted.org/datarobot/. In *R*, you access the DataRobot package. Both come with exceptional introductory information on their

```
# Usage: python datarobot_shared_prediction.py <input-file.csv>
# Note: Before running this, change API_TOKEN to the value on your profile page
# We highly recommend that you update SSL certificates with:
#    pip install -U urllib3[secure] certifi
# This example snippet makes use of the DataRobot API Python client, installable with:
#    pip install "datarobot"
# See https://pypi.python.org/pypi/datarobot/ for more information and documentation.
import sys

import datarobot as dr


API_TOKEN = 'NQ1NDA4NWNmNU1Y2QxZDQxNzNNDdiOnVMeXlRMlZ0cktzV21McEd5ZjFyVhKRFR
nbFhIUk93'
PROJECT_ID = '5f0ca065f688220b6071a4f'
MODEL_ID = '5f4e72fabb594b44b65eac0'
MAX_WAIT = 60 * 60  # Maximum number of seconds to wait for prediction job to finish

dr.Client(endpoint='https://app.datarobot.com/api/v2', token=API_TOKEN)
project = dr.Project.get(PROJECT_ID)
model = dr.Model.get(PROJECT_ID, MODEL_ID)

# Upload dataset to make predictions
pred_dataset = project.upload_dataset(sys.argv[1])

# Make predictions on your data
pred_job = model.request_predictions(pred_dataset.id)
predictions = pred_job.get_result_when_complete(max_wait=MAX_WAIT)
for row in predictions.iterrows():
    print(row)
```

Figure 21.4. Sample Python Code for API Access.

use. Third-party companies, including Talend and Alteryx, have developed tools for connecting to DataRobot APIs.

Of the programming interfaces available for connecting to DataRobot, only the API approach allows access to the prediction explanations, which can be important for low-volume predictions. For example, an employee in charge of the patient intervention plan generated in previous chapters could be provided with more information than simply receiving a message that the patient is likely to be readmitted and has been selected for intervention. This employee could also be supplied with the top three reasons why the patient was flagged, allowing for evaluation of whether or not intervention is likely to be helpful in this case, as well as information for providing feedback to the patient. The system may suggest, for example, that the patient was selected because of their five inpatient visits during the last year, their low body weight (in the 50–75 pounds range), and their two outpatient procedures during the last year.

DataRobot Prime Scoring (not available in student version) creates an approximation of the selected model, available as code in the *Python* and *Java* programming languages. *Prime Scoring* availability depends on DataRobot account type and is not made available in student versions of the system. DataRobot cannot guarantee that this code is as accurate as the original model, but it is often quite closely comparable (in the experience of this book's authors). This Prime-generated code may then be placed into the business workflow. Figure 21.6 shows the *Prime* option display after clicking *Run DataRobot Prime* (RUN DATAROBOT PRIME). The disadvantage of this approach is that it is now an in-house responsibility to integrate and maintain the model code. The advantage, on the other hand, is that it provides vendor independence and allows the use of an organization's servers for processing of new cases. Note that prime may not be run on the 100% version of our model, so Figure 21.5 shows the run on the 64% *ENET Blender*.

The *Prime* job generates a set of rules based on the original model (See Figure 21.6) and automatically suggests the model's lowest optimization measure (*LogLoss* in this case). These settings can be changed by clicking another of the radio buttons if a less complex model is preferred (fewer rules).

At this point, the option is available to **Generate and Download Code**. This option will generate Python code in this case, as shown in Figure 21.7, which may then be implemented within an organization's existing code base.

Batch Scoring uses the DataRobot API to upload and score multiple large files in parallel. The code required to use batch scoring is available at https://github.com/datarobot/batch-scoring.

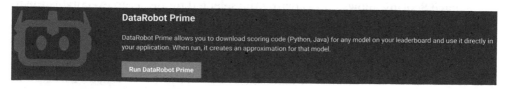

Figure 21.5. DataRobot Prime Screen for 64% *ENET Blender*.

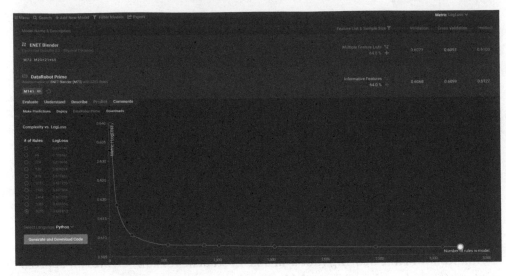

Figure 21.6. DataRobot Prime Model.

```
import calendar
from datetime import datetime
from collections import namedtuple
import re
import sys
import time
import os

import numpy as np
import pandas as pd

PY3 = sys.version_info[0] == 3
if PY3:
    string_types = str,
    text_type = str
    long_type = int
else:
    string_types = basestring,
    text_type = unicode
    long_type = long

def predict(row):
    A1Cresult = row[u'A1Cresult']
    ...
```

Figure 21.7. Sample Python Code from Prime Model.

In-place Scoring allows for exporting the selected model as an executable file to be used in an *Apache Spark* environment. *Spark* is a fast and widely distributed data processing environment. Note that, while this approach is ideal for organizations already using a *Spark* cluster in which scoring of many cases is necessary, it can be slower than other approaches for small case sets due to the overhead involved in deploying *Spark* tasks.

The specifics of how these five deployment strategies work are less important for those who are reading this text as an introduction to machine learning. Nevertheless, the DataRobot approaches do offer some generalizable lessons for understanding how new cases are scored with probability and are then placed into a business process. A final caution is that no general-purpose machine learning platform can explicitly state what actions should be taken based on a given probability or predicted outcome. This information must be programmed as a next step after receiving a probability. For example, in the hospital readmittance case, a probability threshold was chosen such that 62% of patients would be selected for a low-cost intervention plan. The development of the plan, triggering the prompt to move a patient into the intervention queue, and tracking the plan's value to the organization will still be the job of the machine learning analyst working with the assistance of in-house subject matter experts.

21.3 Exercises

1. Why retrain the model with 100% of the data?
2. Select two deployment strategies. What is the difference between them?
3. What is an API Token and what is it used for?

22

Document Modeling Process for Reproducibility

<table>
<tr><td colspan="1">History Repeats Itself</td></tr>
<tr><td>ML principle: "Stress repeatability and efficiency, using scripts for everything" (Williams, 2011, 9).
AutoML relevance: Same for ML and AutoML.</td></tr>
</table>

22.1 Model Documentation

Documenting the modeling process is where projects most often fail. Those attracted by the "search for truth" aspect of machine learning are seldom motivated by the required documentation that follows a machine learning project. Most would much rather create the model, implement it, and then move on to the next business problem; however, proper documentation is critical for others to understand what actions were taken to accomplish project results, as well as the justification for the project to exist. While obvious after extended work on a project, over time, the justifications for adding a step to an organizational process must stand up to scrutiny.

Consider model documentation as an opportunity to do more of the desirable central machine learning work. By attending to the details of articulating project processes while a project remains fresh in mind, an analyst can save future time spent on the project. Work under the assumption that the project will need to be revisited within a year, and think through what information would be helpful to have immediate access to at that time. Implement the system and write documentation that provides all relevant information for future project stakeholders.

Pay attention to the following: Where did the data come from? How was the data processed? What parameters or selections were used when creating and selecting the model? How is the model used within the business?

In this book's example, ideally, the hospital already has a documentation system in place. It needs to be considered how to document the new process(es) in the hospital's system so that those charged with maintaining it can access the necessary information. Without taking these measures, the project may very well fail. Assuming that such a system is successfully in place, the next step is to specify the business problem

Automated Machine Learning for Business. Kai R. Larsen and Daniel S. Becker, Oxford University Press. © Oxford University Press 2021.
DOI: 10.1093/oso/9780190941659.003.0022

in the project documentation. This step should be easy, as this has already been done at the beginning of the machine learning process.

Next, document where the data came from. In this case, it is likely that the data came from the Electronic Health Record (EHR) system for the hospital. It is important to document the exact queries used to access the data as well as the exact code used to transform the data into a machine learning accessible dataset. It is possible that this may have been done in a backward fashion; for example, if yesterday's date were May 15, 2018, the starting point for selecting data cases would be April 15, 2018, beginning with the last patient released from the hospital that day (the starting date is 30 days earlier, as this is the selected timeline for the target). For this patient, moving a month into the future would allow for the examination of whether that patient returned to the hospital while looking a year into the past provides data for their number of inpatient visits. As mentioned, all the programming code used for such transformations must be carefully kept not only to enable future maintenance (implementing changes as necessitated by changes in the environment) but also because the same process must be followed before sending data for scoring.

The next step in documentation is to specify all the steps taken within DataRobot. In this case, that means not using the advanced options, but rather taking the following steps: using *LogLoss* as the optimization criterion, using the autopilot to build the models, selecting the best model based on cross validation, and running that model with 100% of the data. This process has been simplified to illustrate the important point that every step leading to model implementation needs to be detailed. This even includes documenting the DataRobot account used to create the model, as well as the name of the project under that account.

Finally, the business rules for the use of the model and the probability thresholds must be recorded, along with information from the IT group about how the model was set up in the IT environment.

22.2 Exercises

1. Why is documentation so important?
2. Why is documentation so often not created?

23
Create Model Monitoring and Maintenance Plan

23.1 Potential Problems

When documenting the newly installed system, it is also necessary to create a monitoring and maintenance plan. Such plans serve to inform others about what to do in the event of changes in the environment that stand to impact the effectiveness of the model. This chapter is about detecting when the model performance has deteriorated such that the model must be retrained.

Potential environmental changes, either within the business data environment or in the outside world, can be widely varied. For example, there may be changes in data format within the electronic health records (EHR) system (or another database) that provided the original data. Perhaps the system that originally extracted the data from the EHR as comma-separated files may now save files in other formats such as XML or JSON. As such, the values extracted from the system may have been changed in the EHR by the introduction of new codes or the removal of old codes. Perhaps more difficult to detect are real-world environmental changes. Take, for example, that the ailments of diabetes patients may change in a positive direction (lower rates of occurrence). These changes might result from new medications or the detection of deleterious effects caused by interactions between a new medication and other medications. Regardless of its nature, all changes that impact the model's efficacy require the development of strategies for changing the machine learning workflow, but whereas data format changes will require meticulous tracking and addressing the changes before continuing the use of the model, environmental changes may require developing a new model.

23.2 Strategies

The good news is that in such cases, DataRobot will fail rather than attempt to make the best of the available data. If a column is removed from the prediction data, the system fails. This outcome can be expected whether a column is missing from the data or a column name has simply been altered.

To avoid model failure, it is a good idea to rerun the model as soon as sufficient new data is available (business costs permitting). When doing so, it is important

Automated Machine Learning for Business. Kai R. Larsen and Daniel S. Becker, Oxford University Press. © Oxford University Press 2021. DOI: 10.1093/oso/9780190941659.003.0023

to wait until the target value is also available. In the case of the hospital diabetes project, this takes a month, but because data was collected starting a month before model implementation, each day immediately brings a new set of cases available to be added to a modified model training set. In such cases, the most challenging problem to manage may be that the analyst (or team) introduced the change. If the hospital intervention plan works as intended, the patients assigned to the plan will have a lower readmission rate. Retraining a model with these patients presents the problem of introducing target leak by adding a feature stating that a patient was assigned to the intervention plan. Training the model without information on which patients were assigned intervention would likely lead to weaker relationships between features and a target. The model would struggle in this case because more patients are doing better than their features would indicate under the old model. Regardless of the reason for deteriorating model performance, early detection is paramount. One approach for detecting declining performance is through evaluating the training data against new data. The methodology here is to create a new target that specifies whether a case was used to create the original model or whether that case was retrieved from the production system after the model was used for prediction. Figure 23.1 shows an example of how such data might look. This approach does not require waiting for target values to be available, which is a major benefit, especially when rating cases such as loans where it may be a long time before the case outcome becomes known.

Once a sufficient set of production cases are available, machine learning may be run with the source of the data as the target. If the produced model is capable of distinguishing between the two sets of data, this would be an indication that the business context has changed enough to warrant model retraining with access to additional data that includes more recent patient cases. Currently, no clear rules exist for determining what threshold to use for such alerts, but it is recommended to use either the same measure used for model selection or the Matthews Correlation

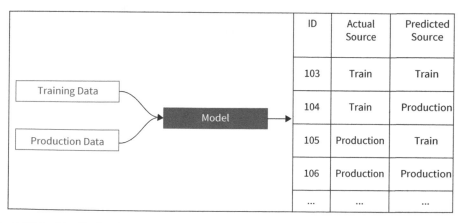

	ID	Actual Source	Predicted Source
Training Data → Model → Production Data →	103	Train	Train
	104	Train	Production
	105	Production	Train
	106	Production	Production
	...	...	...

Figure 23.1. Monitoring System Data.

Coefficient (see Chapter 17.3 for a reminder on MCC). It is also recommended to automate threshold testing and set up message and alert transmissions to signal when the determined threshold is reached.

23.3 Exercises

1. What are some reasons a model needs to be retrained?
2. When would you, as an analyst, recommend to the Chief Analytics Officer that a model is retrained?

24

Seven Types of Target Leakage in Machine Learning and an Exercise

---

Reliable Target Values Drive Everything

ML principle: The reliability of the target values in the training data is a fundamental problem in ML. When errors exist, simpler models may be preferable (Witten, Frank, & Hall, 2011). AutoML relevance: Same for ML and AutoML.

24.1 Types of Target Leakage

Many experts consider target leakage one of the most insidious problems of automated machine learning. In this book, the term "target leakage" (aka data leakage) will be defined in a broader scope than usual, as this provides an opportunity to discuss related issues of importance. Our definition of target leakage considers a target leak to have occurred when the model performance metrics are better than what is possible in a real-world scenario due to the inclusion of *illegitimate* features in the model. This definition is expansive and goes beyond the conventional description, which focuses only on features that are not available at the time of prediction. It is worth noting that feature illegitimacy often depends on both the context of model usage and the reporting of model performance.

The clearest example of target leakage comes from the use of the target itself to predict the target. Take, as an example of this, a party game: you claim to be a great prognosticator of people's ages. You require only one feature to do so. When you ask them how old they were on this date a year ago, no one is impressed that you can add one to their answer, and the impressiveness or validity of your prediction disappears. Here are seven types of target leak:

1. The *model contains one or more features that are not available to the model at the time of prediction*. For example, when building a model of whether a patient who is about to be released from the hospital is likely to be readmitted, the inclusion of their blood-sugar level during their next visit would be predictive. No such test results would be available for patients never again readmitted.

Automated Machine Learning for Business. Kai R. Larsen and Daniel S. Becker, Oxford University Press. © Oxford University Press 2021.
DOI: 10.1093/oso/9780190941659.003.0024

2. *Time is an essential predictor of the target, but the model was evaluated with cases that happened before some cases in the training set.* This type of target leak is especially insidious because the features used to build the model exist at the time of prediction. By allowing the model to "know" the future, it may be aware of a larger variance in the target or a feature that becomes salient only in the future. For example, consider a model designed to predict exercise behavior. We have ten months of daily data ending on February 28. With a traditional validation approach, the model has access to data showing that exercise behaviors tend to increase on and after January 1 due to New Year's resolutions. Alternatively, an appropriate time-aware validation approach would set aside the last two months of data for evaluation. The time-aware approach will provide more accurate performance metrics for the model. Detecting this type of target leak requires careful attention to timelines and is addressed in DataRobot through the option of *Time-aware Modeling*, covered in Chapter 25.

3. *The model contains one or more features that, while available to the model at the time of prediction, do not occur in the real world.* One example encountered in the hospital readmissions example was hidden inside the *discharge_disposition_id* feature and one-hot encoded into a separate feature: whether the patient had *expired* during the visit. This feature was predictive of the target (deceased patients are never readmitted to the hospital), but dead patients also never show up to be released and have the model rate their likelihood of readmission. While the resulting model will work, like target leakage 2 above, it contributes to incorrect performance metrics. Detecting this type of target leak requires domain knowledge and careful evaluation of the included features.

4. *The model contains one or more features that do not make sense for the model's use-cases.* In the hospital readmissions example, a key use-case for the model was to determine which patients would receive home health service or higher levels of service, such as being transferred to a skilled nursing facility (SNF). In the example case, certain features were removed by the exclusion of patients slated for any discharge outcome other than discharge-to-home (example: by removing all patients who had a *discharge_disposition_id* equal to "Discharged/transferred to SNF," an AutoML software will not have the option of creating a one-hot encoded feature to deal with this categorical feature). Detection of this type of target leak requires an understanding of the problem statement along with possible planned interventions or end-use of the model.

5. *The model contains one or more features that interact with the operationalization of the target.* To show how troublesome the *discharge_disposition_id* feature was, note that the researchers who collected and shared the original hospital readmissions dataset likely failed to realize that their coding system for discharged patients gave some patients less time to return than others. With a cutoff of readmittance within 30 days, hundreds of patients who were

transferred to another short-term hospital, rehabilitation units of a hospital, or another inpatient care facility were potentially misclassified. Many, if not all, of these patients were likely under the care of physicians at a hospital for a timeframe ranging from one day to several years, significantly decreasing their natural tendency to be readmitted. Detecting this type of target leak requires careful attention to timelines when assembling training data for a model.

6. *The model was created with the help of knowledge about the target values collected from outside sources.* This type of target leak is mostly a problem in data science competitions. For example, if you go to Kaggle.com and check out the leaderboard for their *Titanic* training competition, you will find that several competitors have created models that 100% correctly predict who lived and died when the *Titanic* sunk. Which of the following is more likely? Is it possible to develop a model that can correctly factor in all the uncertainties of thousands of desperate people fighting for their lives in a situation where there are only enough lifeboats for half the passengers? Or is there a greater likelihood that the person who created the model looked up a list of surviving *Titanic* passengers and submitted the correct answers for the test set? Kaufman et al. (2012) refers to this phenomenon as *external leakage* and discussed the IJCNN 2011 Social Network Challenge in which data scientists were asked to predict whether a set of 8,960 potential relationships existed. Once participants realized that the data came from Flickr, they were able to look up the target value for 60% of the evaluation set. Detecting and protecting against this type of target leakage is exceedingly hard, but when teaching students, inspection of assignment code to ensure no use of outside data is paramount, even to the point of regenerating student models based on reported algorithms and hyper-parameters.

7. *The model was created based on data collected from individuals aware of their own target status.* When surveying people to find the features important in predicting whether one will go to the gym tomorrow, asking about the features as well as the target in the same survey (or even in separate surveys) introduces (same) method bias (Sharma, Safadi, Andrews, Ogunbona & Crawford, 2014). Even with a good research design that separately checks the gym records to see if subjects showed up the next day, odds are that the participant already knows quite well whether he or she will go to the gym the next day due to habit and pre-set schedules. In fact, some research shows that survey methodology often focuses on internal measures of statistical fit rather than external measures— what is used primarily in machine learning. This focus on internal validity of models supported by test cases rather than prediction on cases unknown to the model results in surveys often producing little more than what can be discerned from a simple machine-learning analysis of the survey question text (Arnulf, Larsen, Martinsen & Bong, 2014; Arnulf, Larsen, Martinsen & Egeland, 2018; Gefen & Larsen, 2017).

24.2 A Hands-on Exercise in Detecting Target Leakage

In Chapter 2, the two types of AutoML were introduced: context-specific tools vs. general platforms. Because context-specific tools, such as Salesforce Einstein, are programmed to use only specific features within a larger system, target leakage is generally not a problem. Unfortunately, for every other area of machine learning, both manual and automatic, it is up to the data scientist to address target leakage manually.

To better understand the first type of target leak (for example, *the model contains one or more features that are not available to the model at the time of prediction*), take the following exercise using a dataset from this book. The dataset is found in Appendix A.6 and consists of real data downloaded from Lending Club. The problem statement here is as follows: you want to invest in 36-month loans, which have average interest rates of 12.7%, but there is a high level of risk in that, even during stable economic times, 14% of these loans are eventually charged off. Your goal is to find the loans that have an attractive combination of probability-of-repayment and high interest rates.

Start a new project by clicking the DataRobot logo in the upper left corner and upload the file named *LendingClub_2007_2014_Cleaned_Reduced.csv* (Appendix A.6). Select *loan_status* as the target, and start a *Quick* modeling process. As soon as the preliminary operations are over, you should see the screen displayed in Figure 24.1.

When hovering over the green bars in Figure 24.1 it can be seen that five features are highly predictive of the target (represented by their normalized value scores). The

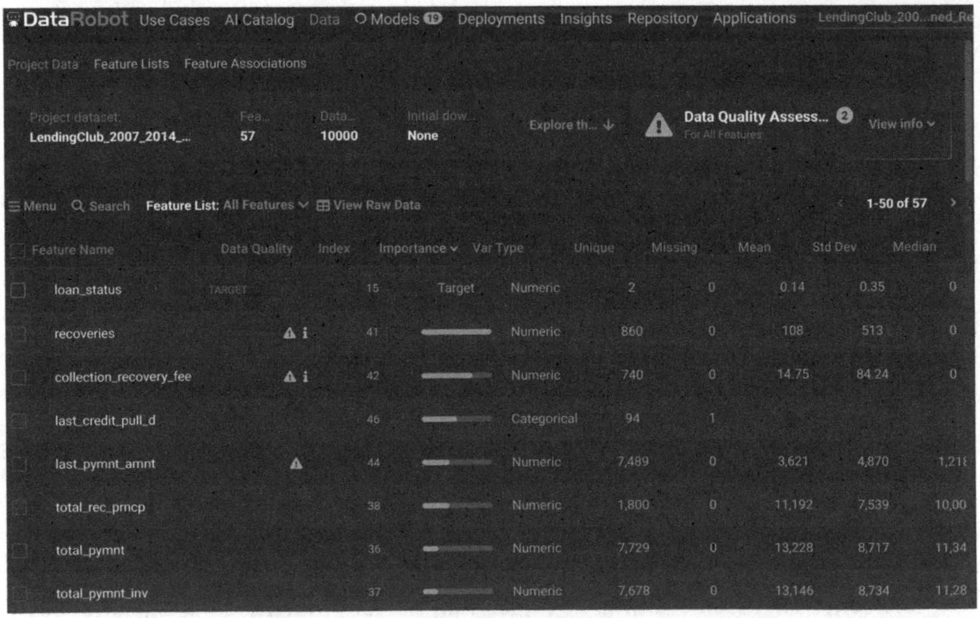

Figure 24.1. Importance Scores for Detecting Target Leakage.

scores give an immediate indication that there may be target leakage in the model. This seems especially likely given that the model seeks to predict a complex human behavior (repayment of a loan). In a case like this, domain knowledge, or at the very least access to a data dictionary, is needed to understand the features. Starting from the top of the list, the most predictive feature, *recoveries*, is defined as "post charge off gross recovery." *Wikipedia* (2018) defines *charge-off* as:

> The **declaration by a creditor** (usually a credit card account) that an amount of debt is unlikely to be collected. This occurs when a consumer becomes severely delinquent on a debt. Traditionally, creditors will make this declaration at the point of six months without payment (para. 1).

This definition grants possible insight into the process of lending on Lending Club as laid out in Figure 24.2. While the entirety of the process may be unclear to those who haven't either borrowed or lent money on Lending Club, it can be reasonably assumed that the process starts with a person wanting a loan and filling out a form on the Lending Club website. Some of the features available (Appendix A.6), such as *purpose*, come from this application. A *purpose* is defined as "a category provided by the borrower for the loan request," the majority of which are classified as *debt consolidation*, *paying off credit card*, and *home improvement*. Find and examine this feature under the *Data* tab (search for it if necessary). Notice that the green importance bar barely registers, which is common for consumer-provided information without target-leakage.

In the second step of Figure 24.2, Lending Club will do due diligence to remove unserious applicants, fraud cases, and borrowers who Lending Club believes are highly unlikely to pay back the loan. These loans are never visible to the data scientist here, which is one reason for caution in generalizing the findings from this Lending Club example to any other setting. Lending Club shares many features from this process, including a categorized version of the lender's credit rating, seen as *grade* and *sub-grade*. These two features are quite predictive. Lending Club also shares several less predictive features, such as information on existing credit lines: for instance, *open_acc* ("the number of open credit lines in the borrower's credit file") and *total_acc* ("the total number of credit lines currently in the borrower's credit file"). Interestingly, Lending Club shares some features in the downloadable files that are

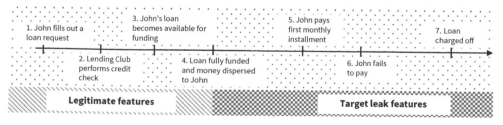

Figure 24.2. Importance Scores for Detecting Target Leakage.

not shown in the manual investing screen outlining the available information at the time for decision making, such as *tax_liens* ("number of tax liens"). For this example, these features can be considered target leakage for a person making investment decisions through the screen shown in Figure 24.3.

In Step 3, Lending Club decides to make John's loan available for funding. New features are now stored, including the interest rate (*int_rate*), which is quite predictive, but does not have a full green bar. It is worth noting that Lending Club likely sets such interest rates based on their own machine learning algorithms. In Step 3, several questions become relevant, including whether other funders and their actions can be observed. Additionally, how fast does the loan get funded? While it does not seem that the dataset at hand enables a wisdom-of-the-crowd approach, this is something to keep in mind in case other Lending Club datasets have the date/time of first release of the loan prospect, as well as the date/time of full funding.

In Step 4, John receives his money and takes all his friends to a hoedown to square dance, spending about half of the cash on whiskey. The moment that loan was fully financed, we are into target-leakage territory. John is right to celebrate. At this point none of his behaviors can be used to evaluate his likelihood of paying back the loan, and, more important, his behaviors cannot be used to predict whether other people like John will pay back their loans.

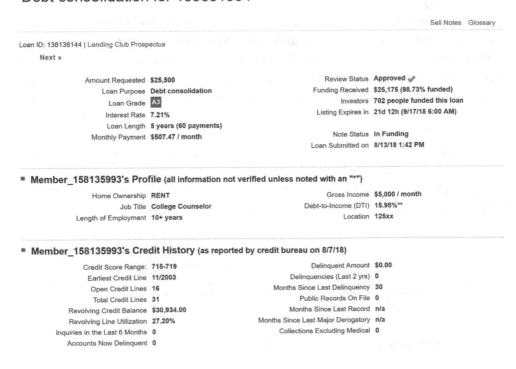

Debt consolidation for 159631904

Sell Notes Glossary

Loan ID: 138138144 | Lending Club Prospectus

Next »

Amount Requested	$25,500	Review Status	Approved ✔
Loan Purpose	Debt consolidation	Funding Received	$25,175 (98.73% funded)
Loan Grade	A3	Investors	702 people funded this loan
Interest Rate	7.21%	Listing Expires in	21d 12h (9/17/18 6:00 AM)
Loan Length	5 years (60 payments)		
Monthly Payment	$507.47 / month	Note Status	In Funding
		Loan Submitted on	8/13/18 1:42 PM

▪ **Member_158135993's Profile** (all information not verified unless noted with an "*")

Home Ownership	RENT	Gross Income	$5,000 / month
Job Title	College Counselor	Debt-to-Income (DTI)	15.98%**
Length of Employment	10+ years	Location	125xx

▪ **Member_158135993's Credit History** (as reported by credit bureau on 8/7/18)

Credit Score Range:	715-719	Delinquent Amount	$0.00
Earliest Credit Line	11/2003	Delinquencies (Last 2 yrs)	0
Open Credit Lines	16	Months Since Last Delinquency	30
Total Credit Lines	31	Public Records On File	0
Revolving Credit Balance	$30,934.00	Months Since Last Record	n/a
Revolving Line Utilization	27.20%	Months Since Last Major Derogatory	n/a
Inquiries in the Last 6 Months	0	Collections Excluding Medical	0
Accounts Now Delinquent	0		

Figure 24.3. Information Available at the Time of Prediction.

Steps 5 and 6 see John still with some of the money he was originally loaned, and he willingly pays his first monthly payment. Unfortunately, after that, another hoe-down wipes him out financially and he is no longer able to pay the installment when the second month arrives. If one frequently downloads data on Lending Club loans, the information on John's initial success and subsequent failure, as he neglects to pay his monthly installments, is available for loans that are still in process. All features providing information on this process are considered target leakage. Examples include *total_rec_int* ("interest received to date") and *total_rec_late_fee* ("late fees received to date").

Finally, in Step 7, the lender has given up any hope of receiving their money from John and, after doing everything they can (legally) to get their money back, resorts to charging off the loan. This feature may not be used to predict the target because not only does it happen after the time of prediction, it *is* the target. In Chapter 5, a point of focus was how to create a target for the Lending Club dataset, and "Charged off" was one of five statuses that would be coded as a bad loan ("True").

24.3 Exercises

1. For the steps in Figure 24.2 that yielded target leakage features, what types of target leakage were they?
2. What is the difference between target leakage types 1 and 3?
3. What is the difference between target leakage types 3 and 4?
4. Why does it matter whether a model has been trained with features from people who already know their target value?

25
Time-Aware Modeling

Panta Rei—Everything Flows

ML principle: Machine learning generally assumes that the data used to build the model has the same distribution as the data on which the model will be applied. While training data is always retrospective, reality always shifts (Witten et al., 2011).
AutoML relevance: Same for ML and AutoML.

There are contexts in which one or more features, while entirely legitimate for modeling, are illegitimate for model evaluation. More specifically, a functional model could be built and put into production using such features, but these features would have occurred at or even after the data in the validation set, introducing a target leakage problem. Because the algorithm had access to the entire distribution of the target over time, the resulting model would "see" that the overall trend in the target changed, and adjust for it in a way that wouldn't be possible in a real-world situation.

One example where time makes an evaluation illegitimate is when the first 20 days after New Year's Day showed a sharp increase in exercise participation. If we evaluate a model through cross validation (random assignment of days to validation folds) and these 20 days are spread out across the validation folds, it gives an unfair advantage to the algorithm during the training of a model relative to keeping these 20 future-days back and evaluating the model on its ability to predict exercise behavior on those 20 days.

25.1 An Example of Time-Aware Modeling

25.1.1 Problem Statement

Scientists (or perhaps just real estate developers) are clear on the relationship between avocado toast prices and low rates of millennial homeownership. It is therefore crucial to establish the best places for millennials to live where this green treasure is highly available and affordable. The avocado dataset of Appendix A.9 comes to us from the Hass Avocado Board through Justin Kiggins, who set out to determine whether the Avocadopocalypse of 2017 was, in fact, real. Simply put, can millennials have their avocado toast and eat it too?

Automated Machine Learning for Business. Kai R. Larsen and Daniel S. Becker, Oxford University Press. © Oxford University Press 2021.
DOI: 10.1093/oso/9780190941659.003.0025

25.1.2 Data

Open avocado.csv from the Appendix A.9 directory in Excel, and sort by the columns Date, Type, and Region.[1] Doing so will show you that there is one average price per weekly date for each type of avocado (conventional vs. organic), as well as one for each location (i.e., Albany, Atlanta, Denver, etc.). Make a mental note of this, and close Excel without saving the file.

25.1.3 Initialize Analysis

Load the avocado.csv file into DataRobot. Once it has been loaded, pick *Average Price* as the target and take note that because DataRobot found a date in the dataset, the Time-Aware Modeling area is no longer unavailable (grayed out) (Figure 25.1).

Click to **Set up time-aware modeling**, and DataRobot will allow selection of the *Date* feature (Figure 25.2, left screen). Click on the orange *Date*, or manually select it and DataRobot will conduct background calculations for average price on each date. It is worth noting the extreme swings in the prices after generating this view (Figure 25.2, right screen). Perhaps there really was an avocado crisis in 2017?

25.1.4 Time-Aware Modeling Background

If presented with the option, pick **Out-of-Time Validation**. To understand DataRobot's approach to time-aware modeling, start by selecting the advanced options (**Show Advanced Options**). Doing so provides the screen in Figure 25.3.

Figure 25.1. Time-Aware Modeling Available.

---

[1] If Excel does not correctly load the file, go to the *Data* tab and manually import it.

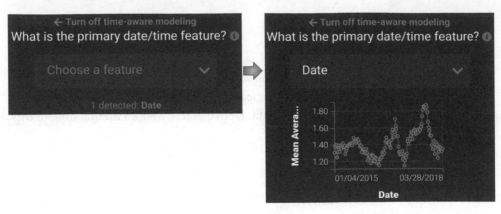

Figure 25.2. Specifying Time-Aware Date.

Taking on one piece at a time from the top, you are asked to choose between *Duration* and *Row Count*. Row count means that the present dataset is one where each training set should be determined by number-of-rows rather than by specific dates. For simplicity's sake, keep the default set to *Duration*.

Next, navigate to the bottom of the screen and observe the blue, green, and dark gray bar named *Backtest 1*. Above it is another blue bar (followed by a red bar) named *Holdout*. These two bars represent how time-aware testing works in DataRobot. First, as is similar in non-time-aware modeling, a holdout sample is locked away (red bar), but, unlike past modeling where 20% of the data was *randomly* selected for the holdout sample, the most *recent* part of the data (16 weeks of data—1,728 observations) is now selected. Firstly, note that this dataset has dates aggregated to weekly data points (one date data point per week). The selected 16 weeks is the period that DataRobot specified under *Validation Length*, as the 112 days suggested to be measured reflect 16 weeks (112 days divided by 7).

Second, notice the *Backtest 1* bar at the bottom of the screen: the rightmost part of the bar is grayed out because DataRobot will (appropriately) abstain from using the part of the sample set aside for holdout for any other purpose. To the left of this gray area is a green rectangle. Green, in this case, indicates the period set aside for validation in a so-called backtest. Finally, note that there is a solid blue bar for both the backtest and holdout, and that the area covered by the bar is the same for both processes. This bar denotes the period of data used to train the model. In this case, it means that the model created for holdout evaluation uses less data than could be used, so that each approach will have access to the same span of time with regard to the date/time range in the dataset, thereby enabling comparable results for the two approaches. Before we put this model into production, it will be crucial to retrain the selected model with all available data.

Two more points to make about this screen (Figure 25.3): First, there is an option to specify a given *Gap Length*, which would appear, if added, in yellow. A gap can be specified if time-gapped features are needed. For example, in this dataset there is a feature containing the *volume* of avocado sold. This feature will be identified later

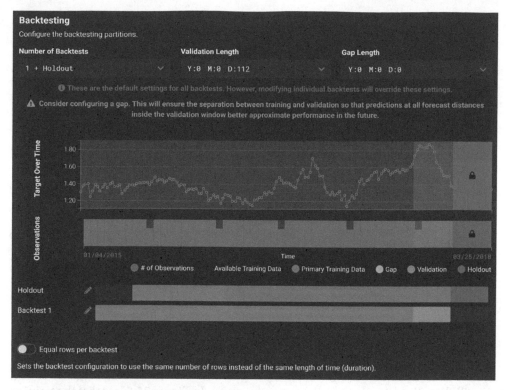

Figure 25.3. Advanced Time Options.

as target-leak, but it would not be unreasonable to time-lag the target. Such time-lagging would mean that for every row available, instead of specifying the avocado price for *that* week, the avocado price for *next* week would be specified. It would then be necessary to enter a gap length of 1 week to allow for the fact that price information is collected a week after sales information. Taking this route would turn this time-aware analysis into a poor man's time series analysis and would not be worthwhile. We cover an appropriate case of time series analysis with the avocado dataset in Chapter 26.

The second point to make about the screen displayed in Figure 25.3 is that it allows for the specification of more than one backtest. Go to the bottom of the screen and specify five backtests, as seen in Figure 25.4. Note that this shrinks the data available to each model such that each model will be comparable in size (shown in Figure 25.4 by the white dotted boxes indicating the period of data available to each algorithm). What this means is that by increasing the quality of the evaluative scheme, the accuracy of the resulting models will likely suffer. Nevertheless, as a test case of time-aware modeling in DataRobot, continuing with five backsets will provide valuable learning. However, for a data scientist frequently working with time-aware models, more backtest segments than the default single backtest conducted by DataRobot will likely not be required after understanding the relationship between validation, backtest, and holdout for a given type of data.

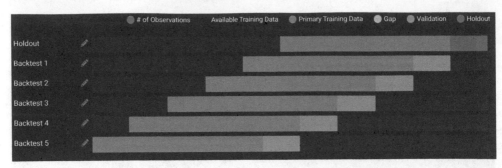

Figure 25.4. Selecting Multiple Backtests.

Figure 25.5. Specific Time Ranges.

A final note before moving on: note that hovering over a part of a fold (or expanding it) will show the date ranges in the respective range. In Figure 25.5, see that the training data for the holdout model starts on July 16, 2016, and ends on December 4, 2017. This feature will be useful for evaluating the final model from this walkthrough against a naïve model in Section 25.1.9.

25.1.5 Data Preparation

Close the *Advanced Options* screen and scroll down to evaluate the features (Figure 25.6). DataRobot has kindly taken the *Date* feature and added a few optional date features. This includes *Day of Month* (the day as a number between 1 and 31 for each date in the dataset), the *Month* (the month as a number between 1 and 12), *Day of Week* (the day of the week as a number between 0 and 6, where 6 is Sunday), and *Year* (the year as a number, i.e., 2015, 2016, 2017).

While the automatically created date-derived features may be sufficient moving forward, it is still worth considering *all* possible date-derived features. To be thorough, click on the *Date* feature and select *Var Type Transform* (Figure 25.7).

Here it will be possible to add two more features based on the *Date* (*Year Day*— day of the year as a number between 1 and 365) and *Week* (week number between 1 and 53).[2] The other date granularisation options already appear in the feature list. It is quite likely that DataRobot is right to exclude these two options from its default, given that it already added *Month* as a number (1–12), and there is little reason to

---

[2] Yes, 53. Contrary to popular opinion, some years have 53 weeks.

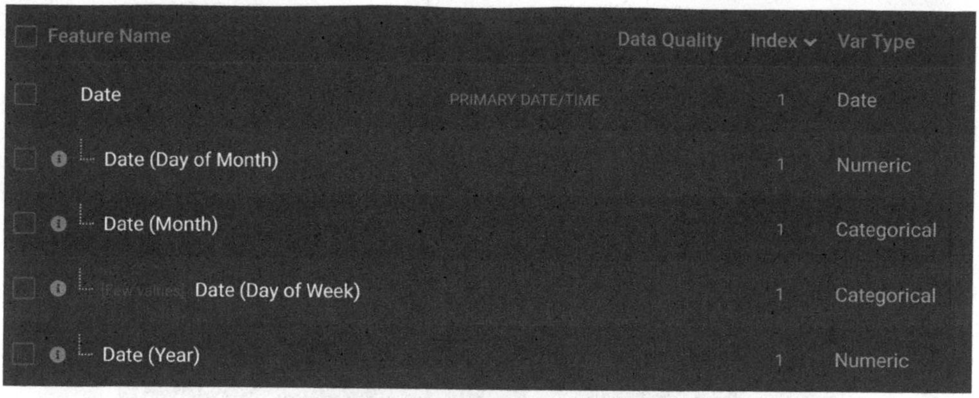

Figure 25.6. Automatically Created Date Features.

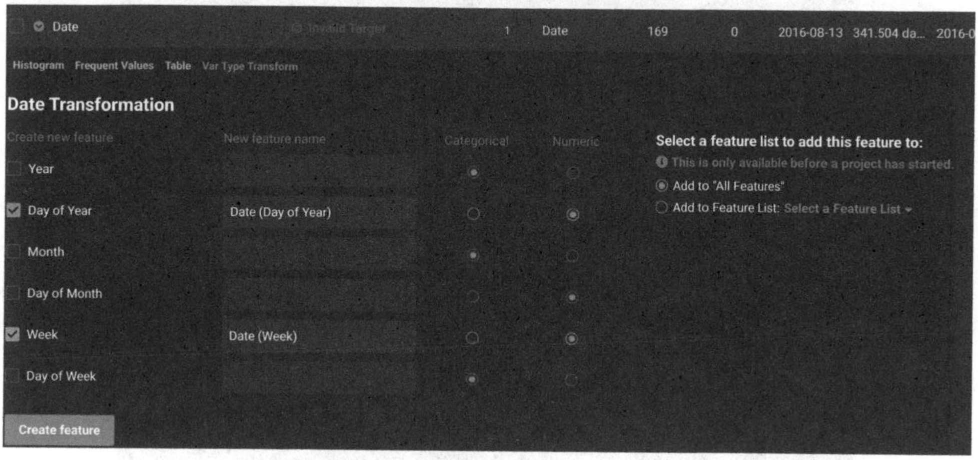

Figure 25.7. Creating Additional Date Features.

believe that avocado prices are specific to a given date (other than National Avocado Day, July 31, of course). Nevertheless, it is good to put any AutoML through its paces and evaluate its decisions on a regular basis. Click **Create Feature**. Next, specific cases of target leakage in this dataset will be identified and evaluated.

In Chapter 24, an example was made explaining how treating longitudinal data as a single dataset is a specific type of target leakage in and of itself. In this chapter's example, that kind of target leak is being protected against by employing time-aware modeling techniques; however, covering this manner of target leakage is not enough on its own—we also need to protect against other forms of target leakage. For example, this dataset contains features specifying the number of avocados sold: *Total Volume* and *Bags Total* (the number of avocados sold in bags of various sizes). These data measures should be treated as a consequence of the pricing decision. As such, the timeline for an avocado sale might go as follows: An avocado of a specific type (*Type, Size*) arrives in a store. It is then priced based on several factors (in this case, mostly unknown factors, but we can imagine that placing a set of avocados in a bag will affect the price), which create the *Average Price* feature (averaged by *Type* and

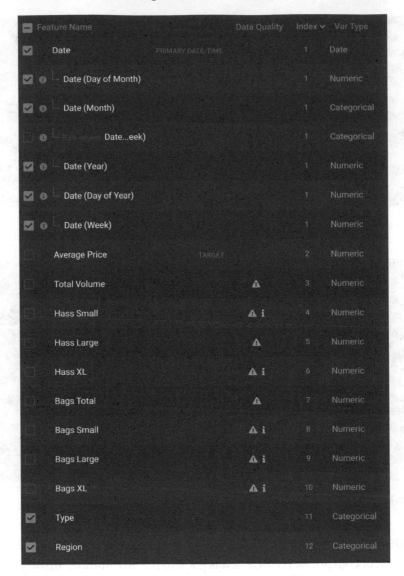

Feature Name		Data Quality	Index ∨	Var Type
☑ Date	PRIMARY DATE/TIME		1	Date
☑ ⓘ ⌐ Date (Day of Month)			1	Numeric
☑ ⓘ ⌐ Date (Month)			1	Categorical
☐ ⓘ ⌐ Date...eek)			1	Categorical
☑ ⓘ ⌐ Date (Year)			1	Numeric
☑ ⓘ ⌐ Date (Day of Year)			1	Numeric
☑ ⓘ ⌐ Date (Week)			1	Numeric
☐ Average Price	TARGET		2	Numeric
☐ Total Volume		⚠	3	Numeric
☐ Hass Small		⚠ i	4	Numeric
☐ Hass Large		⚠	5	Numeric
☐ Hass XL		⚠ i	6	Numeric
☐ Bags Total		⚠	7	Numeric
☐ Bags Small		⚠ i	8	Numeric
☐ Bags Large		⚠ i	9	Numeric
☐ Bags XL		⚠ i	10	Numeric
☑ Type			11	Categorical
☑ Region			12	Categorical

Figure 25.8. Selecting Features.

Region). This process leads to sale information, including *Total Volume.* Are all the features that specify the number of sales then to be considered target-leak?

After careful thought, these features can and should be considered target-leak risks. Take the following example: at the time of pricing a small bag of Hass XL, while it is known that the bag is a small bag that holds extra large avocados, this is not information that makes it into the aggregate data set. The aggregate dataset information notes *how many* small bags of XL avocados *sold*, which is not available data when pricing a bag in real time. The level of analysis would have to be changed to the level of the individual avocado, in which case the avocado's packaging could then become a feature. Figure 25.8 displays the features that were removed because

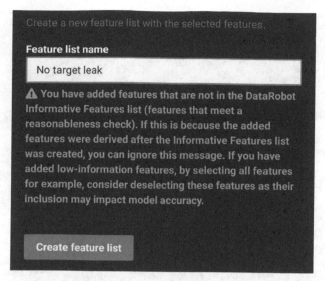

Create a new feature list with the selected features.

Feature list name

No target leak

⚠ You have added features that are not in the DataRobot Informative Features list (features that meet a reasonableness check). If this is because the added features were derived after the Informative Features list was created, you can ignore this message. If you have added low-information features, by selecting all features for example, consider deselecting these features as their inclusion may impact model accuracy.

Create feature list

Figure 25.9. Creating a New Feature List.

of target leakage. *Day of week* has also been removed: since all weekly sales were aggregated on Sunday, there is no meaningful variation in this feature (all rows contain the number six). Change the feature list to "Informative Features" first. After selecting the features to keep, we create a new feature list named *No target leak* (Figure 25.9).

25.1.6 Model Building and Residuals

To begin building the model, set Modeling Mode to Quick and click **Start**. After some time running, return to the *Models* screen to observe the model leaderboard (Figure 25.10).

25.1.7 Candidate Models

To simplify the initial understanding of the model output, change the Metric to *R Squared*, as it provides a commonsense understanding of the extent to which (as a value between 0 and 1) the variance in the target is explained. Go ahead and unlock the holdout data in the rightmost pane. Though it is premature to look at the holdout scores given how little modeling time has been spent on this problem, because this is a learning exercise, it can be unlocked to better understand the model-building process.

As shown in Figure 25.11, DataRobot creates extra models by combining feature lists and reducing features (such as "DR Reduced Feature M15"). Ignoring the model recommended for deployment, we note that when sorting by *All Backtests*, the *Light*

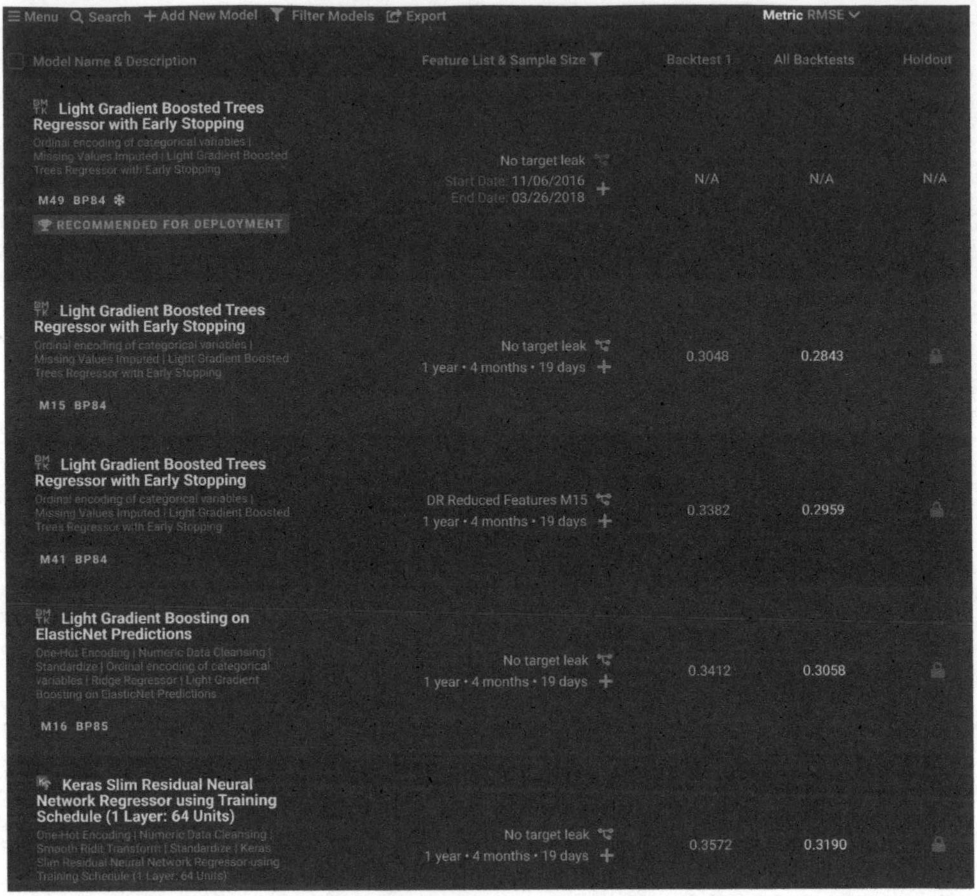

Figure 25.10. Top Model in Leaderboard.

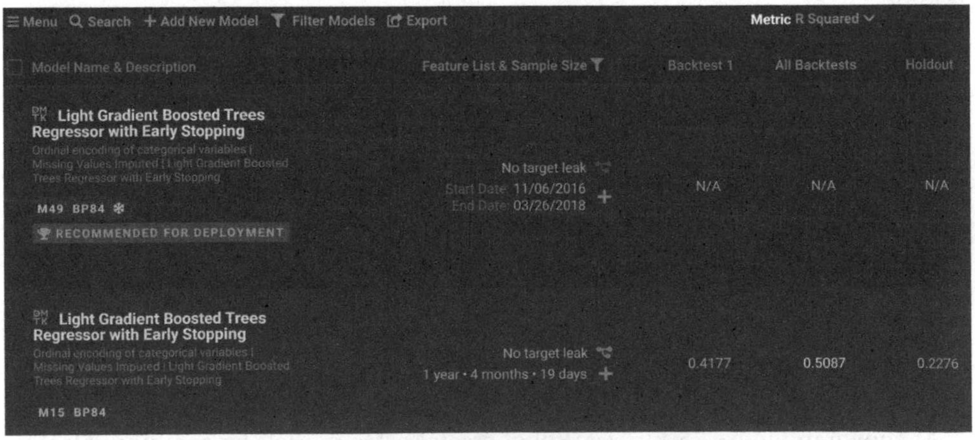

Figure 25.11. Leaderboard Sorted by All Backtests Scores.

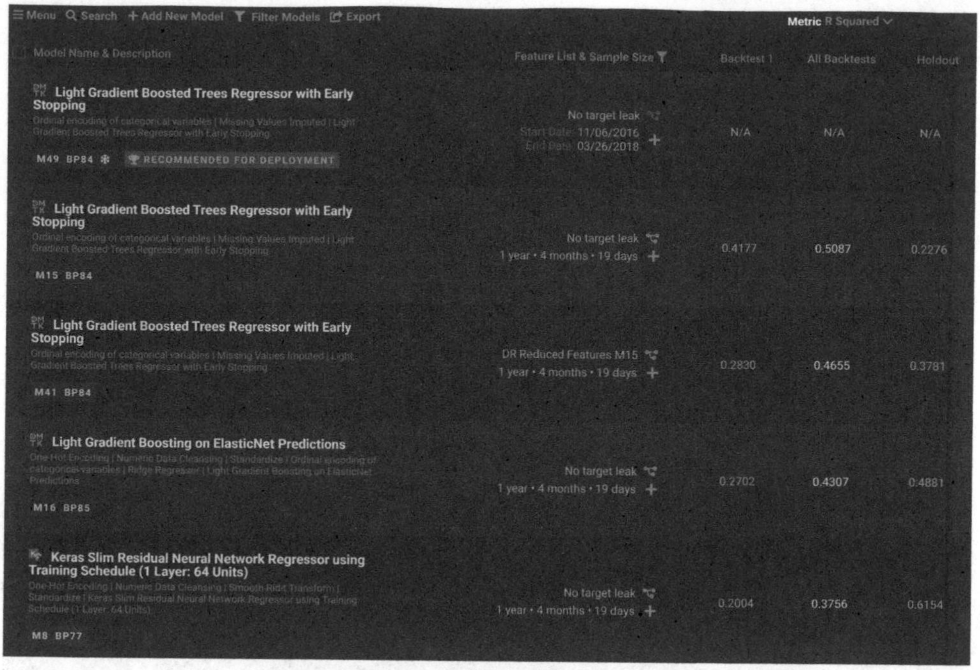

Figure 25.12. Leaderboard Sorted by All Backtests Scores.

Gradient Boosted Trees Regressor with Early Stopping (LGB) is the model at the top of the leaderboard.

When sorting by the *Holdout* column, we also see that some models with atrocious backtest scores have high holdout scores. This variance is suggestive of considerable volatility in avocado prices during the period, which means that the simpler models or models that do not overfit consequently benefit.

Click on the *All Backtests* column name to order by this measure (Figure 25.12). Remember, this analysis has been set to conduct five backtests, so the backtesting column contains the average validation score for those five tests. Note that the same model outperform the rest of the models.

Finally, re-sort by *Holdout* scores (Figure 25.13). Here, a number of models with poor *Backtest 1* scores are at the top of the leaderboard. In this case, we are forced to ignore these and focus our attention on the *All Backtests* scores.

25.1.8 Selecting and Examining a Model

It seems that avocado prices are more difficult to understand than initially expected. One possible reason for this might be a poor theoretical understanding of millennials' avocado hankering patterns and associated missing features. A more likely reason, however, is a deficient understanding of the competitive marketplace for avocados outside of the Hass product line. Because of this level of uncertainty, it

Figure 25.13. Leaderboard Sorted by Holdout Scores.

Figure 25.14. RandomForest Regressor Performance Characteristics.

makes the most sense, in this example, to retreat to the safer bet of the *AVG Blender* model. Scrolling down in the model selection view, the performance characteristics in Figure 25.14 will become visible. If the model does not have All Backtests run, go ahead and click the *Run* option. The model is doing a bit worse than the top models on the holdout sample, but it has performed well on both Backtest 1 and all backtests. Considering the likelihood that understanding and predicting avocado prices is a difficult problem given the presently available data, a somewhat combined like the *RandomForest Regressor* may be a safer decision in the long run. To further understand the problem context as well as the model, a closer examination of the *AVG Blender* can be conducted.

Click on the name of the *AVG Blender*, select *Evaluate* from the model menu, and then select *Accuracy Over Time*. This is a new screen (Figure 25.15) for time-aware modeling. In this view, the performance of the model is shown in terms of its ability to predict avocado prices over time, with a default view showing results

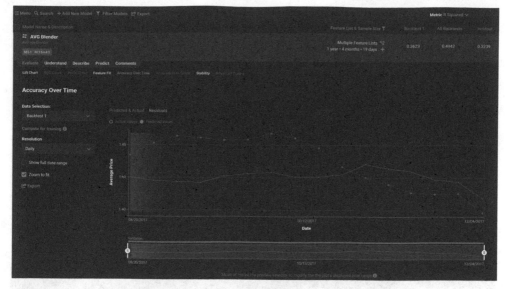

Figure 25.15. AVG Blender Accuracy over Time Screen.

for Backtest 1, in which predicted values are plotted in blue and the actual values in orange. Here, the extent to which time can invalidate or undermine a prediction model becomes apparent. It is immediately visible that the model is not so accurate. In this time frame, the actual price for avocados rises sharply, but the model contains no information allowing it to understand this trend. The model expects the price to flatten out before deflating, mostly missing the upturn that was just hinted at in its last training cases.

Instead, the actual price goes up markedly for three weeks, before staying static for a month and then beginning a two-and-a-half-month downward correction. Now examine the *Holdout* sample (Figure 25.16). This view shows only the holdout time period. Notice that this period continues from where the data in Figure 25.15 ended (a week later, as the data are at the week-level of aggregation).

Remember that *Backtest 1* predictions were about 25 cents off for the first period, after which the actual price crossed below the prediction prices and remained about 5 cents below thereafter. Here the prediction and the actual price can be seen trending together, though the actual price tends to stay slightly above the prediction. Going back to the *Backtest* pulldown, now select *Backtest 2*.

For each of the six validation sets (Figure 25.17), examine the models' performance. Note that these are different models built with the same algorithm using slightly different data, and always validated on different data subsets.

Instead of spending too much time on the individual backtest screens, it can be more efficient to examine all five of them together (Figure 25.18). Select *All Backtests* under *Data Selection*. This shows the whole time period from May 2016 to March 2018, almost two years of evaluation data.

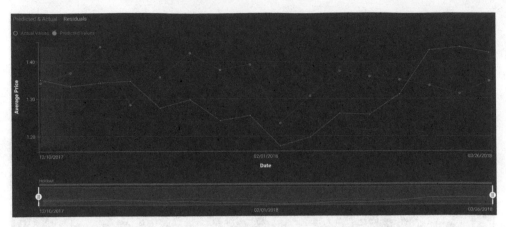

Figure 25.16. Accuracy over Time Screen for Holdout Sample.

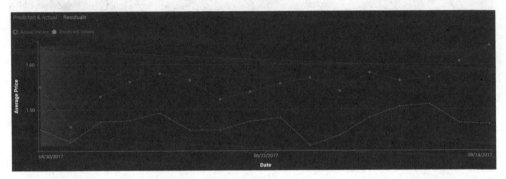

Figure 25.17. Backtest 2 Performance.

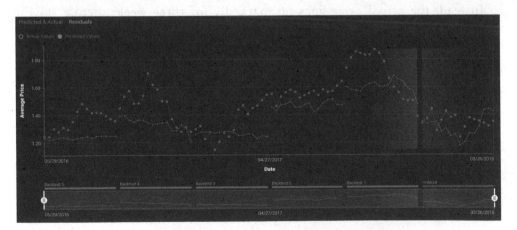

Figure 25.18. All Backtests and Holdout Performance.

While the models do reasonably well, in the cases of Backtest 4 and Backtest 1, they are far off the target, even a week after training the model. The good news is that when considering all models, while the predictions are off by as much as 30 cents, there does not seem to be a trend of the models deteriorating over time. This suggests a certain level of self-correction among the models.

25.1.9   A Small Detour into Residuals

To better understand our models, let us take a detour into the performance metrics. To get the view in Figure 25.19, select *Residuals* (same screen, at the top of the figure). This shows the average of actual values minus their predicted counterparts. When a blue line is above the zero-line, the model underpredicted the price for all sales on that date (on average). The Y-axis denotes the size of the residuals, here shown with an "m" denoting "milli" (thousands of a dollar). After examination of the data with knowledge of what a *residual* is, this screen will satisfy any need for evaluating residuals in the future.

When evaluating the leaderboard, RMSE is still the default measure provided.[3] What does it mean that the *Validation, Backtesting*, and *Holdout* scores are between 0.25 and 0.31? Because the target was the sales price in dollars, this is how far off the actual price the model predictions are on average—but not quite.

Turn now to the *Holdout* metric, for which DataRobot makes a download of the data easily available. Click on the *Predict* from the menu, then *Make Predictions* from the submenu (See Figure 25.20).

For the moment, skip over the suggestion that model accuracy has been affected by the inclusion of holdout data and the many backtest samples, and focus instead on adding *Optional Features*. Add *Average Price, Type*, and *Date*. Then click *Compute Predictions* and download the resulting file when DataRobot has finished

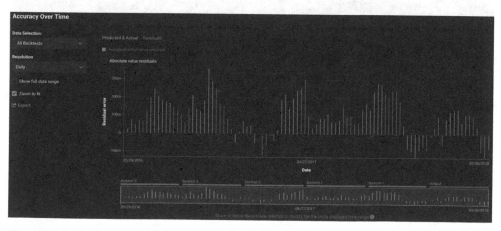

Figure 25.19. Residuals for All Models.

---

[3] Should we select another metric, the order of models may change somewhat. You may try some other metrics and see what happens to your leaderboard order. In this case, the *RandomForest Regressor* is quite immune to metric selection.

its calculations. Open this file in Excel. In the *A.9 Assets Avocado Toast* directory, you will find the file pre-prepared to this point, or you can create it yourself. Note that because DataRobot constantly reinvents and improves its algorithms, your numbers may not fit exactly with the ones in this file.

In Figure 25.21, the file from DataRobot is opened, and, for each row, the predicted price is subtracted from the actual price (*Actual - Prediction* column). These are the *residuals*. The left part of Figure 25.22 shows a visualization of the residuals with a line indicating their distance from zero (zero representing perfect prediction). Residuals show how far off from the actual price every prediction was, where positive numbers, like the residual in cell J6 for conventional avocados in the Albany region, suggest that the actual price was 3 cents lower than the predicted price. The residuals are then squared followed by taking the square root to re-represent negative values (Figure 15.22, right). Column L of Figure 25.21 contains these distance values, representing the inaccuracy between each prediction and the actual price, respectively. One benefit of the absolute differences is that the large outliers are

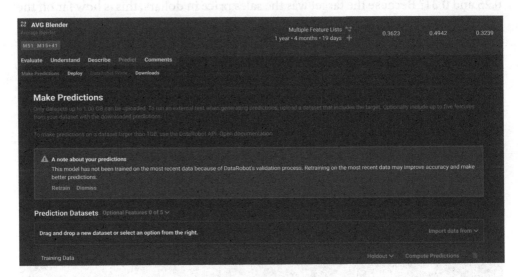

Figure 25.20. Predicting on the Holdout Sample.

			Holdout Data from DataRobot						Our Calculations					
row_id	Average Price	Type	Region	Date	Partition	timestamp	Training Prediction		Actual - Prediction	Squared	SquareRt		Mean of Squared:	0.06836373
16334	1.67	organic	NorthernNewEngland	12/10/2017	Holdout	2017-12-10T00:(	1.717445142		-0.047445	0.002251	0.047445		RMSE:	0.25172154
16758	1.4	organic	RichmondNorfolk	12/10/2017	Holdout	2017-12-10T00:(	1.490738158		-0.090738	0.008233	0.090738		MAE:	0.19284212
6573	0.79	conventional	Houston	12/10/2017	Holdout	2017-12-10T00:(	0.821095387		-0.031095	0.000967	0.031095			
5619	1.29	conventional	Albany	12/10/2017	Holdout	2017-12-10T00:(	1.329197875		-0.039198	0.001536	0.039198			
5937	1.06	conventional	California	12/10/2017	Holdout	2017-12-10T00:(	1.098894918		-0.038895	0.001513	0.038895			
7103	1.14	conventional	NewYork	12/10/2017	Holdout	2017-12-10T00:(	1.252203359		-0.112203	0.01259	0.112203			
5990	1.02	conventional	Charlotte	12/10/2017	Holdout	2017-12-10T00:(	1.259611402		-0.239611	0.057414	0.239611			
7262	1.02	conventional	Orlando	12/10/2017	Holdout	2017-12-10T00:(	1.162578911		-0.142579	0.020329	0.142579			
17341	1.13	organic	Syracuse	12/10/2017	Holdout	2017-12-10T00:(	1.594874742		-0.464875	0.216109	0.464875			
16970	2.27	organic	SanFrancisco	12/10/2017	Holdout	2017-12-10T00:(	2.113291693		0.1567083	0.024557	0.156708			
14744	1.45	organic	Albany	12/10/2017	Holdout	2017-12-10T00:(	1.655942886		-0.205943	0.042412	0.205943			
7633	1.04	conventional	RichmondNorfolk	12/10/2017	Holdout	2017-12-10T00:(	1.064136109		-0.024136	0.000583	0.024136			
7421	1.27	conventional	Pittsburgh	12/10/2017	Holdout	2017-12-10T00:(	1.157654947		0.1123451	0.012621	0.112345			

Figure 25.21. Spreadsheet Containing Holdout Predictions.

immediately visible, the largest being close to the 1.0 line on the Y-axis in the plot. If you click this point in the Excel sheet, you will learn that this point represented a large overprediction of prices in San Francisco in the middle of January 2018.

To further examine the model, the spreadsheet can be sorted by the SquareRt column to find the largest model failures. This yields two useful pieces of information: first, almost all the largest prediction failures were for organic avocados, and the largest misclassifications were for the San Francisco region and the Cincinnati/Dayton region. In Figure 25.23, the absolute differences for Cincinnati/Dayton are visualized with a distinction between organic vs. conventional avocados. While the model is relatively accurate for predicting convential avocados (diamonds), it struggles with the organics (circles).

One potential reason for such prediction problems may be that Cincinnati and Dayton, while only an hour apart by car and similar in many ways, have notably different organic produce consumption patterns. More likely is the reason hinted at by CNN's cost of living calculator, which suggests that housing costs in Dayton are 11% less than in Cincinnati, but groceries are 5% more expensive (CNN, 2018). This calculation might imply that Dayton has a poorer economy, and thus less of a market

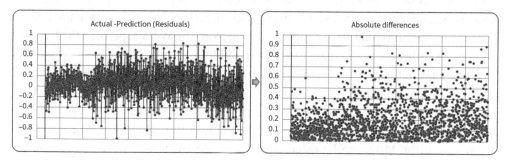

Figure 25.22. Visualization of Residuals and Absolute Differences over Time (X-axis).

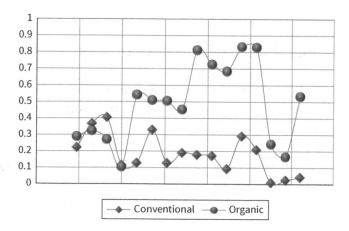

Figure 25.23. Visualization of Cincinnati/Dayton Residuals.

for organics. At the very least, this information suggests that the two markets should be disaggregated and treated separately in future modeling efforts.

A similar analysis should be conducted for the Buffalo/Rochester region, as the largest residuals come from the San Francisco, Cincinnati/Dayton, and Buffalo/Rochester regions followed by the Boise region. However, the fact that the 36 largest residuals are all for organic avocados, which are generally more expensive, suggests there is reason to believe that further economic indicators need to be added to the model.

25.1.10 Model Value

As seen in Figure 25.1, potential models were optimized using *Root Mean Square Error* (RMSE). Now, *squared error* has been calculated as well. The next step is simply to take the average of these and apply the *square root* of the average *squared error*. This yields a number that is arguably close to representing the endpoint average error range (though not completely so).

For simplicity of interpretation, change the *Measure* for the leaderboard to *Mean Absolute Error* (MAE). This is simply the average of the absolute difference between the actual and predicted values. This score turns out to be 0.1928 (about 19.3 cents), meaning that since the average price in the holdout sample is $1.35, the average prediction will be incorrect by 19.3 cents in either direction. To get a sense of the quality of these predictions relative to simply guessing from the average price in the training sample, examine the performance of a naïve model.

Look again at Figure 25.5, and remember that the holdout sample was based on training data starting on July 16, 2016, and ending on December 4, 2017. After opening the training dataset, the average price for that period can be easily calculated at $1.48, which can be treated as a best guess for future (holdout) avocado prices from which the MAE can be calculated. Doing so suggests that the MAE for the naïve model is 27 cents, quite a bit worse than the model score of 19.5—suggesting that the model has an immediate quantifiable value.

25.1.11 Learning about Avocado Price Drivers

After understanding the performance characteristics of this model, an evaluation of the important feature-components of the avocado price problem can be worthwhile. Figure 25.24 shows the *Feature Effects* screen showing that *Type* (conventional vs. organic) is the most influential feature, with a partial dependence varying by almost 50 cents. This is a lot, especially given the knowledge that the model struggles specifically with organic avocados.

Figure 25.25 shows the *Feature Effects* for *Region*. Herein lies the answer to the initial effort of identifying a relationship between avocado prices and millennial

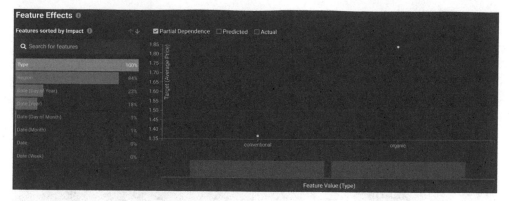

Figure 25.24. Feature Effects for Type.

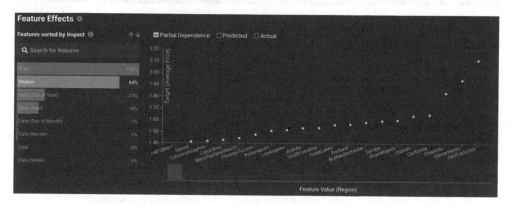

Figure 25.25. Feature Effects for Region.

homeownership. A millennial may be excused for avoiding San Francisco because of its expensive avocados (though there are likely other drivers for lower millennial homeownership in S.F., such as housing prices). In contrast, beyond offering really cheap avocados, Grand Rapids has many attractions, including the Gerald Ford Presidential Museum as well as the Judy Garland Museum, where one can view one of Richard Nixon's Oval Office tape recorders and a pair of magical ruby slippers, respectively. Perhaps this is a more suitable destination for young house buyers? Of course, a true avocado lover might even consider moving to Detroit.

Finally, the *Coefficients* screen from the *Ridge Regressor* model (Figure 25.26) or your best model with the β*i* symbol provides additional useful information for millennial decision-making. First, stick to non-organics for that additional chlorpyrifos high. Second, to drive the prospective house prices further down, move to Houston or Dallas–Fort Worth. Third, turn avocado toast into a special treat reserved for December and February, as those feature coefficients add up.

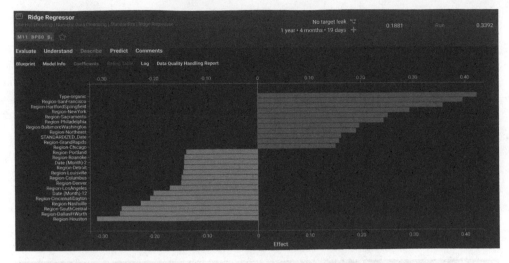

Figure 25.26. Coefficients.

25.2 Exercises

1. Re-run the analysis with the DataRobot default options, thereby leaving more data available for training. How did the results change? Is the model more accurate?

2. Will splitting the analysis up into two datasets, one for each type of avocado, and running separate analyses help the predictive ability of the project? If you believe it will, do it and evaluate the result on the holdout sample.

3. Run this analysis with a cross validation rather than time-aware setup. What happens to your accuracy numbers? Is the model more accurate with cross validation? If so, why? Develop three candidate hypotheses and discuss with a colleague.

26
Time-Series Modeling

26.1 The Assumptions of Time-Series Machine Learning

The core focus of Chapter 25 was time-aware modeling, in which *time* made its first appearance as a significant component in the evaluation of a given model. The content from Chapter 25 is critical for understanding the current chapter. Time-series modeling is the destination of this journey into the vortex of time. Note that this chapter is not about the theory underlying time-series modeling—that would require another book entirely. For a full introduction to time-series theory and approaches, we recommend Ghysels and Marcellino (2018).

A critical principle of machine learning is called *Panta Rei—everything flows—* and is central to understanding time-series analysis. This principle stems from the Greek philosopher Heraclitus through Plato and suggests that we cannot enter the same river twice. To rephrase less philosophically: everything moves and nothing ever stands still. We can no longer assume that distributions in data or outcomes stay the same over time.

Time-series analysis is an attempt to extrapolate the evolution of a complex system and use this information to predict the future. Traditionally, time-series analysis is conducted using approaches such as *autoregressive integrated moving average* (ARIMA), *exponential smoothing*, and *trend analysis*. In any kind of time-series analysis, we encounter a critical need for advanced feature engineering such as *stabilizing the target* (a stationary target is, after all, easier to hit), creating *lagged features* (it is not target leak if it happened in the past), and *detecting periodicity* (for example, seasonal trends) (Schmidt, 2017).

Arguably, the core of such feature engineering comes from creating many different time windows into the past, within which we apply different feature creation approaches (i.e., mean, median, min, max, and standard deviation). Some or all of these new features (e.g., the mean sales over the last three weeks) may, in some cases, be further transformed, such as through logging, creating a truly massive task for an AutoML. The challenge for the AutoML is to decide which features to generate from the potentially infinite features it *could* create. Once the AutoML has created a subset of such features, it must then further test the efficacy of the features and reduce the set.

At the end of the setup process, where the user carefully and skillfully considers the time dimension in setting up the features, and the AutoML has generated a

Automated Machine Learning for Business. Kai R. Larsen and Daniel S. Becker, Oxford University Press. © Oxford University Press 2021.
DOI: 10.1093/oso/9780190941659.003.0026

large set of features, the AutoML has an advantage over traditional approaches like ARIMA. Because the cutting-edge modern algorithms we have explored in earlier chapters are "more expressive" (better able to fit the data without overfitting), we should be able to get better results.

26.2 A Hands-on Exercise in Time-Series Analysis

26.2.1 Problem Context

Focusing on the avocado data used in Chapter 25, recall that the data made available were limited—data on select cities and only from 2015 through 2018 (we retain 2015–2017 for training in this case). One assumption made in this chapter is that the *Total Volume* of each type of avocado sold within a given week at a given market could then be multiplied by the average price per avocado to identify a total sales sum. By performing this calculation, we added a column named *Sales*. Then the sales were added up for each of the 157 available weeks across the avocado types and markets. The top chart of Figure 26.1 shows these sales figures without paying attention yet to time. A regression line fitted to *this* data shows that there is no significant predictive ability in the ordering ($R^2 = 0.01$). However, when we order the sales over time, clear patterns emerge—in this case, showing rising prices over time. With a regression line fitted to this data that explains nearly half of the price ($R^2 = .42$), the importance of time in a business case such as this one becomes clear. This simple regression line in the bottom of Figure 26.1, however, is missing a seasonal pattern that can be seen by splitting the data by year; the sales within each year look like an upside-down U.

If ordering cases by time displays such patterns, it is important to either use time-aware or time-series analysis. Time-series analysis is appropriate when the following contextual notions hold:

1. The order of rows matters.
2. Training data and future data are not similar.
3. Timestamps are available for training and prediction data.
4. In addition to the individual row containing the target we are training the model to predict, past rows allowing time-lagged feature creation are also available during prediction time.

The first two notions easily apply to the avocado case. Figure 26.1 shows the order (ordered by time) is significant, as the ordering of a case determines its likely target value (sales). Say you are interested in future sales figures for 2018. In the upper scatterplot of Figure 26.1, the available data to infer from is the average sales value (between $20 and $21 million). However, examining the trend line for the bottom scatterplot, weekly sales for 2018 can be estimated at an average of approximately $25 million.

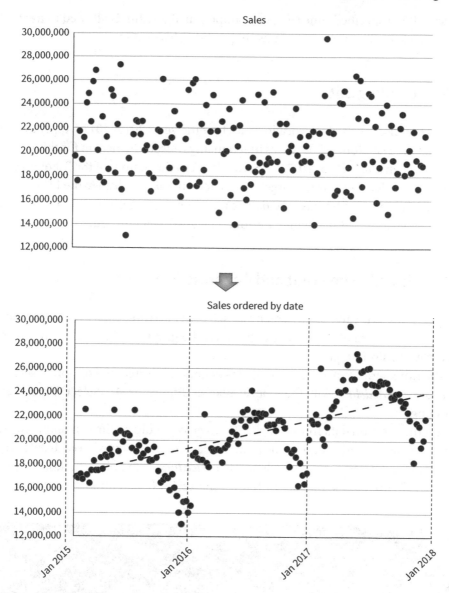

Figure 26.1. Ordering the Target by Time.

Regarding Notion 3, "timestamped data" is accessible in that each sale is recorded as occurring on a given date (summarized at the week level). Seeing the data sorted by time (bottom plot of Figure 26.1), it is also reasonable to assume that the fourth notion holds, and that when preparing to predict for future cases, access to cases from the weeks before the prediction date will also be available.

Given that the data seems appropriate for time-series analysis, we must reassess the rules for target leakage (Chapter 24). Algorithms now need access to the target, as well as to features that were previously flagged as target leakage and removed. To avoid being too liberal with this approach, we set the algorithms to only peek at these features after a specified time lag. For example, an algorithm is allowed to treat sales for last week as a feature that it can use to predict sales next week.

26.2.2 Loading Data

For this exercise, we use the avocado dataset for the years 2015–2017 (Appendix A.9). Note that the DataRobot time-series functionality must be turned on for this exercise. Load the file *avocado 2015–2017.csv*. Scroll down to the bottom of the list of potential features and select *Sales* as the target, then click on *Sales* to display the histogram in Figure 26.2. Note that because the data is no longer aggregated for all locations and types of avocados, the sales figures are quite a bit lower than in Figure 26.1.

26.2.3 Specify Time Unit and Generate Features

Navigate back to the top of the screen and select **Set up time-aware modeling**. Select *Date*, and take note of the similarity between the graph in Figure 26.3 and the one created manually in Figure 26.1.

If the time-series functionality in your system is activated, the option of selecting *Time Series Modeling* will then be available (Figure 26.4). Select **Time Series Modeling**.

With the avocado data from Chapter 25, an error would be thrown upon selecting *Time Series Modeling* because of the multiple data points assigned to each date. There are 41 different cities, each of which has two *price total* data points, making 82 prices per date. Figure 26.5 shows six of these time series (conventional vs. organic for

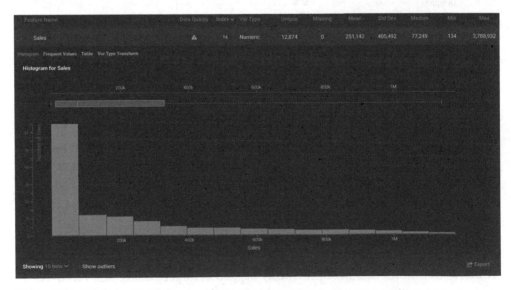

Figure 26.2. Histogram of Sales.

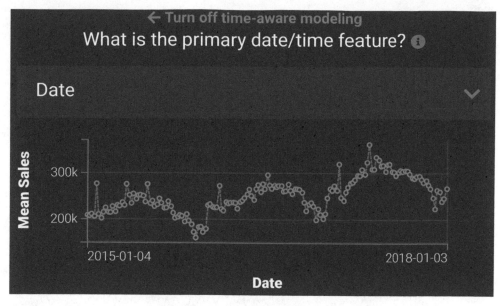

Figure 26.3. Time-aware Modeling Screen.

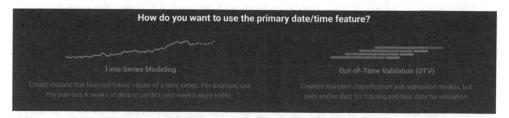

Figure 26.4. Time-aware Modeling Options.

Albany, Atlanta, and Baltimore). To remedy this error, there are two options. Option one: aggregate across cities so that there are only two prices per date. This option allows the *Type* column to be treated as a time-series identifier (resulting in two time series, one for conventional and one for organic). Unfortunately, that works against the original goal of predicting avocado price for each market. The second option is more suitable: aggregating across type (conventional vs. organic), making the 41 *Region*s (cities) available as a time-series ID.

In this case, however, the initial level of analysis is appropriate; so, instead of either of the above measures, a new feature was created (*SeriesId*), for which each unique combination of *Region* and *Type* are given a number between 1 and 82. Given some time, DataRobot will detect this feature as a potential series identifier, allowing you to simply select **Series ID**. This selection will produce the screen in Figure 26.6.

Perhaps the most interesting thing about time-series AutoML relative to regular AutoML is the number of features it will create based on past values of the target. Figure 26.6 shows the modeling options relevant to this task. This view will be

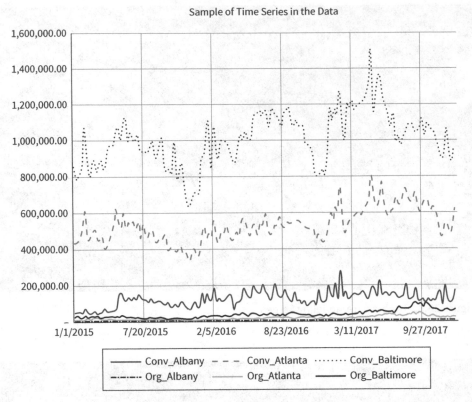

Figure 26.5. Six Sample Time Series (out of 82).

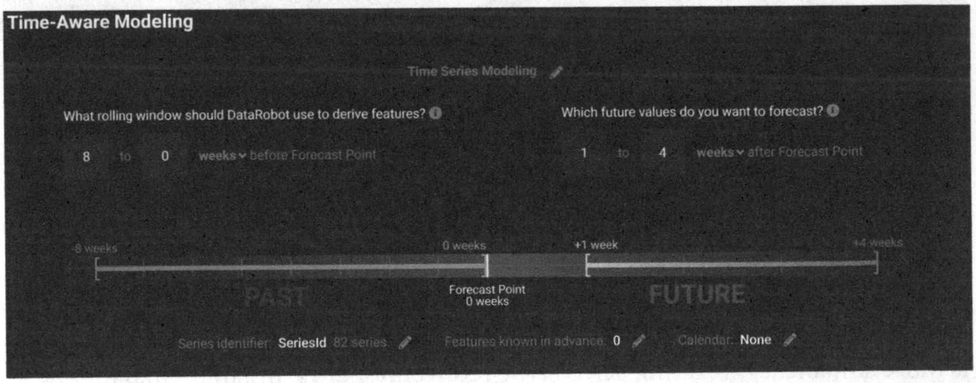

Figure 26.6. Time Series Modeling Options.

covered in further detail later on, but for now, note the pencil icon next to *Features known in advance*. Clicking on this icon brings you down to the Advanced options screen shown in Figure 26.7.

We will ignore the potential for better prediction through enabling cross-series feature generation (the first checkmark). To avoid target leakage, carefully evaluate which features could possibly be known in advance of the forecast point. These

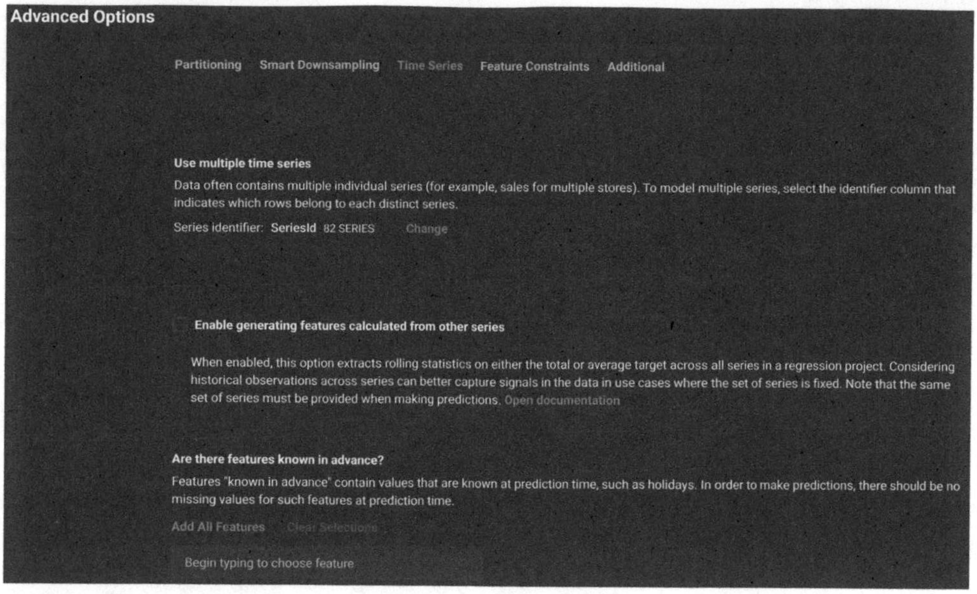

Figure 26.7. Time Series Advanced Options.

features will not have to be "lagged." This means that when generating a training row, in addition to the correct target value, it will contain two types of features:

1. *Features that are known in advance* (features known at the time the target value was generated, in practice at the time of the sale or at the end of week aggregation). These features are just like any other feature without target leak in traditional machine learning.
2. *Features not known in advance*, primarily target values from earlier periods. For example, the most likely feature predicting whether a given person is going to run five kilometers at some point this week is the number of times they ran five kilometers in the last week or during the last four weeks. Such information is not taken advantage of in traditional ML, but is very useful in creating new features in time-series ML.

Start with the first type of feature—those known in advance. These are the only features that were "allowed" for use during the exercise on time-aware modeling in Chapter 25: *Type* and *Region*. However, because a time series has now been created for every unique pairing of these features, they are not likely to improve final prediction accuracy and may decrease accuracy. Therefore, create a feature list containing every feature except *Type* and *Region*. Dropping these two features from the analysis leaves only one remaining feature that is known in advance: *Date*. This feature is already treated appropriately by DataRobot, so no action is needed. Another set of features that may be known in advance are *holidays*. DataRobot allows the upload of

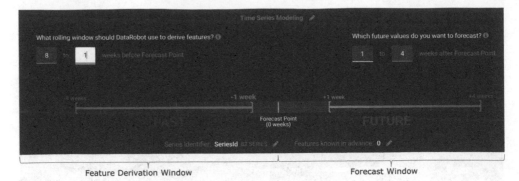

Figure 26.8. Time Series Advanced Options.

a list of holidays. However, because date data is aggregated by week in this case, such holidays would have a minor impact, even the all-important National Avocado Day.

The next choice is to evaluate features to specify which of them are available at the time of forecasting. For example, if I am forecasting store sales for tomorrow, the weather for tomorrow is not yet available, but the weather for yesterday is available. Note the following point: because the data represents week-long aggregations of sales conducted on each Sunday, these aggregations would likely contain data coming in as late as midnight on the US West Coast. At this point, even if the procedure was instantaneous, 24-hour stores on the East Coast would already have been open for two hours of the next week. Given that Hass avocados are sold in a wide variety of stores, it is likely that complete and accurate sales figures would not be available until some time into the coming week, rendering prediction of following week impossible. This means that for any given forecast point, it has to be assumed that the data from the week of the forecast point it is not available. To take this into account in DataRobot, change one of the defaults in the *Time Series Modeling* window (Figure 26.8) to use only features that are a week old.

Given that the DataRobot default for the start of the rolling window is accepted, the tool will create features based on the prior seven weeks. Keep the defaults in the *Forecast Window*. They simply suggest that instead of one forecast price, the system will forecast prices for each of the following four weeks.

Next, set *Modeling Mode* to **Quick** and start the analysis. DataRobot will now train models with two years and 19 days of data. As the process in the rightmost window finishes, click on the link **View more info** and then **Preview derivation log**, shown in part in Figure 26.9.

Upon examining the feature derivation log, notice that DataRobot has detected a trend in the data similar to that showed in Figure 26.1 ("Series detected as nonstationary"). Because it detected the trend, DataRobot will automatically apply *differencing*, that is, changing the target to be the difference in target value from the previous period, as opposed to measuring an *actual* sales value (shown in Figure 26.10). For example, because sales were 17,002,942 in the first week, 16,904,653 in the second week, 17,208,243 in the third week, 16,767,694 in the fourth week,

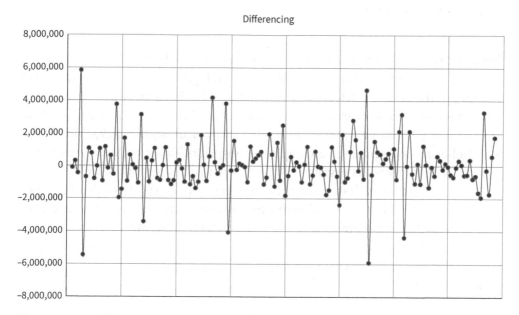

```
Limit on the maximum number of feature in this project is 500
Total number of derived features during the feature generation process is 137
Total number of features removed during the feature reduction process is 72
The finalized number of available features is around 65

Series detected as non-stationary
Multiplicative trend detected
Multiplicative trend without inflated values detected
Detected periodicities:
The window sizes chosen to be: 7 weeks (because the time step is 1 week and FDW is 7 weeks)
Features treated as known in advance:
Features excluded from derivation:
Applying supervised feature reduction to reduce the number of output features
Generating feature "Sales (log)" from "Sales" because multiplicative trend is detected
```

Figure 26.9. Feature Derivation Log.

Figure 26.10. Differencing Applied to the Target Values.

and 22,604,985 in the fifth week, the first four values in Figure 26.10 are −98,289, 303,590, and −440,548 before the sales difference jumps to 5,837,290 at the fourth difference measure. Finding the difference has been proven to be an easier task in machine learning than finding the expected value (Brockwell & Davis, 2013), and the resulting predictions can later be turned into actual predicted values.

Following the differencing by DataRobot, some concerns arise from the resulting chart. What immediately becomes clear are the extreme swings that happen seven or eight times in this dataset. For the most part, these swings are reflective of one outlier value adjusting in the opposite direction.

Secondly, Figure 26.9 shows that a "multiplicative trend [was] detected," and that because of that trend, the sales prices were logged *before* differencing was done.

Feature Name	Data Quality	Index	Importance ⌄	Var Type	Unique	Missing	Mean	Std Dev	Median	Min
Sales (actual)	⚠	36	Target	Numeric	11,808	0	254,241	409,368	79,317	134
Sales (month ...ion) (actual)	⚠	58	▬▬▬▬	Numeric	2,706	0	254,241	408,143	79,441	1,204
Sales (7 week ...seline) (log)		28	▬▬▬▬▬	Numeric	12,054	0	11.10	1.88	11.25	7.29
Sales (7 week mean) (log)		31	▬▬▬▬▬	Numeric	12,054	0	11.10	1.88	11.25	7.29
Sales (7 week median) (log)		32	▬▬▬▬▬	Numeric	6,602	0	11.08	1.89	11.25	7.19
Sales (7 week max) (log)		29	▬▬▬▬▬	Numeric	3,877	0	11.29	1.82	11.47	7.44
Sales (log) (2nd lag)		38	▬▬▬▬▬	Numeric	12,054	0	11.09	1.90	11.27	4.90
Sales (log) (3rd lag)		40	▬▬▬▬▬	Numeric	12,054	0	11.09	1.90	11.27	4.90
Sales (7 week min) (log)		34	▬▬▬▬▬	Numeric	4,057	0	10.88	1.98	11.06	4.90
Sales (log) (4th lag)		42	▬▬▬▬▬	Numeric	12,054	0	11.08	1.90	11.27	4.90

Figure 26.11. Data Window.

Further investigation indicates another worrisome detail: DataRobot has not discovered the periodicity that was so plain to see in Figure 26.1. In all likelihood, this means that the ability to detect the seasonal shapes has been lost when transitioning from three years of available data to 2 years and 19 days. Finally, DataRobot has created a multitude of features (listed as variables in Figure 26.9). Notice that DataRobot has implemented a complex set of priorities for each feature creation type and constantly tests the value of different approaches per Figure 26.11.

After completion of feature engineering, the system has derived several new features, for a total of 66. Several derivations of the seven-week period made available to the system are the most prominent features. Of these, the log of the deviation from the average sales baseline over that seven-week period is the single most important feature. As is often true, the target itself (lagged) is the most important predictor of the target.

26.2.3 Examine Candidate Models

Go now to the *Models* window and change the Metric from *Gamma Deviance* to *R Squared*. R^2 is a bit easier to understand, even though it is not the best measure for evaluating time-series models. It becomes immediately visible (Figure 26.12) that the models are wonderfully predictive, with the *Elastic-Net Regressor (L2/Gamma Deviance) with Forecast Distance Modeling* explaining 99.16% of the prices in the target. While it is good to exercise cautious optimism, in this case, this high score suggests that the problem is, at the least, quite tractable. It does not tell us, however, whether these models are better than straightforward approaches.

For that reason, change the metric once again, this time to Mean Absolute Scaled Error (Hyndman & Koehler, 2006; Masegosa), which compares the performance of each model to a naïve (or baseline) model. What Figure 26.13 shows is that the

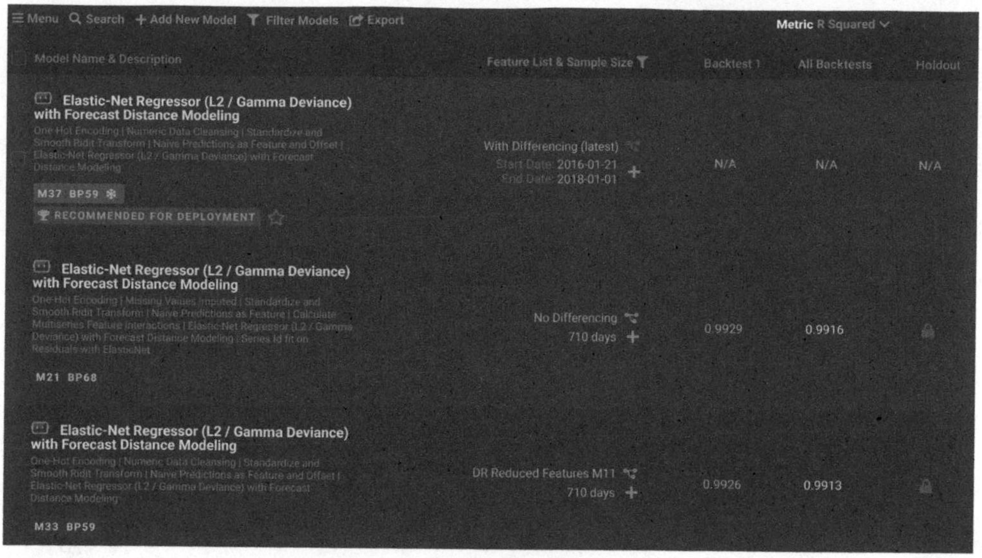

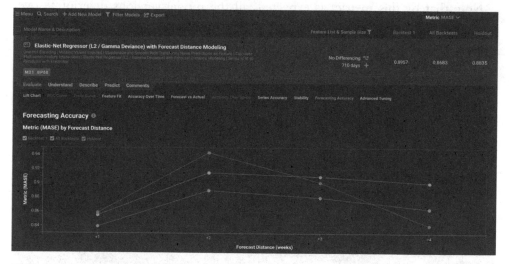

Figure 26.12. Leaderboard Ordered by All Backtests R^2.

Figure 26.13. Forecasting Accuracy for Elastic-Net Regressor on MASE Metric.

model named *Baseline Predictions Using Most Recent Value* (blueprint shown at the bottom of the figure) predicts each sale based on the most recent sales value inside the *Feature Derivation Window* (see Figure 26.8). The performance of the baseline model is set to 1.0, while other models' performance metrics are set relative to the baseline. This makes it so that a model that is better than the baseline has a performance metric lower than 1. Note that DataRobot does not need to run the Baseline Prediction model to calculate MASE, because a feature list containing it is automatically examined earlier in the process.

26.2.4 Digging into the Preferred Model

Shown by the resulting MASE scores, the best-performing model improves upon the baseline model by a bit more than 11 percentage points. Take the best model here then as a baseline for examining some additional screens/views relevant to time-series models. First, release the holdout sample in the right pane,[1] navigate to the *Evaluate* menu, and then to the *Forecasting Accuracy* screen (Figure 26.13).

The *Forecasting Accuracy* screen shows that different versions of the top-performing model all start out well. Over the four weeks into the future that the model forecasts, they consistently beat the baseline model, though diminishing in effectiveness over time until, on the third or fourth day, there is again improvement relative to the baseline. These performance characteristics are especially true for the holdout sample, which does better than the other versions tested against Holdout 1 and the combination of Holdout 1 and Holdout 2. Of course, these scores are against a baseline model, so the scores are as much about that model as it is about the Elastic-Net model. Now, change the Metric to *Mean Absolute Error (MAE)*, as is done in Figure 26.14.

Note that by this metric, as expected, all the model versions deteriorate over time and, on the first day of prediction, range between a mean error of $19,651 and $22,158. On the fourth day, that range shifts to 24,494 and 27,119, quite reasonable for this problem.

Next, navigate to the *Stability* sub-menu to understand how stable the different versions of the model are to dynamic or fluctuating datasets. Figure 26.15 displays that the model is quite stable, and that the average error average across all four days remains within the range of 21,312 to 25,147.

Next, examine the individual time series to better understand within which markets—and for which products—this model struggles. Go to the *Series Accuracy* sub-menu and sort by *Backtest 1* from highest to lowest numbers. In Figure 26.16 we now see that predicting series 21 (conventional avocados in Los Angeles) is the

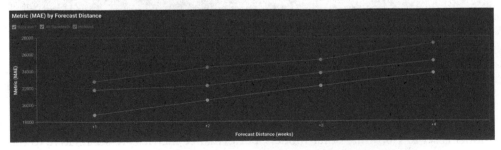

Figure 26.14. Forecasting Accuracy for Elastic-Net Regressor on MAE Metric.

---

[1] Note that the holdout is only released this early in the process for learning purposes, as discussed in earlier chapters.

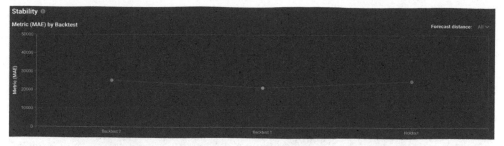

Figure 26.15. Model Stability on MAE Metric.

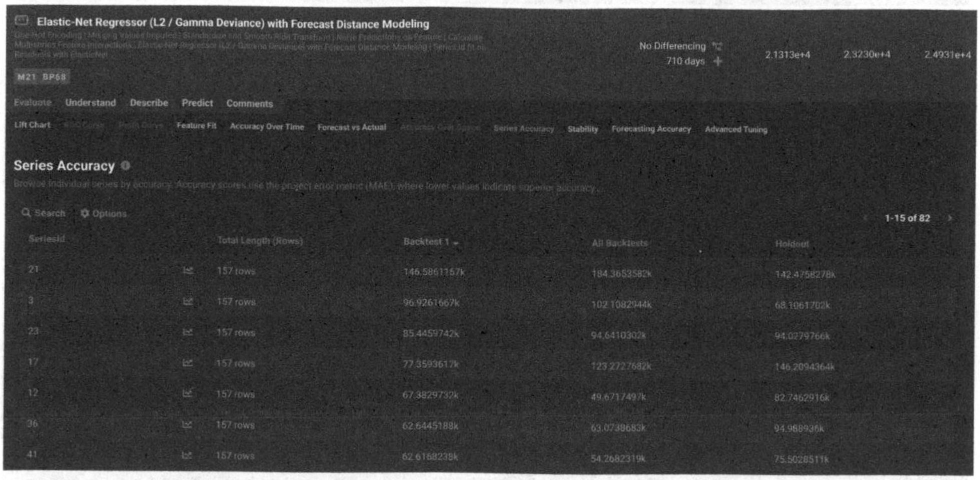

Figure 26.16. Series Accuracy on MAE Metric.

most problematic. Series 3 (conventional avocados in Baltimore/Washington) has the second largest amount of prediction failure.

If sorted by *Backtest 1* but with the lowest errors on top, notice that the best predictions are those made on organic avocados in Boise, where the sales prediction error is on average only $543 off. However, again reserving excitement, examine first the time series for Boise by clicking the graph icon on the row for SeriesId 45. Clicking the icon will bring up the *Accuracy Over Time* screen (Figure 26.17). See from the resulting view that a highly probable cause of this time series' accuracy could be the fact that those salt-of-the-earth Boiseans hardly eat any organic avocados.

Change the value in the pulldown menu under *Series to plot* to 21. Notice that the resulting graphs are quite similar, but that the scale of conventional avocado sales in Los Angeles is also much more extensive (Figure 26.18).

What this exercise makes clear is that MAE is not the right metric to compare predictive success across time series. Go back now to the *Series Accuracy* screen and change the Metric in the upper right corner to MASE. This will explain prediction

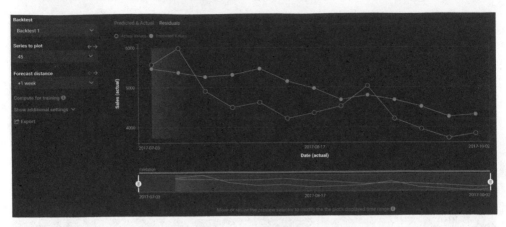

Figure 26.17. Accuracy over Time for Time Series 45 on MAE Metric.

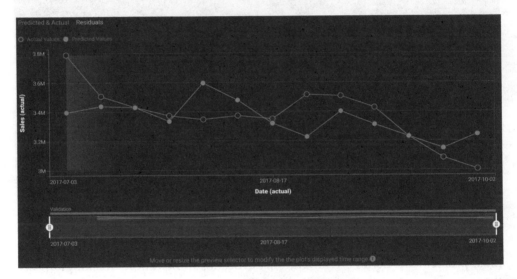

Figure 26.18. Accuracy over Time for Time Series 21 on MAE Metric.

accuracy relative to a baseline model. Focusing on *Backtest 1* again, see that time series 13 (conventional avocados in Detroit) represents the best available prediction. However, this seems to vary depending on whether the focus lies on *Backtest 1*, *All Backtests*, or *Holdout* (Figure 26.19).

More worrisome is the other end of the list, reached by clicking *Backtest 1* again to sort by most substantial MASE numbers first. Doing so shows that SeriesId 29 (conventional avocados, Pittsburgh) is the most challenging prediction with a MASE score of 1.8. Sorting the same way for *All Backtests* shows that SeriesId 69 (organic avocados in Phoenix/Tucson) is another challenging prediction with a MASE score of 3.0, suggesting that the baseline model does three times as well as this advanced

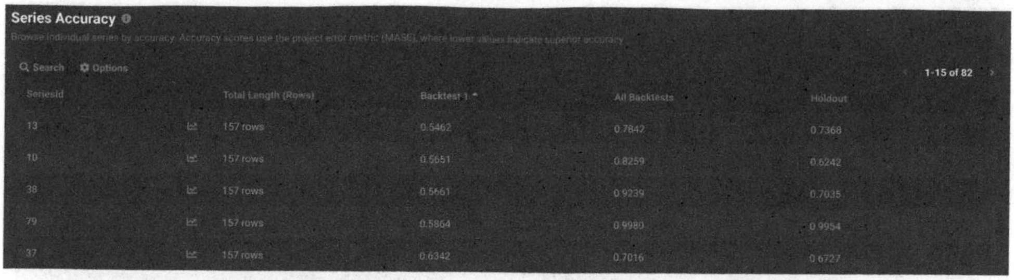

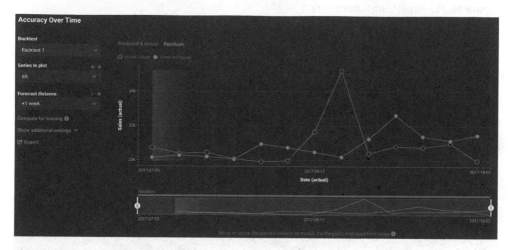

Figure 26.19. Series Accuracy for MASE Metric.

Figure 26.20. Accuracy over Time.

model. Click on the graph icon on the row for SeriesId 69 to see what went so wrong (or well, given the high sales) in Phoenix/Tucson (Figure 26.20).

The *Accuracy Over Time* graph shows that the predictions are not all bad, except or the week of August 27, 2017, for which the model messed up quite substantially: sales unexpectedly went through the roof without the model having any ability to detect or predict it. With such a significant failure, it might be appropriate to dig deep into the original data for Phoenix and Tucson to better understand what happened. Looking into the prediction failure, we found that there was a total solar eclipse on August 21, 2017, that was viewable in Phoenix and Tucson. Perhaps lots of guacamole was consumed to celebrate the event? Again, only the data will tell.

26.2.5 Predicting

Having selected a model, it is now time to move forward to making future predictions. Go to the *Predict* menu and choose *Make Predictions* (Figure 26.21). When offered the option, retrain the model with all the data.

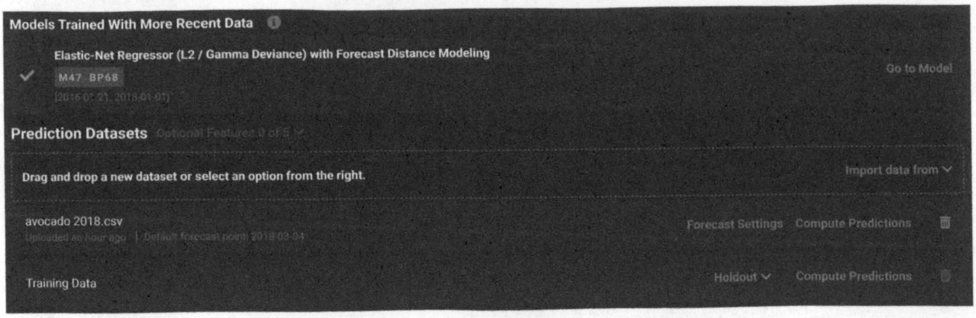

Figure 26.21. Predicting Future Data.

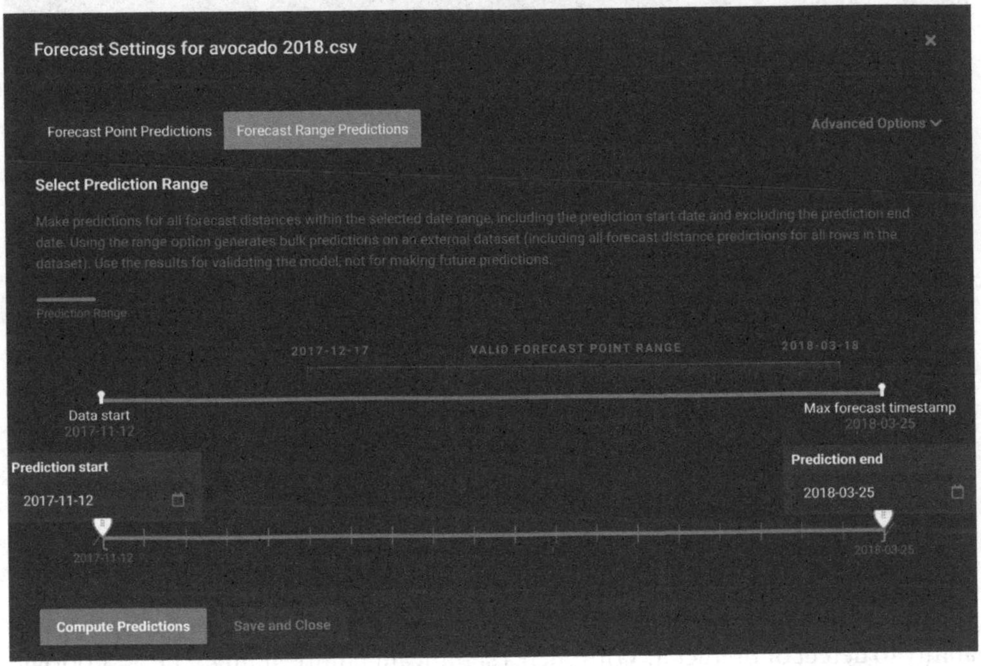

Figure 26.22. Predicting Future Data: Decisions for Predictions.

Once the model is updated, upload the following file: *avocado 2018.csv*, available in folder A.9. Note that this file must be prepped differently for forecasting. The *avocado 2018.csv* serves as an example, but DataRobot also offers an example dataset. First, select **Forecast Settings** followed by the *Forecast Range Predictions* option (Figure 26.22), and insert the first and last date for the rows we have for 2018.

Note that the avocado file also contains data on the previous eight weeks of data. Having access to this past data will enable DataRobot to do the required feature engineering.

26.3 Exercises

1. Going back to the data used for differencing in Figure 26.10, calculate your own differencing scores and examine whether US holidays may have contributed to the biggest difference scores. Did National If Pets Had Thumbs Day play a role?

2. Use your preferred model to predict for the *avocado 2018.csv* file, then go back to time-aware modeling and create another model. Predict the sales with this model and compare the two models to see what benefit was had from the introduction of time-series analytics.

Datasets

A.1 Diabetes Patients Readmissions

Summary

This dataset is a subset from University of California, Irvine's Machine Learning Repository's "Diabetes 130-US hospitals for years 1999–2008 Data Set." In the dataset, the unit of analysis is *patients that visited an emergency room for diabetes-related treatment*. The target is whether the patients returned to the hospital within 30 days of being released and were readmitted (*target: readmitted with values true or false*).

Business Goal
Create a model predicting whether a new patient will be readmitted and provide better understanding of the factors associated with readmission.

Datasets
Original Dataset
Source: https://archive.ics.uci.edu/ml/datasets/diabetes+130-us+hospitals+for+years+1999-2008. The original dataset is available in dataset_diabetes.zip and consists of two files.

Cleaned Dataset
The cleaned dataset is available with the book in the file 10kDiabetes.csv. The dataset contains data on 10,000 patients in:

- 10,000 rows
- 52 columns

Dataset Cleaning Process
This dataset was not originally developed for this book and has been a regular in DataRobot training sessions. It was originally cleaned and reduced by DataRobot staff, making the cleaning process unclear.

Data Dictionary

Feature	Target Leak?	Description
A1Cresult	No	Indicates the range of the result or if the test was not taken. Values: ">8" if the result was greater than 8%, ">7" if the result was greater than 7% but less than 8%, "normal" if the result was less than 7%, and "none" if not measured.
acarbose	No	Indicates whether the specific drug named was prescribed or there was a change in the dosage. Values: "up" if the dosage was increased during the encounter, "down" if the dosage was decreased, "steady" if the dosage did not change, and "no" if the drug was not prescribed.
acetohexamide	No	Indicates whether the specific drug named was prescribed or there was a change in the dosage. Values: "up" if the dosage was increased during the encounter, "down" if the dosage was decreased, "steady" if the dosage did not change, and "no" if the drug was not prescribed.

Feature	Target Leak?	Description
admission_source_id	No	Where did the patient come from? For example, physician referral, emergency room, and transfer from a hospital.
admission_type_id	No	Integer identifier corresponding to 9 distinct What kind of admission was this? For example, emergency, urgent, elective, newborn, and not available.
age	No	Grouped in 10-year intervals: [0, 10), [10, 20), . . ., [90, 100)
change	No	Indicates if there was a change in diabetic medications (either dosage or generic name). Values: "change" and "no change."
chlorpropamide	No	Indicates whether the specific drug named was prescribed or there was a change in the dosage. Values: "up" if the dosage was increased during the encounter, "down" if the dosage was decreased, "steady" if the dosage did not change, and "no" if the drug was not prescribed.
citoglipton	No	Indicates whether the specific drug named was prescribed or there was a change in the dosage. Values: "up" if the dosage was increased during the encounter, "down" if the dosage was decreased, "steady" if the dosage did not change, and "no" if the drug was not prescribed.
diabetesMed	No	Indicates whether this specific diabetic medication was prescribed. Values: "yes" and "no."
diag_1	No	The primary diagnosis (coded as first three digits of ICD9); 848 distinct values.
diag_1_desc	No	The text name of diag_1.
diag_2	No	Secondary diagnosis (coded as first three digits of ICD9); 923 distinct values.
diag_2_desc	No	The text name of diag_2.
diag_3	No	Additional secondary diagnosis (coded as first three digits of ICD9); 954 distinct values.
diag_3_desc	No	The text name of diag_3.
discharge_disposition_id	Yes	Where was the patient discharged to? For example, discharged to home, expired, and not available. See Chapter 24 for information on target leak in this feature.
examide	No	Indicates whether the specific drug named was prescribed or there was a change in the dosage. Values: "up" if the dosage was increased during the encounter, "down" if the dosage was decreased, "steady" if the dosage did not change, and "no" if the drug was not prescribed.
gender	No	Values: male, female, and unknown/invalid.
glimepiride	No	Indicates whether the specific drug named was prescribed or there was a change in the dosage. Values: "up" if the dosage was increased during the encounter, "down" if the dosage was decreased, "steady" if the dosage did not change, and "no" if the drug was not prescribed.
glimepiride.pioglitazone	No	Indicates whether the specific drug named was prescribed or there was a change in the dosage. Values: "up" if the dosage was increased during the encounter, "down" if the dosage was decreased, "steady" if the dosage did not change, and "no" if the drug was not prescribed.
glipizide	No	Indicates whether the specific drug named was prescribed or there was a change in the dosage. Values: "up" if the dosage was increased during the encounter, "down" if the dosage was decreased, "steady" if the dosage did not change, and "no" if the drug was not prescribed.
glipizide.metformin	No	Indicates whether the specific drug named was prescribed or there was a change in the dosage. Values: "up" if the dosage was increased during the encounter, "down" if the dosage was decreased, "steady" if the dosage did not change, and "no" if the drug was not prescribed.

Feature	Target Leak?	Description
glyburide	No	Indicates whether the specific drug named was prescribed or there was a change in the dosage. Values: "up" if the dosage was increased during the encounter, "down" if the dosage was decreased, "steady" if the dosage did not change, and "no" if the drug was not prescribed.
glyburide.metformin	No	Indicates whether the specific drug named was prescribed or there was a change in the dosage. Values: "up" if the dosage was increased during the encounter, "down" if the dosage was decreased, "steady" if the dosage did not change, and "no" if the drug was not prescribed.
insulin	No	Indicates whether the specific drug named was prescribed or there was a change in the dosage. Values: "up" if the dosage was increased during the encounter, "down" if the dosage was decreased, "steady" if the dosage did not change, and "no" if the drug was not prescribed.
max_glu_serum	No	Indicates the range of the result or if the test was not taken. Values: ">200," ">300," "normal," and "none" if not measured.
medical_specialty	No	Specialty of the admitting physician. For example, cardiology, internal medicine, family/general practice, and surgeon.
metformin	No	Indicates whether the specific drug named was prescribed or there was a change in the dosage. Values: "up" if the dosage was increased during the encounter, "down" if the dosage was decreased, "steady" if the dosage did not change, and "no" if the drug was not prescribed.
metformin.pioglitazone	No	Indicates whether the specific drug named was prescribed or there was a change in the dosage. Values: "up" if the dosage was increased during the encounter, "down" if the dosage was decreased, "steady" if the dosage did not change, and "no" if the drug was not prescribed.
metformin.rosiglitazone	No	Indicates whether the specific drug named was prescribed or there was a change in the dosage. Values: "up" if the dosage was increased during the encounter, "down" if the dosage was decreased, "steady" if the dosage did not change, and "no" if the drug was not prescribed.
miglitol	No	Indicates whether the specific drug named was prescribed or there was a change in the dosage. Values: "up" if the dosage was increased during the encounter, "down" if the dosage was decreased, "steady" if the dosage did not change, and "no" if the drug was not prescribed.
nateglinide	No	Indicates whether the specific drug named was prescribed or there was a change in the dosage. Values: "up" if the dosage was increased during the encounter, "down" if the dosage was decreased, "steady" if the dosage did not change, and "no" if the drug was not prescribed.
num_lab_procedures	No	Number of lab tests performed during the encounter.
num_medications	No	Number of distinct generic names administered during the encounter.
num_procedures	No	Number of procedures (other than lab tests) performed during the encounter.
number_diagnoses	No	Number of diagnoses entered into the system.
number_emergency	No	Number of emergency visits of the patient in the year preceding the encounter.
number_inpatient	No	Number of inpatient visits of the patient in the year preceding the encounter.
number_outpatient	No	Number of outpatient visits of the patient in the year preceding the encounter.
payer_code	No	Who paid? For example, Blue Cross/Blue Shield, Medicare, and self-pay.

Feature	Target Leak?	Description
pioglitazone	No	Indicates whether the specific drug named was prescribed or there was a change in the dosage. Values: "up" if the dosage was increased during the encounter, "down" if the dosage was decreased, "steady" if the dosage did not change, and "no" if the drug was not prescribed.
race	No	Values: Caucasian, Asian, African American, Hispanic, and other.
readmitted	**Target**	**Days to next inpatient readmission. True if less than 30, false if 30 or greater.**
repaglinide	No	Indicates whether the specific drug named was prescribed or there was a change in the dosage. Values: "up" if the dosage was increased during the encounter, "down" if the dosage was decreased, "steady" if the dosage did not change, and "no" if the drug was not prescribed.
rosiglitazone	No	Indicates whether the specific drug named was prescribed or there was a change in the dosage. Values: "up" if the dosage was increased during the encounter, "down" if the dosage was decreased, "steady" if the dosage did not change, and "no" if the drug was not prescribed.
rowID	Id	Numeric identifier added to dataset ranging from 1–10,000.
time_in_hospital	No	Integer number of days between admission and discharge.
tolazamide	No	Indicates whether the specific drug named was prescribed or there was a change in the dosage. Values: "up" if the dosage was increased during the encounter, "down" if the dosage was decreased, "steady" if the dosage did not change, and "no" if the drug was not prescribed.
tolbutamide	No	Indicates whether the specific drug named was prescribed or there was a change in the dosage. Values: "up" if the dosage was increased during the encounter, "down" if the dosage was decreased, "steady" if the dosage did not change, and "no" if the drug was not prescribed.
troglitazone	No	Indicates whether the specific drug named was prescribed or there was a change in the dosage. Values: "up" if the dosage was increased during the encounter, "down" if the dosage was decreased, "steady" if the dosage did not change, and "no" if the drug was not prescribed.
weight	No	Weight in pounds.

Exercises

Exercises and processes for this dataset exist inside the book.

Rights

If using for research, please cite: (Strack et al., 2014).

A.2 Luxury Shoes

Summary

This dataset is a subset of Datafiniti's product database. It hosts information about online retail listings for women's shoes and their associated prices. Each shoe will have an entry for each price found for it so that a single shoe may have multiple entries. Data includes shoe name, brand, price, and more. The data is part of a larger dataset that was used to determine brand markup and pricing strategies for luxury shoes.

Changes to the data have been made via data cleansing; see section below.

Business Goal

Predict and set the appropriate selling price for a low-price vendor entering the online shoe market.

Datasets

Original Dataset
Source: https://www.kaggle.com/datafiniti/womens-shoes-prices.
The original dataset is available in the file *luxury-shoes.csv* in the files included.

Cleaned Dataset
Name: luxury-shoes-trimmed.csv
The cleaned dataset contains a high number of columns with null values. The dataset contains data on 10,000 shoes represented in:

- 27,560 rows
- 96 columns

Dataset Cleaning Process
While it is recommended that readers develop their data cleaning skills, the cleaned dataset is also available in the files included.

- The data vendor had not quite removed all non-shoe items. A simplistic solution to this is to filter using a RegEx match on a list of shoe-related keywords (reducing, in this case, the number of rows from 33.8k to 27.5k)
  - Note: this process possibly trims shoe listings that do not contain shoe keywords in the listing title dependent on the words in the RegEx match list. In this case, a sizeable enough sample has been maintained after applying the filter; note, however, that such cleaning should be based on steadfast business logic to not remove otherwise valuable data.
- Using programmatic means, parse the JSON encoded fields into individual features. JSON-encoded features are: *features, SKU, review, quantity, description.*
  - Original notation in JSON: {"key":"Material","value":["Leather"]}
  - Split to a new column *Material* with the value *Leather* for this row.
- The following features still require cleaning (or removal, if deemed unusable):
  - *Prices.offer* (possible target leak)
  - *Height* (result of JSON parse)
  - *Sizes* (result of JSON parse)
    - *Height* and *Sizes* (among others) are outputs from the JSON field parsing that are not notated uniformly across all rows. Some are numeric values while others extract in string-form.

Data Dictionary
Vendor data dictionary: https://datafiniti-api.readme.io/docs/product-data-schema

Feature	Target Leak?	Description
asins	No	Amazon standard identification number
brand	No	Product brand (Ralph Lauren, Nike, Michael Kors, etc.)
categories	No	Product categories (Shoes, Women's Shoes, Clothing, etc.)
colors	No	Available colors for that listing

Feature	Target Leak?	Description
dateAdded	No	Date of listing creation
dateUpdated	No	Date of listing update
descriptions	No	Description from site product page
dimensions	No	Product dimensions
ean	No	European article number
features	No	Listed product features from the product page
id	Id	Product identification number
imageURLs	No	Product image URLs
keys	No	Combination field with possible: brand, identification number, description, style
manufacturer	No	Product manufacturer
manufacturerNumber	No	Manufacturer product identification code
merchants	No	Distribution merchant
name	No	Product name
prices.amountMax	Yes	Maximum listing price (if changed at any point). This is an alternative target if you intend to find out the top price a product may fetch.
prices.amountMin	**Target**	**Minimum listing price (if changed at any point)**
prices.availability	No	Stocking state of the product
prices.color	No	Product color (and sometimes shoe size)
prices.condition	No	Product condition (new, new w/ box, used, etc.)
prices.currency	No	Listing price currency
prices.dateAdded	No	Date of listing creation
prices.dateSeen	No	Date listing was downloaded
prices.isSale	No	Product is or is not on sale
prices.merchant	No	The listing service provider (Amazon, Overstock, Walmart, etc.)
prices.offer	Yes	Currency amount of sale (*'REDUCED 59.87 USD'*)
prices.returnPolicy	No	Return Policy (string)
prices.shipping	No	Shipping price (string and currency values)
prices.size	No	Product size (string values and numerics: S, M, L | 35.5 | $12^{1/2}$)
prices.sourceURLs	No	Listing location URL
reviews	No	Text field for product reviews
sizes	No	Available product sizes
skus	No	Stock keeping unit(s)
sourceURLs	No	Listing location URL
Upc	No	Universal product number
weight	No	Item weight (non-consistent units)

Exercises

Run the **original** dataset with prices_amountMin as the target.
Create feature set removing any empty features and the feature prices_amountMax (target leak)

1. What are the clear (and less clear) features that inform item price in this set?
   - Features like *brand* and *name* seem readily useful. However, Data Robot assigns more significance to aggregate features like *keys* or *description*, string fields that potentially hold important information with further parsing treatment.
2. With *descriptions* and *keywords* associated with price, how can an incoming vendor better market shoes online to justify a higher selling price?
   - Using DataRobot's integrated text analytics, text features related to high or low price can be viewed easily at a glance. It is possible that with further parsing of *description* and *keyword* fields, better relationships can be developed between text data and price.
   - Worth noting is the potential relationship between text data and fields like *brand* either by explicitly naming the brand or by specific word combinations existing only for listings of a certain brand or distributor.
3. Look at the varying data formats of rows within some columns. Considering inconsistencies in how data is formatted, what are the limitations of this dataset? How will these limitations affect an analysts ability to produce accurate and useful prediction models?
   - The data in the set is a product of web-scraping. As such, rows in some columns are not unified in their data structure (example: for column *height*, values could be *5in*, *high heel 10cm*, or *100 millimeters* among other formats).
   - Additionally, rows often do not have data for all columns; of these columns *with* data, not all rows have the same columns accounted for. This is the cause of many null values and makes it difficult for DataRobot to derive relationships needed for a high-quality model.
   - There are few features that are fully present and unified in structure.

Run the **cleaned** dataset with *prices_amountMin* as the target.
This dataset has been prepared to extract JSON field data and remove non-shoe listings. Create a feature set that removes any empty features and the feature prices_amountMax (target leak)
Examine the features prices.offer, Height, Sizes. How can these features be prepared further to increase DataRobot's predictive capabilities? Are there other features apart from these noted that could benefit from additional feature engineering?

1. How does the predictive capability with these fields parsed compared to that of the raw data? Hint: look at model scores as sorted by different metrics.
   The cleaned dataset produces models that vary in effectiveness based on the metric of evaluation. By Gamma Deviance, the models are slightly less accurate. Judging by RSME, the models become somewhat more predictive (by a degree of ~4 dollars). However, even in this case, they are far from the exact dollar amount, calling into question the model's real-world applicability.

Rights

A.3 Boston Airbnb

Summary

This dataset is sourced from publicly available information on the Airbnb website and contains information on Airbnb listings in the Boston metro area. The data has been cleaned and aggregated to improve its usability for predictive analytics.

Changes made through data cleaning:

- Removed columns that caused target leak
- Removed any redundant columns that mirrored data in cleaned columns

Business Goal

Predict and set the appropriate selling price of Airbnb rooms for the city of Boston.

Datasets

Original Dataset
Source: http://insideairbnb.com/get-the-data.html
   Listings.csv can be found under the Boston section of the linked web page.

Cleaned Dataset
Name: *Boston-Cleaned.csv*. The cleaned dataset removes columns that cause target leak as well as a handful of columns with redundant information.

- 3,500+ Airbnb listings
- 68 features

Dataset Cleaning Process
The following steps were taken to optimize the original listings dataset:

- Remove all url-based features
- Remove all pricing related features except price
- Remove non-cleaned features when similar feature is provided by Airbnb

Data Dictionary
The following Airbnb activity is included in this Boston dataset: Listings, including full descriptions and average review score. More information can be found about the dataset at http://insideairbnb.com/about.html. Note that feature descriptions are not available for this data dictionary. They should, however, be relatively easy to discern.

Feature	Target leak?
access	No
accommodates	No
amenities	No
availability_30	No
availability_365	No
availability_60	No
availability_90	No
bathrooms	No
bed_type	No
bedrooms	No
beds	No
calculated_host_listings_count	No
calendar_last_scraped	No

Feature	Target leak?
calendar_updated	No
cancellation_policy	No
city	No
cleaning_fee	Perhaps
country	No
country_code	No
description	No
experiences_offered	No
first_review	No
guests_included	No
has_availability	Perhaps
host_about	No
host_acceptance_rate	No
host_has_profile_pic	No
host_id	No
host_identity_verified	No
host_is_superhost	No
host_listings_count	No
host_location	No
host_name	No
host_neighbourhood	No
host_response_rate	No
host_response_time	No
host_since	No
host_total_listings_count	No
host_verifications	No
house_rules	No
id	Id
instant_bookable	No
interaction	No
is_location_exact	No
jurisdiction_names	No
last_review	No
latitude	No
license	No
longitude	No
market	No
maximum_nights	No
minimum_nights	No
name	No
neighborhood_overview	No
neighbourhood	No
neighbourhood_cleansed	No
neighbourhood_group_cleansed	No

Feature	Target leak?
notes	No
number_of_reviews	No
price	**Target**
property_type	No
require_guest_phone_verification	No
require_guest_profile_picture	No
requires_license	No
review_scores_accuracy	No
review_scores_checkin	No
review_scores_cleanliness	No
review_scores_communication	No
review_scores_location	No
review_scores_rating	No
review_scores_value	No
reviews_per_month	*Perhaps*
room_type	No
security_deposit	No
smart_location	No
space	No
square_feet	No
state	No
street	No
summary	No
transit	No
zipcode	No

Exercises

Run the cleansed dataset with *Price* as the target.

1. The name of the listing appears to be a fairly informative feature for predicting the cost of an Airbnb in Boston. Which keywords indicate a low-cost listing? Which keywords indicate a high-cost listing?
   - Keywords in Blue indicate a lower cost. For example: *Studio, Room*, and *Cozy*, are fairly informative that a property listing price will be low.
   - Keywords in Red indicate a higher cost. Words like *luxury, condo* and *historic* all indicate higher rental costs.
2. What are three ways someone looking to rent a property on Airbnb might use DataRobot to help them
   - A renter can predict the value of their property to price it appropriately with the rest of the market
   - A renter may look at the word cloud data robot produces to determine which words they should use in their text fields and which words they should stay away from.
3. Which neighborhoods should one expect to pay a premium to stay in the city of Boston? Which neighborhoods might one look at to visit Boston on a budget?

   - The South Boston waterfront and Back Bay are the two most expensive neighborhoods in the dataset. Dorchester and Roslindale are the least.

Rights

This work has been dedicated to the public domain with all rights under copyright law waived, including related and neighboring rights, to the extent allowed by law.

You can copy, modify, distribute and perform the work, even for commercial purposes, all without asking permission.

https://creativecommons.org/publicdomain/zero/1.0/

A.4 Part Backorders

Summary

This dataset looks at the issue of goods or parts on backorder, the goal being to predict which inventory items will go on backorder and need to be more properly stocked. The prepared data file contains historical data for the eight weeks before the week for which to predict appropriate inventory levels. The data was taken as weekly snapshots at the start of each week.

The precise origin of the data remains unknown, as the owner of the data has stated some details cannot be made public. This produces some limitations for analysis in that it is difficult to provide specific business recommendations, lacking subject matter knowledge. However, it remains possible to do a general analysis.

Note: Without knowledge of inventory details of the data, it is possible to use inventory SKUs to identify products and develop a taxonomy to create the most accurate predictions. This is important because not all inventory requires the same treatment; large machinery versus small screws will have different inventory cycles. Even without knowing what each SKU represents, it is possible to make assumptions using past sales and forecasts to understand the type of product.

Business Goal

Predict which items will go on backorder and need to be stocked further.

Datasets

Original Dataset
Source: https://www.kaggle.com/tiredgeek/predict-bo-trial

Cleaned Dataset
Dataset name: *downsampled-11000.csv*

- 11,000 rows
- 22 columns

Data Dictionary

Feature	Target Leak?	Description
deck_risk	No	Part risk flag
forecast_3_month	No	Forecast sales for the next three months (units)
forecast_6_month	No	Forecast sales for the next six months (units)
forecast_9_month	No	Forecast sales for the next nine months (units)
in_transit_qty	No	Amount of product in transit from source
lead_time	No	Transit time for product (if available); in weeks

Feature	Target Leak?	Description
local_bo_qty	No	Amount of stock orders overdue
min_bank	No	Minimum recommended amount to stock
national_inv	No	Current inventory level for the part
oe_constraint	No	Part risk flag
perf_12_month_avg	No	Source performance for prior 12-month period
perf_6_month_avg	No	Source performance for prior 6-month period
pieces_past_due	No	Parts overdue from source
potential_issue	No	Source issue for part identified
ppap_risk	No	Part risk flag
rev_stop	No	Part risk flag
sales_1_month	No	Sales quantity for the prior 1-month period (units)
sales_3_month	No	Sales quantity for the prior 3-month period (units)
sales_6_month	No	Sales quantity for the prior 6-month period (units)
sales_9_month	No	Sales quantity for the prior 9-month period (units)
sku	Id	Random ID for the product
stop_auto_buy	No	Part risk flag
went_on_backorder	**Target**	**Product went on backorder**

Notes on features:

1. National Inventory—There is often a positive relationship between inventory and going on backorder (being on backorder indicated no inventory). Also, consider sale swings that deplete inventory faster than the forecast accounts for. These can sometimes be difficult to predict.
2. Local_bo_qty—These represent stock replenishment orders that could not be fulfilled from the local warehouses. There may or may not be national inventory available to cover the order, but if there is, it will be transferred from another warehouse to cover the demand.
3. Part Risk Flag—The part risk is a manual assignment where the business has tagged the part because the part or supplier of the part has an issue (material shortage, etc.). This feature's relationship to backorders is unclear.
4. Perf_6/12_month_avg—This a scale of the product supplier's historical performance. Some suppliers have not been scored and have a dummy value of −99 loaded.
5. National Inventory—The negative value for national inventory means that one of the locations has placed a stock order for more quantity than is available. However, since it is not a customer order, it is not a considered a backorder to be predicted.
6. Does forecast_9_month include forecast_3_month and forecast_6_month?—Yes, the forecast values are a rolling window, so the 9-month includes the 3 and 6-month; the 6-month includes the 3-month value.

Exercises

Run the training data using *went_on_backorder* as a target.

1. Is this data too large to work with in its original state?
   - DR can certainly handle datasets of this size, but to preserve server resources (and practice downsampling in DR), take a random sample of the data.
   - To do so, before pressing the *START* button, open the *show advanced options* panel directly above the feature list. Scroll to section two named *smart downsampling* and change the percentage to 1%. This will downsample the data to a manageable size while maintaining the ratio of items that did or did not go on backorder (roughly 2x *yes* vs. *no*).

2. Which features, looking at the *Feature Effects* panel, inform the target? Analyze these features and consider which of them are realistically usable and which are less so. Why?
   - Note that the SKU feature is high on the list of importance; however, each item likely has an individual SKU, which provides little information on general trends in predicting backorders. The part risk flag features (5) rank as less important. Other than sales and forecasting, national inventory is the other standout feature noted as informative.

3. With the features analyzed, develop suggestions for how the company can use this data to optimize supply chain(s). (Hint: feature combinations producing positive values can be seen in the insights panel named *hotspots*.)
   - Using DR, the SKUs that will go on backorder can be predicted fairly accurately; however, it is still unknown what the inventory represents. The dataset as-is doesn't provide useful information on which to take action without insider knowledge of the part types and business operations.

Rights

The owner of the dataset is not able to release publicly where the data originates from, but the data is available for the following:

- Share—copy and redistribute the material in any medium or format
- Adapt—remix, transform, and build upon the material
- The licensor cannot revoke these freedoms as long as you follow the license terms.

  https://creativecommons.org/licenses/by-nc-sa/4.0/

A.5   Student Grades Portuguese

Summary

This dataset will provide an example of how DataRobot handles small datasets along with the insights it produces for EDA purposes (regardless of model precision). As well, this example will allow for examination of when a regression problem becomes a classification problem.

The data herein were obtained in a survey of students in Portuguese-language courses in secondary school. The set contains potentially interesting social, gender, and study habit information that can be used to predict future performance of the current students and produce a model for future students. Note also that the set is named *Student Alcohol Consumption*. Alcohol consumption is a component of just 2 of 33 features.

An assumption made about the dataset: it is possible that the data was collected mid-semester when students knew their early session grades. Assume that this data was collected at the *beginning* of the session with grade-related fields being recorded later.

Business Goal

To identify students likely to struggle and develop a course of action to help them improve grades and general academic performance.

Datasets

Original Dataset
https://www.kaggle.com/uciml/student-alcohol-consumption

Cleaned Dataset
Dataset name: *student-por.csv*

- 649 rows
- 32 columns

Data Dictionary

Feature	Target Leak?	Description
Absences	No	number of school absences (numeric: from 0 to 93)
Activities	No	extra-curricular activities (binary: yes or no)
Address	No	student's home address type (binary: 'U' - urban or 'R' - rural)
Age	No	student's age (numeric: from 15 to 22)
DAlc	No	workday alcohol consump. (numeric: from 1 - very low to 5 - very high)
Failures	No	number of past class failures (numeric: n if 1<=n<3, else 4)
FamRel	No	quality of family relationships (numeric: 1 - very bad to 5 - excellent)
Famsiz	No	family size (binary: 'LE3' - less or equal to 3 or 'GT3' - greater than 3)
FamSup	No	family educational support (binary: yes or no)
Fedu	No	father edu. (0 - none, 1 - grade 1–4, 2 - grade 5–9, 3 - high school, 4 - uni)
Fjob	No	father's job ("teacher," "health" care, civil "services," "at_home" or "other")
FreeTime	No	free time after school (numeric: from 1 - very low to 5 - very high)
G1	Yes	first-period grade (numeric: from 0 to 20)
G2	Yes	second-period grade (numeric: from 0 to 20)
G3	**Target**	**final grade (numeric: from 0 to 20, output target)**
GoOut	No	going out with friends (numeric: from 1 - very low to 5 - very high)
Guardian	No	student's guardian (nominal: 'mother', 'father' or 'other')
Health	No	current health status (numeric: from 1 - very bad to 5 - very good)
Higher	No	wants to take higher education (binary: yes or no)
Internet	No	Internet access at home (binary: yes or no)
Medu	No	mother edu. (0 - none, 1 - grade 1–4, 2 - grade 5–9, 3 - high school, 4 - uni)
Mjob	No	mother's job ("teacher," "health" care, civil "services," "at_home" or "other")
Nursery	No	attended nursery school (binary: yes or no)
Paid	No	extra paid classes within the course subject (binary: yes or no)
Pstatu	No	parent's cohabitation status (binary: "T" - living together or "A" - apart)
Reason	No	why that school (near "home," school "reputation," "course" pref. or "other")
Romantic	No	with a romantic relationship (binary: yes or no)
School	No	school ("GP" - Gabriel Pereira "MS" - Mousinho da Silveira)
Sex	No	student's sex (binary: "F" - female or "M" - male)
StudyTime	No	weekly study time in hours (1 - <2 h., 2 - 2–5 h., 3 - 5–10 h., or 4 - >10 h.)
TravelTime	No	commute time in mins(1 - <15 m., 2 - 15–30 m., 3 - 30–60 m., or 4 - >60 m.)
WAlc	No	weekend alcohol consumption (numeric: from 1 - very low to 5 - very high)

Exercises

Run the dataset with *G3* as the target.
Sort by Cross Validation and run the Feature Effects and Feature Impact for the highest ranking model.

1. The default number of cross validation folds in DataRobot is 5. What are the benefits and drawbacks of increasing the number of folds for small datasets? Additionally, the default percentage of holdout

data in DataRobot is 20%. When can an analyst afford (and not afford) to use this 20% of data as holdout (no longer available for model construction)? These settings can be modified in the *Advanced Options* field *before* starting autopilot.

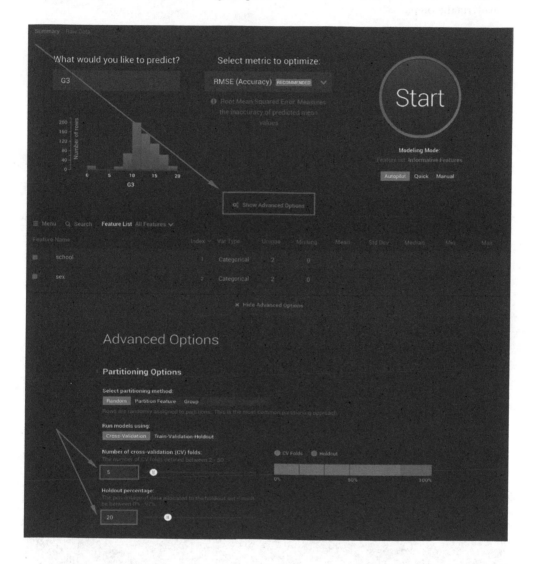

- Generally, 5-fold cross validation is best, as it avoids fold overlap and model overfit. However, with a small dataset, increasing the number of folds allows for more data to be utilized in creating our models.
- For a small dataset, models are less accurate as they have limited training data. Therefore, it is necessary to have every row possible available for model learning/creation. For this reason, increasing the number of folds to maximize available rows is beneficial; however, be wary of creating a model that overfits the sample. This is the purpose of holdout—to test a model outside of the validation sample to examine overfit levels.

- To derive the best results within the confines of a small sample, run DR on the data twice: once on the data with 20 folds *and* 20% holdout. Examine models that do not overfit the data (by releasing the holdout), then rerun the data with *no holdout* and 20 folds using the models that were just found not to overfit the sample.

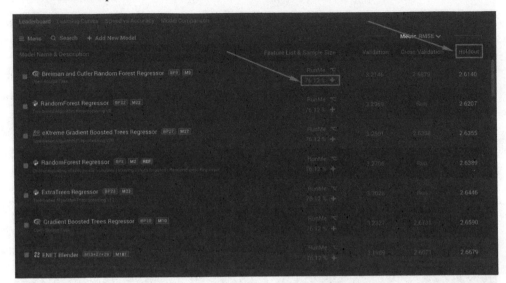

First, run with 20% holdout and 20 fold cross validation. See the % of total data that is used for model construction (in this case: 76.12 made up of 100–20% for the holdout, ~4% for .05 of the remaining 80%).

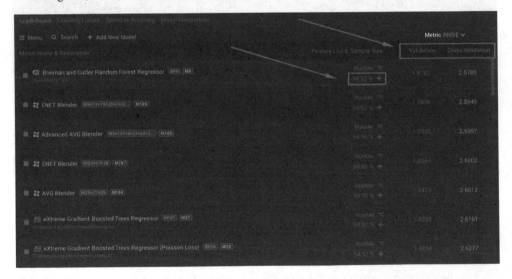

Second run with 0% holdout and 20 fold cross validation (we can see a small increase in CV score). Note the significant increase in data used for model training, now 94.92%

2. How does this settings combination affect the usefulness of single validation (not cross valida-tion)? Single validation is simply one fold being used to evaluate the model. When the folds become smaller, so does the validation sample. As such, in a small dataset, it loses representative ability in judging model performance.

3. DataRobot proposes RMSE as the default metric for this AutoML case. What sorts of problems can be well-judged by RMSE as an optimization metric? RMSE measures the absolute value distance of points from the best-fit regression line produced by the model. This metric is best for numeric pre-diction problems (regression problems). It also explains the model error in meaningful units within the scale of the target feature.

4. How well does the best model predict student performance? The best models have a standard error of 2.xx in either direction from the correct value on a scale of 20. Notice as well that there are no scores below a score of 5. The models may not predict the exact score of a student, but they can serve to predict general performance.

5. Would these models be more predictive with a larger dataset?
   - Looking at the learning curves tab, with so few data points, the models are only run with the max-imum data available rather than stepwise with different quantities withheld. With only 649 rows and the fact that blender models are not able to outperform other models, there is cause to believe that more data would allow for better grade prediction.

6. What are conclusions and suggestions that can be drawn from the *feature impact* and *insights* panels?
   - The insights panel offers an easy-to-interpret dashboard of informative features and the weight they have (to scale in points) on a student's final grade. For instance, *CONST_SPLINE_HIGH_ failures* accounts for a 1.6 grade point decrease when present.
   - With continued data collection (or greater sample size), the models would have more data to draw stable conclusions from. A larger sample size is more preferable to continued data collection if possible to avoid any time-related effects that are not intended to be modeled.
   - Using these panels, EDA assumptions can be made for behaviors which should either be rein-forced or discouraged.

Rights

A.6 Lending Club

Summary

This is a dataset from Lending Club. Lending Club is a peer-to-peer lending platform that also supplies data on all of their loans. Lending Club categorizes loans by the associated risk of default and then assigns the loan a rating: a grade and a sub-grade. These assigned grades are highly correlated with the interest paid on a loan. This dataset contains a total of 120 other attributes specific to each loan; some of these attributes will be useful for predicting a default status, some will be harmful to the model, and others will have no impact.

Business Goal

Eliminate target leak and clean the data to create an accurate model to implement for a hedge fund. This hedge fund is considering investing $40 million/year in loans on LendingClub.com. These loans are an appealing investment with interest rates averaging 12.7% for 36-month loans. However, 14% of these loans are charged off.

Building a model to screen out the riskiest borrowers that can be automated to choose which loans to fund.

Dataset

Original Dataset
Source: https://www.lendingclub.com/info/download-data.action

Cleaned Datasets
Name(s):

- *LendingClub_2007_2014_Cleaned_Original.csv*
- *LendingClub_2007_2014_Cleaned_Whole.csv*
  (avoid to protect your DataRobot processing allotment)
- LendingClub_2007_2014_Cleaned_Reduced.csv (used in this example)

Data Cleaning Process
All loans in these datasets are 36-months loans. The focus of this case is on loans originating between 2007 and 2014 to ensure that all loans have reached maturity (either fully paid back or charged off). The loans can have one of four values relevant to the target feature: *Fully Paid, Charged off, Does not fit credit policy: Fully Paid*, and *Does not fit credit policy: Charged off*. The target created in *LendingClub_2007_2014_Cleaned_Reduced.csv* contains only loans that fit the modern lending club policy. The target values are therefore: 0 = Fully Paid and 1 = Charged off.

Eliminating Target Leak
The Lending Club platform includes attributes seen in Figures A6.1 and A6.2, showing information available to the lender at the time making an investment deciding on a given loan. The Feature list in DR allows for filtration of any data columns that provide insight beyond the date on which a loan originated. By removing these attributes before uploading to DataRobot, necessary to eliminate target leak, each CSV file will also be reduced in size by 90%.

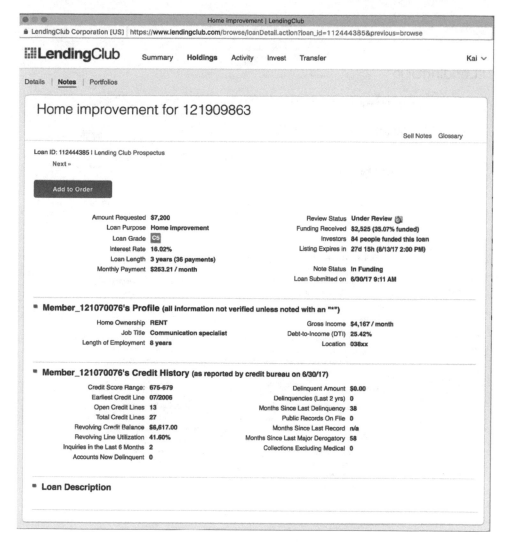

Figure A6.1. Information Available at the Time of Prediction.

Figure A6.2. More Information Available at the Time of Prediction.

Data Dictionary

Feature	Target Leak?	Description
acc_now_delinq	No	The number of accounts on which the borrower is now delinquent.
acc_open_past_24mths	Yes	Number of trades opened in past 24 months.
addr_state	No	The state provided by the borrower in the loan application.
all_util	Yes	Balance to credit limit on all trades.
annual_inc	No	The self-reported annual income provided by the borrower during registration.
annual_inc_joint	Yes	The combined self-reported annual income provided by the co-borrowers during registration.
application_type	Yes	Indicates whether the loan is an individual application or a joint application with two co-borrowers.

Feature	Target Leak?	Description
avg_cur_bal	Yes	Average current balance of all accounts.
bc_open_to_buy	Yes	Total open to buy on revolving bankcards.
bc_util	Yes	Ratio of total current balance to high credit/credit limit for all bankcard accounts.
chargeoff_within_12_mths	Yes	Number of charge-offs within 12 months.
collection_recovery_fee	Yes	Post charge-off collection fee.
collections_12_mths_ex_med	Yes	Number of collections in 12 months excluding medical collections.
delinq_2yrs	No	The number of 30+ days past-due incidences of delinquency in the borrower's credit file for the past two years.
delinq_amnt	No	The past-due amount owed for the accounts on which the borrower is now delinquent.
desc	Yes	Loan description provided by the borrower.
dti	No	A ratio calculated using the borrower's total monthly debt payments on the total debt obligations, excluding mortgage and the requested LC loan, divided by the borrower's self-reported monthly income.
dti_joint	Yes	A ratio calculated using the co-borrowers' total monthly payments on the total debt obligations, excluding mortgages and the requested LC loan, divided by the co-borrowers' combined self-reported monthly income.
earliest_cr_line	No	The month the borrower's earliest reported credit line was opened.
emp_length	No	Employment length in years. Possible values are between 0 and 10 where 0 means less than one year and 10 means ten or more years.
emp_title	No	The job title supplied by the Borrower when applying for the loan.
funded_amnt	No	The total amount committed to that loan at that point in time.
funded_amnt_inv	No	The total amount committed by investors for that loan at that point in time.
grade	No	LC assigned loan grade. Shows up as *Rate* in Figure A6.2.
home_ownership	No	The home ownership status provided by the borrower during registration or obtained from the credit report. Our values are: RENT, OWN, MORTGAGE, OTHER.
initial_list_status	Yes	The initial listing status of the loan. Possible values are – W, F.
inq_fi	Yes	Number of personal finance inquiries.
inq_last_12m	Yes	Number of credit inquiries in past 12 months.
inq_last_6mths	No	The number of inquiries in past 6 months (excluding auto and mortgage inquiries).
installment	No	The monthly payment owed by the borrower if the loan originates.
int_rate	No	Interest rate on the loan.
issue_d	No?	The month which the loan was funded. While LendingClub does not provide this feature at the time of prediction, the month and year of prediction may be provided the model.
last_credit_pull_d	Yes	The most recent month LC pulled credit for this loan.
last_pymnt_amnt	Yes	Last total payment amount received.
last_pymnt_d	Yes	Last month payment was received.
loan_amnt	No	The listed amount of the loan applied for by the borrower. If at some point in time, the credit department reduces the loan amount, then it will be reflected in this value.
loan_status	**Target**	**Current status of the loan. Also listed as *loan_is_bad* in Chapter 5. TRUE = bad loan.**
max_bal_bc	Yes	Maximum current balance owed on all revolving accounts.

Feature	Target Leak?	Description
mo_sin_old_il_acct	Yes	Months since oldest bank installment account opened.
mo_sin_old_rev_tl_op	Yes	Months since oldest revolving account opened.
mo_sin_rcnt_rev_tl_op	Yes	Months since most recent revolving account opened.
mo_sin_rcnt_tl	Yes	Months since most recent account was opened.
mort_acc	Yes	Number of mortgage accounts.
mths_since_last_delinq	No	The number of months since the borrower's last delinquency.
mths_since_last_major_derog	Yes	Months since most recent 90-day or worse rating
mths_since_last_record	No	The number of months since the last public record.
mths_since_rcnt_il	Yes	Months since most recent installment accounts opened.
mths_since_recent_bc_dlq	Yes	Months since most recent bankcard delinquency.
mths_since_recent_inq	Yes	Months since most recent inquiry.
mths_since_recent_revol_delinq	Yes	Months since most recent revolving delinquency.
next_pymnt_d	Yes	Next scheduled payment date.
num_accts_ever_120_pd	Yes	Number of accounts ever 120 or more days past due.
num_actv_bc_tl	Yes	Number of currently active bankcard accounts.
num_actv_rev_tl	Yes	Number of currently active revolving trades.
num_bc_sats	Yes	Number of satisfactory bankcard accounts.
num_bc_tl	Yes	Number of bankcard accounts.
num_il_tl	Yes	Number of installment accounts.
num_op_rev_tl	Yes	Number of open revolving accounts.
num_rev_accts	Yes	Number of revolving accounts.
num_rev_tl_bal_gt_0	Yes	Number of revolving trades with balance >0.
num_sats	Yes	Number of satisfactory accounts.
num_tl_120dpd_2m	Yes	Number of accounts currently 120 days past due (updated in past 2 months).
num_tl_30dpd	Yes	Number of accounts currently 30 days past due (updated in past 2 months).
num_tl_90g_dpd_24m	Yes	Number of accounts 90 or more days past due in last 24 months.
num_tl_op_past_12m	Yes	Number of accounts opened in past 12 months.
open_acc	No	The number of open credit lines in the borrower's credit file.
open_acc_6m	Yes	Number of open trades in last 6 months.
open_il_12m	Yes	Number of installment accounts opened in past 12 months.
open_il_24m	Yes	Number of installment accounts opened in past 24 months.
open_il_6m	Yes	Number of currently active installment trades.
open_rv_12m	Yes	Number of revolving trades opened in past 12 months.
open_rv_24m	Yes	Number of revolving trades opened in past 24 months.
out_prncp	Yes	Remaining outstanding principal for total amount funded.
out_prncp_inv	Yes	Remaining outstanding principal for portion of total amount funded by investors.
pct_tl_nvr_dlq	Yes	Percent of trades never delinquent.
percent_bc_gt_75	Yes	Percentage of all bankcard accounts > 75% of limit.
policy_code	Yes	publicly available policy_code = 1.

Feature	Target Leak?	Description
pub_rec	No	Number of derogatory public records.
pub_rec_bankruptcies	No	Number of public record bankruptcies.
purpose	No	A category provided by the borrower for the loan request.
pymnt_plan	Yes	Indicates if a payment plan has been put in place for the loan.
recoveries	Yes	Post charge-off gross recovery.
revol_bal	No	Total credit revolving balance.
revol_bal_joint	Yes	Total credit revolving balance.
revol_util	Yes	Revolving line utilization rate, or the amount of credit the borrower is using relative to all available revolving credit.
sec_app_chargeoff_within_12_mths	Yes	Number of charge-offs within last 12 months at time of application for the secondary applicant.
sec_app_collections_12_mths_ex_med	No	Number of collections within last 12 months excluding medical collections at time of application for the secondary applicant.
sec_app_earliest_cr_line	Yes	Earliest credit line at time of application for the secondary applicant.
sec_app_inq_last_6mths	Yes	Credit inquiries in the last six months at time of application for the secondary applicant.
sec_app_mort_acc	Yes	Number of mortgage accounts at time of application for the secondary applicant.
sec_app_mths_since_last_major_derog	No	Months since most recent 90-day or worse rating at time of application for the secondary applicant.
sec_app_num_rev_accts	Yes	Number of revolving accounts at time of application for the secondary applicant.
sec_app_open_acc	Yes	Number of open trades at time of application for the secondary applicant.
sec_app_open_il_6m	Yes	Number of currently active installment trades at time of application for the secondary applicant.
sec_app_revol_util	No	Ratio of total current balance to high credit/credit limit for all revolving accounts.
sub_grade	No	LC assigned loan subgrade. Shows up as *Rate* in Figure A6.2.
tax_liens	Yes	Number of tax liens.
term	No	The number of payments on the loan. Values are in months and can be either 36 or 60. Our dataset contains only 36-month loans, so this feature will be excluded by DataRobot.
title	Yes	The loan title provided by the borrower.
tot_coll_amt	Yes	Total collection amounts ever owed.
tot_cur_bal	Yes	Total current balance of all accounts.
tot_hi_cred_lim	Yes	Total high credit/credit limit.
total_acc	No	The total number of credit lines currently in the borrower's credit file.
total_bal_ex_mort	No	Total credit balance excluding mortgage.
total_bal_il	Yes	Total current balance of all installment accounts.
total_bc_limit	Yes	Total bankcard high credit/credit limit.
total_cu_tl	Yes	Number of finance trades.
total_il_high_credit_limit	Yes	Total installment high credit/credit limit.
total_pymnt	Yes	Payments received to date for total amount funded.
total_pymnt_inv	Yes	Payments received to date for portion of total amount funded by investors.
total_rec_int	Yes	Interest received to date.

Feature	Target Leak?	Description
total_rec_late_fee	Yes	Late fees received to date.
total_rec_prncp	Yes	Principal received to date.
url	Yes	Months since most recent 90-day or worse rating at time of application for the secondary applicant.
verification_status	Yes	Months since most recent 90-day or worse rating at time of application for the secondary applicant.
verification_status_joint	Yes	Months since most recent 90-day or worse rating at time of application for the secondary applicant.
zip_code	No	Zip code. Partial zip code provided.

Rights

"Do not use data provided by Lending Club, provided in any manner whatsoever, for any competing uses or purposes. You further agree that you have never used data, provided in any manner whatsoever, from Lending Club in the past to compete with the products or services of Lending Club"
Statement from Lending Club accessed September 17, 2017

A.7 College Starting Salaries

Summary

This dataset serves as a cautionary example of applying DataRobot to a dataset that is not robust. The data herein is a joined set obtained from Payscale, Inc. via the *Wall Street Journal*. It takes note of early- and mid-career average salaries of US colleges/university graduates. Data includes school name, school type, and salary information broken into sub-fields (10th, 25th, 75th, and 90th percentiles).

Business Goal

Predict starting median salary of prospective universities (as a parent or incoming student).

Datasets

Original Dataset
Source: https://www.kaggle.com/wsj/college-salaries.
Names:

- *salaries-by-college-type.csv*
- *salaries-by-region.csv*

Cleaned Dataset
Name: *college-salaries_joined.csv*

- 268 schools/records
- Eight features (dictionary below)
- Features can be simplified down to 4, dropping percentile statistics

Data Dictionary

Feature	Target Leak?	Description
Mid 10th Percentile Salary	Yes	10th percentile avg. salary of graduates mid-career
Mid 25th Percentile Salary	Yes	25th percentile avg. salary of graduates mid-career
Mid 75th Percentile Salary	Yes	75th percentile avg. salary of graduates mid-career
Mid 90th Percentile Salary	Yes	90th percentile avg. salary of graduates mid-career
Mid-Career Med. Salary	Yes	Median salary of graduates mid-career
School Name	No	Name of university or college
School Type	No	Category of school (*party, liberal arts, state, Ivy League, engineering*)
Starting Med. Salary	**Target**	**Median salary of graduates at start of career**

Exercises

Run the joined dataset with *Starting Median Salary* as the target.
Create feature set removing the percentile features—these are duplicates of the aggregate mid-career median salary feature—remove as well the feature Mid-Career Med. Salary (target leak).
*DataRobot does not allow features with currency variable types to be used as a target. To fix this, go to the menu and select create f(x) transformation and create a new feature called Numeric Starting median salary and set it equal to Starting Median Salary * 1. Use Numeric Starting Median Salary as your target.*

1. Judging by model validation and cross validation scores, how predictive are the models?
   - It is clear, looking at RMSE, that these models have quite large margins of error.
2. Can this dataset realistically be used to predict starting median salary for a university?

   - This is a good example of the lower-bound limits of machine learning regarding available data. DataRobot (and machine learning in general) requires a larger training set upon which the computer can draw relationships to be effective.

Rights

Data is displayed publicly at the following locations. It is not explicitly noted whether or not it is under copyright of any sort.
Links:
http://online.wsj.com/public/resources/documents/infoSalaries_for_Colleges_by_Region-sort.html
http://online.wsj.com/public/resources/documents/infoSalaries_for_Colleges_by_Type-sort.html

A.8 HR Attrition

Summary

This case contains two datasets to be compared against one another: a general "Simulated Set" and an "IBM Simulated Set."

Simulated Set
This sizeable dataset is a record of 14,999 employees including HR-related details, and whether or not these employees left the company. Features include satisfaction and performance levels, time spent at the company, salary, division of work, and more. The dataset is simulated, but is robust and varied

enough to provide an interesting look at how machine learning can inform HR efforts to increase employee retention.

IBM Simulated Set

This dataset was produced by IBM data scientists for practice modeling and exploratory analysis. It includes similar features as the first set, but differs in having about 2x as many features per individual (~35). This set is, however, slimmer than the first, having only 10% as many data points.

Business Goal

Predict which employees are at risk of leaving. Who needs special attention to be retained?

Datasets

Simulated Set
Origin: https://www.kaggle.com/giripujar/hr-analytics
Name: *hr-attrition.csv*

- 14,999 rows
- 9 columns (dictionary below)

IBM Simulated Set

Origin: https://www.kaggle.com/pavansubhasht/ibm-hr-analytics-attrition-dataset
Name: *ibm-hr-attrition.csv*

- 1,470 rows
- 34 columns (dictionary below)

Data Dictionaries
Simulated Set

Feature	Target Leak?	Description
average_montly_hours	No	Average number of hours worked per month. Note typo in original feature name
last_evaluation	No	0 to 1 numeric rating of employee performance at last review
left	**Target**	**Binary – did the employee leave**
number_project	No	Number projects the employee has been assigned
promotion_last_5years	No	Binary – was the employee promoted in the last five years
salary	No	Categorical salary (i.e., high, medium, low)
sales	No	String value division of work (i.e., sales, support, management, hr, etc.)
satisfaction_level	No	0 to 1 numeric rating of satisfaction (i.e., .55 - > 55% satisfied)
time_spend_company	No	Number of years spent as company employee
Work_accident	No	Binary – has the employee had a work-related accident

IBM Simulated Set

Feature	Target Leak?	Description
Age	No	Age of employee
Attrition	**Target**	**Binary of whether or not they left the company ("Yes" or "No")**
BusinessTravel	No	String value noting frequency of business travel
DailyRate	No	Daily pay rate in dollars
Department	No	Department in which they work (HR, R&D, etc. string value)
DistanceFromHome	No	Distance between home and office (in miles)
Education	No	Scale 1–5 (1 "Below College" 2 "College" 3 "Bachelor" 4 "Master" 5 "Doctor"
EducationField	No	Field of study (string value: technical degree, medical degree, etc.)
EmployeeCount	No	Count of employees (always 1 for each row)
EmployeeNumber	No	Employee identification number
EnvironmentSatisfaction	No	Scale 1–4 satisfaction with working environment
Gender	No	Binary value ("Male" or "Female")
HourlyRate	No	Hourly pay rate in dollars
JobInvolvement	No	Scale 1–4 level of involvement in daily work
JobLevel	No	Scale 1–5 level of seniority within company
JobRole	No	Job role title (string value: "Sales Executive," "Laboratory Technician," etc.)
JobSatisfaction	No	Scale 1–4 level of satisfaction with job
MaritalStatus	No	Marital status (string value: "Single," "Married," "Divorced")
MonthlyIncome	No	Monthly income in dollars
MonthlyRate	No	Monthly rate of pay in dollars
NumCompaniesWorked	No	Total number of companies worked for in employee career
Over18	No	Binary value for over age of 18 (Y/N)
OverTime	No	Binary value for having received overtime at any point (Y/N)
PercentSalaryHike	No	Percent salary increase of current position since beginning in that pos.
PerformanceRating	No	Scale 1–4 rating employee performance
RelationshipSatisfaction	No	Scale 1–4 rating employee satisfaction with professional relationships
StandardHours	No	Standard weekly working (bi-weekly?) working hours (always 80 for all)
StockOptionLevel	No	Scale 0–3 ranking available stock options for employee
TotalWorkingYears	No	Total working years for entire career
TrainingTimesLastYear	No	Scale 0–6 number of trainings received in previous year
WorkLifeBalance	No	Scale 1–4 noting work-life balance (1 is low, 4 is high)
YearsAtCompany	No	Number of years working at current company
YearsInCurrentRole	No	Number of years in current role
YearsSinceLastPromotion	No	Years since receiving last promotion
YearsWithCurrManager	No	Number of years working under current manager

Exercises

Simulated Set
Run the dataset with *left* as the target.
Sort by *Cross Validation* and run the *Feature Effect* and *Feature Impact* for the highest ranking model.

1. Take a look at the *feature impact* pane. What are the key indicators of an employee deciding to leave?
   - *satisfaction_level, time_spend_company, number_project, average_montly_hours,* and *last_evaluation* are the most predictive features.
2. Now take a closer look at these features in the Feature Effects, noting the trend line. What story do these charts tell? How is loyalty fostered, according to this data?
   - Looking only at satisfaction level, positive cases of *left* spike at very low levels, a chunk at mid-level (.35–.45), and ever-so-slightly between .75 and .9.
3. Click now to the *Insights* pane and then on the horizontal red/blue bar chart. Here, DataRobot weighs the correlation of specific variables with the target (*left*). How do these conclusions compare to your own?
   - DataRobot applies coefficients to specific ranges of variable outcomes. Note that this frame only displays insights for some models. Be aware of the selected model and how the scoring results for that model compare to the top model available.

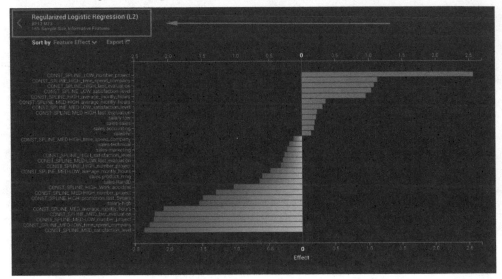

In this case, the model selected (Regularized Logistic Regression (L2)) uses only 16% of the available data and ranks significantly lower than top models.

-Note: Look also at the *Hotspots* tab to see the most common cases of positive target variable outcomes. Be aware here as well which model these insights are derived from.

4. Clicking back to *Models* and selecting the winning model, navigate to the *ROC Curve* tab. Note the very high level of accuracy of this model; testing understanding of the charts and metrics in this tab, explain briefly what information each chart provides, include a general note on the predictive metrics and a summarizing statement about the model, as well as possible ideas for why the model is so cleanly divided.

IBM Simulated Set
Run the dataset with *attrition* as the target.
Sort by *Cross Validation* and run the *Feature Effects* and *Feature Impact* for the highest ranking model.

1. Look at the *Feature Effects*; which features that have a relationship to *attrition* can be addressed by a manager? Which variables are out of such control?
   - Features that concern an employee's career history (i.e., *total working years*, or *number of companies in career*) are impossible to change unlike features such as *workplace environment satisfaction*.
   - Note: features that cannot be changed may inform other business problems like how to structure hiring criteria. Employees who have fewer years of professional experience may be more likely to quit, which can be a factor in how to intelligently hire new team members.
2. Take a look at the *feature impact* pane. Compare the number of features in the IBM set to those of the first set. How does the added level of granularity affect our ability to identify employees at risk of leaving the company?
   - Disregarding level of model predictability, the IBM model provides potentially more telling exploratory data analysis (EDA) opportunities by identifying more specific components of employee burn-out.
   - It is possible that, with more test cases, the IBM dataset could produce a more accurate model. This can be seen in the *learning curves* section. However, with so few features, the IBM set is only run once using all available points.

Rights

Simulated Set
You are free to:

Share—copy and redistribute the material in any medium or format
Adapt—remix, transform, and build upon the material for any purpose, even commercially.

The licensor cannot revoke these freedoms as long as you follow the license terms.
https://creativecommons.org/licenses/by-sa/4.0/

IBM Simulated Set
You are free to:

Share—To copy, distribute and use the database.
Create—To produce works from the database.
Adapt—To modify, transform and build upon the database.

As long as you:

Attribute—You must attribute any public use of the database, or works produced from the database, in the manner specified in the ODbL. For any use or redistribution of the database, or works produced from it, you must make clear to others the license of the database and keep intact any notices on the original database.
Share-Alike—If you publicly use any adapted version of this database, or works produced from an adapted database, you must also offer that adapted database under the ODbL.
Keep open—If you redistribute the database, or an adapted version of it, then you may use technological measures that restrict the work (such as DRM) as long as you also redistribute a version without such measures. https://opendatacommons.org/licenses/odbl/summary/

A.9 Avocadopocalypse Now?

Summary

This dataset is a subset of the Hass Avocado Board data aggregated by Justin Kiggins.

Business Goal

Examine the best place for millennials to live so that they can have their avocado toast and also afford their own house.

Datasets

Original Dataset

Source: https://www.kaggle.com/neuromusic/avocado-prices.
Original source: http://www.hassavocadoboard.com/retail/volume-and-price-data
Original description of data: "The table below represents weekly 2018 retail scan data for National retail volume (units) and price. Retail scan data comes directly from retailers' cash registers based on actual retail sales of Hass avocados. Starting in 2013, the table below reflects an expanded, multi-outlet retail data set. Multi-outlet reporting includes an aggregation of the following channels: grocery, mass, club, drug, dollar and military. The Average Price (of avocados) in the table reflects a per unit (per avocado) cost, even when multiple units (avocados) are sold in bags. The Product Lookup codes (PLU's) in the table are only for Hass avocados. Other varieties of avocados (e.g. greenskins) are not included in this table."

Cleaned Dataset

Datasets:
For Chapter 25 on time-aware modeling: *avocado.csv*.
For Chapter 26 on time series modeling: *avocado 2015-2017.csv* and *avocado 2018.csv*.
The cleaned dataset for time-aware analysis is available with the book in the file avocado.csv. The dataset contains data on 18,249 avocado purchase patterns in:

- 18,249 rows
- 12 columns

The cleaned dataset for time series analysis is available with the book in the file avocado 2015-2017.csv. The dataset contains data on 12,874 avocado purchase patterns in:

- 12,874 rows
- 14 columns

Dataset Cleaning Process

This dataset was not originally developed for this book and has been a regular in DataRobot training sessions. It was originally cleaned and reduced by DataRobot staff, making the cleaning process unclear.

Data Dictionary (Time-aware Modeling)

Feature	Target Leak?	Description
Average Price	**Target (time-aware)**	The average price of a single avocado
Bags Large	Yes	Total number of large bags sold
Bags Small	Yes	Total number of small bags sold
Bags Total	Yes	Total number of bags sold
Bags XL	Yes	Total number of extra large bags sold
Date	No	The date of the observation
Hass Large	Yes	Total number of avocados with PLU 4225 sold
Hass Small	Yes	Total number of avocados with PLU 4046 sold

Feature	Target Leak?	Description
Hass XL	Yes	Total number of avocados with PLU 4770 sold
Region	No	The city or region of the observation
Sales	**Target (time series)**	**Product of Average Price and Total Volume for each region and each type.**
SeriesId	No	Unique identifiers for each series (one series per city and type combination). **Only available in time series data.**
Total Volume	Yes	Total number of avocados sold
Type	No	Conventional or organic avocados

Exercises

Exercises and processes for this dataset exist inside the book.

Rights

Released Under Database: Open Database, Contents: © Original Authors. Permission to use for book given by Justin Kiggins on August 24, 2018.

Optimization and Sorting Measures

Most of these optimization and sorting measures were taken from the DataRobot documentation. Many originated from Stackexchange (2018).

Display	Full Name	Description
AMS@15%tsh	Approximate Median Significance	Measures the median of estimated significance with a 15% threshold.
AMS@opt_tsh	Approximate Median Significance	Measures the median of estimated significance with an optimal threshold.
AUC	Area Under the (ROC) Curve	Measures the ability to distinguish the ones from the zeros.
Coldstart MAD	Mean Absolute Deviation	Measures the inaccuracy of predicted mean values; for recommendation systems, cold-start (previously unseen) uses only Coldstart MAE.
Coldstart RMSE	Root Mean Squared Error	Measures the inaccuracy of predicted mean values when the target is normally distributed; for recommendation systems, cold-start (previously unseen) users only.
FVE Binomial	Fraction of Variance Explained	Measures deviance based on fitting on a binomial distribution.
FVE Gamma	Fraction of Variance Explained	For Gamma deviance.
FVE Poisson	Fraction of Variance Explained	For Poisson deviance.
FVE Tweedie	Fraction of Variance Explained	For Tweedie deviance.
Gamma Deviance	Gamma Deviance	Measures the inaccuracy of predicted mean values when the target is skewed and gamma distributed.
Gini	Gini Coefficient	Measures the ability to rank.
Gini Norm	Normalized Gini Coefficient	Measures the ability to rank.
LogLoss	Logarithmic Loss	Measures the inaccuracy of predicted probabilities.
MAD	Mean Absolute Deviation	Measures the inaccuracy of predicted mean values. Steps: 1. Calculate mean. 2. Calculate each prediction's absolute distance from the mean (deviation from the mean). 3. Add deviations together for a total sum. 4. Divide sum by number of predictions.
MAE	Mean Absolute Error	Measures the inaccuracy of predicted mean values.
MAPE	Mean Absolute Percentage Error	Measures the percent inaccuracy of the mean values.
MASE	Mean Absolute Scaled Error	*For time series models only.* Measures relative performance with respect to a baseline model.
NDCG	Normalized Discounted Cumulative Gain	Measures the ability to rank graded items.
Normalized MAD	Mean Absolute Deviation	Measures the inaccuracy of predicted mean values, normalized by user ID.
Normalized MAE	Mean Absolute Error	Measures the inaccuracy of predicted mean values, normalized by user ID.

Display	Full Name	Description
Normalized RMSE	Root Mean Squared Error	Measures the inaccuracy of predicted mean values when the target is normally distributed, normalized by user ID.
Poisson Deviance	Poisson Deviance	Measures the inaccuracy of predicted mean values for count data.
R Squared	R Squared	Measures the proportion of total variation of outcomes explained by the model.
Rate@Top10%	Rate@Top10%	Response rate in the top 10% highest predictions.
Rate@Top5%	Rate@Top5%	Response rate in the top 5% highest predictions.
Rate@TopTenth%	Rate@TopTenth%	Response rate in the top tenth highest predictions.
RMSE	Root Mean Squared Error	Measures the inaccuracy of predicted mean values when the target is normally distributed.
RMSLE	Root Mean Log Squared Error	Measures the inaccuracy of predicted mean values when the target is skewed and log-normal distributed.
Tweedie Deviance	Tweedie Deviance	Measures the inaccuracy of predicted mean values when the target is zero-inflated and skewed.

The following table describes weighted metrics. The weights are the result of smart downsampling and/or specifying a value for the Advanced Options weights parameter. The metric then takes those weights into account.

Display	Full Name	Description
Weighted AUC	Area Under the (ROC) Curve	Measures the ability to distinguish the ones from the zeros
Weighted FVE Binomial	Fraction of Variance Explained	For binomial deviance
Weighted FVE Poisson	Fraction of Variance Explained	For Poisson deviance
Weighted FVE Gamma	Fraction of Variance Explained	For Gamma deviance
Weighted FVE Tweedie	Fraction of Variance Explained	For Tweedie deviance
Weighted Gamma Deviance	Weighted Gamma Deviance	Measures the inaccuracy of predicted mean values when the target is skewed and gamma distributed
Weighted Gini	Gini Coefficient	Measures the ability to rank
Weighted Gini Norm	Normalized Gini Coefficient	Measures the ability to rank
Weighted MAPE	Mean Absolute Percentage Error	Measures the percent inaccuracy of the mean values
Weighted LogLoss	Logarithmic Loss	Measures the inaccuracy of predicted probabilities
Weighted MAD	Mean Absolute Deviation	Measures the inaccuracy of predicted mean values
Weighted MAE	Mean Absolute Error	Measures the inaccuracy of predicted mean values
Weighted Normalized MAD	Mean Absolute Deviation	Measures the inaccuracy of predicted mean values, normalized by user ID
Weighted Normalized MAE	Mean Absolute Error	Measures the inaccuracy of predicted mean values, normalized by user ID
Weighted Normalized RMSE	Root Mean Squared Error	Measures the inaccuracy of predicted mean values when the target is normally distributed, normalized by user ID

Display	Full Name	Description
Weighted Poisson Deviance	Weighted Poisson Deviance	Measures the inaccuracy of predicted mean values for count data
Weighted R Squared	Weighted R Squared	Measures the proportion of total variation of outcomes explained by the model
Weighted RMSE	Root Mean Squared Error	Measures the inaccuracy of predicted mean values when the target is normally distributed
Weighted RMSLE	Root Mean Log Squared Error	Measures the inaccuracy of predicted mean values when the target is skewed and log-normal distributed
Weighted Tweedie Deviance	Weighted Tweedie Deviance	Measures the inaccuracy of predicted mean values when the target is zero-inflated and skewed

More on Cross Validation

Sampling has generally been used to select smaller datasets (samples) that mirror the characteristics of a population (the entirety of the group being studied). In machine learning, sampling is used both to create datasets that will be used to build models and datasets used to evaluate models to ensure that machine learning findings are generalizable to contemporary data *and* capable of predicting future behaviors and events (customers, clients, website visitors, weather, etc.). The benefit of sampling is, for very large datasets, the preservation of processing power and time spent in analysis. In such cases, it is critical to make sure that enough rows are retained for effective prediction-making. In Chapter 16.1, a method called *learning curves* is discussed for using machine learning to understand how much data is enough. There are also cases where the dataset is what can be called an *unbalanced* dataset. An unbalanced dataset occurs when one value is underrepresented relative to the other in what is called a binary target (two target values, for example, "yes" and "no"). Unbalanced datasets are common in machine learning.

A typical example might be training datasets whose target values indicate whether someone is afflicted by a specific disease or whether someone clicked on or bought a specific product advertised to them. It is common in such cases to downsample only the rows from the majority class (for example, ad-clickers, but this does require you to put weights on the rows you keep, an advanced topic not covered in this book) so as not to lose any of the few cases in the minority class (non-ad-clickers). In most tools, this often means applying a filtering tool to create two tables, one for each class of target, before downsampling the majority class. Then, the tables will be joined back together again with a union.

In machine learning, random sampling is baked into the core of the process. The available data is almost always randomly sampled into several groups to evaluate the success of a model. The first set of data that extracted is the *holdout sample*. This set of data will be used for the final evaluation of the model(s) produced. For the AutoML tool used in this book, this is most often 20% of the available data. Think of this data as being locked into a safe for examination at the very end of the project to evaluate the true accuracy of the top-scoring machine-learning model. There are often multiple rounds of adjusting the data and the model before the model is at its highest level of predictive capability possible. Throughout this process, the data in the holdout sample remained hidden and locked away. Once the final business decisions are ready to be made using the model, this data can be released and used to evaluate the expected model performance. Before releasing the holdout sample for evaluation, other samples will be used for validating models, so let us start with a demonstration of the whole process.

Figure C.1 demonstrates the principles of holdout, validation, and cross validation. On the left, it shows the full dataset, in this case, the first three columns of a 25-row dataset, the smallest dataset possible for clean splitting with the sampling percentages used. The three columns are, in order, a *unique identifier*, a *feature* used to predict the target, and the *target*. While this dataset size is below the threshold for running machine learning, the principle is the same as with a larger dataset. Imagine that each row represents 1,000 rows in a 25,000-row dataset. The following steps are conducted in validation, cross validation, and holdout sample creation and use. These concepts will be explained as the appendix continues as they are best explained in context:[1]

1. Randomize the order of the data and select a *holdout sample*. In this case, 20% of the data is set aside and locked up to minimize the temptation of checking it while building the model (illustrated in Figure C.1 in dark gray). The remaining data is split into a set of *folds* (another word for this would be "groups"). Five or ten folds is the most common number. An appropriate number of folds (not too few or too many) balances the processing power needed for cross validation with the retaining as much of the data for model building as possible. In this example, five-fold validation will be used

---

[1] Note that the order presented here is conceptual and that a machine learning system does not have to conduct these steps in the same way.

Step 0: Randomize data and pick holdout sample and folds.

10993	0	0
10457	0	0
10527	0	1
11043	0	0
10638	0	1
10970	0	0
10440	1	1
11029	0	1
10815	0	0
10812	0	1
10795	0	0
10313	0	0
10407	0	0
10817	1	0
10306	0	0
10634	1	0
10281	2	0
10681	0	0
10386	2	0
10668	0	0
11048	0	0
11045	0	0
10818	0	0
10544	1	0
10353	1	0

Step 1: Build model with combination of folds 2+3+4+5, validate on fold 1.

Fold			
Holdout (20%)			
Fold 1 (16%)	10970	0	0
	10440	1	1
	11029	0	1
	10815	0	0
Fold 2 (16%)	10812	0	1
	10795	0	0
	10313	0	0
	10407	0	0
Fold 3 (16%)	10817	1	0
	10306	0	0
	10634	1	0
	10281	2	0
Fold 4 (16%)	10681	0	0
	10386	2	0
	10668	0	0
	11048	0	0
Fold 5 (16%)	11045	0	0
	10818	0	0
	10544	1	0
	10353	1	0

Step 2: Build model with combination of folds 1+3+4+5, validate on fold 2.

Fold			
Holdout (20%)			
Fold 1 (16%)	10970	0	0
	10440	1	1
	11029	0	1
	10815	0	0
Fold 2 (16%)	10812	0	1
	10795	0	0
	10313	0	0
	10407	0	0
Fold 3 (16%)	10817	1	0
	10306	0	0
	10634	1	0
	10281	2	0
Fold 4 (16%)	10681	0	0
	10386	2	0
	10668	0	0
	11048	0	0
Fold 5 (16%)	11045	0	0
	10818	0	0
	10544	1	0
	10353	1	0

Figure C.1. Cross Validation Principles. First Steps.

as it is easier to visualize. Given that 80% of the data is left after removal of the holdout, 16% of the data is left for each of the five folds.

2. Ignore the holdout sample for the moment and focus on the remaining five folds. First, set aside Fold 1 (illustrated in yellow), combine the rows in the remaining four folds (2–5), and use these rows to create a model of which features (columns) drive (explain) the target. Once that model is prepared, it is given access to all the data in Fold 1 (yellow) (not including the target column). The model is now employed to predict the actual value in the target column. Once those predictions are complete, the machine learning system compares the true target value inside Fold 1 to its predicted target values and calculates a variety of success metrics. Assuming a binary target (zeros and ones, as in this example), the *Accuracy* measure may be used to see how many of true zeros the model predicted as zero values and how many true ones the model predicted as one values. If it is correct in 3 out of 4 cases, the accuracy is 0.75 (or 75 percent). This will later be referred to as the *Validation Score*, though any number of other measures of success can be used as well (most are a bit more mathematically complex). Obtaining this score often includes a significant cost of processing power. If the dataset in question is sufficiently large, the model validation process sometimes ends here, as further cross validation may be prohibitively costly regarding time or machine processing.

3. Step 3 only occurs if cross validation is deemed appropriate and valuable for a given model. In AutoML, this will often happen automatically for the top models if the dataset is below a certain size. This step and the following (Steps 2–5) are conducted tandem as a single process, *cross validation*. Here, the validation sample is no longer Fold 1, but rather Fold 2, now hidden from the algorithm. The remaining four folds (1, 3, 4, and 5) are combined into one table and used for algorithm training. Once that algorithm has created a model, the model is applied to the validation sample (Fold 2) and, as in Step 1, predicts the state of the target variable for each row and then calculating success metrics (in this case *Accuracy* score). Let's assume this one was right 2/4 times—an accuracy of 0.50.

4. Step 4 is not pictured in Figure C.1; however, it follows the same actions in Step 2. The validation sample is moved down one more step and is now Fold 3. Training is conducted with the combined folds 1+2+4+5. Validation is run against Fold 3, this time with an accuracy of .25 (1/4 rows are correctly assigned).

5. In Step 5, the validation sample is moved down to fold 4. Training is conducted with the combined folds 1+2+3+5. Validation is run against Fold 4 with an accuracy of .75 (3/4 of rows are correctly assigned).

6. In Step 6, the validation sample is moved down to Fold 5. Training is conducted with the combined folds 1+2+3+4. Validation is run against Fold 5 with an accuracy of .25 (1/4 rows are correctly assigned).

7. Overall accuracy for cross validation is calculated. It is worth noting that every row in the (non-holdout) training set is used five times, four times to help construct a model and one time to evaluate another model for which it was not active in constructing. The overall model accuracy is calculated by checking the true target value for all 20 rows against their predicted values. In this case, the number of correct predictions was 3+2+1+3+1 = 10 out of 20 correct—an accuracy of 0.50 (50 percent). Further coverage of evaluation of models will come in Chapter 17, but for now, this should be readily apparent as an abysmal accuracy. Random assignment of values for the target variable would produce an expected accuracy of 0.50. Thus, the model is no better than a blind guess.

8. Finally, with feedback from validation/cross validation, improvements can be made to the dataset and Steps 2–6 can be run once more to test new iterations. With the data scientist satisfied that they have improved the model as much as they are capable, the selected algorithm is trained on all five folds, and a completed model is created. This model is then used to predict the target of the rows in the holdout sample, and a final accuracy is evaluated and communicated to stakeholders involved in the project.

References

Allen, M. (2018, July 17, 2018). Health Insurers Are Vacuuming Up Details about You—And It Could Raise Your Rates. *Morning Edition.*

Ampil, C., Cardenas-Navia, L. I., Elzey, K., Fenlon, M., Fitzgerald, B. K., & Hughes, D. (2017). Investing in America's data science and analytics talent: The case for action. Retrieved from pwc.com/us/dsa-skills.

Arnulf, J. K., Larsen, K. R., Martinsen, Ø. L., & Bong, C. H. (2014). Predicting survey responses: How and why semantics shape survey statistics on organizational behaviour. *PloS One, 9*(9), e106361.

Arnulf, J. K., Larsen, K. R., Martinsen, Ø. L., & Egeland, T. (2018). The failing measurement of attitudes: How semantic determinants of individual survey responses come to replace measures of attitude strength. *Behavior Research Methods,* 1–21. doi:https://doi.org/10.3758/s13428-017-0999-y.

Aschwanden, C. (2017, April 13, 2017). Can Science Help Runners Break The Marathon's 2-Hour Barrier. Retrieved from https://fivethirtyeight.com/features/can-science-help-runners-break-the-marathons-2-hour-barrier/.

Baker, R. S., & Inventado, P. S. (2014). Educational data mining and learning analytics. In: Larusson J., & White, B. (eds.) *Learning Analytics* (pp. 61–75). New York: Springer.

Bano, M., & Zowghi, D. (2015). A systematic review on the relationship between user involvement and system success. *Information and Software Technology, 58,* 148–169.

Bergstra, J. S., Bardenet, R., Bengio, Y., & Kégl, B. (2011). *Algorithms for hyper-parameter optimization.* Paper presented at the Advances in Neural Information Processing Systems.

Berry, M. J. A., & Linoff, G. S. (2004). *Data Mining Techniques: For Marketing, Sales, and Customer Relationship Management* (2nd ed.). Indianapolis, IN: Wiley.

Breiman, L. (2001). Statistical modeling: The two cultures (with comments and a rejoinder by the author). *Statistical Science, 16*(3), 199–231.

Breiman, L., & Friedman, J. H. (1985). Estimating optimal transformations for multiple regression and correlation. *Journal of the American Statistical Association, 80*(391), 580–598.

Brockwell, P. J., & Davis, R. A. (2013). *Time Series: Theory and Methods.* New York: Springer.

Burns, M. N., Begale, M., Duffecy, J., Gergle, D., Karr, C. J., Giangrande, E., & Mohr, D. C. (2011). Harnessing context sensing to develop a mobile intervention for depression. *Journal of Medical Internet Research, 13*(3), e55.

CNN. (2018). Cost of Living: How Far Will My Salary Go in Another City?

Copeland, R., & Hope, B. (2016, Dec. 22, 2016). The World's Largest Hedge Fund Is Building an Algorithmic Model From its Employees' Brains. *The Wall Street Journal.*

Davenport, T. H. (2006). Competing on analytics. *Harvard Business Review, 84*(1), 98.

Davenport, T. H., Harris, J., & Shapiro, J. (2010). Competing on talent analytics. *Harvard Business Review, 88*(10), 52–58.

Davenport, T. H., & Harris, J. G. (2007). *Competing on Analytics: The New Science of Winning.* Cambridge, MA: Harvard Business Review Press.

Davenport, T. H., & Patil, D. J. (2012). Data scientist: The sexiest job of the 21st century. *Harvard Business Review,* 70.

Domingos, P. (2012). A few useful things to know about machine learning. *Communications of the ACM, 55*(10), 78–87.

Durden, T. (2012, August 8, 2012). From Chicago to New York and Back in 8.5 Milliseconds. *ZeroHedge.*

Franklin, V. L., Waller, A., Pagliari, C., & Greene, S. A. (2006). A randomized controlled trial of Sweet Talk, a text-messaging system to support young people with diabetes. *Diabetic Medicine, 23*(12), 1332–1338.

Frino, A., Mollica, V., & Webb, R. I. (2014). The impact of co-location of securities exchanges' and traders' computer servers on market liquidity. *Journal of Futures Markets, 34*(1), 20–33.

Garcia, D., & Sikström, S. (2014). The dark side of Facebook: Semantic representations of status updates predict the Dark Triad of personality. *Personality and Individual Differences, 67*, 92–96.

Gefen, D., & Larsen, K. R. (2017). Controlling for lexical closeness in survey research: A demonstration on the technology acceptance model. *Journal of the Association for Information Systems, 18*(10), 727–757.

Ghysels, E., & Marcellino, M. (2018). *Applied Economic Forecasting Using Time Series Methods.* New York: Oxford University Press.

Guynn, J. (2015, July 1, 2015). Google Photos Label Black People "Gorillas." *USA Today.*

Guyon, I., Bennett, K., Cawley, G., Escalante, H. J., Escalera, S., Ho, T. K., . . . Statnikov, A. (2015). *Design of the 2015 ChaLearn AutoML challenge.* Paper presented at the Neural Networks (IJCNN), 2015 International Joint Conference on.

Guyon, I., Chaabane, I., Escalante, H. J., Escalera, S., Jajetic, D., Lloyd, J. R., . . . & Sebag, M. (2016). *A Brief Review of the ChaLearn AutoML Challenge: Any-time Any-dataset Learning Without Human Intervention.* Paper presented at the Workshop on Automatic Machine Learning.

Hendershott, T., & Riordan, R. (2013). Algorithmic trading and the market for liquidity. *Journal of Financial and Quantitative Analysis, 48*(4), 1001–1024.

Hu, G., Sun, X., Liang, D., & Sun, Y. (2014). Cloud removal of remote sensing image based on multi-output support vector regression. *Journal of Systems Engineering and Electronics, 25*(6), 1082–1088.

Husain, H., & Handel, N. (2017, May 10, 2017). *Automated Machine Learning—A Paradigm Shift That Accelerates Data Scientist Productivity @ Airbnb. Medium.com.*

Hyndman, R. J., & Koehler, A. B. (2006). Another look at measures of forecast accuracy. *International Journal of Forecasting, 22*(4), 679–688.

Isaac, W., & Dixon, A. (2017, May 13, 2017). Why Big-Data Analysis of Police Activity Is Inherently Biased. *Salon.*

Jean, N., Burke, M., Xie, M., Davis, W. M., Lobell, D. B., & Ermon, S. (2016). Combining satellite imagery and machine learning to predict poverty. *Science, 353*(6301), 790–794.

Kaufman, S., Rosset, S., Perlich, C., & Stitelman, O. (2012). Leakage in data mining: Formulation, detection, and avoidance. *ACM Transactions on Knowledge Discovery from Data (TKDD), 6*(4), 15.

Kirilenko, A., Kyle, A. S., Samadi, M., & Tuzun, T. (2017). The flash crash: High-frequency trading in an electronic market. *The Journal of Finance, 72*(3), 967–998.

Kosinski, M., Stillwell, D., & Graepel, T. (2013). Private traits and attributes are predictable from digital records of human behavior. *Proceedings of the National Academy of Sciences, 110*(15), 5802–5805.

KPMG. (2017). *Building Trust in Analytics.* Retrieved from https://home.kpmg.com/lv/en/home/media/press-releases/2017/02/business-executives-lack-confidence-in-generating-trusted-insigh.html.

Le, Q., & Zoph, B. (2017, May 17, 2017). Using Machine Learning to Explore Neural Network Architecture. Retrieved from https://research.googleblog.com/2017/05/using-machine-learning-to-explore.html.

Masegosa, A. D. (2013). *Exploring Innovative and Successful Applications of Soft Computing:* IGI Global.

McClendon, L., & Meghanathan, N. (2015). Using machine learning algorithms to analyze crime data. *Machine Learning and Applications: An International Journal (MLAIJ), 2*(1).

Mochal, J., & Mochal, T. (2012). *Lessons in Project Management.* New York: Apress.

Ostrov, B. F. (2017, March 31, 2017). Kaiser Campaign Slashes Opioid Prescriptions. *89.3 KPCC.* Retrieved from http://www.scpr.org/news/2017/03/31/70369/kaiser-campaign-slashes-opioid-prescriptions/.

Provost, F., & Fawcett, T. (2013). *Data Science for Business: What You Need to Know About Data Mining and Data-Analytic Thinking.* Sebastopol, CA: O'Reilly Media.

Riley, D. (2017, April 30th, 2017). Report Reveals Facebook Document That Could Help Advertisers Target Insecure Kids. *SiliconANGLE.*

Risley, J. (2016, March 24, 2016). Microsoft's Millennial Chatbot Tay.ai Pulled Offline after Internet Teaches Her Racism. *GeekWire.*

Ross, J. S., Chen, J., Lin, Z. Q., Bueno, H., Curtis, J. P., Keenan, P. S., . . . & Vidán, M. T. (2009). Recent national trends in readmission rates after heart failure hospitalization. *Circulation: Heart Failure,* CIRCHEARTFAILURE. 109.885210.

Schmidt, M. (2017). Automated Feature Engineering for Time Series Data. *KD Nuggets News.*

Sharma, R., Safadi, M., Andrews, M., Ogunbona, P. O., & Crawford, J. (2014, December 14-17). *Estimating the magnitude of method bias on account of text similarity using a natural language processing–based technique.* Paper presented at the International Conference on Information Systems, Auckland, New Zealand.

Shearer, C. (2000). The CRISP-DM model: The new blueprint for data mining. *Journal of Data Warehousing, 5*(4), 13–22.

Shore, J. (2004). Fail fast [software debugging]. *IEEE Software, 21*(5), 21–25.

Sirmacek, B., & Unsalan, C. (2011). A probabilistic framework to detect buildings in aerial and satellite images. *IEEE Transactions on Geoscience and Remote Sensing, 49*(1), 211–221.

Stackexchange. (2018). A List of Cost Functions Used in Neural Networks, Alongside Applications. Retrieved from https://stats.stackexchange.com/questions/154879/a-list-of-cost-functions-used-in-neural-networks-alongside-applications.

Steiner, C. (2010, September 9, 2010). Wall Street's Speed War. *Forbes.*

Stephens-Davidowitz, S. (2017). *Everybody Lies: Big Data, New Data, and What the Internet Can Tell Us about Who We Really Are.* New York: HarperCollins.

Strack, B., DeShazo, J. P., Gennings, C., Olmo, J. L., Ventura, S., Cios, K. J., & Clore, J. N. (2014). Impact of HbA1c measurement on hospital readmission rates: Analysis of 70,000 clinical database patient records. *BioMed Research International, 2014.* Epub 2014 Apr 3. PMID: 24804245; PMCID: PMC3996476.

Turban, E. (1990). *Decision Support and Expert Systems: Management Support Systems* (2nd ed.). New York: Macmillan.

Wang, D., & Murphy, M. (2004). Estimating optimal transformations for multiple regression using the ACE algorithm. *Journal of Data Science, 2*(4), 329–346.

Watson, H. J. (2014). Tutorial: Big data analytics: Concepts, technologies, and applications. *Communications of the Association for Information Systems, 34*(1), 1247–1268.

Wikipedia. (2018). Charge-off. Retrieved from https://en.wikipedia.org/wiki/Charge-off.

Williams, G. (2011). *Data Mining with Rattle and R: The Art of Excavating Data for Knowledge Discovery.* New York: Springer.

Wirth, R., & Hipp, J. (2000). *CRISP-DM: Towards a standard process model for data mining.* Paper presented at the Proceedings of the 4th international conference on the practical applications of knowledge discovery and data mining.

Witten, I. H., Frank, E., & Hall, M. A. (2011). *Data Mining: Practical Machine Learning Tools and Techniques* (3rd ed.). Burlington, MA: Elsevier.

Index

Note: Page numbers followed by *f* or *t* indicate a figure or table on the designated page

Printed in the USA/Agawam, MA
May 12, 2021

774510.035